MW00774883

THE
NAMESAKE

A Biography of
THEODORE ROOSEVELT, JR.

ROBERT W. WALKER

Brick Tower Press
New York

Brick Tower Press
1230 Park Avenue
New York, NY 10128
Tel: 212-427-7139
bricktower@aol.com • www.BrickTowerPress.com

The Brick Tower Press colophon is a registered trademark
of J. T. Colby & Company, Inc.

**Library of Congress Cataloging-in-Publication Data
is on file with the Library of Congress**

Robert W. Walker
The Namesake

Trade Paper Edition, 2014
Library of Congress Control Number: 2008933418

Cover design and typesetting by
The Great American Art Company

ACKNOWLEDGMENTS

Having been a World War II buff all my adult life, I had read about many of Theodore Roosevelt Jr.'s combat exploits, including his mention in Cornelius Ryan's book, *The Longest Day,* and I watched the movie that followed. I felt that his heroics had been exaggerated because of who he was. But when I read Mrs. Ted's wonderful autobiography, *Day Before Yesterday,* I was hooked and began searching for a biography on Ted. Many biographies of others and histories mentioned him, but, at the time, I could not find a book on just him. Having retired from law practice, I decided Ted's biography would be a worthwhile project. I had read that during WW II Ted's military aide was Captain Marcus O. Stevenson (Stevie) from Texas, and I set about trying to find him. Unfortunately "Stevie" was deceased, but, luckily, I found his son, Marcus O. Stevenson, Jr. The younger Mr. Stevenson had saved all of his father's clippings and notes and was extremely kind in boxing them up and sending them to me. Stevie, Jr. said that his father had intended to write a book about Ted, but somehow never got around to it. Thank you very much Mr. Marcus O. Stevenson, Jr. Your material permitted me to write a much more accurate description of Ted's WW II service.

In the 1960s, Dr. Laurence Madaras entitled his PhD dissertation *The Public Career of Theodore Roosevelt, Jr.,* in which he accurately wrote about Ted's campaigns for public office, his work as Assistant Secretary of the Navy, and his years as Governor General of Puerto Rico and the Philippines. A special appreciation is owed to Dr. Madaras for giving me permission to use his learned dissertation as a cited source, as well as his kindness in discussing Ted with me by phone and sending me copies of several articles relating to Ted which he had in his personal files.

Mr. Werner Kleeman, a 4th Infantry Division D-Day veteran, is due a special acknowledgement. While Mr. Kleeman did not personally know Ted well, he put me in contact with Major James Fiset and a number of other WW II 4th Division veterans that had served with Ted during the war. Of course, these crusty old World War II heroes had many interesting Ted Roosevelt stories to tell. Mr. Kleeman also furnished me photographs and allowed me access to books in his personal library, including a rare book entitled *D Day at Utah Beach* given to him by his French friend, Michel de Vallavieille, who was the book's author.

Mr. Theodore Roosevelt, IV furnished several pictures used in the book, and recommended a series of scrapbooks compiled by his grandmother, Mrs. Theodore Roosevelt, Jr., as a source for other pictures. Mr. Wallace Dailey, Curator of the Theodore Roosevelt Collection at Harvard University's Houghton Library recommended certain material in the collection that was used, and Dr. John Gable, Executive Director of the Theodore Roosevelt Association provided me with several articles I used as sources. Fred and Max Osborn provided pictures of the graves of Ted and Quentin Roosevelt in the American Military Cemetery in Normandy. The Center for Military History provided a copy of the letter Ted wrote to the Big Red One at the time he was relieved as its Assistant Division Commander.

The 4th Division Association and the 1st Division Association were both kind in assisting in locating veterans with anecdotes about Ted, and both the American Express Company and the American Legion furnished copies of minutes and resolutions concerning him.

The staffs at the Library of Congress; the New York Public Library; the National Archives and Records Administration; the Franklin D. Roosevelt Library; the Eisenhower Center; the Sagamore Hill National Historic Site; the Florence-Lauderdale Public Library; the Vanderbilt University Library; and the University of North Alabama Library were most accommodating in giving me access to their archives, books, and periodicals. Mrs. Christine Box and her staff at the Sheffield Alabama Public Library were especially helpful and courteous in obtaining many books and periodicals through the Alabama Library Service that I used in my research. I could not have written this book without Christine's help.

Ms. Kris Szebenyi, did the copy editing for this book. Thank you, Kris, for doing such a good job.

Last, but certainly not least, thanks to my daughter, Margaret Cheryl Bennett, my son, Ben Walker, and my good friends Henry Prater, Jim Smith and Robert S. Terry, for listening to my ramblings, doing some editing, and making thoughtful suggestions- well, sometimes thoughtful.

SALUTE

Some of them were called "Flappers." Others were said to be "Doughboys." In their younger days they thought it was "hep" to flavor their discourse with expressions like "Hello, Daddy-O," "Doodly Squat," "The Cat's Meow," and "Bee's Knees." But rather than being flighty and immature, as might have been supposed, they were responsible and energetic, and had a vision for the future. Among their many accomplishments were: amending the Constitution to give women the right to vote and guiding the Country through the Great War, Prohibition, and the Great Depression. Perhaps, however, their greatest achievment lay simply in how they raised their kids, for they instilled in them the values and discipline that would one day save the freedom of the world. This salute is to the remarkable American World War I Generation.

AUTHOR'S NOTE

Because several members of the Roosevelt family had similar or even identical names, I offer this explanation to aid the reader.

When the name Theodore Roosevelt, Sr. or TRSr. is used, it refers to former President Teddy Roosevelt's father. In life, Teddy's father never used "Sr." with his name and it is used here merely to clarify.

Theodore Roosevelt, TR, Theodore, Teedie, and Teddy all refer to the former President.

Theodore Roosevelt, Jr., TRJr. and Ted refer to the subject of this book..

Eleanor Roosevelt was Ted's wife and she is named many times as simply, "Eleanor." Occasionally she is referred to as Mrs. Ted and Mrs. TRJr.

There is a second Eleanor Roosevelt mentioned in this book. The few references to Ted's first cousin, Eleanor Roosevelt, who married her own distant cousin, Franklin Delano Roosevelt, are made in such a way as to make it obvious that Mrs. FDR is the subject of the event described.

Another name that could possibly confuse the reader is Quentin Roosevelt. There are two Quentin Roosevelts involved in the book. Ted's brother, Quentin, was killed in 1918, during World War I. When Quentin is mentioned in a setting occurring prior to 1919, the reference is to Ted's brother. Any mention of Quentin with respect to events subsequent to 1919, means Ted's son, Quentin.

CONTENTS

To all those wonderful educators
who tried to teach me English.

1
TAPS

BEFORE THE FUNERAL BEGAN, the body of Brigadier General Theodore Roosevelt, Jr. lay in state on the small, olive drab trailer that had been used to transport his personal belongings from place to place as the division advanced. As a contingent of his men on their way to the front passed by the wooden, flag draped coffin, one of them remarked, "He would be sore as hell if we slowed down one minute because of him." Later, just as the service began, a column of replacements moving up was allowed to stop and watch. The officer in charge told them it would be something they would never forget.

Promptly at 2100 hours, in the twilight of the long Normandy summer afternoon, with the rumble and rattle of artillery and small arms fire heard in the distance, Lt. Col. Park Hunt of the division staff, a close friend of General Roosevelt's, led the cortege between a break in the hedgerow, and into the American Army Cemetery near St. Mere Eglise. After Col. Hunt came the Flag Bearers with the American and the 4th Division Flags. Marching at slow step, the 4th Division Band followed, playing Chopin's "Marche Funebre." Then came respectively, two chaplains to conduct the service, an army half track bearing Gen. Roosevelt's coffin, and the eight enlisted men selected as pallbearers. The family, represented by Ted's son, Captain Quentin Roosevelt of the 1st Division, together with the general's aide, Captain Marcus O. Stevenson, and his driver, Sergeant Kurt Show, walked behind the pallbearers, Then came Generals Bradley, Patton, Collins, Hodges, Huebner, Barton, and some five or six other general officers as honorary pallbearers. Following the generals marched an honor company, all old timers, representing every unit in the 4th Infantry Division. Many officers and men from other divisions were there, including a group from the nearby First Infantry Division. Gen. Roosevelt had served in the 1st Division during World War I and for the first twenty months of World War II, and he had many friends in the Big Red One. Also present were more than a hundred French civilians, some wearing tricolor armbands with the Cross of Lorraine, marking them as members of the

French resistance. The service started with the band playing a hymn, "The Son of God Goes Forth to War." The chaplains led prayer, and an Honor Guard, composed of some of the men that had landed with Ted in the first wave at Utah Beach on D-Day, fired a salute. "Taps" was played and echoed in the distance, and Ted Roosevelt's body was lowered into the ground. He was the second of Teddy Roosevelt's sons to be buried in the soil of France. Afterwards, some of the French civilians filed by and tossed beautiful Normandy Roses into the open grave. [1]

Quentin Roosevelt thought the service was "a warriors funeral in every since of the word," but the egotistical George Patton criticized the contents of the prayers, and the formation of the Honor Guard. He called the funeral a flop, except that "towards the end of the service, our anti-aircraft guns near Coutances opened on some German planes and gave an appropriate requiem to the funeral of a really gallant man." Patton said all the photographers wanted to take pictures of him, so he got in the rear. [2]

The events described above took place on July 13th, 1944.

During World War II most of the high-ranking American officers commanding combat units larger than a battalion were professional soldiers. Many of them were ring knockers, West Pointers. Ted Roosevelt was not a West Pointer, nor was he a professional soldier. He was a Harvard man and, besides being the son of one of the icons of American history, he was the cousin of both the sitting President and the First Lady. He was essentially a civilian on active duty, similar to a draftee, except that he had a reserve officer's commission and combat experience from World War I. It was only natural that some of the top brass, all with many years on active duty, found it difficult to accept Ted as a true contemporary and equal. They felt he had not paid his dues, and had obtained the rank of Brigadier General because of who he was, the old "he was born with a silver spoon in his mouth" syndrome. Ted was well aware of this prejudice and had, in fact, written his wife that everybody loved him except his own high command, and, in another letter, that Gen. Collins, the Corps Commander, didn't have much use for him. General Bradley, the commander of all American ground forces in France, and General Patton, soon to lead the Third U.S. Army across France and into Germany, both claimed to have been responsible for Ted being fired as Assistant Division Commander of the 1st Division in August of 1943, less that a year before his death. [3]

Ted's heroics in combat were legend among the Doughboys and GIs. During the course of two world wars the United States awarded Ted the Congressional Medal of Honor, the Distinguished Service Cross, the Silver Star with three Oak Leaf Clusters, the Bronze Star with V device, the Distinguished Service Medal, the Legion of Merit, and the Purple Heart with one Oak Leaf Cluster. The Republic of France awarded him the Legion of Honor (Chevalier), the Legion of Honor

(Officer), the Croix de Guerre with five palms, the Medaille de la Reconnaissance de la France Liberee, and two Fourrageres. Belgium presented him with the Grand Cross of the Order of the Crown, and the Croix de Guerre with Palm. He had other decorations from Montenegro, China and Tunisia.[4]

Even though he was awarded every medal offered by the United States to the foot soldier for combat heroism, and was the most decorated citizen-soldier in American annals, and is second only to Douglas MacArthur in awards to all the soldiers who ever served, today, other than some of the rapidly vanishing World War II generation, very few people have ever heard of Theodore Roosevelt, Jr. Those who claim to know who he was, say only that he must have been Teddy Roosevelt's son, or that he was the fellow with arthritis played by Henry Fonda in the movie, *The Longest Day*. Hopefully the following narrative will offer some insight as to whether Ted has, on his own merit, earned a significant place in American history, perhaps as the "Fourth Roosevelt," or is destined to remain, like the offspring of many famous people, merely a blurred face in the crowd.

Taps Source Notes

1. Mrs., TRJr. p. 456–59; Capt. Marcus Stevenson notes; *Time Magazine* 7/24/44; *New York Herald Tribune* 7/15/44; *New York Times* 7/14/44; *San Antonio Evening News* 7/14/44.

2. Blumenson, *Patton Papers,* p480–81; Mrs. TRJr. p. 456–59

3. TRJr letters to Eleanor of 8/24/43 & 5/14/44, LOC c-61; Bradley, *A Soldiers Story* (paperback) p. 162; Blumenson, *Patton Papers,* p. 303–309.

4. Official Army Records.

PREAMBLE

Dutch by blood, Nicholas von Rosenvelt (1658–1742) was the common ancestor of President Franklin Delano Roosevelt and President Theodore Roosevelt. FDR descended from Nicholas' son Jacobus, and Teddy from another son, Johannes. Nicholas was raised in New Amsterdam, and was the first of his family native-born in the land that would become the United States of America. While still a boy, his name was changed from von Rosenvelt to Roosevelt, and the town of New Amsterdam became New York City. As a young man, Nicholas wandered into the upstate area to trap mink and other fur bearing animals, and there he sired his eight children. Later in his life, Nicholas, along with Johannes and some of his other children, returned to New York City, where he made a meager living operating a mill.

Johannes Roosevelt, on the other hand, was more successful financially than his father, and made a small fortune in the construction business and in the manufacture of linseed oil. Several generations later, Cornelius Van Schaak Roosevelt emerged from the Johannes Roosevelt genealogical line. CVS, as he was called, was intelligent, ambitious, energetic, and very conservative. He accumulated great wealth by securing control of the moderately successful family-owned investment company of Roosevelt and Son, and then he funneled the company's assets into land speculation and the plate glass business.

Theodore Roosevelt, Sr.[1813–1878] was one of five sons born to CVS and his wife. Wealthy from his father's enterprise, but having no desire to add to his own financial worth, TRSr did little with respect to income-producing activities. He lived the good life and enjoyed his father's money. He loved traveling, especially with his family, taking them on several overseas sojourns, and he enjoyed mixing socially with the New York elite. However, he had a strong sense of noblesse oblige and, aside from his family, his principal interests were philanthropic. He was a tireless worker for many charities, especially the Newsboys Lodging House, and was one of the founders of the American Museum of Natural History, the Metropolitan Museum of Art, and the New York Orthopedic Hospital.

There is a touching story that some years after TRSr's death, Teddy Roosevelt, then the governor of New York, was attending a governor's conference when he was approached by Governor Brady of Alaska. Brady told Teddy that he wanted to shake his hand, not because he was the governor of a great state, or a war hero, or because he was a famous author, but because he was Theodore Sr.'s son. Brady went on to explain that he had been a homeless child in New York when Theodore Sr. took him off the streets, found a family out west willing to take him in, paid for his transportation there, and then checked on his progress from time to time as he grew up. The Alaskan Governor gave Theodore Sr. credit for the success he had made of his life. There must have been many similar stories, for when TRSr died over two thousand people attended his funeral, many being former newsboys, orphans, and others he had helped.[1]

On a trip to Georgia in 1850, when he was 19 years old, Theodore Sr. met Martha (Mittie) Bulloch, a beautiful southern belle raised on the Bulloch Hall Plantation near Roswell, Georgia. He fell madly in love with Mittie and they were married in 1855. The Bulloch family had to sell four slaves to pay for their elaborate wedding. Besides being a strikingly handsome woman, Mittie brought a fervid and zestful personality into the otherwise staid Roosevelt family. While Margaret Mitchell always claimed that GoneWith theWind was pure fiction, Roswell is only a few miles from Atlanta, and many of the old timers in and around Atlanta and Roswell claimed that Scarlet was patterned after Martha Bulloch and that Tara was actually the Bulloch Hall Plantation.[2]

TRSr and his bride made their home in New York City, where all four of their children were born. Anna, the oldest, nicknamed both Bamie and Bye, was born in 1855. She was three years senior to the next child, and was very much the "older sister" to her siblings, being almost like a second mother to them. Bamie was intelligent to the point of being shrewd, and extremely loyal to the Roosevelt clan. An affliction with scoliosis did not prevent Anna from becoming the solid rock in the family, the one the others could always count on for assistance when there was a problem. It is said that after Teddy became president, he had such respect for her insight and judgment that he never made an important decision without first seeking her council. Bamie surprised the whole family when, at age forty, she announced that she had found the love of her life and would soon marry William Sheffield Cowles, a career naval officer. She referred to him as Mr. Bearo. Anna and her Mr. Bearo had only one child, William Sheffield Cowles, Jr. Bamie died in 1931.[3]

The next child delivered by Mittie was Theodore Roosevelt[1858–1919], called Teedie when a youngster, and, of course, Teddy later in life. Even when only a boy Teedie was energetic to the point of hyperactivity. It seemed that he was always enthusiastically and intensely engaged in some activity: be it reading, observing the flora and fauna, horseback riding, hunting, or some other of his many interests. Some believe he got this kinetic trait, which served him well all through life, from his mother. What makes Teddy's high energy level somewhat surprising, is the fact that he suffered from chronic asthma, and had very poor eyesight. He got his first pair of glasses at age thirteen and was delighted at how his improved vision made him more aware of his immediate surroundings. Thereafter, he kept several pair of glasses close at hand so that he would always have an extra pair handy. The asthmatic condition was another matter. Especially when small, Teedie would have such severe asthma attacks that his parents feared for his life. They took him to many medical practitioners hoping to find a cure, or at least to moderate the problem. Some of the remedies prescribed were unusual by today's standards. For example, science had discovered that a puff of strong tobacco smoke would sometimes terminate an asthmatic episode. For some period of time his parents had TR puff on a strong cigar when he began to have an attack. His asthmatic condition improved some as Teddy grew into adulthood, but it never left entirely. Teedie's accomplishments as president are legendary, and include: vastly increasing the acreage devoted to national parks, sanctuaries, and other conservation projects; obtaining some measure of public protection against corporate abuse through anti-trust legislation; getting Congress to pass the Pure Food and Drug Act and the Meat Inspection Act; winning the Nobel Peace Prize for his hands on work in negotiating a peace to the Russo-Japanese War; enlarging the U.S. Navy; completing the Panama Canal; and guiding the United States to the position of being accepted by the other nations as a world power.[4]

Elliott was the third child born into the TRSr family. All the things that Teddy was, Elliott was not. Ellie, as he was called, began having seizures as a teenager and developed an horrific alcohol problem as a young adult. In 1882, he married Anna Hall, who, before her untimely death in 1892, bore him two sons and a daughter. Elliott was in and out of hospitals and sanatoriums until he died in 1894, at the age of thirty-four. Elliott Jr., the first born child to Elliott and Anna, contracted scarlet fever and died while still a toddler. Gracie Hall Roosevelt, the other son, grew to adulthood, served honorably during World War I, but died some years later of acute alcoholism.

The only daughter born to Elliott and Anna had protruding teeth, a receding chin, and was called "Granny" by some of the members of the family. After her mother died, the little girl was shuttled around and raised by a combination of grandparents, and uncles and aunts. Teddy's wife, Edith Roosevelt, must have seen something in the pathetic child that the others overlooked, for she told the family that sometimes an ugly duckling grew up to be a swan, and insisted that they send the her off to a good private school to give her the best chance of overcoming the tragedy of her parents' deaths and her unattractive appearance. That unattractive, orphaned daughter of the alcoholic Elliott Roosevelt was destined to marry her own distant cousin, Franklin Delano Roosevelt, and to serve as First Lady of the United States for over twelve years. She was a tireless worker in the causes in which she so fervently believed, and is today remembered as one of America's most admired women. Better known to the public by her middle name, Anna Eleanor Roosevelt did grow up to be a swan.[5]

Corinne, or Conie, born in 1861, was the youngest of Theodore Sr.'s children. Corinne, much like her beautiful and vivacious mother, was outgoing and always the life of the party. Conie married Douglas Robinson and had four children; she remained supportive of Teddy all of her life. Later in life Conie worked with Bamie in the reconstruction of the Roosevelt home in New York City where she, Bamie, Teedie, and Ellie grew up. Conie died in 1933. She was the only one of the children that lived to see their distant cousin, Franklin Delano Roosevelt, and their first cousin, Eleanor Roosevelt, become President and First Lady.[6]

Growing up, Theodore Sr.'s children lived the life of the wealthy. They were educated by the best private tutors, spent summers in New England or Oyster Bay, had trips abroad, servants, a big warm house, and expensive clothes. These were some of the advantages of being a Roosevelt.

Almost like a fifth child in the TR Sr./Mittie household was little Edith Kermit Carow, affectionately known as Edie. Edith's parents, Charles and Gertrude Carow, lived nearby. Edie, Teedie, Ellie, and Conie played together almost daily. Mittie realized that the Carows were poor, at least by Roosevelt standards, and arranged for Edie to attend kindergarten with Corrine and Elliott. There is a famous photograph taken in 1865, showing the Abraham Lincoln funeral procession going down Broadway in New York, on its way to Springfield for the burial. In the background of the photo is the CVS home with two little heads looking down from a second floor window. The heads were those of Teddy and Elliott Roosevelt. Teddy was seven and Elliott was four at the time. It is said that shortly before the photo was made, Edith Carow had been a third small head peering out, but she got scared of the soldiers marching by and all the horses, and, when she started to cry, Teddy and Elliott put her in a closet so that they could watch the proceedings in peace.[7]

Charles Carow had at one time been in the shipping business, but had a tragic fall, and suffered a permanent head injury. His business failed and he turned to drink. From the time Edith was six, Charles Carow never worked, but he was good to her, doing such things as telling her stories, teaching her Latin and horseback riding, and taking her to the theater. He enkindled in her an abiding interest in literature and nature, and somehow found a way to send Edith to a very good private school. She studied English, arithmetic, philosophy, and other subjects. Charles Carow was largely responsible for little Edie developing into an intelligent and cultured young lady.[8]

Teedie and Edie had been together so much that by the time the Roosevelts left for a European vacation in 1869, they were almost like brother and sister. He was eleven and she was eight. During the year the Roosevelts were away, Edie and Teedie wrote to each other often. When the family returned from abroad, the children immediately took up where they had left off, and were a group again. In fact Conie and Edie had become best friends, even though they were opposites personality wise. Conie was an extrovert, while Edith was on the introverted side. The two girls would remain the best of friends all of their lives.[9]

As the teenage years approached for Teedie and Edie, their relationship naturally began to change from brother/sister to boy/girl. They both took dancing lessons and loved to dance. They both had an interest in nature and enjoyed taking long walks together to look at the plants and animals. Both were literary. Edith especially enjoyed Shakespeare and nature books; Teddy had a curiosity about almost everything. They both read profusely.

In 1874, Mittie and TRSr acquired Tranquility, a summer home in Oyster Bay on Long Island. Each summer, Edith would visit them at Oyster Bay for as long as a month at a time. The kids always had a wonderful time. When they became teenagers, they ducked for apples, pulled molasses candy, put on theatrical productions for the adults, swam, and rode horses. For activities such as nature walks in the woods and rowing, they often paired up, Conie with one of the neighborhood boys and Teddy with Edith. Teddy named his little rowboat the *Edith*.[10]

In the fall of '76, Teddy enrolled as a freshman at Harvard. In those days only about one American in five thousand went to college. By this time, Elliott was beginning to have seizures, and the family had a sense of foreboding about his future. Shortly after Teddy's enrollment, TRSr wrote him to the effect that he considered Teddy to be the scion, and trusted him to look after the family business.[11]

TR fit right into college life, and was quite the man about campus. His grades were excellent, and he was, in time, inducted into Phi Beta Kappa. He was admitted into Porcellian, the most prestigious of the Harvard clubs, and worked on one of the campus newspapers, eventually becoming editor. Because of his family's wealth, TR had a great deal more money to spend than the average Harvard student. He bought only the most fashionable clothes and boarded his horse at a private stable. Edith and the TRSr family visited Teedie at Cambridge for several days during the spring of his freshman year. Immediately after the visit was over, Edith wrote Teddy a nice letter thanking him for showing her such a good time. Upon returning home for Christmas and summer vacations, Teddy would court Edie and have fun with his friends and family.[12]

On one occasion in the summer of 1877, Teddy, Edie, Conie and Ellie spent some time at the New Jersey home of Edie's grandfather, Brigadier General Daniel Tyler of Civil War fame. Beginning when he had been a small boy, Mittie told Teedie spellbinding stories of the heroic Civil War exploits of her two Confederate brothers, James Dunwoody Bulloch and Irvine Bulloch. The brothers, Teddy's uncles, feared federal government prosecution after the war and made their homes in England. Teddy did, however, get to meet them when the family went to Europe in 1869, and on several other occasions when his uncles would slip into the United States for brief periods. TR had been enamored with heroes, soldiers, and wars since the days of Mittie's stories. He enjoyed the few days spent with a real war hero immensely.[13]

When TR arrived home for the 1877 Christmas break, he found that his father was having some stomach problems, but the family considered it to be minor and saw no reason to be concerned. Shortly after Christmas, however, TRSr was diagnosed with terminal cancer. Knowing that there was nothing Teddy could do, the family did not tell him the seriousness of his father's condition, and allowed him to returned to his studies. Theodore Roosevelt Sr. died on February 9, 1878. The family was devastated. When his father's estate was settled, Teddy's share amounted to about $125,000. This provided him with a fixed income of approximately $8,000 per year, not bad by modern standards, and a fortune in 1878.[14]

Shortly after TRSr's funeral, Bamie had occasion to introduce her good friend, Sara Delano, to her distant cousin, James Roosevelt, a widower twice Sara's age. James was a descendant of old Nicholas von Rosenvelt through Nich's son, Jocobus. Sara and James were married a few months after they met. They would name their only child Franklin Delano Roosevelt.[15]

As grief stricken as he was over his father's death, TR returned to Harvard and went on with his education. He later said that his father was "the best man I ever knew." When summer vacation began in 1878, Teddy resumed his courtship of Edith. He even remembered her seventeenth birthday in early August and sent her a gift. Friends and family were beginning to look upon the couple as kind of engaged to be engaged. However, on August 22nd they went off together and something happened between them that completely altered their relationship. While there has been speculation as to what actually occurred, neither of them ever revealed the secret. Edith said only that TR had not been nice, and Teddy said that Edith had had an off day. For whatever the cause, they broke up, and were no longer a twosome.[16]

After the fall 1878 college term began, Teddy undertook the writing of his first book, *The Naval War of 1812*. That same fall, he was invited to a private home in the exclusive Chestnut Hill section of Boston for a social weekend. There he met a beautiful blue eyed blond named Alice Hathaway Lee and fell passionately in love.

He and Alice went for carriage rides, walks, picnics and, their favorite entertainment, dancing. Probably because her family thought she was too young, Alice declined TR's first marriage proposal, but he was not deterred and continued his wooing. By the fall of 1879, the New York Roosevelts and the Bostonian Lees began to visit each other, and almost immediately Mittie and Alice struck up a warm friendship. A formal engagement was announced in January. The wedding would take place in October, 1880, several months after TR's graduation from Harvard.[17]

Edith accompanied Mittie and the other Roosevelt family members to Teddy's wedding. At the reception she danced, laughed, and seemed to have a wonderful time. TR and Alice honeymooned for two weeks at Tranquility, and decided to take a second honeymoon in Europe the following summer. They also made plans to build their dream house on the ninety-five acres that Theodore had acquired in a rural area of Long Island, near the village of Oyster Bay. It would be called Leeholm. An architect was hired and a house plan was completed. The newlyweds established their residence in New York City, and the young Harvard graduate enrolled in the Columbia University School of Law. He spent the remaining weeks of 1880 writing, reading and studying law.[18]

The year 1881 was a very busy one for TR. *The Naval War of 1812* was completed and published, and is still today considered a standard authority on the naval aspects of that war. An interest in politics he had first exhibited at Harvard blossomed, and he dropped out of law school to run in his district as the Republican candidate for a seat in the New York General Assembly. Teddy had truly found his element. He was elected, re-elected twice, and served three consecutive one-year terms. The legislative session began in January of each year and ended when ever business was finished, usually in June. Between sessions he wrote quite a lot, read, did some hunting, and he and Alice went on that delayed European honeymoon.[19]

Over the next few years, Edith maintained her close friendship with Corrine and Bamie. She saw Alice often, but they were never close. Alice wondered why. On at least one occasion when Alice was visiting in Boston, Teddy took Edie for a carriage ride, just the two of them, but the times were Victorian, and they were old friends. Edith busied herself with reading, visiting with Conie, Bamie, and other friends, attending art exhibits, Bible readings, and occasionally going dancing or engaging in some other social activity, but there was never a serious suitor. Charles Carow died in 1883. Early in 1885, Edith, her mother, and her only sibling, Emily, made plans for an extended visit in Europe. They had even talked of permanently moving to Europe, probably Italy, because the cost of living was so much cheaper there. They would leave in the spring of 1886. Edith was preparing herself for life as a *feme sole*.[20]

Except for weekends, TR was required to be in Albany while the Assembly was in session. His wife had gotten pregnant in 1883 and was in the third trimester of her pregnancy when the 1884 legislative session began. Alice moved in with Mittie as her time for childbirth approached. As usual, Teddy came home on Friday, February 8th, after the legislative session was adjourned. Alice appeared to be having a normal pregnancy. While TR's mother, Mittie, was running a fever, she was not thought to have any serious health problems. Mrs. Lee, Alice's mother, as expected, arrived to join her daughter at Mittie's on Monday. TR returned to Albany by train Tuesday morning. Alice went into labor a few hours after Teddy left, and shortly gave birth to Alice Lee Roosevelt, a normal, healthy baby girl. A telegram was immediately sent to Albany informing Teddy of the birth, and that mother and daughter were doing fine. Just as TR was being congratulated by his fellow assemblymen, a second telegram arrived giving him the shocking news that an emergency existed at home. Leaving immediately, TR arrived at Mittie's house about midnight to find his wife dying from Bright's disease and Mittie terminally ill with typhoid fever. He left Alice's bedside only once, to see his mother one final time. Mittie died at 3:00 a.m. February 14th and Alice died at 2:00 p.m. that same day. Alice never got to spend a night in Leeholm; it was still just a blue print.[21]

After a double funeral, Teddy turned the care of his new baby girl and the responsibility of seeing to the completion of Leeholm over to Bamie, and he returned to Albany to finish out the legislative term. In an effort to deal with his grief, he immersed himself in the work of the legislature, and then attended the Republican National Convention in Chicago. At this convention, TR handled himself well and established himself on a national level as an up-and-coming, young Republican politician. He also met and made a life-long friendship with Henry Cabot Lodge. Afterwards, still devastated over his loss, he would write, "The light went out of my life forever."[22]

Several months before Alice died, TR had traveled out west to the Dakota Badlands on a hunting trip, and, while there, made an investment in a cattle ranch. After the political convention in Chicago was adjourned, Theodore was still in a bewildered and depressed state. Wanting to let time do its job as the great healer, he acquired a gaudy wardrobe of cowboy's garb, including a silver bowie knife from Tiffany's; alligator cowboy boots; silver spurs; a ten-gallon hat; a silver belt buckle; and leather chaps, and headed back to the Dakota Territory. Over the next eighteen months, he wrote, meditated, read, hunted, and established the Maltese Cross and the Elkhorn cattle ranches. His total investment in the cattle business was by then over eighty thousand dollars. To the tough, hard-drinking, hard-living locals in the Badlands, TR was something of an enigma. At first they laughed at him and considered him a dandy, until the occasion in a local bar when an intoxicated cowhand, with a six-shooter in each hand, laughed at him and intimated that he was a sissy. TR knocked him out cold with one blow. The story got around, and thereafter he was treated with more respect.[23]

Between his activities in the West, Teddy made several trips back to New York to see little Alice and visit friends and family, but he never saw Edie Carow. Then, one September day in 1885, he accidentally, or on purpose, bumped into her at Bamie's house. When Teedy and Edie saw each other, whatever had happened on 8/22/1878 was instantly forgotten and a surreptitious courtship began. He extended his stay in New York by several months, and changed the name of Leeholm to Sagamore Hill. It is unusual for intelligent, educated adults to keep a romantic relationship concealed, but until November 17, 1885, when he gave her a pearl necklace, a ring, and a watch, and they became engaged, TR and Edith would not go out in public together. Even then, they kept their engagement a secret. They didn't tell anyone, not Bamie, Conie or even Edith's mother. To Theodore, there was a flaw in his character if he allowed himself to have amorous feelings for another woman, when Alice had been dead for only a year and a half. In fact, he didn't believe in second marriages, and didn't want anyone to know he was serious about Edie. During this time, Edith was living with her mother, and Teddy stayed at Bamie's house during his New York visits. It is impossible to believe that Bamie and Gertrude didn't have at least some suspicions of the romantic involvement of their brother and daughter.[24]

Exactly when and where their marriage would take place required some thought and planning. Edith, Gertrude, and Emily had already made arrangements for their extended European trip, and her mother and sister were counting on her. Edith didn't see how she could back out now. Also, Theodore's future plans were uncertain. He was undecided as to whether he would return to Dakota and continue in the ranching business, and/or pursue a career as an author, or take Bamie's advice to move back east and become politically active again. They finally came to the conclusion that Edith would go on to Europe with her mother and sister, and that, in a year or two, after Theodore had made his decision as to what path to take with respect to a career, he would meet Edith in London and they would wed.[25]

TR headed back to the Badlands in March of 1886, and the Carows sailed for Europe a month later. Out West, Teddy tended to his cattle and resumed his other normal activities. He missed Edith and often thought of their approaching marriage. They corresponded by letter frequently. On the Fourth of July, Teddy was asked to speak at the celebration in the town of Dickinson, Dakota Territory. He held the crowd spellbound, telling them that Americans were lucky to be living in such a bountiful land, and that everyone should work and do their part. He said that wealth was important, but that honesty, truthfulness and other traits of character were more important. The editor of the local newspaper was so impressed by his oratory that he predicted TR would be President of the United States one day. Teddy responded, "If your prophecy comes true, I will do my part to make a good one." His decision had been made. He would make his permanent home in New York, and go back into politics, but, at least for the time being, he would also retain his cattle ranching investments. Theodore returned to New York for a month in August to do some political groundwork and some research on a new book he was writing, then he went back to the Badlands for two months. In an early September issue of the *New York Times,* there appeared an unauthorized item announcing the engagement of TR and Edith. A week later, the paper ran a correction stating that a mistake had been made and that they were not engaged. Where the *Times* got its original information about an engagement is not known. Theodore often told his friends in the Badlands about Edith and showed them her picture. It may well have been that somehow news of the engagement reached New York from the Dakota Territory. Apparently, either Bamie or Conie had the corrective notice run. Now TR was in a real predicament with his friends and relatives in New York, and especially with his sisters. He had purposely kept from those closest to him the news of his commitment to Edith, one of their very best friends. TR immediately wrote both sisters a contrite letter confirming his upcoming marriage, and giving them his lame explanation of why the engagement had been kept secret. As a gesture of appeasement, he offered to let Bamie keep and raise his young daughter as her own.[26]

Arriving back in New York City in early October, Theodore ran as the Republican candidate for mayor. Two other candidates were in the race. He campaigned hard and did his best, but could not overcome the fact that he had been away from the City so much since 1884, he was almost like a non-resident candidate, and came in third. Shortly after the election TR and Bamie sailed for England for his wedding. They arrived on November 13, 1886. On the trip over, Teddy and Bamie were introduced to Cecil Spring-Rice, a career diplomat for the British government. The warm friendship that developed between TR, Edith and "Springy" would last for the rest of their lives. Edith was busy with the wedding, and TR, for the next two weeks, began a busy schedule of social events arraigned by Springy. The marriage was solemnized in a private ceremony on December 2, 1886, in London, with Springy as best man. Teddy and his bride then left for a $3\frac{1}{2}$ month honeymoon. They began in Dover, continued to Paris, Lyons, Marseilles, and to Italy where they visited with Gertrude and Emily for several weeks before returning to London for more dinners, parties, and other social engagements. In keeping with his energetic personality, Theodore wrote several magazine articles on hunting and ranching during his honeymoon. Edith was pregnant when the couple arrived back in New York on March 27, 1887. TR and his new spouse discussed what to do with little Alice. Edith insisted that they take her and raise her as one of their own. Shortly after landing, they picked up Alice from Bamie, and thus she became the first child in the Theodore/Edith household.[27]

By now TR had been away from his ranches for more than six months, and he was anxious to go back and check on things in the Badlands. He had heard of the severe winter the Dakota Territory experienced during his absence, but, upon his return, found the frigid conditions had been even worse than he expected. There had been weeks with temperatures forty degrees below zero, and snow and ice several feet deep. The cattle losses were as high as 75%. Mother Nature had made the decision for him with respect to the ranching business. TR rounded up his surviving cattle and liquidated his herds. In the end, he lost most of his $80,000 investment, and he returned home in late May, 1887. After his cattle ranching fiasco, TR would rarely return to the Badlands, and then for only brief hunting trips.[28]

In late spring, Edith and Theodore spent their first night in Sagamore Hill, the house that would remain their family home until their children, one by one, left to lead their own lives. It was to be home to Edie and Teedie until they died. The structure has over twenty rooms, twelve being bedrooms, and is of an uncertain architectural style. The ceilings are high, and the numerous windows and open areas give an impression of a big, old, drafty house. But there is also an impression of stability and safety, like a granite storm cellar against a tornado. Hides and heads from Teddy's many hunts line the walls and cover the floors, but there are not nearly as many hunting trophies as there are books. Hundreds, perhaps thousands, of books are on shelves and tables throughout. Sagamore Hill is not, in appearance, a warm and cozy family home. It is more like a big, old, drafty, but yet warm, and friendly boarding house, where you can get all the wholesome food you can eat, a large sleeping room, and can sit on the porch in a rocking chair and chat with the other boarders. In actuality, however, during the time it was occupied by the Roosevelt family it was a wonderful and cozy family home, and a home where there was a constant stream of houseguests, many being the movers and shakers of the late-nineteenth and early-twentieth centuries. It was also a home away from home for TR's and Edith's close friends, especially Henry Cabot Lodge, and Springy.[29]

The young couple settled into married life at Sagamore, and awaited the birth of their first child. In the mornings, Teddy would work on his fourth book in the study, while Edith would see to the running of the house. Afternoons were mostly private times for the couple to spend together. Walking in the woods, rowing in the bay, and swimming were some of their favorite activities. As Edith's pregnancy neared term, the valetudinarian Gertrude was not feeling well and had to cancel the trip she and Emily planned to make to be with her daughter for the birth of her first child. Edith then arranged for the nurse from her own childhood, Mame, to be with her to assist with the new baby. Mame's real name was Mary Ledwith. She migrated to the United States from Ireland in the 1840s, and worked for the Roosevelt and Carow families for many years. By the time of Mame's death, she had known five generations of those families, and helped raise many of them. The birth of Edith's baby was not expected until the latter part of September, and Mame had not yet arrived when, on September 12th at 9:00 p.m., Edith went into labor. Theodore's cousin, West Roosevelt, a physician who lived nearby, was immediately summoned, and at 2:15 a.m. on September 13th, 1887, Edith gave birth to her first child.[30]

Preamble Source Notes

1. Collier p 16–34 & Family Tree; McCullough p 47.
2. Collier p 31; McCullough p 47.
3. McCullough p 88, 362; S. Morris p 21.
4. Hagedorn p 272; McCullough p 96, 112, 118, 364–365.
5. Collier p 62 84, 87; Cook p 64, 214–215; McCullough p 369; S Morris p 142.
6. Collier Family Tree; McCullough p 369.
7. Collier p 38; S. Morris p 14–16.
8. S. Morris p 20, 72.
9. S. Morris p 3, 23, 27, 41.
10. McCullough p 115; S. Morris p 33, 44, 47, 52, 64.
11. Collier p 44; McCullough p 198–205.
12. McCullough p 198–207; S. Morris p 55–56.
13. McCullough p 74; S. Morris p 14, 17, 45, 56; Renehan p 13.
14. Collier p 46–48; McCullough p 205.
15. Collier p 53–54.
16. Collier p 47, 51; S. Morris p 58.
17. Collier p 51, 57–58; Kerr p 8; McCullough p 220.
18. Hagedorn p 6; Collier p 52–56.
19. Collier p 57–58; McCullough p 257, 272.
20. S. Morris p 68–71, 79–83.
21. Collier p 62; McCullough p 283.
22. Collier p 64; McCullough p 288, 310–312.
23. Collier p 65–66; McCullough p 312–334.
24. S, Morris p 79–91.
25. McCullough p 355; S. Morris p 83.
26. Collier p 71; McCullough p 345; S. Morris p 83, 89–90.
27. S. Morris p 93–106.
28. Ibid p 107.
29. S. Morris p 107; Renehan p 9–11.
30. Roosevelt, T R, Jr., *All in the Family* p. 24; S. Morris p 15, 111–112.

3
AND ALONG CAME TED

In recent years the descendants of old CVS had failed to produce a male child, so when Edith gave birth to the $7^1/_2$ pound Theodore Roosevelt, Jr., there was great rejoicing. One of Teddy's uncles was so excited that he decorated his wagon and drove it around in celebration of the coming of a baby Dutch boy. Everyone in the family was ecstatic, but the happiest of all was three-year-old Alice. She pulled her chair up to her new brother's bedside and refused to leave him unless her colicky, "howling polly parrot" could go with her. Alice sat by Ted's crib and heard and saw everything. She was amazed when she saw him nursing and said, "Baby eats mama." Since Kermit, the next child to be born into the TR family, would not arrive until October of 1889, Alice had Ted practically all to herself to play with for the next few years, and a special brother/sister bond developed between them. Alice was as devoted to Ted as Bamie had been to Teddy, and TRJr returned the affection. The strong sibling attachment which Ted and Alice had for each other lasted well into their adulthood, when each had a family of their own. Alice was away from Ted for three weeks each spring and three weeks each fall while she visited her Lee grandparents in Boston. When she returned from these trips, Ted would be so happy to see her that he would run round and round in joy, and try to hug her and kiss her. As children will do, there were some hurtful remarks made from time to time by one of them to the other. As an example, when Ted was five and Alice eight, he told her she had had a sweat nurse, referring to the fact that Alice's mother died when she was a newborn and TR and Bamie had hired a wet nurse for her to suckle.

On one occasion, Ted crawled under an old pile of lumber and got stuck, and Alice crawled right under and pulled him out. Once she probably saved his life when Ted lost his balance and started to fall from a third story window. Alice grabbed his feet and held on until help arrived. Later, Ted, remembering his fun times with Alice, wrote of a game they played with toy monitors made for them by their father. They were opponents in the re-creation of the Battle of Mobile Bay. Ted had Alice's monitor in trouble from play shell hits, and he clamed her ship had hit a mine. To prevent her ship from sinking, Alice said, "Ted! My monitor has gone to bed. It always goes to bed at six o'clock and it's half-past six now!"[1]

Thinking back upon Ted's infancy and childhood, Teddy wrote: "How well I remember when we were fitting up our nursery for Ted! And he was such a cunning baby . . . I can see him now, hanging on the little nursery gate and begging to be taken off to extra-nursery excitement; and if his request were granted, his arms and legs were waved with frantic jubilance as he was borne off, making him about as easy to carry as an electric starfish. Then when he slept by us in a crib he would begin what his mother called his 'hymn to the light,' at dawn; and, when he was old enough, if I was unwary enough to give the least sign of being awake, he would swarm into bed with me and gleefully propose 'a story,' keeping a vigilant watch on me for any sign of sleepiness on my part while I told it." TR also wrote, "Ted is the most loving, warm-hearted gallant little fellow who ever breathed . . . I often show him and Alice books; the great, illustrated Milton, the *Nibelungenlied,* or hunting books; and Ted knows any amount of poetry from Scott to Longfellow. I tell them how I hunted the game whose heads are on the wall; or of Washington crossing the Delaware, or of Lincoln or Farragut. We have most entrancing plays in the old barn, and climbing trees in the orchard, and go to Coopers Bluff; Ted usually having to come back part of the way piggy-back. He wears big spectacles, which only make him look more like a Brownie than ever; and delights in carrying a tin sword, at present, even in his romps. It is an awe inspiring sight to see him, when Alice has made a nice nest in a corn-stack, take a reckless header in after her, with sword and spectacles, showing a fine disregard both of her life and his own."[2]

Ted was lucky to have been heir to his father's energy and enthusiasm for life in general, and for the task at hand in particular. From the time he was a baby, almost everything he did was lighting quick and with great vigor. He was asthmatic when young, and his eyesight was poor because his eyes did not work in unison. These conditions may have also been passed down from Teddy. The asthma was, however, not nearly as severe as was that of his father's. Ted got his first pair of glasses when he was five and wore glasses until age nineteen, when he underwent a successful operation to correct his vision.[3]

The Roosevelt home always contained hundreds of books of all types, including: the classics, history, novels, poetry and science. Both Edith and TR loved to read, and did so at every opportunity. Sometimes Teddy read two books a day. As soon as Ted reached the toddler stage his parents allowed him to join Alice in the daily storytelling and reading time. Ghost stories were the favorite with the children, but history was often the subject read to them. Stories and books such as Robin Hood, Daniel Boone, Custer's Last Stand, Gettysburg, The Battle of Mobile Bay, and The Alamo were read. Theodore delighted in telling the children stories about famous war heroes. He probably got this from his mother, who told her sons stories of the Civil War exploits of her two heroic brothers many times. Oftentimes their parents recited Longfellow, Keats, Shelly, Kipling, or the works of other poets to the children. TR's favorite time to recite was when the children were in his room watching him get dressed for dinner. Ted said, later in his life,

> If you want the child to like Shakespeare or the Bible or whatever it may be, interest the child in it, read it to him, explain it to him. Long before we could read to ourselves, long before we knew how to read, we had already memorized quite a lot of poetry from having it recited to us by our father and mother.

Many people claimed that Ted could remember more poetry than anyone they knew, and after he was grown he would sometimes recite poems in conversations and speeches. There are a number of accounts of him reciting some poem while in the heat of battle during World War I and World War II.[4]

Except for the fact that he was born into a wealthy family, the early years for TRJr were typical for a boy growing up in the 1890s. He went to bed each night with Buffy Bob and Trixie Wee, two small china elephants, and he collected an assortment of things, including Bibles, and bird eggs. Once Ted spotted a bird nest high in a tree, and climbed up to discover the nest had eggs in it. He retrieved one of the eggs, and put it in his mouth for safekeeping as he descended. On the way down, he slipped and fell, causing the egg to break in his mouth. He often drank warm milk squirted into his silver cup right from the cow's teat. He enjoyed playing tricks on his siblings, like putting toads down in their clothes. There is an amusing story involving the big porcelain bathtub on the second floor at Sagamore Hill. Mame, their Irish nanny, used to put Ted in the tub with his toys. When his bath was finished and the stopper pulled, the draining water made a gurgling sound. Mame told Ted that the noise was the "faucet lady" and for him to look down into the drain and try to see her. Thereafter, when Ted chanced to see a nun, he thought he had seen the "faucet lady."[5]

Over the years at Sagamore, Ted and his brothers and sisters had quite a variety of pets. Besides dogs and cats, they had ponies, rats, guinea pigs, chickens, a badger, a coyote, an eagle, a macaw and once a black bear cub and a mountain lion. But perhaps the strangest pet of all was Ted's horseshoe crab. Two flying squirrels slept in Ted's bedroom, unless one of the dogs that also slept there chased them out. One of the many features at Sagamore was the pet cemetery that the Roosevelts started and maintained over the years. It was marked by a stone that was engraved "Faithful Friends," and most of the family's pets were buried there.[6]

Like many boys, Ted was especially attached to his dogs, and particularly to Jack. Jack was a Manchester terrier given to him by a friend of his father. The little canine was the first "inside" dog in the Roosevelt family. Jack slept with Ted and would crawl under the covers and sleep alongside his feet. Edith was not by nature an animal lover, but she was very attached to Jack. Teddy was President when Jack died, and the family had him buried at an appropriate spot on the White House lawn. At the end of Teddy's full term as Chief Executive, the family moved back to their old homeplace, and, in the process, had Jack disinterred and reburied at Sagamore Hill. Ted wrote of Jack's second funeral and how they used a wheelbarrow for a hearse. Teddy, Edith and all four of the boys solemnly walked behind as their beloved little dog was transported into the pet cemetery, each of them feigning sorrow. Then, almost simultaneously, Teddy and Edith were struck by the humor of the event and burst out laughing. At that, Ted, Kermit, Archie, and Quentin also saw the humor in what was going on and took up the chuckle. The whole family loved the mutt, and the comedy they saw in the situation was how they wanted to remember him. They were never able find another "Jack Dog." Ted expressed his fond memories of the many family canines when he wrote that in the "happy hunting ground where the dogs are now, there are plenty of rabbits to chase, and garbage cans are open to all, and numerous kind-hearted cooks abound."[7]

While Ted was devoted to Alice, he idolized his father and was determined to live up to Teddy's image and example. It is not unusual in life for there to be a compulsion or competitiveness on the part of a son to live up to, or even outdo, his father. The fact that Ted was named after his father, and was smaller in statue than TR, (As an adult Ted stood no more than 5'6") may have caused him to have had something like a Napoleonic complex that elevated this natural competition between father and son into almost an obsession. While Ted was a very smart boy, he probably lacked his father's immense intellect. Had IQ tests been common back in the 1800s, TR may well have tested in the genius range. Intelligence aside, Ted certainly never attained his father's perspicacity when it came to politics. Being his firstborn son, Teddy pushed Ted from infancy, talking to him about duty, honor, country and excellence. Ted remembered,

My father believed very strongly in the necessity of each boy being able and willing not only to look out for himself but to look out for those near and dear to him. This gospel was preached to us all from the time we were very, very small.

His father told him,

Ted, every man should defend his country. It should not be a matter of choice, it should be a matter of law. Taxes are levied by law. They are not optional. It is not permitted for a man to say that it is against his religious beliefs to pay taxes, or that he feels that it is an abrogation of his own personal freedom. The blood tax is more important than the dollar tax. It should not therefore be a voluntary contribution, but should be levied on all alike.

TR encouraged all of his children, but especially Ted, to give their all in any activity they undertook, be it games, athletics, education, hunting, or other endeavors. Teddy spent an inordinate amount of time with Ted and his other children. Besides reading books and poetry to them, he was just one of the gang when it came to play. In fact, Edith called her spouse her "oldest and worst child." When the neighborhood kids came over, which was often, there were sometimes as many as twenty children. TR played games with them, swam, camped, hiked, climbed and romped with them. Teddy was the brains of the horde. He taught the children to swim by throwing them into deep water and then pretended they had to swim or sink. He thought up games for all to play, and when they played follow the leader, he, of course, was the leader. Many years later, in an address to the Recreation Congress in Atlantic City, Ted described some of the games his father had invented for the kids, saying:

I remember more of our family tribal customs. We have a delightful thing at home called a "point to point" walk. In the first place, I think that one of the reasons why all of this works out well with us is because every one in the family enjoys it, grownups as well as the younger children. The "point to point" walk was really an invention of my father's. It wasn't thoroughly approved of by my mother!

What you did was this: You took a starting point, let us say by the old barn. Then you picked up another point, perhaps two miles away, a big tree or a house or the top of a house. And then all of you went directly from one point to the other, without turning aside for anything. If you came to a barn, you couldn't go around the barn—you had to go through it or over it. If you came to a pond, you couldn't go around the pond—you had to swim it.

Then we would all go bathing. I remember one time we were on a picnic and had no bathing clothes with us, and father let us go in in our ordinary clothes, Of course, you can realize, to begin with, that that was a perfect joy to the children. We got back and Mother observed our condition, Mother did not see it in quite the same light that father did!—

Then we got to the house and the tragedy started! I don't know how it is with your mothers, but my mother had an invention of the evil one which was called peppermint. And, furthermore, it was fallaciously disguised by being poured over a lump of sugar, on the theory that that made it palatable. It didn't. If anything, it made it worse. We got back to the household, and the first thing mother said was that we must all have peppermint at once. I have never known, to this day, whether that was because she really thought we needed it physically, or whether she thought it was good discipline for us. Anyway when notice was served on us, we galloped out to father, because we felt that father had been *particeps criminis* and he ought to stand up for us. We found him out on the piazza. Mother, meanwhile, was upstairs going through the medicine closet. We said, "Father, need we have peppermint? Mother is going to give us peppermint. Won't you ask her not to?"

And I can just see father, He said, "My dear, I will not. I will be very fortunate if your mother doesn't give me peppermint."

TR did these things to physically and mentally toughen the children, and especially Ted. Ted loved the fact that Teddy was as much or more of a companion than a father, but Alice didn't. She looked on some of her father's play as an ordeal. Alice once told a friend, "Poor TRJr, every time he crosses the street, someone has something to say because he doesn't do it as his father would. And if he navigates nicely, they say it was just as TR would have done it." Ted spent a good part of his life trying to live up to what he perceived to be his father's expectations of him, the namesake. He had an impossible goal. By age five, he was beginning to show signs of nervousness.[8]

Other than for short periods away for hunting or politics, Theodore was at home writing, reading, and playing with the children from the time Ted was born until the spring of 1889, when he was appointed to the U.S. Civil Service Commission by President Benjamin Harrison. TR had campaigned for Harrison during the 1888 election and got the appointment because of his political efforts. The new job required him to be in Washington, D. C. during the week, and he took a temporary residence there. Edith was pregnant with Kermit at the time, so she delayed moving the family to Washington until almost Christmas. Prior to moving, she and TR had Kermit christened. When Ted, who was only twenty-six months old, spied the minister dressed in a surplice, he raised quite a ruckus by exclaiming loudly, "Man in Nana's clothes. Man in Nana's clothes" Edith finally had to remove him from the room. Although Edith and the children would spend summers at Oyster Bay, Washington would be their primary residence for the next six years.[9]

Everyone adjusted well to Washington. Edith was by nature somewhat on the reserved side, but during these first years in the nation's capital, she proved herself to be a gracious and charming wife for the man who, very early in the twentieth century, would be the President of the United States. Alice was becoming a tomboy and her parents began having a difficult time keeping tabs on her. She would rather be wearing boy's clothes and playing in the streets, than be at home sitting around in a nice, clean dress. Kermit was only two months old when the family relocated to Washington, but even at this early age it was easy to see that he was more attached to his mother than either Ted or Alice had been. Ted was Ted. Quick in mind and body, and already wanting very badly to be like his father. Once Alice told Ted that 'Mr. Roosevelt' was their father. Jumping at the chance to compare, Ted said, "Ted is Misser Roosevelt too!" but then added with a look of despair, "but Ted got no mufstache. Ted got muffin but a mouf!" Not many years later, Mame heard Ted describing his father, "A little mufstache, and white teeth, and black hair, and very short, a nice smell of cologne, and wears glasses and gray trousers, and white feet with bones in them and red slippers. And that's my Papa." And later Alice came upon him giving a speech on the back porch to an audience of the hired help. He had a coin in one hand and a loaf of bread in the other and was speaking on the evils of free silver.[10]

While residing in the nation's capital, Edith and TR took the children to Rock Creek Park almost every Sunday afternoon. There they did most of the same things they did when at Oyster Bay, because, at that time, Rock Creek Park was more or less in the country. They looked at the flowers and wildlife, pulled the kids in wagons, swam in summers, skated in winters, walked barefoot, picnicked and hiked. Ted reminisced on those six years that the family resided in Washington, when he wrote that he would frequently walk to work with Teddy, and on the way his father would tell him stories about famous historical events in such a way that he would always remember them. "During every battle we would stop and father would draw out the full plan in the dust with the tip of his umbrella." Teddy's dramatic manner in telling stories of history's great battles and heroes would almost mesmerize the impressionable Ted, and he would daydream that he was one of the principal participants in the event his father was describing. On occasions when TR rode the streetcar to work, Ted and Alice would often ride their bicycles and meet Teddy at Farragut Square when he was on his way home in the evening. During this period, Ted began to show for the first time that he, as a small boy, would not be a "A little Mr. Goodie two-shoes." The Roosevelts resided in a rather small home with no spare rooms. Ted's bedroom was actually meant to be a dressing room just off the master bedroom in which Teddy and Edith slept. Senator Henry Cabot Lodge gave Ted a small hand organ, which he dearly loved to play. Ted usually woke up around five-thirty each morning and delighted in playing his organ as soon as it began to get daylight. After a few days of being awakened by the sound of organ music, his parents came down on him and forbid any hand organ-playing until after breakfast.[11]

Ted's first and only full sister, Ethel, was born in 1891, followed by his brother Archibald in 1894. Ted awoke during the excitement of Archie's arrival, and he woke Alice. Together they were allowed to go in and see the newborn infant. They said it was "better than Christmas." TRJr presented his "little brother in a blanket" his own silver baby's cup as a gift. [12]

Summers spent at Sagamore were great fun for the children, and eagerly anticipated by the entire family. TR spent as much time as he could there, if he wasn't off on a hunt or doing some type of political campaigning. The Roosevelt children and their neighborhood cousins and friends enjoyed being outside playing games, swimming, boating, hiking, picnicking, camping, and riding. Teddy was usually the only grown-up in the group. Ted attributed his father's time and attention to the children as TR's way of insuring that the children grew up to be robust and righteous with the ability to answer the country's needs. If this was TR's goal, he was successful. Of the kids who regularly participated in these activities, six of them were either wounded or killed during wartime service. [13]

One day, when Ted was six, he accompanied his father on a hunt in the woods near the house. Teddy spotted a possum high in a tree and shot it. Witnessing this incident greatly impressed young Ted. When he got back home he told his mother that he, "Had seen a fella killed for the first time," and then launched his career as a author by writing on a blank page in an old book a brief story entitled, "How We Shot My First Possum."

The Fourth of July was always a big occasion at Sagamore Hill. Being the patriots and historians that they were, Teddy and Edith allowed the children to shoot firecrackers, Roman candles, and rockets all day long. On one occasion in 1899, the festivities started at 4:00 a.m. when either Ted or Kermit, but most likely Ted, set off a bunch of giant firecrackers and woke up the rest of the family. Teddy, remembering his own childhood and believing in the proper celebration of the birthday of the country, held his temper and allowed the fireworks to continue. The Fourth of July was a special day for TRJr, he got to lead the neighborhood children in the festivities instead of his father. [14]

The Roosevelt children did not have the opportunity to get to know their Carow grandparents. Their grandfather, Charles Carow, died before they were born, and grandmother Gertrude Carow had resided in Europe since before Teddy and Edith were married. She was able to visit the children only one time before her death in 1894. However, Alice's Lee grandparents were good to all the Roosevelt children and the whole brood looked on Mr. and Mrs. Lee as their own grandparents. One time the Lees gave Alice and her siblings a pony named Grant, along with a pony cart. They all loved pony Grant, and especially Ted. He always rode the little animal just as fast as its short legs would go. Later, the family got a second pony for the children. They named that one Algonquin, and he was transported back and forth between Washington and Oyster Bay, wherever the family happened to be. [15]

By 1894, TR was beginning to tire of his job on the Civil Service Board. He felt he had accomplished a lot, but was ready to move on to some new challenge. The election for mayor of New York was coming up in the fall, and Teddy wanted badly to run for the office. Edith was opposed to this, however, and Teddy complied with her wishes and did not enter the race. Later Edith expressed remorse because of what she decided was her unwarranted interference in a career decision her husband was entitled to make. The Republican candidate, William Strong, won the election and, in the spring of 1895, offered TR the appointment as President of the New York City Board of Police Commissioners. Teddy resigned from his job in Washington and accepted the appointment. The family left the nation's capital and moved back to Oyster Bay, but maintained a second residence in New York City. The 3½ years following this move back to Sagamore Hill were among the happiest of Ted's life.[16]

It was about the time the Roosevelts moved back to Oyster Bay that TR Jr first began to tell his friends and relatives that he wanted to be a soldier when he grew up. Apparently, no one in the family took him seriously except Kermit. Kermit responded that Ted was just going to be an ordinary man with "'bunnies" like their father. The matter was dropped and did not come up again until some years later, when Ted was at an age to be seriously considering a career.[17]

All the Roosevelt children dearly loved life at Sagamore Hill, and had many sentimental memories of growing up there. In later life Ted wrote, "Sagamore is the offspring of the years as surely as is a reef of coral. Wings and rooms, pictures and furniture. Each tells a story in the same fashion as the rings in the trunk of a great tree." Ted christened the room on the second floor where Teddy kept his rather extensive firearms collection as the "gun room." The "North Room" on the first floor had been added to the house when Teddy was president and was by far the largest room in the house. Teddy insisted that all of the materials used in the construction of the North Room be made, grown or mined in the United States, or one of its possessions. Reminiscing, Ted later wrote that to him the North Room was the warm and snug family room. He would always picture it with Teddy poking the fire with an iron trident in one hand and a book in the other and with his mother quietly sitting on the sofa sewing.[18]

Edith and the children frequently attended church services at the small Episcopal Church in Oyster Bay. Ted recalled that, after church, a typical Sunday lunch would consist of "thick black bean soup powdered with grated eggs, with golden brown cornbread steaming hot so that butter melts without spreading, roast beef flanked by brown potatoes, spinach, and vanilla ice cream with thick dark chocolate sauce." While the land use in the immediate area would change in the coming years, at that time Sagamore Hill was located in a rural area where most of the land was in pasture and cropland, with many scattered patches of woods. Part of the land surrounding Sagamore was farmed, and Teddy and Edith employed the services of a gardener to take care of their yard and raise a small vegetable garden in season. Ted, even though he was only $7\frac{1}{2}$ years old, was already showing an interest in horticulture, and he liked nothing better than to don his overalls and help tend the garden or hitch a ride on some old farm wagon that happened to be passing by. Years later Ted sadly remembered Davis, the old Sagamore Hill gardener who had lost all of his children. They mistook mercury for sugar at a play tea party. The old man's favorite expression was "let it be." Ted's love for planting and growing things would surface again years later when he owned his own home.[19]

The Roosevelt's nearest neighbors were the families of their cousins, Emlen Roosevelt and West Roosevelt. Emlen's daughter, Christine, and sons, George and Jack, were almost the same ages as Alice, Ted, and Kermit respectively, and West's daughter Lorraine and son Nicholas were the same ages as Ethel and Archie. The cousins did everything together. They swam, rode horses, played hide and seek and other games. Camping was one of their favorite group activities, with or without Teddy. Nicholas Roosevelt recalled that TR's and Edith's children were an independent lot, wanting to do everything for themselves. Each even built his or her individual campfire and prepared his or her own food, claiming that none of the others could cook as well. One Fourth of July, Ted, Kermit, George and Jack sneaked over to a neighbor's house just after daylight, and shot off a large number of firecrackers. Naturally the neighbors complained to the parents for their rude awakening. As the Fourth of July approached the following year, Emlen told George and Jack they could not go out with Ted and Kermit that year. Not to be deterred, early on the morning of the fourth, Ted and Kermit climbed up one of the posts to George's and Jack's second floor bedroom, quietly got them up, and persuaded them to come out for some early morning shenanigans. After the boys finished and were on their way back home, they saw Emlen coming down the path with a switch in his hand. Not wanting to interfere in what they considered to be a family matter between George, Jack and their father, Ted and Kermit disappeared into the woods.

The Emlen Roosevelt family always ate a big country breakfast at 7:00 a.m., while Teddy Roosevelt's family did not eat their similar breakfast until 8:00 a.m. Very often the kids from both families would eat breakfast at Emlen's at 7:00 and then make it over to Teddy's by 8:00 to eat a second hardy breakfast.[20]

To have been a little fellow, TRJr had a ravenous appetite. His love for good food was apparent from the number of times it was mentioned in his writings later in life. In one instance, Ted confessed of how he and Kermit purloined a pound of guava jelly out of the family pantry and ate all of it in their secret hiding place out behind the icehouse. This was one time when crime did pay because it was never discovered, nor did they get sick from eating so much jelly. Ted recalled another occasion when he and Kermit, then ages six and eight, made plans to explore the upper stories of Sagamore Hill. To insure they would have plenty to eat, they made another a raid on the pantry and absconded with a supply of food including candy, cookies, crackers, prunes and sugar. For lack of a better place, they hid the food under a pillow in the spare bedroom. Knowing that Edith would never stand for what they had done, they took their father into their confidence and told him about their secret food stash. Teddy assured the boys he would not tell their mother. True to his word, Teddy honored his commitment to the boys and did not reveal the secret to Edith. Some time passed and Ted, Kermit and Teddy forgot all about the food cache until one day when a guest came to stay in the spare bedroom and the food was discovered by Edith. The boys instantly realized they were in serious trouble, and, when confronted by their mother, they admitted the act but slyly passed the buck on to Edith's "oldest and worst child" by telling her that their father had known of the location of their provisions all along.[21]

Teddy felt that he should stay most nights in the city to properly perform his job on the Police Commission, so Edith and the children frequently stayed weeknights in the city with him. Alice loved the city life, but Ted would rather have been at Oyster Bay. In New York, Alice and Ted took dancing lessons at Ms. Dodsworth's and music lessons in Brooklyn. Most of the time Teddy had a plainclothes policeman take them over to Brooklyn for their music lessons. Sometimes the officer would bring them to police headquarters after their lessons were over. They always had a wonderful time at the police headquarters because they were allowed to look at mug shots, see the jail, and watch the police officers come in and out as they did their jobs. On one occasion Alice had a rather serious infection involving her jawbone and was confined to Roosevelt Hospital for a time. After she got better, she and Ted would slip away from her room and explore unusual places in the hospital. Once, they made it into the refrigerated room where cadavers were kept and dissected by the medical students.[22]

When Ted was nine, Teddy bought him his first real firearm, a Flobert rifle (a small caliber weapon designed for target shooting). TR brought the weapon home one night after it was too late to go outside and test it out. Sensing Ted's disappointment at having to wait until the next day to shoot his new rifle, TR took Ted and the new rifle upstairs to Ted's bedroom, put a shell in the chamber, and, after mutual promises not to tell Edith were exchanged, fired the rifle into the ceiling. Afterwards, one summer day Ted and some of his cousins were out shooting their rifles at whatever targets of opportunity happened to be spotted. Out of wickedness they fired a number of rounds into the TR family bathhouse in which Teddy's brand new bathing suit was hung. A day or two later Teddy went into the bathhouse, changed into his swimming attire and went for a swim, failing to notice the numerous bullet holes in his new suit from which small spots of naked skin showed like polka dots.

Following right in his father's footsteps, Ted, during his pre-teen years, was something of a puck, a real Huckleberry Finn. As an example, Ted and Kermit once drank an enormous quantity of water to get their stomachs to swell. Then they showed their stomachs to Edith and Mame in order to create panic among the women. Ted, and who ever else he could get to go with him, liked to hide in bushes along the road and throw green apples and pinecones at wagons and buggies as they came by. On one unlucky day, Ted and his cousins George and Jack Roosevelt were engaged in this pastime when down the road came a carriage from the train station with one passenger aboard. Each boy made an accurate throw, hitting the driver and knocking the passenger's hat off. Both the driver and passenger gave chase, but the boys knew the terrain and made good their escape. Later when Ted got home, he was horrified to see that the passenger was Colonel Andrews, who was to be an overnight guest of his father's. At dinner that night, with the whole family around the table, Col. Andrews described the apple-throwing incident, adding that he was sure that Ted was not involved. There was a silence at the table as everyone looked at Ted. They knew. Theodore Roosevelt, Jr. was a very mischievous boy. He was quick to anger, but quick to forgive and forget.[23]

Ted did not receive any formal public or private school education until the fall of 1896, when Edith enrolled him in the one-room Cove Neck School, a public school near Oyster Bay. While a few of the students were the offspring of wealthy residents, most of them were children of the common folk of the area, gardeners, coachmen, farmers, etc. The teacher, Ms. Hawkshurst, was herself the daughter of an old time Oyster Bay commoner. Ted was small for his age, recited poetry, wore glasses, and from home had been taught the golden rule and the idea of politeness, especially to girls. This type behavior and appearance was just not the norm at the tough, obdurate Cove Neck School, and he was considered to be a sissy by his classmates. Ted talked to his father about his problems in adjusting to public school. Teddy, no doubt thinking of the time years before when he stood up for himself in the bar in the Dakota Badlands, told him, "You can be just as decent as you wish, provided you are prepared to fight. If you fight hard enough, you are perfectly certain to secure the respect of your playmates for your virtues." A few weeks later Ted was accosted by Pete Gallager, one of his primary antagonists. This time, he held his ground and whipped Gallagher. As far as Ted was concerned, chivalry and decency prevailed. Thereafter his classmates looked on him with more respect.[24]

By the time the 1896 presidential election approached, Teddy had been President of the New York Board of Police Commissioners for over two years. He had accomplished a lot, and had received quite a bit of good local publicity. The crime rate in the city was down, as was corruption within the police department. Teddy was a very ambitious politician, and felt that to further his political career he should get out of New York and back into the national political picture. This meant going back to Washington. He campaigned for William McKinley, the Republican candidate, and when McKinley soundly thrashed Democrat William Jennings Bryan in the fall presidential election, Teddy immediately began a lobbying campaign to get himself appointed Assistant Secretary of the Navy. President McKinley delayed in making the appointment for a while, but finally in April, 1897, gave TR his much sought after appointment. Resigning as police commissioner, he left for the nation's capital. Teddy had made the right move, but he could not have known that he had just stepped into a political rocket that would, within three short years, propel him from being well known only in New York and the Dakota Badlands, to holding the most prestigious political office in the world.

De ja vu to the time when TR had been appointed to the Civil Service Board, Edith was pregnant and postponed moving the family to Washington until October. In the interim Teddy stayed with the Henry Cabot Lodges when in Washington, returning to Sagamore on weekends and holidays when he could get away.

While the Fourth of July was always a special occasion at Sagamore Hill, the Independence Day celebration in 1897 was extra special. There was unrest in Cuba; the Cubans were almost in open revolt against the oppressive Spanish dominance. Many Americans, including TR, were calling for war against Spain. Teddy told President McKinley that he intended to be personally involved in the fighting if war should come about. Some of the animosity created by the American Civil War had waned, and, in anticipation of war with Spain, a sense of patriotism and excitement was beginning to spread across the country. Another event which made the holiday significant that year, although there was no way anyone could have been aware of it at that time, was that Bamie's old friend Sara Delano Roosevelt and her fifteen-year-old son, Franklin Delano Roosevelt, were houseguests at Sagamore for the occasion. Franklin was a very handsome, outgoing, and elegant lad, but somehow he just did not fit in with the rough-and-tumble life of Ted, Teddy, and the rest of the TR clan. A few years later Franklin would refer to himself as "F. D. Roosevelt." Someone in the TR household, most likely Alice, claimed that the "F. D." stood for "feather duster." Kermit would eventually become a close friend of FDR's, and Teddy had a pleasant, almost fatherly relationship with him, probably because they shared a keen political instinct. However, Edith, Ted and the other children would remain political enemies of FDR for the rest of their lives.[25]

Ted had suffered from recurring headaches for several years, but by Christmas time 1897 the headaches had increased in frequency and intensity to the point that they were debilitating. His parents were very concerned about him. They had him examined by a number of physicians, but none of them could find the cause of the problem. Then, about the middle of January, Edith came down with a fever and a host of other aches and pains. When she had not improved by the middle of February, Alice was hurried off to visit Bamie in New York to lessen the load on the young mother. Ted would have been sent with her, but he was too sick to move. Edith's problem was diagnosed as an abscess of the psoas muscle, and she was classified as critically ill. After surgery in early March, she slowly began to improve. In the meantime, Ted showed some improvement, and he was then sent to join Alice at Bamie's. While in New York, Ted was examined by Dr. Alexander Lambert, a personal friend of TR's. Dr. Lambert reported that the boy was suffering from nervous prostration brought on by the way Teddy constantly drove him to perfection and Ted's desire to live up to his father's expectations. A treatment of diet and exercise was prescribed.

TR was shocked at this diagnosis and responded by writing to Dr. Lambert, "Hereafter I shall never press Ted either in body or mind. The fact is that the little fellow, who is peculiarly dear to me, had bidden fair to be all things I would like to have been and wasn't, and it has been a great temptation to push him." In a letter Teddy wrote William Sheffield Cowles, he said, "I guess I have pushed him a little too hard, or rather that everybody had, for being a bright, amusing little fellow he is favored and petted by all kinds of people **** with the result that he becomes self-conscious, and his nerves have finally given away." When TR eased up, Ted was soon on the road to recovery. In reminiscing about her children years later, Edith wrote that Ted was more affected by his father's constant pushing than the other children because by the time the others came along Teddy was busy with other things.[26]

On February 15, 1898, 264 Americans were killed when, while making a "courtesy call," the U.S.S. Maine blew up and sank in Havana Harbor. The public cry for war escalated into a demand. President McKinley ordered an investigation by a Naval Court of Inquiry, and delayed asking Congress to declare war until he had an opportunity to view the results. The Court reported on March 21st that the ship sank as the result of an external explosion but was not able to place responsibility on any particular person, group or country. As far as public opinion in the United States was concerned, Spain was the culprit. War was declared on April 19th. Congress, realizing that the regular American Army was small and unprepared for war, authorized the recruitment of three voluntary cavalry regiments to boost the Army's strength. Teddy, because of his political connections, was offered the command of one of these new regiments, but he had had no military experience and did not feel himself qualified for the job. He, therefore, declined in favor of his friend, Colonel Leonard Wood. TR was to be a Lieutenant

Colonel and the second in command. On May 6th he resigned his appointment as Assistant Secretary of the Navy, purchased for himself a beautiful blue Cravenette cavalry uniform from Brooks Brothers, and departed Sagamore Hill for San Antonio, Texas, where his regiment, the First United States Volunteer Cavalry Regiment, was to form for training purposes. Ted, now at the impressionable age of eleven, was apprehensive about his father leaving for battle. But at the same time he was proud of him and wanted to go with him, not to fight, but to clean his guns and be of assistance in any way he could. Ted knew that not every boy had a father that had actually seen battle.[27]

Applications to join the new regiment came in from all over the country: north, east, south, and west, but the only official sign-up stations were in the Arizona, New Mexico, and the Oklahoma Indian Territories, so most of the applicants accepted were Indians, cowboys, professional hunters, and miners from that general area of the country. However, some Ivy League college men were approved, along with men from other colleges, and a smattering of men from all sections of the U.S. The Regiment soon acquired the nickname "Rough Riders." It originally had an authorized strength of 790 officers and men, but this was later increased to one thousand. One of the Native American Rough Riders was a descendent of the famous Chickasaw chief, George Colbert. Eighty-four years before Chief Colbert had ferried the renowned Tennessee Volunteers across the Tennessee River as that bedraggled army trekked south on the Natchez Trace toward New Orleans for one of the decisive battles of the War of 1812, and General Andrew Jackson's appointment with history.

Like their second in command, most of the Rough Riders had no previous military training. To be approved and accepted into the new regiment an applicant had to be in excellent physical condition and appear to have a personal toughness that would allow him to hold up under extremely harsh conditions. The training, which was completed in about $2\frac{1}{2}$ weeks, consisted of: instruction in basic military duties, mounted drill, dismounted drill, guard duty, rifle and pistol instruction, and skirmish drills.

At the end of May, the Regiment was moved by rail to Tampa, Florida, the port of embarkation, and sailed for Cuba on June 13th. Landing in Cuba on June 22nd, the troopers were moving on foot toward Santiago when, on June 24th, they were engaged in a firefight by a contingent of the Spanish Army. This engagement lasted about two hours and resulted in eight Rough Riders being killed and thirty-four wounded. A few days later, Leonard Wood was made brigade commander, and TR was promoted to full colonel and given command of the Regiment. Pushing on toward Santiago, by late morning of July 1st, the regiment found itself at the base of Kettle Hill and San Juan Ridge. A number of the men had dropped out due to illness and heat exhaustion, and a detail had been left behind to guard supplies and equipment. The unit was down to less than half of its authorized strength when orders to support an advance up Kettle Hill were received. Now began what TR referred to as his "Crowded Hour." Ted would refer to it as the time when his father "approached the gates of paradise." Under heavy fire and upon his mount "Little Texas," Teddy led the reckless, famous charge of the Rough Riders up Kettle Hill. To those of his troops that hesitated, he urged them on by yelling, "Are you afraid to stand up when I am on horseback?" With his men now following behind, TR continued leading the assault against the Spanish regulars entrenched at the top. When the summit of Kettle Hill had been secured and the enemy troops either dead, captured or fleeing in terror, TR scrutinized San Juan Ridge and saw that the U.S. regulars there were taking casualties from the well dug in Spaniards. Although still under heavy fire, Teddy wheeled Little Texas in the direction of the ridge, and led the Rough Riders in its capture. While there remained scattered small arms and artillery fire, the battle was essentially over. The Rough Riders suffered eighty-nine killed and wounded. TR's arm had been grazed by a bullet, the heel of his boot had been hit, and an exploding artillery shell had thrown dirt in his face, but otherwise he went unscathed in the fierce fight. The battle had been well covered by the press, who immediately dubbed Teddy a great American hero. After the battle, the Rough Riders were left in stifling, disease-ridden Cuba for another month, and they got back to the U.S. then only because Teddy put public pressure on the Secretary of War to bring them home. After sailing back to the U.S., the Regiment disembarked at Montauk Point, Long Island, on August 15th.[28]

Meanwhile, at home, TR Jr prayed for his father's safety and read intently every news account of his father's exploits he could get his hands on. When word got back to Sagamore that Teddy was safe and of his heroism, the family was elated and proud, especially Ted. Hearing that his father had been hit in the boot heel, Ted wanted him to, "save the boot" as a battle souvenir. The events of the Spanish-American War in general, and his father's actions in particular, were permanently etched in Ted's mind and would remain so for the rest of his life.[29]

It is interesting to speculate on what motivated TR to perform his valiant actions on that July 1st day and to consider the factors involved. Psychologists claim that why humans do what we do is often not the result of a carefully thought-out plan, but is an impulsive reaction to an unexpected situation, and that the reason different people may react differently to the same situation is because of each individual's heredity, life experiences, and physical health, i.e. one person may run away while another person may stand and fight. While Teddy was without question the principal beneficiary of his own heroism, when the facts are considered there is no reasonable way he could have planned his conduct like a chess game. A battle was in progress; there was no way to foresee what may occur next. The Rough Riders were not given the order to advance on Kettle Hill until the moment before TR mounted Little Texas to begin the charge. Also, when the Rough Riders began their assault up Kettle Hill there was a unit of U. S. regulars on the slope ahead of them. These regular troops should have led the assault, but they froze and allowed Teddy's men to pass through them. It is not impossible, and may very well be probable, that TR had considered in advance the likelihood that he would find his unit in a dangerous battle situation and had determined to throw caution to the wind if and when this circumstance arose. Teddy was a thrill seeker, an example being the frequent big game hunts he went on, and on one occasion killing a cougar with a knife so the hunting dogs would not get hurt fighting with the wild beast. No doubt, at San Juan and Kettle his adrenaline was flowing. His actions were those of a man excited and possessed.[30]

Also with respect to motivation, consideration must also be given to the fact that Teddy felt a sincere obligation to the country. He was a patriot in every since of the word. This is evidenced by his constantly drilling into his sons that they had a moral duty to answer their country's call for help. It is well known that Teddy's father, Theodore Roosevelt, Sr., had declined to serve in the Union Army during the Civil War, and paid another man to serve in his place. TR was ashamed of his father for this. He felt that his father disgraced the family name and wanted to set a better example for Ted, Kermit, Archie, and Quentin, than TRSr had set for him. Many times, Teddy said that he would rather have to explain why he had gone to war than have to explain why he had not.[31]

To suggest that Theodore Roosevelt would endanger the lives of his men for his own personal gain is almost irreverent to consider, but this point of view is bolstered by the fact that the Spanish-American War was well covered by newsmen and the papers were calling for Teddy's election to the governorship of New York within a few days after the San Juan battle. Also, Teddy met with Henry Cabot Lodge and other political cronies to plan a governors race just as soon as he was able to get away from the Rough Riders at Montauk Point. Thinking he was helping TR politically, one of his most trusted Rough Riders, Buck Taylor, said in a speech, "He kept every promise he made to us and he will to you. When he took us to Cuba he told us ***. We would have to lie out in the trenches with the rifle bullets climbing over us, and we done it ***. He told us we might meet wounds and death and we done it, but he was there in the midst of us, and when it came to the great day he led us up San Juan Hill like sheep to the slaughter, and so will he lead you." On many occasions TR proudly referred to the fact that his regiment took heavy casualties.[32]

The Rough Riders were quarantined at Montauk Point for several days after debarking. TR, at his earliest opportunity, took a temporary leave of a few days to visit with his family and meet with political advisors. At the conclusion of his leave, he went back to his men for the next three or four weeks, seeing to their needs and arranging for their discharge from the army. Edith, Alice, Ted and Kermit made an overnight visit with Teddy and the Regiment the first week in September. It was hard to tell who was the most delighted with the visit, Ted or Alice: Ted, with being around real live heroes and sleeping in his father's tent, or Alice, flirting with the young Rough Rider officers.[33]

The First United States Volunteer Cavalry Regiment was still at Montauk Point when, on September 13th, 1898, it was formed in a hollow square and called to attention for the last time for the formal mustering out ceremony. With Teddy in the center, one of the Rough Rider sergeants stepped forward and presented him with a reproduction of Frederick Remington's famous bronze, "The Bronco-Buster." This gift from the enlisted men would remain Theodore's most-prized possession until he died. In a final address to his troops, Teddy reminded them that the Regiment was American through and through because it was composed of all races that made America great. Then, as the men filed by, many in tears, TR shook hands with each of them.[34]

Shortly after the famous San Juan battle, Theodore was recommended for the Congressional Medal of Honor, which he desperately wanted. He thought it would help his political career, but then throughout his life TR delighted in the public accolades that came his way. He lobbied for the MOH award, writing letters and contacting influential people, and obtaining affidavits to support his heroism. The award was denied him at that time, probably because of the embarrassment he caused the Secretary of War and the President when he went public with the deplorable conditions the Rough Riders were living in before they were brought home from Cuba. There can be no doubt that Theodore's acts on that July 1st day were deserving of the nation's highest award for valor, and it was finally posthumously awarded to him 103 years later by President Bill Clinton.

With the Rough Riders disbanded, Teddy got down to the serious business of pursuing the Republican nomination for governor. His quest was successful and there followed a rigorous campaign before the general election. On November 8th, TR eked out an eighteen thousand vote victory over his Democratic opponent and became the Governor-Elect of the State of New York.

Customarily each Christmas Eve afternoon there was a program at Cove Neck School. The kids recited and sang and TR made a short talk followed by the distribution of the presents from under the tree. Edith always made inquiries to determine what gift would please each individual child. The gift from TR and Edith was the best one many of the children got. Everyone knew TR would be going to Albany, but during the program this year one of the Gallagher children recited a poem that made the event special for TR and Edith. The poem included the lines: "We'll send you to the White House for the gallant deeds you've done," This brought the house down with applause. Soon thereafter, Ted was withdrawn from Cove Neck School, the only public school he would ever attend, and once again Edith and the family moved their residence, this time into the Governor's Mansion in Albany. Their new home was somewhat larger than Sagamore Hill, but the architecture was similar. At the January 2, 1899 inauguration Teddy spotted Ted sitting in the gallery of the Assembly Chamber and blew him a kiss. The crowed roared its approval.[35]

Before the family was settled in good, Ted was enrolled in the first form at the Albany Academy, a military school for boys that taught kindergarten through high school. The school was established in 1813, and it had a reputation of providing its students with a quality education while encouraging vigorous athletic participation. A course in boxing was offered, and Ted availed himself of the opportunity. He proved to be a very good boxer by several times bloodying the instructor's nose while they were sparring in the ring. Continuing the propensity he exhibited at Cove Neck School, Ted was not hesitant to engage in a little extracurricular fisticuffs when he thought it was justified, like the time he came home from school all muddy and scuffed-up from having a fight with a bigger boy. He told his father that the other boy had made a face at him and hollered, "Your father's a faker." It was a close fight, Ted said, but he had won. Teddy bared his teeth and grinned his approval.

Unlike in Cove Neck School, Ted was now associated with the children of the wealthy, or at least the moderately wealthy, but like in Cove Neck, he made many lasting friends there, one being Mort Deyo, who later became a Navy Admiral. Shortly after his enrollment, Ted and seven or eight of his schoolmates formed "The Boy's Junior Athletic Club." All the club members were about the same age. They would meet frequently and play team sports, primarily football and hockey. Even though he was small for his age, TRJr was a tough competitor and gave a 100% effort in all the contests. George Cantine, who was a member of the little club, remembered Ted as being "personable and lovable" and a "born leader." Unlike his father, who never played team sports, Ted thoroughly enjoyed team play and the camaraderie that resulted. After playing football, hockey or some other sport, the boys would sometimes go over to the Governor's Mansion to warm up, or go over to one of the other boy's houses for cookies and milk. Ted especially loved cookies and would stuff his pockets full when he left. One time Teddy agreed to speak to the members of the little club. Ted was to introduce him. TR was concerned as to whether his son would be embarrassed or in some way resentful to have his governor-father speak, and was in a quandary as to how the handle the situation. Ted put him at ease when, before they arrived at the meeting, he told Teddy, "Please, Father, don't pay any attention to me or talk about me when we get there."[36]

While the winter temperature in Albany is somewhat colder than on Long

Island, Ted and his siblings, except for possibly Alice, thoroughly enjoyed their two-year stint there. Naturally, summers were still spent at Sagamore Hill. While in Albany, Ted carried on much the same life he lived at Oyster Bay except that he was in an urban environment rather than his customary, uninhibited, rural surroundings. He continued his interest in nature, and added an eagle egg and an ostrich egg to his bird egg collection. To protect his valuables from the curious hands of his younger siblings, he kept them locked in a cabinet. At Easter one time, TR and Edith decided to give Ted and his brothers and sisters a lesson: that sometimes the obvious is not so easy to see or detect. To emphasize the point, during the Easter egg hunt they put one egg in plain view; it was the last one found.[37]

TR and Edith were very young to be Governor and First Lady of any state, and especially one as large and as important as New York. Besides being young, they were ambitious and energetic. To further public relations, they often entertained in the Governor's Mansion. When a social event was in progress, the children were supposed to stay upstairs and out of the way, but sometimes they would sneak downstairs and get into mischief. One time while guests were at the mansion, the Roosevelt youngsters went outside in their sleepwear and had a snowball fight, to the amusement of the guests, but to the embarrassment of their parents. Another time, one of them, considering his tendency for pranks it was probably Ted, slipped downstairs and hid a billiard ball in a bowl of fruit. A distracted guest picked it up and, thinking it was a piece of fruit, tried to bite into it. Probably the most embarrassing incident, as far as TR and Edith were concerned, occurred on the first really warm night after a bitter cold winter. With the mansion full of important people, a foul odor permeated the dwelling. An investigation revealed that the decaying droppings from all the little rabbits, guinea pigs, and other varmints Ted and his siblings kept in the basement were the cause.

During the first days of the twentieth century, Governor Roosevelt began to consider his options for the future, political and otherwise. He could run for re-election for another two-year term as governor, or he could earn his living as a writer or teacher; in fact he had declined at least one opportunity to teach several years before. Another choice was to get into national politics in some way. TR had had his eyes set on the presidency since San Juan Hill, but the question was how was the best way to get there. Republican William McKinley was the current President, and he would certainly seek a second term in the fall general election. Teddy could bide his time by seeking re-election as governor, but that would still leave him two years short of the 1904 general elections, or he could work toward a position in McKinley's cabinet, perhaps as Secretary of War. Another option was to seek the Republican nomination for Vice President. The vice-presidency was historically a do-nothing job with little chance to keep oneself in the public eye. He knew the V-P nomination was his for the asking, but Edith was against it. She felt being Vice President would not aid in his quest for the presidency in 1904, and besides, it paid $2,000 less per year than the New York Governor's job. What to do? What to do?

When the Republican National Convention opened in June, 1900, Edith and his close friends and advisors were under the impression that TR would decline the VP nomination, but his heroics of two years before had not been forgotten by the delegates. The nomination was practically thrust upon him. TR made a fiery speech and got caught up in the excitement of the hour. The convention band played, "There'll Be a Hot Time in the Old Town Tonight." There was pandemonium. "We want Teddy!" "We want Teddy!" "We want Teddy!" His party called! His country called! How could he refuse? After a vigorous campaign in the fall, the McKinley-Roosevelt Republican ticket soundly defeated the William Jennings Bryan-Adlai E. Stevenson Democratic ticket. TR was VP.[38]

Ted remained a student at the Albany Academy until the 1901 spring school term was over, and then he joined his mother and siblings at Sagamore Hill for the summer. TR was there some of the time, but was away campaigning a good bit. Almost a teenager now, Ted was certainly not a handsome young man; some would say he was "pug ugly." He was still small for his age, but he was wiry, strong, quick, and he had a lot of stamina. Alice was almost grown, and was driving her parents crazy with her antics.[39]

Summer was again a fun time for the kids, with the usual swimming, boating, riding, fishing, tennis, shooting, and other activities. Toward the end of summer, Ted began to prepare for a major event in his life. He had been enrolled as a student at Groton School in Massachusetts and would be leaving the parental nest in early fall. The last days of September were busy ones for him as he got ready to leave. Ted was not enthusiastic about going away to school. When the time came, Edith accompanied him to Groton and got him unpacked and settled in. He had just celebrated his thirteenth birthday.

Groton, in 1900, was an exclusive boarding school for boys, established by Teddy's old friend, Endicott Peabody, in 1884. It was located about forty miles from Boston. The school sought to enhance the intellectual, moral and physical life of its students. All three of Ted's brothers would follow him there in later years.[40]

For the first month or so away from home, Ted did not adjust well. He was extremely homesick and had fights with many of the other boys, whipping most of them. One reason for his unhappiness was because he had not begun school until he was nine years old, and the frequent changes in schools had left him scholastically behind his classmates. By late November, however, he was getting his feet on the ground and was over his homesickness. He was applying himself to his studies, singing in the school choir, and he was captain of his dormitory football team. Ted wrote his mother that his clothes were in good condition "excepting that one pair of pants was split up the middle and one jacket had lost a sleeve in a scuffle," and that he ruined another pair of pants when he "sat down in a jam pie at a cellar spread."[41]

The upper classmen at Groton had a tradition of punishing the younger boys who had in some way failed to live up to the strict standard of conduct expected of a student there. The punishment was referred to as "pumping," and consisted of a stern lecture on the failed conduct followed by holding the offender under a running faucet for a time, making him cough and spit. Ted was pumped twice during his first months of enrollment. His cousin, Franklin Delano Roosevelt, who had preceded him to Groton, was never pumped.[42]

As the March 1901 inauguration day approached, the family moved from Albany to the nation's capital. The move, however, had little effect on Ted at Groton. The plans were for him to catch a train to Washington for the inauguration festivities. His mother wrote him to be sure and wear his best clothes. Edith was waiting at Washington's Union Station when Ted's train pulled in. Looking him over, she immediately saw that his attire was mismatched. When questioned, Ted said that he had done as his mother instructed. He had worn his best trousers, his best vest, and his best jacket. Nobody had a better time at the reception following the formal inauguration of Teddy as Vice President than Ted. He mingled and talked to guests, just like an adult. He even drank two glasses of champagne, claiming he thought he was drinking "fizzy water." After the event concluded, Ted returned to Groton to finish out the spring term. By now his grades had improved dramatically; he stood third in his class and was participating in the school boxing and wrestling programs. In his weight class he was very good in both sports.[43]

After officially assuming the duties of Vice President on March 4th, Theodore presided over the Senate only until March 8th, when the Senate was adjourned until December. TR, Edith and all the kids, except Ted at Groton, packed up and went home to Oyster Bay for an extended stay. Ted joined them there as soon as the spring term was over. Before the weather turned summer hot, TR took all of his children, all of their contemporary cousins, and their mothers on an all-day beach picnic. Ted described their food that day as being, "baked clams and cinders, and sandwiches and sand."

In early September, Edith and all the children went to the Adirondack Mountains for a before school starts vacation. TR was to join them later in the week. Shortly before Teddy was to arrive, word was received that President McKinley, who had been visiting in Buffalo, had been shot by a would-be assassin. Theodore immediately went to the President's bedside, only to discover that

McKinley was doing well and was expected to fully recover. Based on this medical information, TR joined his family in their remote mountain cabin. Then word was received that the President had worsened and that his condition was critical. Teddy again departed for Buffalo. This time, because of the almost inaccessible area their cabin was in, the initial leg of the journey was by wagon, and then by train. Before he arrived, President McKinley died. Theodore, at a younger age than any previous President, had made all the right moves and had now achieved his goal in life, even if by default.

Just after Teddy was sworn in, a newspaper reporter ran into Ted and asked him whether he was more pleased to have killed his first deer or to be the son of the President of the United States. Even though he was only fourteen, he sensed a loaded question and responded, "I have no time to answer such questions."[44]

After Mrs. McKinley vacated the executive mansion, TR and his clan moved in. This was the first time that young children had occupied the presidential home, and the White House staff didn't know what to make of it. The children played all over the house and the furnishings. Their games included: leapfrog on the fine furniture, roller-skating on the nice hardwood floors, walking on stilts, and ponies on the elevator and in the children's bedrooms. Ted was probably glad to get back to the quiet life at Groton to begin the fall term and play some more football. He was now fourteen but not much taller or heavier than in the past year. Early on in the fall term, Ted had a fight with a schoolmate who called him "the first boy in the land." The remark offended him. He must have thought the boy was making fun of him for being the President's son.

Football practice started and, as always, Ted played as hard as he could on every down. In one game he broke his collarbone but went ahead and played the rest of the game without letting anyone know he was hurt. Later that same season, he got some of his teeth knocked loose. Teddy became so concerned over Ted's football injuries that he wrote the headmaster, Endicott Peabody, to express his concern. Later, TR would write that Ted was, "a regular bull terrier and devoted to his mother and sisters, and although I don't believe he is quarrelsome among his friends, he is everlastingly having sanguinary battles with outsiders."***"In most branches of sport he has already completely passed me by."*** "he can certainly take horses over jumps which I would not care to."[45]

The fall term flew by. When TRJr went home for the Christmas holidays, it was, for the first time, to the Roosevelt's new home in the White House. The kids all hung their stockings from the mantel in the library. The day after Christmas Edith, Ted and the rest of the children went on a three-day excursion on the Presidential yacht, "Dolphin." They would lazily cruise down the Potomac for a while, and then stop, anchor, and eat a shore lunch of roasted oysters or some other delicious seafood. They all enjoyed the trip immensely.[46]

The new year began with TR's first official public reception, followed the next night by his first Cabinet Dinner. Then, on January 3rd, Alice made her debut with a coming-out ball at the White House. She was almost eighteen now, smoked and ran with the fast wealthy crowd to the dismay of her father and stepmother. Her party was the premiere social event of the Washington holiday season. Alice and Edith were pictures of beauty in the latest fashions. Alice wanted champagne served, but her father put his foot down, so there was no alcohol. Ted was probably sorry he didn't get another chance to claim he thought it was fizzy water. Among the guests were Alice's cousin, Franklin Delano Roosevelt, and several of her old boyfriends, including Payne Whitney. Alice was already showing signs of a dislike for FDR. She refused to dance with him, claiming she preferred older men like the Rough Riders to her handsome, charming cousin.[47]

When the holidays were over, Ted returned to Groton to begin the 1902 spring term. He had a cold and had not been feeling well, but he wrote his mother a long letter on January 20th saying, "I am nearly all well. I am taking malt and cod liver oil a thick stuff which is 'solemnly' doled out to after meals by the nurse." He went on to ask Edith to send him his black winter suit, some stamps and writing material, and to inform him who sent him a box of apples. The apples did not have the name of the sender, and he didn't know who to send a "thank you" note to. He also wrote,

> I spoke to the Rector about my tooth and said if it was dangerous for fearing it turning black that I could go in and I guess any way if you ask him but it will be expensive and bothersome as I will have to neglect lessons according to the number of times I go in what is the name of the dentist perhaps I might go in to grandmas* some Friday after noon go back Sunday and get it all through with. Could you please write and tell me what to do.
> (* Refers to Alice's grandmother, Mrs. Lee, who lived in Boston)

Ted adopted his father's habit of often drawing on his letters little scenes relevant to something in the letter. On this particular letter to Edith he drew a little scene of the nurse passing out medicine to the Groton students. Ted was very wrong about being "nearly all well," however, for by early February he was critically ill with pneumonia, and, this being a time before penicillin, there was doubt as to whether he would survive. Upon learning of the seriousness of his condition, Edith immediately went to his bedside and was followed the next day by the President. They remained with their son for a week, until he was much improved and out of danger. As soon as he could travel, Ted went to the White House for a while to convalesce.[48]

Early in 1902, Edith wrote a revealing letter to close family friend, Cecil

Spring-Rice, in which she briefly described each of her children. She wrote, "****
Ted is a good boy and stands well at school. Kermit is odd and independent as
always, and Ethel is just a handful. She is a replica of Mrs. Cowles. Archie we call
'the beautiful idiot' and Quentin is the cleverest of the six." Kermit was Edith's
favorite and he was devoted to her, but in the letter it was obvious that she
recognized his weaknesses. Kermit was somewhat of a loner. He either liked a
person very much or didn't want anything to do with him or her. There was no
in-between. He was the only one of the TR children to become good friends with
FDR. Kermit's later life was tragic. He left his wife, took up with a mistress, and
developed an awful drinking problem, similar to that of his Uncle Elliott. What a
compliment Edith paid to Ethel in comparing her to Mrs. Cowles, (TR's sister
Bamie) and in this comparison she very accurately described her daughter. Ethel
was the loyal, compassionate, down-to-earth member of the family. She kept her
cool when things were tough and had lots of common sense. She was a good
student, and helped the younger children with their studies. She taught Sunday
school and could manage the home when her mother was away. Ethel would retain
these fine qualities until the day she died. Edith failed to give Archie his due when
she called him "the beautiful idiot." Archie certainly had above average intelligence,
even though he may have lacked the superior intellect of the other children. But
Archie had a moral quality of character about him that was ingrained in his
personality. Ted had some of this quality too, but not to the extent as Archie.
Quentin did not live long enough into adulthood to reveal how he would have
turned out, but it would appear that he carried his father's great intelligence and
imagination, and he had a wonderful outgoing personality. If there had been a
future President among the children of TR and Edith, it would have been
Quentin.[49]

After TRJr recovered from his illness and returned to school, he wrote a poem
entitled "The Norman Baron's Prayer"

Would God I might die my sword in my hand
My gilded spur on my heel
With my crested helmet on my head
And my body closed in steel
Would God when the morning broke
I might by my friends be found
Stiff in my war worn harness
Ringed by dead foes all around

He was obviously daydreaming about his father when he wrote this lyric.

Teddy at San Juan and Kettle Hills can be pictured when it is read. He submitted his poem to *Harpers Magazine* using a pseudonym, but it was not published.[50]

When the spring school term was over, Ted went back home to Oyster Bay for the summer to the usual sports and fun times. This year the family had a new and unusual pet, a macaw named Eli. Eli and Ted took an immediate liking to each other. The big bird liked nothing better than to get on Ted's shoulder and then walk all over his head, arms, etc. TR wrote that the bird was "gorgeous," but had a strong beak that could probably "bite through boiler plate." Early in the summer Ted, his father, and cousins George and Phillip Roosevelt rode horses all one night in a heavy rain to go spend the night with Ted's great uncle, Robert Barnwell Roosevelt, who lived 35 miles from Sagamore Hill. After dawn broke, the local residents recognized the dirty, wet President and party and waved and cheered as they rode by. Leaving Uncle Barnwell before daylight the following morning, they got back home just in time for lunch. Edith had been concerned about the trip since they departed at night, in a heavy rain, with no escorting secret service men. When they returned, she welcomed her "oldest and worst child" with an acid, "I am glad to see you safely home, Mr. President!"

In July, Ted, his father, brother Kermit, and several cousins went on a four day hunting and fishing trip to Great South Bay. They had planned the trip for months and had a great time. Writing about the trip years later, Ted remembered the sound of the waves slapping against the sides of the boat and said, "We sat patiently in ell grass blinds and felt the thrill when the first birds circled down, half seen in the gray of the early dawn." Before the summer was over, Ted, Kermit, TR and cousin Phillip went camping at Ted's favorite camping spot, a secluded area several miles from Sagamore at the end of Lloyd's Neck. After the sun went down, they could hear a fox yapping in the distance and other sounds of the night. TR cooked them steaks over an open fire. After eating, they spread Navajo blankets on the ground and relaxed around the campfire, taking turns telling hunting, fishing and ghost stories.[51]

Nearing fifteen, Ted was maturing emotionally and mentally, if not in body size, and he was beginning to have some serious thoughts about the course his life would take and about how being the eldest son and namesake of such a famous father would affect his life. He already knew from experience that there would be some positive and some negative influences because of who his dad was. Deciding that the negative outweighed the positive, he told TR's good friend, Jake Riis, that he would be glad when his father was through holding office because he "was sick and tired of it." One day when talking to one of the good citizens of Oyster Bay, Ted accurately foresaw the future when he asked the old man, "Don't you think it handicaps a boy to be the son of a man like my father, especially to have the same name?" When asked to explain what he meant, Ted replied, "Don't you know there can never be another Theodore Roosevelt? I will always be honest and upright, and I hope someday to be a great soldier, but I will always be spoken of as Theodore Roosevelt's son."[52]

Later in the fall Ted attended a State Dinner at the White House, and handled himself like a veteran at the lofty affair. He shook hands all around, conversed intelligently with the guests, and generally conducted himself like an adult. After dinner he excused himself to go horseback riding with Ethel.

When he returned to school to begin his third year at Groton, Ted wrote his mother of an amusing incident. The boys were having a crude picnic in the woods, feasting on jelly, sardines, chocolate, and crackers. One of the boys took more than his share of jelly and quickly put it into his mouth. Ted and some of the others made him open his mouth, then they took out the jelly and gave it to another, unsuspecting boy. Ted closed his letter with, "I am glad I was not the other boy."[53]

One day when Ted was in Washington for Christmas vacation, he, General Leonard Wood, and Bob Ferguson, an old Spanish-American War buddy of TRs, went for a three-hour horseback ride. Another time Ted, Teddy, and several of the children were out riding their assortment of horses and ponies when the skittish horse ridden by a cavalry colonel coming to meet them was spooked when he came in sight of the menagerie of people and animals headed toward him. The Colonel's horse bolted and ran away to the cheers and delight of the Roosevelt bunch. Ted said that the Roosevelt family, all riding together, reminded him of the "Cumberbatch family in the Caldecott drawings." (Randolph Caldecott was a well-known late 19th century English artist, primarily known for his humorous illustrations in Children's books.)[54]

Even though he was busy taking care of the country, Teddy still occasionally got away to partake of his favorite sport, hunting. On one occasion, when he went to Colorado on a hunting trip, he wrote a letter to Ted at Groton describing in detail how the dogs trailed a cougar and treed it several times, only to have it escape. Finally they got the big predator hemmed up and a vicious fight erupted in which several of the dogs were injured. Fearing the wild animal might kill one of the dogs, Teddy pulled out a knife he had borrowed from Ted, jumped into the middle of the affray, and stabbed the cougar in the heart. Ted was impressed with the story and wrote his father back that stabbing of the big cat with his knife would make the knife more valuable.[55]

When the spring term was over, Teddy decided it was high time Ted learned something of the beloved Dakota Badlands, and he sent Ted and one of his cousins to Deadwood, South Dakota to spend some time with his old friend, Seth Bullock. Bullock was a character straight out of the old west. A former marshal with several notches on his pistol grip, Seth was the epitome of the rough, tough, no nonsense cowboy. In the Badlands, the boys drove, rounded up and branded cattle, and generally did the work of real cowpunchers. They slept under the stars, and ate chuck-wagon food. While Ted was in Deadwood, TR wrote him, "I do not have very much hope of your getting a great deal of sport on this trip, and anything you do get in the way of furred or feathered game and fishing I shall count as so much extra thrown in; but I feel the trip will teach you a lot in the way of handling yourself in a wild country, as well as of managing horses and camp outfits, of dealing with frontiersmen, etc. It will therefore fit you to go on a regular camping trip next time."

Summer vacation that year was not all spent working as a cowhand, however. Ted spent part of the summer at Sagamore where he participated in the usual fun sports with his friends Alec Russell, Ensign Hamner, and George and Jack Roosevelt. Alec was the son of the Presbyterian minister at Oyster Bay, Hamner was a member of the crew of the "Sylph," a small navel vessel assigned for the use of the President, and George and Jack were Ted's cousins. TR wrote of the kid's activities on one of those summer days saying, "This afternoon, for instance, was rainy, and all of them from George, Ted, Lorraine and Ethel down to Archibald, Nicholas and Quentin, with the addition of Alex Russell and Ensign Hamner, came to get me to play with them in the old barn. They pled so hard that I finally gave in, but upon my word, I hardly knew whether it was quite right for the President to be engaged in such wild romping as the next two hours saw. The barn is filled with hay, and of course meets every requirement for the most active species of hide-and-seek and the like." Another time, Ted and Lorraine wrote a play. All of the children had parts. The production took place on a neighboring cousin's tennis court to an audience of parents, grandparents and neighbors. Ted and Lorraine had the starring rolls as George Washington and Cleopatra, but all the kids were in it. Quentin, dressed in pink tights, played cupid.[56]

Back at Groton for the fall term, Ted was doing extremely well with his studies and was still involved in the game of football. His coaches told him that because of his small size they were inclined to put him on the third team, but would give him a chance to make the second squad if he thought he was not being given a fair chance to perform on the higher level. Ted wanted some fatherly advice on this and immediately sent his dad a letter marked "Hurry! Hurry!" on the envelope. TR considered the matter and responded, in part:

I am proud of your pluck, and I greatly admire football, though it was not a game I was ever able to play myself, **** there is always the chance of your being laid up. Now, I should not in the least object to your being laid up for a season if you were striving for something worth while ***** But I am by no means sure that it is worth your while to run the risk of being laid up for the sake of playing in the second squad when you are a fourth former, instead of when you are a fifth

former. I do not know that the risk is balanced by the reward. ***** I believe
in rough manly sports. But I do not believe in them if they degenerate into the
sole end of any one's existence. I don't want you to sacrifice standing well in
your studies to any over athleticism; and I need not tell you that character counts
for a great deal more that either intellect or body in winning success in life.
Athletic proficiency is a mighty good servant, and like so many other good
servants, a mighty bad master. Did you ever read Pliny's letter to Trajan, in
which he speaks of its being advisable to keep the Greeks absorbed in athletics,
because it distracted their minds from all serious pursuits.

He went on to tell Ted that he was proud of the fact that he could play football,
box, ride, shoot, walk, and row as well as he could, but should not devote a major
portion of his energies to sports. Ted, however, loved football and continued to
play despite his father's advice. Near the end of the season he suffered a severe
ankle injury that required medical treatment.

The Roosevelts celebrated Christmas at the White House again in '03. Family
friend, Bob Ferguson, and Edith's sister, Emily Carow, were guests for the holidays.
At 7:00 a. m. on Christmas morning, all the kids, including Ted and Alice, went
into their parent's bedroom to sit around and talk and to see what Santa had put
in their stockings. Then, after their usual hearty breakfast, they all went into the
library where the bigger toys and gifts for each child had been placed on separate
tables. Teddy was reminded of the Christmases of his childhood.[57]

During this holiday season, Ted began thinking and talking seriously about
going to the Unites States Military Academy or the Naval Academy and making
the Army or Navy a career. Growing up, he had always been enamored with war
and warriors. This came from the many stories his father told him about his
Grandmother Roosevelt's heroic brothers, and other tales of famous battles, and
from Teddy's Spanish-American War experiences, and the way people glorified TR
all the years since the Spanish-American War ended. As a child, Ted spent many
hours playing soldier and sailor with wooden guns and little wooden ships. TR was
a romantic when it came to war and believed every able-bodied male citizen had
a military obligation to the country when needed. He, however, was not
enthusiastic about one of his sons becoming a professional soldier or sailor. Teddy
had never concealed the fact that he thought little of most of the regular Army and
Naval officers he had come in contact with. He found them to be unimaginative
and indolent from long years of service with little or no chance for promotion. In
his opinion, being a professional military man was just an easy way to diddle away
time, waiting on retirement. But Ted persisted and wrote off for applications from
both service schools. When the forms arrived, TR reluctantly sent them on to Ted
at Groton, with the following letter:

White House, Jan. 21, 1904
Dear Ted;

"This will be a long business letter. I sent you the examination papers for West Point and Annapolis. I have thought a great deal over the matter, and discussed it at great length with mother. I feel on the one hand that I ought to give you my best advice, and yet on the other hand I do not wish to seem to constrain you against your wishes. If you have definitely made up your mind that you have an overmastering desire to be in the Navy or the Army, and that such a career is the one in which you will take a really heart-felt interest—far more than any other—and that your greatest chance for happiness and usefulness will lie in doing this one work to which you feel yourself especially drawn—why, under such circumstances, I have but to say. But I am not satisfied that this is really your feeling. It seemed to me more as if you did not feel drawn in any other direction, and wondered what you were going to do in life or what kind of work you would turn your hand to, and wondered if you could make a success or not; and that you are therefore inclined to turn to the Navy or Army chiefly because you would then have a definite and settled career in life, and could hope to go on steadily without any great risk of failure. Now if such is your thought, I shall quote to you what Captain Mahan said of his son when asked why he did not send him to West Point or Annapolis. "I have too much confidence in him to make me feel that it is desirable for him to enter either branch of the service."

I have great confidence in you. I believe you have the ability and, above all, the energy, the perseverance, and the common sense, to win out in civil life. That you will have some hard times and some discouraging times I have no question; but this is merely another way of saying that you will share the common lot. Though you will have to work in different ways from those in which I worked, you will not have to work any harder, nor to face periods of more discouragement. I trust in your ability, and especially, your character, and I am confident you will win.

In the Army and the Navy the chance for a man to show great ability and rise above his fellows does not occur on the average more than once in a generation. When I was down to Santiago it was melancholy for me to see how fossilized and lacking in ambition, and generally useless, were most of the men of my age and over, who had served their lives in the Army. The Navy for the last few years has been better, but for twenty years after the Civil War there was less chance in the Navy than in the Army to practice, and do, work of real consequence. I have actually known lieutenants in both the Army and the Navy who were grandfathers—men who had seen their children married before they themselves attained the grade of captain. Of course the chance may come at any time when the man of West Point or Annapolis who will have stayed in the Army or Navy finds a great war on, and therefore has the opportunity to rise high. Under such circumstances, I think that the man of such training who has actually left the Army or the Navy has even more chance of rising than the man who has remained in it. Moreover, often a man can do as I did in the Spanish War, even though not a West Pointer.

This last point raises the question about you going to West Point or Annapolis and leaving the Army or Navy after you have served the regulation four years (I think that is the number) after graduation from the academy. Under this plan you would have an excellent education and a grounding in discipline and, in some ways, a testing of your capacity greater than I think you can get in any ordinary college. On the other hand, except for the profession of an engineer, you would have had nothing like special training, and you would be so ordered about, and arranged for, that you would have less independence of character than you could gain from them. You would have had fewer temptations; but you would have had less chance to develop the qualities which overcome temptations and show that a man has individual initiative. Supposing you entered at seventeen, with the intention of following this course. The result would be that at twenty-five you would leave the Army or Navy without having gone through any law school or any special technical school of any kind, and would start your life work three or four years later than your schoolfellows of today, who go to work immediately after leaving college. Of course, under such circumstances, you might study law, for instance, during the four years after graduation; but my own feeling is that a man does good work chiefly when he is in something which he intends to make his permanent work, and in which he is deeply interested. Moreover, there will always be the chance that the number of officers in the Army or Navy will be deficient, and that you would have to stay in the service instead of getting out when you wished.

I want you to think over all these matters very seriously. It would be a great misfortune for you to start into the Army or Navy as a career, and find that you had mistaken your desires and had gone in without really weighing the matter.

You ought not to enter unless you feel genuinely drawn to the life as a lifework. If so, go in; but not otherwise.

Mr. Loeb told me to-day that at 17 he had tried for the army, but failed. The competitor who beat him in is now a captain; Mr. Loeb has passed him by, although meanwhile a war has been fought. Mr. Loeb says he wished to enter the army because he did not know what to do, could not foresee whether he would succeed or fail in life, and felt the army would give him "a living and a career." Now if this is at the bottom your feeling I should advise you not to go in; I should say yes to some boys, but not to you; I believe in you too much, and have too much confidence in you."[58]

Several other long, discouraging letters followed every week or two until Ted buckled under to his father's pressure and abandoned his ideas of a military career. Instead, he decided to follow in TR's footsteps and work toward a degree from Harvard University. From his letters to Ted, the real reason Teddy did not want Ted to go the West Point or Annapolis is obvious. He had visions of Ted following him into the White House and thought a military career was not the way to get there. In a sense, he was pushing his namesake again. In one of his letters to Ted he wrote, "Of course the chance may come at any time when the man of West Point or Annapolis who will have stayed in the Army or Navy finds a great war on, and therefore has the opportunity to rise high." He must have thought the chances of having a "great war" were slim. That is, however, exactly what happened to Dwight Eisenhower and had previously happened to Ulysses S. Grant. Every one can look back at decisions made in life and say "what if" and "what if," so how Ted's life would have developed had he gone on to one of the service academies and put in thirty-five or forty years of active duty is, at best, speculative.

Alice had grown into a strikingly beautiful and rebellious young woman. She had a mind of her own and refused to conform to the restrained lifestyle desired of her by her father and stepmother. Besides smoking, she went to the tracks and bet on the horses, played poker, raced fast cars, and often stayed out to the wee hours with her rich friends. TR and Edith were beside themselves with worry. When a well-known writer asked about her, TR made his famous quip, "I can do one of two things. I can be President of the United States or I can control Alice. I can't possibly do both." On another occasion when a demented man claimed TR wanted to see him about marrying Alice, and had to be forcibly stopped by the secret service from entering Sagamore Hill, the President remarked: "Of course he's insane. He wants to marry Alice." Not to be outdone, Alice came up with one of the classic remarks, which she in later years became famous for, saying that her extremely extroverted father "wanted to be the corpse at every funeral, the bride at every wedding, and the baby at every christening." Later, a kind of truce was made between Teddy and Alice when he sent her as his personal representative on two public relations trips, one to Porto Rico and the other to the Philippines, Japan, China and Korea. Alice handled herself well on both missions and received compliments from her father and others for her good work.[59]

Before the spring school term was over Ted hurt his rib and dislocated his thumb at spring football practice. He also met and took to the theater a girl named Octavia Tonet. Ted was going on seventeen and the hormones were working. He found Octavia to be "very interesting!"[60]

With the end of the term came the end of Ted's education at Groton. He decided to forgo spending his junior and senior years there, and instead to study under a tutor at home. His hope was to be admitted to Harvard University as a freshman and graduate in the fall of 1908. TR wrote one of his friends that Ted was discontented at his progress at Groton and felt it was possible to cover the last two years of high school in one year of hard study at home. He said that Ted intended to work in the railroad industry after graduating from college. One of the first things to happen after Ted got home in June was that he and Kermit both came down with the mumps, and both were kept isolated for a couple of weeks in the southeast bedrooms. After recovering from his illness, TRJr took time to go hunting in the Canadian backwoods. One night, while in Canada, he heard a grunting sound not far away. Stalking toward the sound, he got a clean shot and killed an enormous bull moose with a horn spread of fifty-six inches.[61]

By June, '04, there was less than a year remaining on what should have been McKinley's second term. Teddy had every intention of seeking the presidential nomination at the upcoming Republican National Convention. He was a shoe-in of course, and easily received the nomination. During the four month long campaign before the general election in November, Ted often acted as a kind of informal secret service man by positioning himself near his father and keeping a sharp eye out on the crowd for anyone that appeared suspicious. On election night, before the returns came in, things were tense around Teddy's headquarters. These were the days before reliable polls, and election results were not known until the votes were hand-counted. Alice and Ted were particularly nervous about the outcome and took their anxiety out on each other by continually bickering and insulting one another. When the returns showed a landslide victory for TR, the tension instantly transposed itself into a celebration. A great weight had been lifted from TR's shoulders. Up until this point he felt that he was President only because of another man's death. Now he would be President in his own right and not by default. In his exuberance, Teddy surprised Edith, his children, friends and everyone else when he announced to reporters, "Under no circumstances will I be a candidate for or accept another nomination." In the years to come, he would regret very much having made this rash pledge.[62]

With the election over, Ted turned his focus to preparing for the Harvard entrance exams. He worked under the tutelage of Mathew Hale, a relative of Alice's birth mother. Hale would later become a well-known Boston attorney and chairman of the Progressive Party in Massachusetts. Young Mr. Hale did his job well, for Ted passed his exams with several points to spare. When not cramming for the exams, Ted played a lot of tennis. Sometimes his tennis opponent was none other than the President of the United States. Teddy was a pretty good player, but not really in his namesake's class. Ted delighted in dropping the ball just over the net when he caught his father on the back line, telling TR that the extra legwork would help hold his weight down. When time permitted, Ted would get in some horseback riding; he especially liked to ride at night when the ground was covered with snow. He also attended some of the many social functions he was invited to. Once, he, TR, Ethel and Matt Hale went to one of the New York theaters to see the *Yankee Consul*. Ted found the play to be very funny and enjoyed the outing thoroughly. He got his first tailcoat and became good friends with the pretty, young debutante daughter of the Secretary of the Navy, Paul Morton.[63]

Teddy's formal inauguration in the spring was uneventful, except that many of the Rough Riders marching in the military escort were drunk from making the party rounds in Washington. In the inaugural procession Alice and Ted rode in the carriage with Edith. A few carriages behind the First Lady came Bamie, with Franklin Delano Roosevelt and his bride-to-be, Eleanor Roosevelt, who was the daughter of TR's deceased brother Elliot, and was Alice's, TR Jr's, Kermit's, Ethel's, Archie's, and Quentin's first cousin.[64]

Just as he had five years before when he left home to go to Groton, in the fall of 1905 Ted packed up his clothes and enrolled as a freshman at Harvard University. He had a room in Claverly Dormitory on the campus. This time things were different. He was no longer an insecure boy; now he was a confident young man of eighteen. There was none of the dread of leaving home as before, nor was there homesickness. Besides starting classes, one of the first things he did after he got to Cambridge was to try out for the Harvard freshman football team. Even though he was only 5'6", 130 pounds, and the smallest player on the field, he not only made the team, he made first string end. In one of the freshman games that fall he made a number of nice defensive plays, including a spectacular touchdown saving tackle to hold Harvard's defeat to a 5–0 score. As far as the newspapers were concerned, Ted was the star of the game. Later that fall, when they played their archrival, Yale, Ted played his usual end position, despite having previously broken a thumb and bruised his rib cage. To make matters worse, his nose was broken during the game. Because the President's son was playing, the game attracted more than the normal amount of publicity. Some of the reporters present thought Yale ran an inordinate number of plays around Ted's end in an attempt to injure him. Ted talked with some of the opposing players after the game and found them to be nice guys. He was positive that in running at his position so much, they were just trying to take advantage of his size and pre-game injuries, rather than because of some kind of evil intent to do him harm. One of the nice things that resulted from the Harvard-Yale freshman game that year was that Ted had a chance to renew his friendship with his old friend from Albany Academy, George Cantine. George and Ted had played a lot together when TR was Governor, and now George was a freshman at Yale. They continued to meet after the Harvard-Yale varsity games for the following two years. George said that Ted "had lots of guts and a fighting heart though he was a lightweight. He was a great exponent of team play, while a brilliant individual athlete himself."[65]

One thing that surprised Ted when he started college was the way the newspaper reporters followed him around and constantly harassed him by taking pictures and asking him silly questions. It had not been like that at the more private, more isolated Groton, but the activities of the President's eldest son were news and sold newspapers. Cambridge was actually a suburb of Boston, and the reporters had ready access to the Harvard campus. Being aware of Ted's propensity to fight, when TR heard about Ted's problems with all the reporters, he wrote him,

> Attract as little attention as possible, do not make a fuss about the newspaper men, camera creatures, and idiots generally, letting it be seen that you do not like them and avoid them, but not letting them betray you into any excessive irritation, I believe they will soon drop you, and it is just an unpleasant thing that you will have to live down. Ted I have had an enormous number of unpleasant things that I have had to live down in my life at different times and you have begun to have them now.
> You can never in the world afford to let them drive you away from anything you intend to do, whether it is football or anything else, and by going about your own business quietly and pleasantly, doing just what you would do if they were not there, generally they will get tired of it," also "Avoid any fuss if possible.

Whether Ted took his father's advice or simply evidenced great restraint and maturity for a young man, the harassment was handled very well by the Harvard freshman as there were no incidents where a reporter got decked or had his camera broken over his head.[66]

While Ted was by now accustomed to living away from home, he was not accustomed to the freedom that college life bestows on its students. Besides his studies and football, Ted took part in numerous social activities. He, against his father's advice, joined the Polo Club. TR remembered the members of the Polo Club as being a bunch of slackers, and he wrote Ted that he had heard unfavorable things about that particular club, and that he, "looked with suspicion upon all freshman societies." He went on to state, "Popularity is a good thing, but is not something for which to sacrifice studies or athletics or good standing in any way; and sometimes to seek it overmuch is to lose it." With his father's approval, however, Ted was accepted as a member in the Porcellian Club. This had been Teddy's club when he had been a student at Harvard twenty-five years before and he thought it was the best club at the school.[67]

With all his extracurricular activities, TRJr's grades during his first term in college were poor. He almost flunked out of school and was placed on scholastic probation. Teddy advised Ted to move out of his dorm and into a quiet room off campus, one more conducive to study, and to concentrate on his studies rather than on athletics and social life. In college, Ted never set out to make all A's and be inducted into Phi Beta Kappa like his father. He later in life described his college goal, "When I was young and in Harvard, I crammed my work into three years, as I was anxious to get out and test my own ability to stand up on my own feet in the real world." Studying hard in the spring, Ted managed to pull his grades up enough to get off of probation. He was allowed to stay in school and was elevated to the sophomore class.[68]

For many months, Ted's sister Alice, now age 21, had been in love with Nicholas (Nick) Longworth, a thirty-six year old congressman from Ohio. With the hearty approval of TR and Edith, the couple announced their engagement in December. Nick descended from wealthy, highly regarded parents, and was related to the Lafayette family in France. The marriage took place in February, in the East Room of the White House, before more than seven hundred invited guests. It was one of the most elaborate affairs in the history of the executive mansion. Ted served as one of the ushers and escorted his mother into the East Room shortly before the ceremony began. As soon as the marriage vows were completed, Alice made an emotional gesture when she turned, went over to her stepmother, kissed her, then said something to her and kissed her again. It was obvious to all that she was saying "thank you" for filling the shoes of the mother she never knew and for being understanding and providing such tender loving care for the past nineteen years. At the reception that followed there was none of the usual protocol, as the distinguished guests, family, reporters, aides, White House staff, and servants all shared together in the champagne and hors d'oeuvres.[69]

Franklin Delano Roosevelt was one of the guests at Alice's wedding, but probably felt like an outcast. Teddy, Ted, Nick, and some of the other guests were members of the Porcellian Club at Harvard. Traditionally when a club member married, a room called the "Brothers' Room" was set aside where only members met to toast the groom, sing club songs, and discuss old times. The club's elderly black steward had been brought down from Cambridge to tend bar for this special meeting. Although his father, James Roosevelt, had been a member of Porcellian, FDR had been denied membership, so when the club alumni met in the "Brothers' Room" in the White House, young Franklin could only mingle with other of the guests and act as if he didn't know what was going on in one of the adjoining rooms.[70]

Shortly after his nineteenth birthday, Ted and several of his Harvard friends, including one named Shaun Kelly, were fooling around in the Boston Common one night when an undercover policeman mistook them for robbers. When the policeman, who was not in uniform, made what Ted and his friends took to be a threatening approach, they thought the policeman was a robber. Shaun pushed or hit the officer, resulting in the policeman having a broken nose and a laceration on his head. Naturally, the boys were arrested; however, charges were dropped against all of them but Shaun. Later, Ted testified in behalf of Shaun at the trial. Because of who Ted's father was, this otherwise minor incident was given wide press coverage in both Boston and New York.[71]

When football practice started in the fall, Ted was right back in the middle of the action, playing as hard as he could on every down. He made the Harvard varsity squad and was playing second string end. In a game against Phillips Exeter Academy on October, 12th, he injured his knee and was unable to play again for two weeks. Soon after, he was hurt again, this time with a broken ankle and a broken nose. The ankle was misdiagnosed as a sprain and never recovered its full strength. Ted's days of playing football were over. Few athletes, then or now, play with Ted's enthusiasm, stamina and desire. While he was no longer on the football team, his college athletic career was not over because in the spring the University Athletic Committee appointed him second assistant manager of the Harvard crew.[72]

Even though he was almost legally an adult, TRJr had not lost the dare devil trait he had exhibited all his life. This showed in the way he rode horses and played football. When he was at Sagamore for Thanksgiving holidays, still hurting from his football injuries, he and one of his friends were horse-playing and accidentally fell three floors down an elevator shaft. The only thing that saved their lives was that somehow both young men managed to grab the elevator cable and break their fall by sliding down on it. Their hands were badly skinned and burned.[73]

All of his life Ted had been constantly exposed to books of various kinds and in college developed a real love for both literature and poetry. He always kept handy one of the classics, such as Horace or Virgil, or a book of poems by Kipling, Keats, Shelley, Byron, etc. One of the courses on his schedule was Latin. As the course proceeded, Ted hardly cracked a book and was totally unprepared when he went in to take the final examination. On the exam the professor designated one of the Latin epics for each student to translate. Because of his lack of preparation, Ted was unable to do the literal translation called for, but, from his extensive readings, he had an independent knowledge of the basic story described in his assigned epic. Thinking fast, and relying on his love of poetry, he wrote the basic epic story as a poem in blank verse form and then made a note on his paper that he had done this because the requirement of meter prevented him from doing an exact translation. This was a lie of course, but the professor bought it and gave him an A. Archie, with his high ideals as to character, would have taken an F in the course rather than have committed this pious fraud.[74]

Over the years many people made the comment that TRJr could recite more poems than anyone else they knew, and he read, recited, and wrote poetry throughout his life. Only a few of his own compositions have survived, and very few were actually published. In the latter part of 1906, Ted submitted a poem that was accepted for publication by *Scribner's Magazine* entitled "Sunset of the Marsh," as follows:

Apollo drives his bitted stallions down
Far o'er the golden path across the waves
Which rise and fall in ceaseless undulation
From where the shore juts, with its pebbly points
Thrust forward in the darkening waters
The vesper wind, with soft and soothing touch
Lisps through the reed-beds in the level marsh,
Through which the silent, silver creeks
Trace strange, symbolic figures;
And now the glorious, burnished road has gone-
Melted into the emerald of the water
Slow sinks the burning splendor,
And naught is left of all the Sun-God's glory
But the dim wonder of the afterglow
And the green clouds of dreamland.

When he submitted the poem, he used the pen name "Jacob Van Vechten" because he didn't want to take any chance that his poem might be published simply because it was written by the President's son. Whatever he accomplished in life, Ted wanted to do it through his own efforts and ability. Another of his poems was published in the April 7, 1932 edition of The Evening Star, a newspaper located in Washington, D.C.[75]

Teddy could see that his namesake was maturing as his years in college passed, and he developed a great confidence in Ted's opinions and judgement on various important matters that confronted the presidency. As an example, TR discussed with TRJr what might be done about the economic and political problems facing the small Caribbean nations, and sought his advice on the problems between Russia and Japan. He trusted his oldest son to keep confidential their frank discussions, especially those with respect to the abilities and loyalty of some of America's most important politicians, including Robert LaFollette, a Republican Senator who later joined the Progressive Party, and Charles Fairbanks, who served as Teddy's vice-president during the 1905–1909 term.

While Ted was growing in age and experience and certainly now had more serious thoughts, he still enjoyed the activities of normal young men. He loved to go to the theater, especially when pretty young Gladys Butler was sitting beside him, and he had great fun occasionally doing some outlandish thing, like the time he made a 135-mile trip in a balloon.[76]

Knowing that his son had been busy with his social life, the Harvard crew, football, making reasonably good grades and at the same time taking extra courses when he could squeeze them in, the President was quite proud of Ted. He wrote his namesake in early '08, congratulating him on his successes, but also reminding him not to mimic TR's own apathy toward the end of his college career. Something, probably his father's letter, spurred Ted into action to do the craziest thing he had ever done. Deciding that a little fishing trip was in order, and not telling anybody where he was going, or when, or if he would return, he cut 38 straight classes. The Harvard Dean wrote TR, "Dear Mr. President, You may know where your son Ted is, we do not." When he returned from his escapade, he was placed on probation again. Teddy was infuriated. He told his son that he "was a shame and disgrace," and would never amount to anything. But by now Ted was a confident young man and knew his own abilities and limitations. After returning from his R & R, he strenuously applied himself to his studies and made no grade lower than B+ for the next three months. He made the Dean's List, and received his BS degree at June graduation, thirty-three months after first enrolling as a freshman. Ted had accomplished his goal.[77]

Through with school, Theodore Roosevelt, Jr. was ready to spread his wings and make a name for himself in the real world, but having just felt his father's wrath for cutting so many classes, he pacified TR by taking a job with U.S. Steel Corp. in Minnesota, working under one of Teddy's old friends. However, within only a month or two Ted resigned from this job to accept a trainee's job with the Hartford Carpet Corporation. Robert Perkins, the President of Hartford Carpet, had been a member of the Porcellian Club during his Harvard days and gave Ted his new job. Starting at the bottom, Ted would be a mill hand working fifty-five hours each week, at a salary of seven dollars per week. He intended to work hard and knew that if he was found to be a deserving employee he would be moved around to other, better, jobs within the company. He had the chance to learn the carpet business from the ground up and considered this new job to be an opportunity to gain business experience, and at the same time receive fairly frequent pay raises. Ted reported to work that first day, October 1, 1908. He would be working out of the company's mill in Thompsonville, Connecticut.[78]

Quentin, TRJr's youngest brother, had recently been enrolled in a new boarding school, but was unhappy and was having a rough time adjusting to his new surroundings. When Ted went back East to begin his new job, he learned of Quentin's problem and after completing his first day's work at the carpet company, wrote Quentin the following big brother's letter of encouragement:[79]

Dear Quentin,

Well, you and I both are starting on new phases in our lives. There'll
be a lot of unpleasantness for both of us at the beginning but all one has
to do is to keep up a brave front, behave like a man and it will pretty soon
pass and people will take you at your true worth. The boys who jolly you
will stop and the news papers that cartoon me will lose interest. After all it
is all in the days work and one must accept the bitter with the sweet.
Do they play football at your school? If so you ought to have a lot of
fun this autumn as you have a very good build for the game.
Tomorrow I start in my blue coveralls as a regular wage earner. The
mills are great big affairs with fully four thousand men working in them.
Well goodby & best luck.
Your affectionate brother
Ted.

Along Came Ted Source Notes

1. LOC c-56; S. Morris p 112; Kerr p 20; Hagedorn p 17; Collier p 75; Roosevelt, TRJr., All In The Family, p 46, 52–53.

2. Kerr p 21; S. Morris p 137; Morrison, Vol. 8, p 1430.

3. Kerr p 21; Brands p 216.

4. Roosevelt, Theodore, An Autobiography, p 345; Kerr p 57; McCullough p 74; AA p 3; TRJr's speech to Recreation Congress on 10/19/26, FDR Library; Personal interview with Major Fiset.

5. Roosevelt, TRJr., All In The Family, p 10, 13–15, 40, 57–59.

6. TR Collection bms Am 1834.1[343]; Roosevelt, Theodore, An Autobiography, p 342; Roosevelt, Mrs. T Jr.. p 40; Kerr p 30–31.

7. Adams p 139; Roosevelt, TRJr., All In The Family, p 66–68.

8. Roosevelt, TRJr., Average Americans, p 1–7; Kerr p 76; S Morris p 146–148; Hagedorn p 20, 22 & 33; Brands p 381; Roosevelt, Mrs. T Jr. p 41; TRJr's Speech to Recreation Congress on 10/19/26, FDR Library.

9. Hagedorn p 19; S. Morris p 121.

10. Hagedorn p 20–21; Longworth p 13.

11. Roosevelt, Theodore, An Autobiography, p 337; Roosevelt, TRJr., Average Americans, p 3; Collier p 84; Adams p 138.

12. Hagedorn p 25; S. Morris p 150–151.

13. Roosevelt, TRJr., Average Americans, p 4–5.

14. Roosevelt, TRJr., All In The Family, p 187; Hagedorn p 83.

15. Hagedorn p 26, 30; S. Morris p 146; Kerr p 28–29.

16. Collier p 94.

17. Hagedorn p 43.

18. Adams p 137; Hagedorn p 19.

19. Roosevelt, Theodore, An Autobiography, p 345; Hagedorn p 49; Roosevelt, TRJr., All In The Family, p 15, 36; Cheney p 29.

20. Roosevelt, Nicholas, p 34; Roosevelt, TRJr., All In The Family, p 22–23, 168.

21. Roosevelt, TRJr., All In The Family, p 23; Adams p 142.

22. S. Morris p 162; Longworth p 14, 40.

23. Hagedorn p 41; Roosevelt, TRJr., All In The Family, p 99, 168; Collier p 78.

24. S. Morris p 163; Brands p 307; Hagedorn p 47.

25. S. Morris p 166–168.

26. S. Morris p 170–171; Brands p 336; Hagedorn p 50; Morrison Vol. 2 p 803.

27. S. Morris p 171–174; Harbaugh p 101.

28. Harbaugh p 105–106; Collier p 98–100.

29. Brands p 382; S. Morris p 182.

30. Collier p 125.

31. Roosevelt, TR Jr., Average Americans, p 6

32. Harbaugh p 105, 111.

33. S. Morris p 185.

34. Harbaugh p 107.

35. Hagedorn p 77; S. Morris p 192.

36. Cheney p 30; LOC c-56; Roosevelt, Mrs. T Jr.., p 42.

37. TR Collection bMS Am 1834 1073–1075; Adams p 140.

38. S. Morris p 196, 203–205; Collier p 109–110.

39. E. Morris p 252.

40. Ward, Before the Trumpet, p 183.

41. Hagedorn p 103; Roosevelt, Mrs. T Jr.. p 42; Kerr p 97.

42. Ward, Before the Trumpet, p 183.

43. S. Morris p 207–208; Kerr p 102.

44. Hagedorn p 110, 124.

45. E. Morris p 252; Brands p 431; Morrison Vol. 3 p 490.

46. Time Magazine 7/24/44 p 21.

47. S. Morris p 229–230; Renehan p 48.

48. LOC c-8; Longworth p 47.

49. S. Morris p 233, 298–299; Collier p 126.

50. Collier p 126.

51. Kerr p 104–108, 123; Hagedorn p 112, 154, 180.

52. Snyder; Hagedorn p 145.

53. S. Morris p 251; TR Collection 87M-100.

54. Roosevelt, Mrs. T Jr. p 41; Kerr p 112.

55. Brands p 406; TR Collection 87M-100.

56. Hagedorn p 263; Kerr p 120–123.

57. Kerr p 126–128, 140–141.

58. Kerr p 142–145.

59. Collier p 118; Kerr p 72–73; Wagenknecht p 177.

60. LOC c-8.

61. Morrison Vol 4, pages 977 & 1274; TR Collection bMS Am 1834.1[342]

62. Collier p 129–130; Longworth p 64.

63. Kerr p 150, 158–161; Hagedorn p 139.

64. S. Morris p 282–283.

65. TR Collection clipping file; Roosevelt, Mrs. T Jr. p 42; LOC c-56 & c-63.

66. Brands p 560; Kerr p 178.

67. Kerr p 180.

68. Brands p 561; Snyder.

69. S. Morris p 303–305; Hagedorn p 265.

70. Ward, First Class Temperament, p 46–47.

71. Roosevelt, Mrs. T Jr. p 43.

72. TR Collection clipping file; Roosevelt, Mrs. T Jr. p 42.

73. Morrison Vol 5 p 860.

74. Roosevelt, Mrs. T Jr. p 42.

75. Vanderbilt University Library, Scribner's Magazine Jan., 1907 p 23; LOC c-63.

76. E. Morris p 53; Brands p 504, 529, 635, 683; Harbaugh p 194; TR Collection clipping file.

77. Morrison Vol 6 p 944; Roosevelt, Mrs. T Jr. p 42–43; NY Times 7/14/44; Collier p 141.

78. Schriftgiesser p 245; Morrison Vol 5 p 799; NY Times 7/14/44.

79. TR Collection 91M-50.

AND ALONG CAME ELEANOR

As can well be imagined, Theodore Roosevelt, Jr., single and at age twenty-one, was one of the most eligible bachelors in America. Besides being the son of the President of the United States and a Harvard graduate, he was entertaining, witty, obviously ambitious, and not afraid to get his hands dirty working hard to accomplish something on his own. It seemed he was constantly in the news concerning something he had done at Harvard, his job, or some social event. The publicity that Ted received might well be compared to the news coverage given to the comings and goings of John F. Kennedy, Jr. in the 1980's and early1990's. When, in October, 1908, only days after beginning his new job at the Hartford Carpet Corporation, Ted accepted an invitation to attend a house party at the Arthur Dodge home in Simsbury, Connecticut, he had no way of knowing that this event would be any different from the many other weekend parties he had attended. While he was at the railroad station in New Haven waiting on the local train to Simsbury, he was introduced to another of the guests. She was an attractive, perky, nineteen year-old, and her name was Eleanor Butler Alexander. Eleanor was destined to share with Ted the last thirty-four years of his life.

Eleanor Alexander was born in New York City to Henry Addison Alexander, a prominent New York attorney, and Grace Green Alexander. Eleanor's maternal grandfather was Albert Green, an ultra-conservative Republican who had made a fortune in the wholesale dry goods business. Eleanor's forebears were some of America's foremost pioneers and founders. While they did not realize it for a time, Ted's mother, Edith, and Eleanor were actually very distant cousins, proven by the fact that they each had four ancestors on the Mayflower, the same four!

The first three years of Eleanor's life were spent with her mother and father in New York. Then her parents were divorced and Eleanor and her mother Grace spent the next two years with Grace's parents in California. They then moved to Rome, followed shortly by moving again, this time to Paris. Henry followed them there, where he and Grace were remarried and where the family lived for the next six years. In Paris, Eleanor attended American schools and spent her summers vacationing in Scotland. In 1900, when Grace and Henry divorced for the second time, Eleanor and her mother returned to New York. There, Eleanor studied at Miss Keller's School and then at Miss Spence's School for Girls, where she graduated in 1907. Her upbringing was entirely different from Ted's; she was raised in a structured, well supervised home where grace and manners were emphasized as opposed to the out-of-doors, let-freedom-ring style of Ted's early life.[1]

Even though Eleanor and Ted had a number of mutual friends and Eleanor was a good friend of Ted's sister, Ethel, prior to running into her at the station Ted was not aware that Eleanor existed. But Eleanor knew well who Ted was from all the news coverage of his activities, social and otherwise. At their brief initial meeting in New Haven, Eleanor did not want to jump to any conclusions, but she assumed Ted would be conceited and that she would not like him. That night, however, they were seated next to each other for dinner, and struck up an interesting conversation. After dinner they declined to participate in parlor games with the other guests, preferring to sit on the steps and talk. They were together a good bit the next day at the hares and hounds game (An outside game, also called the paper chase, often played at house parties. The guests chosen as hares were given a head start and left a trail of scrap paper representing the scent of a rabbit for the other guests, the hounds, to follow and try to catch the elusive hares.). They said goodbye when Ted had to leave to get back to his job in Thompsonville. It was obvious to everyone that they were smitten with each other, but the Victorian morals of the day being what they were, he called her "Miss Alexander," and she referred to him as "Mr. Roosevelt." After the Dodge's house party, they did not see or hear from each other for a couple of months, when Eleanor attended Ethel Roosevelt's coming out dance at the White House.[2]

Ethel's debut party was the premiere social event of the 1908 Washington, Christmas holiday season, and the White House was crowded with the guests. As soon as the festivities began, Ted sought out Eleanor and danced with her as many times as he could. Eleanor was afraid she and Ted danced together so much that they had attracted everyone's attention. Theodore Jr. planned to return to the carpet mill by train the next day, and his return route would take him through New York City. When he found out that Eleanor would also be returning to New York the next day, he suggested that they ride back together and asked her what train she would take. Eleanor inadvertently gave him the wrong train. Ted boarded the train Eleanor named at the Washington Union Station and walked its length twice looking for her. Eleanor, not realizing her mistake, wondered why Ted did not meet her as they had planned. Soon, however, the misunderstanding was cleared up and they began to correspond with each other by mail. On some of his letters to her, Ted drew amusing little scenes depicting some of the work done at the carpet mill.

But they still called each other "Mr. Roosevelt," and "Miss Alexander" until Ted finally got up the courage to begin one of his letters with "Dear Goldilocks." Eleanor was insulted by this salutation. She considered it to be an undeserved familiarity and did not answer the letter, or the others that followed.

The next time Ted and Eleanor saw each other was several months later at the prestigious Tuxedo Autumn Ball in Tuxedo Park, New York. Ted found out that Eleanor would be at the dance, but he did not know she had changed her hairstyle. He looked and looked for her on and around the dance floor but did not recognize her. He even cut in on two other girls thinking they were Eleanor. Finally he got their mutual friend, Suydam Cutting, to point her out to him. When Ted cut in, Eleanor wasted no time in telling him of her annoyance at his addressing her as "Goldilocks." She soon got over her irritation, however, because before the party was over she said yes to his suggestion that they see each other on weekends when he could afford the price of a ticket from Thompsonville to New York and then back to Thompsonville. With this, the Victorian etiquette was relaxed and their discrete courtship began.

The papers were constantly reporting on some romance Ted was allegedly having with one woman or another, some of whom he didn't even know. Both Ted and Eleanor wanted to avoid the publicity that they knew would surround them if reports of their dating relationship surfaced. As often as possible on Saturdays, Ted would catch a train for the eight-hour trip to New York, and spend a properly chaperoned Saturday evening with Eleanor. On Sunday, they would go alone for long walks, sometimes in the snow, or go to someplace where they were not likely to encounter anyone they knew. On at least one occasion they went unchaperoned to a little tearoom. Eleanor said that being there alone with a man made her feel like a Jezebel. About this time in their relationship, Ted gave her the sobriquet "Bunny." This was the first of several nicknames he christened her with over the years, but it remained the one he used in their most intimate times. As when his father was courting his mother twenty-two years before, Ted kept his developing love life a secret from everyone, including his own family, for a number of months.[3]

While Ted was in love, Eleanor was not so sure. She liked Ted, but, as her mother pointed out, there was a world of family and political difference between the genteel home life and conservative views of Eleanor's people and the progressive politics and, what Grace perceived to be, the uncultured life style Ted descended from. Not only that, but when Ethel invited Eleanor to spend a weekend at Sagamore Hill, she saw for herself the huge contrast between her sedate home environment and that of the Roosevelts'. Things were anything but calm at Sagamore with all the outdoor games and the banter before, during, and after meals. Even after the Roosevelts had retired for the evening they would think of something they had forgotten to tell the others and get up out of bed for more conversation out in the hall. Eleanor was also perturbed at Edith for having chided her for wearing white kid gloves to the Roosevelt's home in rural Oyster Bay. Finally Eleanor's aunt, Netty McCook, decided her niece could do a lot worse than to marry the son of a former President of the United States and talked some sense into Eleanor and Grace. She told them, "Go home and thank God on your knees," referring to Ted's amorous pursuit. By this time, Ted had been promoted by his employer from wool sorter to the company's sales department and was such a good salesman that his earnings jumped to between $150 and $200 per month, a tidy sum in those days, especially for such a young man. He proposed marriage. She said yes, and a formal announcement of the couple's engagement was made in February, 1910.[4]

With their engagement now public, there was no more privacy. Reporters were constantly hounding them for stories, and their friends and even strangers were calling and knocking at the door to wish the young couple happiness. Ted was used to people being interested in his private life, but Eleanor was not and her mother was horrified. Grace somehow blamed Ted for having such a famous father and when anyone insinuated to her that Eleanor was lucky to be engaged to Ted, she was quick to respond that he was the one that was lucky.[5]

When Teddy's presidential term was up in early spring of '09, the now former President and his son Kermit left on an extended writing and hunting safari to Africa. They would not return to the United States until June 18th of the following year. Ted had been invited to go with them, but he had Eleanor and his job to think about and declined the invitation. In order to make sure Teddy and Kermit got back home in time for the wedding, June 20th was selected as the wedding date, and the engaged couple proceeded with their marriage plans. They would live in San Francisco, due to Ted's transfer to the Hartford Carpet Company's west coast office. When the wedding day finally arrived, it was a scorcher with temperatures well into the 90's. The 5th Avenue Presbyterian Church in New York City was packed with guests, including five hundred of the Rough Riders. A crowd lined the streets outside the church. The marriage ceremony was performed by Dr. Henry Sanders, a Baptist minister and a friend of the bride. The Reverend Gordon Russell, a Methodist friend of Ted's, assisted.[6]

The reception was held at the Manhattan home of Eleanor's aunt and uncle, Mr. and Mrs. Charles Alexander. The Rough Riders had a rip-roaring time and ate most of the hors d'oeuvres and wedding cake. Ted was determined that they would have a honeymoon safe from the eyes of the reporters and the curious, so he composed an elaborate escape plan that worked like a charm, at first. When the couple left the Alexander home amid the customary shower of rice and well wishes, they jumped into a car and sped off. The New York police blocked all the pursuing traffic. They took the ferry at 125th St. and then caught a train to Philadelphia, where they registered in a hotel as Mr. and Mrs. Winthrop Rogers and spent their wedding night. The next day they boarded a train for Chicago and registered there at the Blackstone Hotel, again as Mr. and Mrs. Winthrop Rogers. The newspapers were full of stories of the wedding and speculation as to where they had gone on their secret honeymoon. A few minutes after checking into the Blackstone, there was a banging on the door of their room; they had been recognized. When the knocking continued, Ted opened the door, and, grinning the famous Roosevelt toothy grin, said to the newsman standing there, "I can't talk with you now, I'm busy," and shut the door. From then until they reached the St. Francis Hotel in San Francisco, the newlyweds were able to avoid the journalists and curious, with the help of the hotel staff and by using freight elevators, and service doors.

Shortly after they checked into the St. Francis, the desk clerk called to say that a group of reporters was waiting to see them. Ted told the clerk that he and Eleanor would agree to an interview with only one of the waiting reporters and that the group must select which one of them would conduct it. John Francis Neylan, the political writer for the *San Francisco Bulletin,* was selected. Ted told Mr. Neylan that all the publicity they had been getting because of who his father was was bothersome, and that all they wanted was to stand on their own feet and be left alone to begin their marriage in a normal way. The articles in the papers the next day were not offensive to Ted and Eleanor and thereafter they were left alone. John Francis Neylan later became a close personal friend to Ted and Eleanor and, many years later, wrote a touching booklet memorializing Ted. He entitled it *Beyond the Call of Duty.*[7]

After staying at the St. Francis for a couple of weeks, the young couple spent two weeks at the beach house of some friends. There they swam, surfed, hiked, rode horses, canoed in the lagoons, and generally had a wonderful time. Their host, Stewart Edward White, was a world-class shooter, and he gave them instructions in marksmanship.[8]

With the honeymoon over, the couple returned to San Francisco and rented a house at 1942 Pacific Avenue, overlooking the Golden Gate Bridge, and in August Ted began calling on prospective carpet customers. As a factory representative, it was Ted's job to make sales calls on retailers and wholesalers of carpets rather than to directly contact consumers. He would pack up carpet samples and travel around the San Francisco area showing the samples to prospective customers and explaining to them the benefits of the Hartford carpets. Ted worked hard, was an exceptionally good salesman, and was earning handsome commissions.

They settled into married life. One of the first things they did was hire a Chinese houseboy and start having friends over for small dinner parties. Ted joined the prestigious Pacific Union Club, began to dabble in local Republican politics, and made his first political speech. He spoke on the civic duties of ordinary citizens. Soon he was running a Republican district in San Francisco. In the upcoming California Republican Primary, Ted backed the progressive Hiram Johnson, who was seeking the nomination for governor. Johnson was not given much chance to win and had been virtually ignored by the press. However, he defied the odds and won both the primary and the later general election, and, as a Republican, became Governor of California.[9]

By November, Eleanor was pregnant with their first child. Ted's work was close enough that most days he could come home for lunch. His interests were home, job, and politics, in that order. By early 1911, Teddy, after a three year respite from the presidency, was having serious thoughts about seeking the Republican nomination for President at the 1912 convention, and planned a trip to California for the dual purpose of visiting with his son and daughter-in-law and making some political contacts. Ted acted as the advance man for his father and by the time Teddy, Edith, Ethel and Quentin came out in the spring, he and Governor Johnson had already arranged for the former President to make a number of speeches and meet with many important Californians. Eleanor's and TRJr's house was turned into a temporary political headquarters. During the ten days the former president and family were there, the house was running over with political cronies, friends, and newsmen. Dinner parties were held every night with as many guests as could be accommodated. Eleanor did a beautiful job managing all the dinners, reporters, and visitors, even though she was not accustomed to that kind of chaos.

Contrary to later years, in the early 1900s almost all babies were born at home, instead of a hospital. True to the times, Eleanor delivered Grace Green Roosevelt in the rented home on Pacific Avenue on August 8, 1911. Besides being Ted's and Eleanor's first child, Gracie was Theodore's and Edith's first grandchild. From the first time he saw her, Ted was enthralled with the new baby and loved to hold her in his arms and play with her. It soon became a habit for him to have her on his lap for a half hour each night before Gracie's bedtime.[10]

At some point during the nearly two years they lived in California, Ted made the decision that he wanted to devote himself to a career in politics. He felt that to properly prepare himself for this, he must first earn a lot of money. He did not want his family's living to depend on whatever salary he might earn from holding some elected office. Even though he had worked his way up to office manager, his earning power was limited with the Hartford Carpet Co. Ted was also aware that he would be more help to Teddy's quest for the presidency if he were in New York, rather than in California, so he accepted an offer to join the New York investment banking firm of Bertron, Griscom & Co. as a bond salesman. In early 1912, Ted,

Eleanor, and Gracie packed up and moved the family residence from the rented house in San Francisco into a rented house on East 74th St. between Lexington and 3rd Ave., in New York City. The family would, however, spend a considerable amount of time at Sagamore Hill, at least until the Republican convention in June. While staying at her in-law's house, Eleanor, in her book *Day Before Yesterday,* tells of a visit to Sagamore Hill by Lillian Russell, the silent film star. One day Eleanor and Ms. Russell were sitting on the porch chatting while Eleanor was sewing a little corduroy coat for daughter Gracie. Ms. Russell noticed that she was having trouble putting in the sleeves. After watching Eleanor struggle for a few minutes, the famous actress suddenly exclaimed, "Give me that," then grabbed the coat and expertly showed Eleanor how to finish it. Lillian Russell was the Marilyn Monroe of her day. Eleanor was surprised that she would know how to do such a menial job as sew. [11]

True to his word, Teddy declined to seek the Republican nomination for president in '08. William Howard Taft, an ultra-conservative, received the nomination and was subsequently elected President in the general election. The Republicans lost heavily in the 1910 off year elections, and the Taft supporters blamed the losses on Theodore. They said that the popular former President had given his personal support only to progressive Republicans and had failed to properly succor President Taft. Now, in 1912, Teddy was campaigning for the Republican presidential nomination. The only way to get the Grand Old Party's presidential nod would be to usurp Taft's bid for a second term. A vicious fight was going on within the Republican Party. Besides the philosophical differences between the conservatives and the progressives, Teddy personally did not like Taft. At one time they had been friends, but now he considered the President to be a dull, overly formal stick in the mud. On one occasion Taft, along with his entourage of aides and secret service men, attended a funeral in New York in which Teddy and Eleanor were also in attendance. Toward the end of the service, Taft and his assemblage got up and noisily departed. When asked if it was customary for a President to leave a funeral ahead of the coffin, Teddy remarked that it was not, but that "Taft probably thought there should be a precedence even between corpses."

Teddy had run for the Republican presidential nomination in several of the state primaries held in 1912, and had won a clear majority of the popular vote. However, not all states had Republican Primaries and Taft had control of the party machinery. When the Republican Convention was held, Taft received the nomination. Teddy then bolted the Republican Party and accepted the presidential nomination of the Progressive Party a.k.a. Bull Moose Party. Thus Teddy became a third party nominee for president, like Ross Perot or George Wallace of more recent years. In the general election in November, Woodrow Wilson, the

Democratic nominee, was elected President, but Teddy polled a half million more votes than Taft and finished second. The results of this election caused an even wider rift in Republican ranks. The Taft forces claimed that Teddy cost Taft the election, and the TR supporters thought that their man deserved the Republican nomination and that had he received it, he would have beaten Wilson in the general election. Both sides were probably correct.[12]

Early on into this political turmoil came Ted, trying to help his father politically and sell bonds at the same time. Many, if not most, investors considering the purchase of bonds were conservative Republicans and, therefore, were supporters of William Howard Taft. Often, Ted would make a call on a prospective bond buyer and then be rebuffed when the client found out that he was Teddy's son. Refusing to allow himself to become discouraged, Ted plugged away and continued to make sales calls.

TRJr had enjoyed a drink of liquor all of his adult life, but during the period of time after Teddy's defeat he began drinking so heavily that it was having an effect on his personal life. After the workday was finished, he often stayed out late at New York clubs partying with friends, rather than going home to his family. Eleanor made the best of the situation. When Ted ate with friends at a club instead of attending the family Christmas dinner at Sagamore Hill, Teddy became concerned that his oldest son might be following in the footsteps of his uncle Elliott. Edith, however, was livid. In her anger, she said Eleanor didn't realize the seriousness of the situation and that she wished Ted and Eleanor had stayed in California. On an occasion in 1913, when Edith was called to Italy to tend to her sister Emily, who was sick, Ted, Eleanor, Gracie, and Eleanor's mother all piled into Sagamore Hill for a vacation and to visit with Teddy. At the same time, Ted's brothers Archie and Quentin were home from school. When Edith heard about all the people visiting in her home, she wrote Kermit that his brothers had lit on Teddy "like vampires, filing the house with people they want to know, using Father as a bait!" It didn't bother TR though; he loved the company. Ted and his mother were never as close as Ted was to his father. If Edith had been forced to rank her children according to where each of them stood in her affections, Kermit would have been her favorite, with Ted and Alice at the bottom. Edith's extreme reaction to Ted's drinking problem may well have been one of the events leading to the slight but permanent annoyance that developed between Ted and Eleanor on the one hand, and Edith on the other. While they loved each other, after Ted's marriage there was never a totally free and relaxed relationship between the TRJrs and Edith. Teddy loved and admired Ted, but with TR's intellect, accomplishments, and dominant personality, he unintentionally, but consistently, overshadowed Ted. Teddy also loved Eleanor, at one time writing that Eleanor was a very, very rare girl, and was just as sweet as Edith.[13]

Ted and Eleanor, Ethel, and Alice remained close to each other all their lives. Eleanor and Ethel had been friends for many years, and Alice and Eleanor hit it off well from the first time they met. Alice knew that Eleanor had been a protected, only child, and admired how she fit into the energetic, almost hyper, Roosevelt clan.[14]

Whatever problems Ted's excessive drinking may have caused, he got them under control, and his bond business boomed. By the end of 1913, his income had more than doubled. Still, even though he was earning a very good living, he had not accumulated enough to be as financially independent as he felt was necessary to permit him to run for public office. Not only that, in June, 1914 Eleanor gave birth to their second child, Theodore Roosevelt III.[15]

Next to his wife, his children, his father, and possibly Alice, Ted was closer to his brother Kermit than any other person in his life. Being born only 24 months apart, they grew up together and shared many personal and family experiences. By early 1914, Kermit was employed as an engineer aiding in the construction of a railroad in Brazil when Ted wrote to him with the suggestion that he come home and that they go into some type of business together. Ted did not know that Kermit had other plans, including his upcoming marriage to Belle Willard, the daughter of the U.S. Ambassador to Spain. When Kermit turned him down, Ted resigned his job as a bond salesman with Bertron, Griscom & Co., and accepted an offer made to him to become a partner in the Philadelphia investment-banking firm of Montgomery, Clothier and Tyler. He would be the manager of the company's New York office. Ted was pleased with his new business arrangement from the very first. Both Bob Montgomery and George Tyler had family connections with the Roosevelts, so Ted was personally acquainted with at least some of his new business associates. With his usual vigor and enthusiasm, he went right to work and saw a dramatic increase in his income. The negative impact of Teddy's Bull Moose flop had lessened in the ensuing two years, but Ted's new financial success was mainly attributable to the favorable business climate at the time and his own hard work. Keeping sight of his goal to eventually enter the political arena, Ted and Eleanor cut costs every way they could. They saved and invested every penny possible. The clothes they wore were store-bought rather than tailor-mades and they didn't even own an automobile. Most nights, they stayed at home and read a good book, rather than going out. Their entertaining usually consisted of having a few close friends over for dinner.[16]

Christmas of 1914 was so very typical for the Roosevelt family at Sagamore Hill. Ted, Eleanor, Gracie, and Theodore III were there along with Ted's brothers, Archie and Quentin, and sisters, Alice Roosevelt Longworth and Ethel Roosevelt Derby, and their husbands, Nick Longworth and Dick Derby. They all, old and young alike, hung their stockings on Christmas Eve and early the next morning went into Edith's room and sat around on the bed and on chairs and talked. The only members of the family who were not there for the Christmas festivities were Kermit and Belle. They were still in South America. Belle was recovering from a miscarriage and was not able to travel. Not long after the coming of the new year, Eleanor became pregnant with child number three.[17]

On June 28, 1914, Archduke Ferdinand was assassinated, setting unstoppable war wheels in motion. The initial fighting in what history would label "The Great War," (a.k.a. World War I, and The War to End All Wars) began in August, 1914. Immediately upon the outbreak of hostilities, Teddy, Ted, and a few other farsighted individuals realized the danger a European war posed for the United States, and began calling for an increase in military appropriations and preparedness. Some of them, including TR and TRJr, even called for compulsory military training for all able-bodied men, but neither President Woodrow Wilson, nor Congress, nor for that matter the majority of Americans paid heed to these warnings. As customary in times of peace, the American army was small, ill equipped, and not in the least prepared for military action on a global scale. The only military training provided for civilians at that time was summer camps for high school and college students, similar to the ROTC summer camps of recent years. The output of these camps would be only a drop in the ocean with respect to the need for junior officers should the United States be drawn into a global war. On May 10, 1915, two days after a German submarine torpedoed and sank the American liner Lusitania, Theodore Roosevelt Jr., and fourteen other young New York business and professional men met to discuss their concern for the sinking and for the country's lack of military preparedness. Ted wrote that, "They felt that it was only a question of time until we would be called to the colors, and realized most keenly the fact that it is one thing to be willing and quite another to be able to take your part."[18] As an outcome of this meeting, the group, all college graduates from Harvard, Yale, Princeton, or Hamilton, sent, under their own signatures, the following telegram to President Wilson:

The undersigned citizens of New York express their conviction that national interest and honor imperatively require adequate measures both to secure reparations for past violations by Germany of American rights and sure guarantees against future violations. We further express the conviction that the consolidated judgement of the nation will firmly support the government in any measures, however serious, to secure full reparations and guarantees.

The message was widely publicized by the newspapers and radio and it received a great deal of favorable public support and comment.[19]

Within days, a second meeting of the group took place, this time attended by approximately one hundred young New Yorkers. As a result, a three-man committee, composed of Ted, Phillip Carroll, and Grenville Clark, was appointed to come up with a recommendation as to what action the group could take to enhance the military preparedness of the country. The committee decided that summer training camps similar to the student camps of 1913 and 1914, but open to attendance by older men were needed. They felt that this in itself would at least partially accomplish their goal. Teddy's old friend from the Spanish American War days, Major General Leonard Wood, was Commander of the Army in the Eastern United States and had been instrumental in the success of the previous student camps. Wood was contacted by the committee and enthusiastically promised, not only his personal support, but also the support of the War Department.

At General Wood's urging, the War Department issued General Order No. 38, dated June 22, 1915. This order authorized civilian training camps similar to the ones envisioned by Ted and the other members of the group. Attendance at the camps would be voluntary with eligibility limited to civilian men age forty-five and under. Arrangements were made for the first camp to be held at Plattsburg Barracks near Plattsburg, New York, for a five-week period beginning August 10th. There was no provision in the order for the army to pay travel expenses, uniforms, or food; therefore, each trainee would have to bear his own expenses. The average individual cost for the five-week training period was one hundred dollars. Regular army officers would serve as instructors, battalion and company commanders, and executive officers. An attendance of approximately one hundred men was expected at the first camp. Enrollment applications were printed and publicity was given to the project. There was an overwhelming response and it soon became obvious that the undertaking, which came to be known as the "Plattsburg Movement," would spread far beyond the State of New York. Soon, other camps were set to be held near Chicago, at Fort Sheridan Washington, and at the Presidio in California.[20]

Twelve hundred trainees, including Theodore Roosevelt, Jr. and his brothers Archie and Quentin, were in attendance when the first Plattsburg camp opened. Others attending the first camp included a Congressman, a former Secretary of State, the Police Commissioner of the City of New York, along with college professors, farmers, bankers, lawyers, businessmen, journalists, artists, and others. Forty New York policemen attended with the view that the training would help them deal with any terrorist problems that might arise. The trainees were organized into eight companies of 150 men each, with each company having its own company street and mess hall. Two battalions of four companies each were formed. Strict army discipline was enforced. Training began with a cold shower at 5:15 a.m. and continued until 10:00 p.m. with few breaks or rest periods. The men were instructed in rifle firing and maintenance, the manual of arms, close order drill, physical training, cover and concealment, battle formations and tactics, range estimation, defensive tactics and the use of trenches, use of artillery and cavalry, communications, first aid, and hygiene. Interspersed with the classroom instruction were demonstrations of correct methods. There were also many field and night problems where aggressor forces were utilized. The final week concluded with a 65-mile forced march, with practical problems popping up at unexpected times, some requiring the use of point, rear, and flank protection. Ted proved to be an outstanding trainee and was given a reserve commission as a 1st Lieutenant at the end of camp.[21]

Toward the end of the initial camp former President Theodore Roosevelt spoke to the assembled trainees and cadre. Also in attendance were several thousand citizens from the Plattsburg area. He viciously attacked the Wilson administration for its policies in general, and especially for its failure to properly prepare the United States militarily. The speech was given wide press coverage. President Wilson was also invited to speak at the camp, but he declined. Although General Wood had nothing to do with the contents of Teddy's speech, his friendship with the Roosevelts was well known, and the Wilson administration rebuked Wood for affording Teddy the opportunity to orate. Some historians believe that this was the reason General John J. Pershing, rather than General Wood, was selected to lead the American forces in Europe during World War I.[22]

After the conclusion of the 1915 camps, Ted and a group of other training camp participants got together and formed the Military Training Camps Association. Ted served on the executive committee and was secretary of the enrollment committee. The purpose of the organization was to embolden the government to continue to provide a reasonable amount of military training for civilians and to encourage civilian men to take advantage of the opportunity to receive the training offered. By 1916, the Association was calling for compulsory military training for all able-bodied men. The enrollment committee, under Ted's leadership, was hard at work compiling mailing lists of prospective members. A brochure describing the Association and application forms were prepared and mailed to high school and college graduates, and the participants in the first camps. The initial enrollment in the Military Training Camps Association was approximately forty-two hundred men. Branches of the organization sprang up at many locations across the country. Similar to the mood of the country prior to the Spanish-American War, patriotism was in vogue and a clamor for war against Germany was spreading. Some of the clubs arranged for target practice sessions and held weekly or monthly meetings where regular army officers would speak on various military subjects. The experience Ted gained from being involved in the organization and operation of the Training Camps Association would be invaluable to him in a major project he and a few others would undertake shortly after the conclusion of World War I.

Through the efforts of the Training Camps Association and a few other groups and individuals, on June 3, 1916, Congress passed The National Defense Act which authorized the Secretary of War to establish camps for the military training and instruction of civilians. Under this new law, the federal government would pay for subsistence, uniforms, and other expenses, and also sell to the trainees, at cost plus ten percent, all quartermaster and ordinance supplies and equipment necessary for proper training. Pursuant to the act, some twelve training camps were conducted in 1916 with a total attendance of over sixteen thousand men. The camp planners had expected an even larger number of trainees, but attendance was held down because of the necessity to concentrate US troops on the Mexican border, and also because of a threatened railroad strike.[23]

In February 1917, the Association sponsored a nationally distributed magazine entitled *National Service*. The new magazine was an independently incorporated business and, therefore, owned by stockholders. The original editorial and managing board was composed of TRJr, Nelson Doubleday, and a few others. Besides reporting news of interest to supporters of national preparedness, the magazine offered subscribers interesting correspondence courses involving various military subjects. Also early in 1917, with the encouragement of the Association, Captain Ralph Parker, a regular army officer, gave a series of lectures on military subjects in the New York area and in several other eastern cities. Captain Parker's talks were well received and attended by hundreds of interested men.

More civilian training camps were planned for 1917, but the United States' entry into the First World War resulted in their cancellation and replacement by Officer Training Camps. The difference being that the trainees in the OTCs were on active duty in the army. The civilian training camps that grew out of the original meeting of Ted and the other young New Yorkers, did, however, contribute a great service to the country. Many of the attendees, including Theodore Roosevelt, Jr., were awarded commissions and many others benefited from their training at the camps by being better prepared to take officer examinations. Ted said, "These camps in themselves furnished the nucleus for the selection of the commissioned personnel for the national army, and furnished, furthermore, the system by which the great mass of our junior officers were chosen and educated." Most of the junior officers that commanded the company and platoon size units that fought in France in World War I attended one or more of the civilian training camps.[24]

After attending the 1915 military training camp, Ted went back to hard work at Montgomery, Clothier, and Tyler. In October, Eleanor gave birth to their third child, Cornelius Van Schaack Roosevelt, obviously named after Ted's great-grandfather. TR III and little Cornelius were born so close together that their parents called them the "old baby," and the "new baby." The family, not so little any more, continued to live skimpily, and invest and save all they could. By the end of the year, Ted's share of the Montgomery, Clothier, and Tyler profits amounted to more than $150,000. In placing himself in a position to earn such a large sum in the investment banking business, it was necessary that Ted cultivate friendships with people of great wealth, many of whom had supported Taft in 1912. Teddy called Ted's new, wealthy friends "plutocrats," but he seemed to understand the reason for Ted's actions. Edith, however, was not so tolerant, nor was Ted's sister, Ethel Derby. Grace Vanderbilt was asked to be baby CVS Roosevelt's godmother. At the baby's christening, Edith and Ethel attended but, being discretely rude, they sat alone on the sofa and refused to go upstairs to look at the presents.[25]

With the dawn of 1916, more and more American citizens were convinced of the inevitability of war. Even though war clouds were gathering, 1916 would be little different than 1915 for Ted and his family. Eleanor was busy with her household and child raising duties, and Ted was busy earning large profits from his investment banking business, as well as trying to help his father politically and work with the Training Camps Association. At some point in either '15 or very early in '16, Teddy set his ambitious sights on the 1916 Republican presidential nomination. Since his third party efforts of 1912 had alienated many influential Republicans, it was necessary for him to rebuild some of the political bridges he had burned. Ted spent a great deal of time meeting with and encouraging his wealthy, important friends in the banking and finance business to support his father. Not enough bridges could be re-built, however, and the effort came to naught. The nomination went to Charles Evans Hughes. Hughes was subsequently defeated in the 1916 general election by the incumbent president, Woodrow Wilson. The majority of the voters were somehow under the impression that Wilson would keep the United States out of the war in Europe.[26]

As the months slipped by, citizen parades in support of military preparedness began to spring up across the country. In May, one of the largest parades ever held in New York City took place in support of the cause. Eleanor, at Ted's urging, recruited about twelve hundred women, including her mother-in-law Edith, to march under the banner of "Independent Patriotic Women of America." The ladies were all dressed in white, and were very impressive as Eleanor led them down Fifth Avenue.[27]

Archie graduated from Harvard in June and promptly went to work for Bigelow Carpet Company, the successor company to Ted's old employer, Hartford Carpet Company. Later in the summer, Ted, Archie and Quentin attended a session of the training camp in Plattsburg. This year, the training included instruction in trench construction and how to go "over the top." At the end of camp, Ted received a reserve commission as a major in the infantry and Archie that of a first lieutenant.

Ted's promotion and Archie's commission were made pursuant to recommendations by the regular army officers conducting the camp. Quentin was considered too young for a commission, but he didn't care, his real interest was in aviation.[28]

President Woodrow Wilson was determined to keep the United States out of the war, even though a public outcry for war with Germany was growing louder by the day. In January, 1917, Germany officially notified the United States that any ship, American or otherwise, carrying supplies or equipment which might be used to fight a war would be sunk. The President promptly broke off diplomatic relations with Germany. On February 19th, Major Douglas MacArthur, who was then with the Army General Staff in Washington, D.C., had night duty when a message was received that General Funston, the officer originally picked to command all US forces sent to fight in France should the country be drawn into the war, had suddenly died in San Antonio, Texas. As duty officer, MacArthur was required to deliver the message to the Secretary of War, Newton Baker. When he arrived at Mr. Baker's residence, he discovered that a social event was in progress, with President Wilson in attendance. After delivering his message, MacArthur was asked by Baker and Wilson to step into another room. There they asked for his personal recommendation as to who should be given the assignment of leading the troops in France now that General Funston was dead. Without hesitation MacArthur named General John J. "Black Jack" Pershing. How much weight MacArthur's recommendation was given in the eventual selection of Pershing is unknown.[29]

In early spring, German submarines sank three American ships. Congress declared war on Germany on April 6, 1917. Ted and Eleanor had, by then, a net worth of over $500,000; this was more than enough for the nest egg they felt was needed for Ted to devote full time to some elected office. But now his political ambitions would have to be put on hold.[30]

The world would never be the same.

Ted's brother Archie had fallen in love with Grace Lockwood, a beautiful girl from Boston. Eight days after war was declared, the entire Theodore Roosevelt clan gathered in the bride's home city to celebrate the young couple's wedding. The marriage vows were exchanged at the Emmanuel Church. This was the first time that Ted and his family had been with his parents, and all of his brothers and sisters and their families for over a year. All of the previous weddings and get-togethers had been happy occasions with much joy and laughter, but Archie's and Grace's wedding was different. Everyone put on a good front, but with the war situation there was an uneasy feeling which they could not ignore. There was no way any of them could have known that this would be the last time the Theodore Roosevelt family would all be together. A few days after the wedding, Ted and

Archie were placed on active duty status as instructors at the army base at Plattsburg Barracks, New York.[31]

All of the Roosevelt men, including Teddy, and two of the Roosevelt women wanted desperately to get to France, where much of the fighting was going on. And they wanted to get there as fast as possible. Teddy had been sending messages to President Wilson for months. He told the President that in the event of war he wanted to raise a volunteer cavalry unit similar to the Rough Riders, except that it would have a cadre of regular army officers. His idea was that after his men were trained, he would take them to France to fight the Germans. Wilson and TR were long time political enemies and were certainly not personal friends. Wilson said privately, "I really think the best way to treat Mr. Roosevelt is to take no notice of him. That breaks his heart and is the best punishment that can be administered." It is doubtful that the President ever seriously considered giving approval to TR's ridiculous request. To allow the former President to raise the proposed unit and take it to France would help the Republicans politically no matter how the unit performed in battle. The fact that TR had been openly critical of the Wilson administration from its beginning didn't help. Teddy, being fifty-nine years old, not in the best of health, and having no military training or experience except for what little he received in 1898, gave Wilson a perfect, non-political reason to deny the request. Wilson waited until May, as if the matter was under consideration, before notifying TR of the denial. While his conversations and writings up until his death didn't show it, Teddy may have had a touch of senility at the time, or maybe he was just having a difficult time admitting he wasn't so young any more. With all his intelligence and political savvy, it's hard to believe Theodore seriously thought his idea had a snowballs chance of approval. But he bemoaned the fact that he was not allowed to have a second war until the day he died.[32]

At Plattsburg Barracks, Ted and Archie picked up army scuttlebutt that very soon General Pershing would take the first contingent of an American Army to France, and they were determined to be in the first group to go. For one of the few times in his life, Ted asked his father for help.[33] With Teddy's romantic view of war, Ted didn't have to ask twice. In response, TR wrote the following personal letter to General Pershing:

May 20th, 1917
  "My dear General Pershing,
  **** I write you now to request that my two sons, Theodore Roosevelt, Jr., aged 27, and Archibald B. Roosevelt, aged 23, both of Harvard, be allowed to enlist as privates with you, to go over with with the first troops. The former is a Major and the latter a Captain in the Officers Reserve Corps. They are at Plattsburg for their third summer.

My own belief is that competent men of their rank and standing can gain very little from a third summer at Plattsburg, and that they should be utilized as officers, even if only as Second Lieutenants. But they are keenly desirous to see service; and if they serve under you at the front and are not killed, they will be far better able to instruct the draft army next fall or next winter, or whenever they are sent home, than they will be after spending the summer at Plattsburg.

The President has announced that only regular officers are to go with you; and if this is to be the invariable rule, then I apply on behalf of my sons that they may serve under you as enlisted men, to go to the front with the first troops sent over.

Trusting to hear that this request has been granted, and with great respect, I am,

Very sincerely yours,

Theodore Roosevelt

P. S. If I were physically fit, instead of old and heavy and stiff, I should myself ask to go under you in any capacity down to and including a sergeant; but at my age, and condition, I suppose that I could not do work you would consider worth while in the fighting line (my only line) in a lower grade than brigade commander.[34]

Either accidentally or on purpose, Teddy's letter shaved two years off of Ted's age and promoted Archie from first lieutenant to captain. In neither his brief military career nor during his eight year career as vice president and president did Theodore come in contact with many regular army officers that he considered to be industrious and intelligent soldiers. He thought most of them were lazy and lacked ambition. Besides perhaps General Leonard Wood, the professional officer which Teddy admired most was "Black Jack" Pershing. TR personally observed Captain John Pershing's exemplary performance in leading the all black 10th Calvary Regiment as it fought along side of the Rough Riders at San Juan Hill in 1898. When he was President, TR had been instrumental in furthering Pershing's career by promoting him from captain to brigadier general, bypassing 862 officers with senior dates of rank. How could Pershing refuse TR's request? The request was promptly granted with no loss of official rank. Ted remained a major and Archie a first lieutenant.[35]

With it now assured that Ted would soon be getting overseas orders, Eleanor let her husband know that she had every intention of going to France herself, so she could be close to him and at the same time in some way contribute to the war effort. Her mother, Grace Alexander, was willing and able to care for Gracie, TR III, and Cornelius, ages 5 years, 3 years, and 18 months respectively. Eleanor's aunt, Mrs. Alice Green Hoffman, owned a large house in Paris that would be available for her to live in and for the Roosevelt men to use as a family headquarters if they had occasion to be in the French Capital. In many military conflicts prior to World War I, it had not been all that unusual for women to become camp followers so they could remain close to the soldiers. Ethel Derby, Ted's sister, was also thinking of following her husband when he went "over there." However, Ethel had been in France with her husband a year earlier and now had a new baby, so she changed her mind. Ted reluctantly agreed to his wife's plan, subject to him first arriving in France and having an opportunity to look things over to make sure it was safe for Eleanor to come. There was, however, one other major complication. TR, apparently sensing what some of the wives were contemplating, announced emphatically that no Roosevelt woman would follow her husband to France. While Teddy was certainly the patriarch, he almost never told members of the family what to do. Except for possibly Ted, he normally let them live their own lives without interfering. No one wanted to disobey him, but Eleanor had a strong will of her own.[36]

Eleanor's old family friend, General J. Franklin Bell, was in charge of the Governor's Island Port of Embarkation and, as such, was responsible for the preparation of passenger lists for ships about to depart for France. Ted and Archie wanted to be certain they were on the very first ship to sail for France after they received their formal overseas orders. In an effort to insure this, Ted asked his wife to go to see General Bell and request that he please put them on the first available ship subsequent to their orders being issued. Eleanor promptly, but reluctantly, made an unannounced visit to the General's quarters, only to find that the he was out but was expected back soon. Not wanting to reveal to Mrs. Bell the purpose of her visit, she made small talk for the next two hours. When the General finally returned, Eleanor wasted no time in begging him to help get Ted and Archie on the first available ship. The old General looked at her sternly and said, "And so he has sent you to fix things up with me, has he." Eleanor, thinking she had blown it, in a quivering voice said, "yes." The General said OK, he would help. In describing this event and how relieved she was at the General's response, Eleanor said, "I burst out laughing. So did the General. So did the General's aide, Captain George C. Marshall."[37]

With General Bell's assistance, four days after receiving overseas orders Ted and Archie were given additional orders to report on board the ship "Chicago" the afternoon of June 20, 1917 for immediate departure to Bordeaux. Archie and Ted spent their last few days in the States at Sagamore Hill with their own families, and with Edith, Teddy and Quentin. Alice came up from Washington. When the embarkation day arrived, they all had a melancholy lunch and Eleanor accompanied Ted to the ship. She sat with him on deck until she knew she was about to break down, and then she left. The "Chicago" sailed as scheduled. (Ted in *Average Americans,* a book he wrote after the war, gives his sailing date as June 18th, while the Official Army Records give the sailing date as June 14th. With respect to the army date, there are many things that can snafu an Army date, such as the ship being delayed for days, or schedule adjustments being made, or army inefficiency. Eleanor, in her book *Day Before Yesterday,* gives Ted's departure date as the same day as their 7th wedding anniversary. The fact that it was their anniversary would have stuck hard in Eleanor's mind, so that is the date accepted as accurate.[38]

Of the four Roosevelt brothers, Kermit inherited less of Teddy's passion for battle than the others. He wasn't enthusiastic about going, but then he didn't want to be left behind. The only military training Kermit had had was a few weeks at Plattsburg in the spring of 1917; he was not, therefore, qualified for a commission in the U. S. Army. Feeling that he had run out of favors from General Pershing, Theodore contacted some of his influential British friends for help with getting Kermit a commission and to the war front. Teddy was successful, and Kermit was commissioned in the British Army with orders to proceed to England for training and then to the Middle East for action in Iraq against the Turks. Shortly after Kermit's orders were received, he, Belle and their small child, Kim, sailed for the United Kingdom. From there, Belle and Kim would continue on to her parent's residence in Spain.[39]

Quentin, by June, 1917, had completed his second year at Harvard and had fallen in love with Flora Payne Whitney, the beautiful daughter of the aristocratic and extremely wealthy Harry Payne Whitney and wife, Gertrude Vanderbilt Whitney. Failing the eye exam for the army, the resourceful Quentin memorized the eye chart for the flying service and with his father's help, was admitted into the army flight training course. After a few weeks of flight instruction at Mineola Air Base on Long Island, he received overseas orders. With his family and fiancÈe at the dock to see him off, Quentin sailed for France on July 23rd. Packed with his gear was a copy of his favorite poem, Alan Seegar's "I have a Rendezvous with Death."[40]

Now all four of the sons of Edith and Theodore Roosevelt were in harm's way.

Soon after Ted debarked at Bordeaux and looked things over, he cabled Eleanor telling her not to come to France and that he would let her know if and when it was OK. However, shortly after getting Ted's cable, Eleanor learned that in the near future the federal government planned to adopt a regulation prohibiting wives of American soldiers from going to the war zone. Knowing that if she was going to get "over there," she had no time to lose. She immediately contacted a ranking official with the YMCA and offered to work for them in France as a full time volunteer. The YMCA accepted her proposal and immediately got her on the passenger list of the ship "Espogne," scheduled to depart for France in four days.

Now she was really in a bind. Her husband and her father-in-law had both forbidden her journey, but Eleanor was determined. She first cabled Ted that she was en route to France. That afternoon she went to Sagamore Hill and explained to her father-in-law what her plans were. When she had finished, there was a long pause, then TR said, "Darling, I see you have made up your mind. I don't know anything I can do to help you, but if you can think of something you must let me know." Eleanor knew that he had not changed his mind and given her his consent, but simply didn't want to have a family fuss over something she was going to do no matter what his wishes were. Whatever anger the former President felt was short lived, however, when, not many days later, Teddy was asked by a newsman to comment on a report that President Wilson's son-in-law was going to France to work for the YMCA. The old political wizard, with all of his aplomb and pride, bared his teeth and said, "How very nice. We are sending our daughter-in-law to France in the YMCA!" Eleanor had been forgiven, at least by the czar of the family. She sailed on July 24th, still concerned about Ted's reaction. Three weeks later, the regulation prohibiting wives traveling to France was put into effect. Not long after Eleanor's departure, Ethel's husband, Dr. Richard Derby, embarked for France, as did cousins George, Phillip and Nicholas Roosevelt.[41]

Along Came Eleanor Source Notes

1. Roosevelt, Mrs. T Jr. p 11–32.
2. Ibid p. 11,35,45.
3. Ibid p. 45–46.
4. Roosevelt, Mrs. T Jr. p 46–47, 60; LOC c-55.
5. Roosevelt, Mrs. T Jr. p 48.
6. Roosevelt, Mrs. T Jr. p 50; Hagedorn p 296.
7. Collier p 163; Roosevelt, Mrs. T Jr. p 50–51; Stevie's Notes; Neylan.
8. Roosevelt, Mrs. T. Jr. p 52
9. Roosevelt, Mrs. T Jr. p 53; Morrison Vol 7 p 332; LOC c-55 & c-63.
10. Roosevelt, Mrs. T Jr. p 56–57; S. Morris p 373.
11. Roosevelt, Mrs. T Jr. p 58, 64; Schriftgiesser p 245; LOC c-71.
12. Roosevelt, Mrs. T Jr. p 65.
13. Brands p 737; Hagedorn p 296; S. Morris p 393.
14. Felsenthal p 144; Longworth p 175.
15. Collier p 171; Roosevelt, Mrs. T Jr. p 65.
16. Collier p 171; Harbaugh p 455.
17. Collier p 181.

18. Roosevelt, T Jr., Average Americans, p 8; S. Morris p 402–404.

19. Roosevelt, Mrs. T Jr. p 70.

20. Perry p 1–38.

21. S. Morris p 407; Perry p 1–38.

22. Perry p 38–55.

23. Ibid p 55–100.

24. Roosevelt, T Jr., Average Americans, p 11; Perry p 100–134.

25. Collier p 183–184; Roosevelt, Mrs. T Jr. p 65.

26. Collier p 186; Hagedorn p 352.

27. Collier p 186; Roosevelt, Mrs. T Jr. p 68; S. Morris p 408.

28. Collier p 186; LOC c-55.

29. MacArthur p 46–47.

30. Collier p 196.

31. S. Morris p 412; LOC c-55.

32. Miller, Nathan p 286; Collier p 188–189, 195.

33. Roosevelt, T Jr., Average Americans, p 18.

34. Pershing Vol 1 p 23.

35. Roosevelt, Mrs. T Jr. p 72; Renegan p 131–132.

36. Roosevelt, Mrs. T Jr. p 76–77; Hagedorn p 386.

37. Roosevelt, Mrs. T Jr. p 73–74.

38. Roosevelt, T Jr., Average Americans, p 19–20; Collier p 197; Roosevelt, Mrs. T Jr., p 74.

39. Renehan p 143, 177.

40. Renehan p 138–145.

41. Roosevelt, Mrs. T Jr., p 76–77, 83.

5
LAFAYETTE, WE ARE HERE

The Atlantic crossing was uneventful until they approached the coast of France and began to pass vessels that had been torpedoed by German submarines. Their ship, the Chicago, was not a designated troopship, so the passenger list included a number of French nationals returning home from work in the United States. On board Ted and Archie took French lessons from Felix, a chauffeur by trade, who was returning home to France.

Debarking at the City of Bordeaux in the latter part of June, the brothers immediately caught a train to Paris, where Ted cabled Eleanor not to come to France until she heard further from him. Then they reported to General Pershing at American Expeditionary Force Headquarters. Upon inquiry by the General, both Ted and Archie requested duty with troops rather than an assignment to a staff position. The American Army CO assigned them to the First Expeditionary Division, headquartered in the town of Gondrecourt. Ted was assigned duties with the advanced billeting detail, and Archie was posted to the 16th Infantry Regiment.

On July 4th, a rousing welcome was given by the citizens of Paris to the first arrivals of an American Army that would soon descend on France in the hundreds of thousands. During the celebration, a battalion of the 16th Infantry Regiment paraded through the Paris streets and an American colonel on Pershing's staff named C. E. Stanton was called upon to speak. Suffering a momentary loss of words, he uttered the only thing he could think of, "Lafayette, we are here!" The French took this to mean that the Americans were there to save France and as a way to repay the French for all the help they had given during the American Revolution, and they went wild with joy. Actually, at that point in time, the United States Army was small and untrained. There was not even one American division anywhere close to being ready for combat. It would take at least six months of intensive training before the A. E. F. (American Expeditionary Force) could make any substantial contribution to the war effort. On July 6th, the First Expeditionary Division was re-designated the First Infantry Division.[1]

The First Infantry Division, perhaps better known to the public as the " Big Red One," or simply the 1st Division, was an already famous old army unit, but it had been recently robbed of many of its regular army officers and enlisted men for assignment as cadre to new divisions being formed. The build-up of the American Army presently underway would increase its strength from the thousands to the millions within a little over one year. During World War I the 1st Division consisted of the 16th, 18th, 26th, and 28th Infantry Regiments, together with the Division Artillery and other supporting units, such as an Engineer Battalion, Signal Battalion, Medical units, and MP units. Each regiment contained four battalions, and each battalion was made up of four companies. While the unit strength varied from time to time, the Division, when at full strength, had a total of about 28,000 officers and men, and each battalion approximately one thousand to twelve hundred personnel. The 16th and 18th Infantry Regiments were designated as the First Brigade and the 26th and 28th as the Second Brigade. The vacancies created by the transfer of the old regulars would be filled by new and untrained enlistees and draftees.

Leaving Paris by train on the morning of July 5th, Ted arrived in Gondrecourt at 1:00 p.m. and was directed to the private home of an elderly French couple for his lodging. His room was very comfortable, and furnished with a nice feather bed. One of the first people he met after arriving in the area was Major Leslie "Whitey" McNair, who was also assigned to the billeting detail. Ted and McNair worked together arranging housing for the incoming troops and palled around together when time permitted. They became good friends. Whitey told Ted a lot about his young son, Douglas. Years later, during World War II, while serving as Chief of Infantry of the United States Army, Lieutenant General Leslie McNair was killed by an errant American bomb in Normandy, France. Two weeks after the death of his dad, Colonel Douglas McNair was killed in action in the Pacific.

As the soldiers making up the units of the 1st Division arrived, they would be housed in small towns and villages in the Gondrecourt vicinity for training purposes. Ted wrote of his impressions of the quaint countryside around Gondrecourt:

These small French villages in the north of France resemble nothing that we have in our country. They are charming and picturesque, but various features are lacking which to the well-ordered American mind causes pain. To begin with, there is no system of plumbing. The village gets all its water supply from the public fountains. This naturally makes a bath an almost unknown luxury. Many times I have been asked by the French peasants why I wanted a bath, and should it be winter, was I not afraid I would be taken sick if I took one. Around these public fountains the village life centers. There the chattering groups of women and girls are always congregating. There the gossip of the countryside originates and runs its course. There is rarely electric light in the small towns, and enormous manure piles are in front of each house and in the street. The houses themselves are a combination affair, barn and house under the same roof. The other features that are always present are the church and cafÈ. Even in the smallest town there are generally charming chapels. The cafes are where the opinions of the French nation are formed.

He also observed that most villagers had no desire to stray far from their homes, some never getting more than a few miles away, and that many of them lived in the same dwellings that had been occupied by their distant ancestors. The rural French were frugal, saving every scrap of wood and metal for future use, rather than being wasteful like many Americans. When the local citizens found out the Americans were coming, some thought they would be uncivilized barbarians right out of the wild west with the cowboys and Indians and were afraid of them. On one occasion, Ted introduced his friend, Colonel William J. Donovan, to a French officer and in the course of the introduction commented that Col. Donovan was from Buffalo. The Frenchman responded that he knew of Buffalo, that it was a very wild place where great animals were hunted. Donovan later became known as "Wild Bill Donovan," and is credited with being the father of the CIA.[2]

In a letter he wrote to his wife only a few days after arriving in the training area, Ted observed that the Americans were already fraternizing with the *poilu* and with the French girls and women, and he was afraid that this familiarity might create problems. The letter went on to discourage Eleanor from coming to France, stating that while he had not received an answer to the cable he sent to her several days ago,

> The more I see of the situation here the more I am sure that for the present at any rate, it would not be wise for you to come over here. I am sure I will not be able to see you at all. No women are allowed anywhere near the training area and I will not be allowed to go to Paris.
>
> I guess it is really the termination of the war before we will get a chance to see one another. I however believe that there will be a certain number of months in this continent before we are sent back home. In such case I want you to come over right away and I will see if I can get a furlough and go traveling to Italy, Spain, etc. and join the troops again before they go on the transports.
> With much much love, Ted

Then Ted received Eleanor's cable informing him she was on her way to

France. He said that his spouse must have promised him she would not come until he gave her the OK in "the Pickwickian sense."[3]

With new untrained recruits arriving daily, Ted continued to work on arranging housing. The officers were generally billeted in private homes in the area, while the enlisted men were placed in barns and farm sheds. The barns and sheds were crude, but were dry and the soldiers slept on the hay. This arrangement was not too bad until winter arrived. Smoking and fires were prohibited inside of the structures because of the danger of setting the hay afire. At this time the army uniform was woolen, olive drab in color and the pants looked like riding breeches with wrapped leggings. The steel helmets were copied from the British. The Big Red One was up to full strength by July 14th and training began in earnest on July 15th.

Ted began to feel a little discouraged because he was still not attached to any specific unit, until July 19th, when Colonel Duncan, the Commander of the 26th Infantry Regiment, met with General Sibert, the Division Commander. Duncan told Sibert that one of his battalion commanders was incompetent and was going to be relieved. He asked the General if he had an extra major to try-out as a battalion CO. Sibert replied, "Yes, Why not try Roosevelt?" Ted reported to Col. Duncan that day, and the next day took command of the 1st Battalion, 26th Infantry Regiment, billeted in the village of Boviolles. It is not possible to measure how important this event was in the life of Theodore Roosevelt, Jr. Just as his father had found his niche in politics, Ted had found his forte, and would in time develop the skills to enable him to do something as well, or better, than any man alive, that being to lead, inspire, guide, and assuage front line troops in combat.[4]

The fact that TRJr had been given command of a combat battalion, untrained though it may have been, caused great resentment among the other officers in the 26th Infantry Regiment, especially the senior ranking officers. They felt that he got the command because of his name and who his father was, and not because of his ability and experience. Even the noncommissioned officers and the other enlisted men doubted his ability to perform competently in combat. Roosevelt's assignment was accepted by the officers and men in the battalion with a "resignation of despair." The men in the other battalions began to refer to the 1st Battalion as the, "White House Battalion." Within two months, however, the men of the 1st Battalion would proudly refer to themselves as the "White House Battalion." As the training progressed the morale in Ted's battalion improved remarkably; they considered themselves to be the best battalion in the regiment. They probably were. Ted was proving to the men that he knew his business and he devoted himself to it with unending energy. He exhibited patience and common sense, and a real concern for the welfare of the troops.[5]

Besides the 1st Division, also in the Gondrecourt area was the combat experienced French *Chasseurs Alpins* Division. The Frenchmen had been sent there for the purpose of assisting in the training of the Big Red One. Technically, the *Chasseurs* were not a part of the infantry, although their work was the same. They considered themselves better soldiers than the regular French infantry and often derided them in word and song. Their uniforms were dark blue with silver buttons. Rather than the regular French cap, they wore a blue beret, and were commonly referred to as "Blue Devils."[6]

A normal day's training would begin at the 0600 reveille, followed by one hour for breakfast and policing. Then the troops were marched to a nearby training area where they would follow a strict training schedule all day, having lunch in the field. They would return to the battalion area in late afternoon for formal retreat and supper. "Taps" was sounded at 2200. Training took place regardless of the weather conditions and included: close order drill; assembly, disassembly and firing of the rifle, pistol, and machinegun; bayonet practice; forced marches with full field equipment; trench construction; construction of barbed wire entanglements; basic tactics; physical training; gas mask instruction; mortars; and grenades and rifle grenades; among other subjects. The Americans, being from a baseball playing country, were especially adept at throwing grenades. The French had built an elaborate system of practice trenches in the vicinity of Gondrecourt, nicknamed by the doughboys, "Washington Center." Much of the training was conducted in this trench system, learning how to fight defensively in trenches and how to "go over the top" when on offense.[7]

TRJr applied his own methods of leadership to the prescribed training schedule for his battalion. He was a strict disciplinarian and kept himself and his men in top physical condition. He never asked his men to do something he did not do himself and was with them night and day, supervising, teaching, and encouraging. When a soldier disobeyed an order or committed some other egregious act calling for punishment, Ted usually applied his own brand of creative penalty, rather than blacken the man's military record with a court martial. As an example, on one occasion while the battalion was on a long march with full field equipment, he noticed a man whose pack just didn't look right. Upon inspecting the pack Ted discovered that the man had put hay in the pack, rather than his personal equipment as ordered, so his load would be light. Ted ordered the man to fill his pack with rocks and finish the march with a pack much heavier than those of the other soldiers.

In the course of the training, the newly appointed battalion commander purchased drums, fifes, and trumpets, and had a battalion marching band formed. The little band would march at the head of the column and play appropriate songs as the battalion marched along. To make a point, he had it play loudly when they were passing another unit or going through a town. The band also played at reveille, retreat, during close order drill, and during ceremonies. Ted said he "always got a thrill of conscious pride going through a town, the troops marching at attention, colors flying, bugles playing, drums beating, and the women and children standing on the streets and shouting." He knew that the band would contribute to the *esprit de corps* of his unit. Except when marching, the members of the band would train alongside the other soldiers. One cold winter day he discovered that rather than being outside training, as they were supposed to be, the members of the band were inside by the stove. Ted made them go outside, climb up in trees and play as loud as they could while the rest of the battalion continued training.[8] After the war, one of the doughboys serving under Ted wrote:

> In those days there were a thousand men who called him 'the old man' and went out and died under his inspiring leadership. He hiked with them, although he had a horse to ride; he ate their 'monkey meat' and hardtack, although he might have had better; and he would have died just like they did unless God had seen fit to save him for other things. [9]

Believing that idleness was an enemy of men in training, the young major encouraged his troops to participate in sports when time and place permitted. He had his wife in Paris purchase, with their own money, a variety of items for the morale of the men including: a phonograph and records, a complete baseball outfit, a dozen pairs of boxing gloves, a dozen soccer balls, six basketballs, twelve barrels of soft drinks and ten pounds of pipe tobacco. Eleanor was able to find all the items Ted requested and had them sent to the battalion by the YMCA. Besides sport competitions, Ted created competition between the smaller units in the battalion in every way he could think of. As examples, he created contests between the platoons for the fastest to turn the men back into their billets and turn them out again, with or without full field equipment, and the best platoon at close order drill, and bayonet exercises. The prizes were almost negligible, such as being excused from reveille, but the squads, platoons and companies competing were enthusiastic and took pride when they won.[10]

During the course of the war, Ted acquired two animals that would mean a lot to him and his family for years to come. As a major he was entitled to a mount but was not satisfied with the one furnished to him by the army. He wrote Eleanor to please look around Paris and find him a good horse. After looking and looking, she found a spirited little mare named Tamara. Eleanor liked the horse, thought her suitable for Ted, and had it sent to him. Tamara was housed in the army stables throughout the war and Ted rode her when the occasion arose. Once during a regimental parade, Ted, mounted on Tamara, was leading the 1st Battalion along the parade ground when the horse spooked and bolted forward into the rear ranks of the battalion ahead before Ted could get her under control. Later, during the last days of the war, the men in Ted's unit presented him with Caesar, a beautiful German Shepherd they had captured from the Boche. After the war, Ted had both animals shipped home to Oyster Bay. Caesar and Tamara remained cherished members of the Roosevelt family until they died. Both animals were buried in the Roosevelt's pet cemetery, Tamara beside Little Texas, Teddy's horse from the Spanish-American War.[11]

There were men from all walks of life in Ted's battalion. There were newsmen, politicians, writers, and farmers to name a few. There were also men who were in the army only as a way to keep out of prison. A few of the doughboys in the 1st battalion were what would be termed "colorful characters." Ted's favorite was Sergeant Murphy. Murphy was an Irishman who had been in the Division for many years. Before the war was over, Ted would have many "Sgt. Murphy stories" to tell. Once observing the sergeant drilling his platoon, Ted heard him order, "Squads right bee Jesus." Another time, Ted complimented him on the way his platoon was throwing hand grenades, Murphy responded, "Sor-r, that and slope (sleep) is all they can do." The old sergeant often told his men that they acted like a flock of sheep. On one occasion a neighboring battalion had an early 4:00 a.m. first call. Sgt. Murphy mistook this call for the 1st Battalion call and had his platoon to turn out and "fall in." At the same time he found out his mistake, he discovered one of his men did not turn out and was still asleep in the barn. Murphy had the man pulled out and thrown in the nearby icy creek, stating that even though the fall in order was wrong, that man's place was with the platoon and not in the sack and he should be punished. Sgt. Murphy was older than most of the men in the 1st Battalion and was not physically able to stand up to the rigors of combat, so when the Battalion was ordered to the front, Ted would have Murphy stay behind with the kitchen detail. One night when the Battalion was moving up, Ted recognized Murphy's somewhat stooped silhouette against the moonlit sky. The grizzled sergeant had slipped into the ranks and was slogging his way forward with the rest of his platoon. "Sergeant Murphy!" "Sor-r?" And Ted ordered him to the rear with the mess detail. One night, however, Murphy managed to get himself picked to go on a combat patrol. On this foray, he killed an enemy soldier, saved his lieutenant's life, aided in the capture of a prisoner, and earned his country's second highest combat medal, the Distinguished Service Cross.[12]

By the middle of August, Ted's brother Kermit had completed his military training in England and stopped over in Paris on his way to the Middle East. Ted and Archie, who had been transferred to Ted's battalion, took a day off from their duties and went to Paris to see Kermit and Eleanor. After Ted and Archie returned to their unit, Kermit made his way to 1st Battalion Headquarters in Boviolles to say a final goodbye before resuming his journey. While he was there visiting with

Ted and Archie, to their surprise Quentin walked in. The four Roosevelt brothers had an unexpected, unforgettable reunion. It was the last one they would ever have.[13]

Ted had been working long hours training his men, keeping up with the required paperwork and performing his other administrative duties. About the only interruption from the drudgery of training would be a German plane that would occasionally fly over and drop bombs, although it never hit anything of importance. The American antiaircraft guns would shoot at the plane but they never hit anything either. Later, Ted and a number of other American field grade officers were ordered to spend a couple of days with French officers of corresponding rank in the quiet Pont-a-Mousson sector of the front. Ted wrote of this, his first combat experience:

> This is a rest sector, and there was little to indicate that war was raging. Occasionally a shell would whistle over, and if you exposed yourself too much some Hun might take a shot at you with a rifle.
>
> Pont-a-Mousson, the little French village, was literally in the French front lines, and yet a busy life was going on there. There I bought cigarettes, and around the arcade of the central square business was much as usual. A bridge spanned the river right by the town, where everyone crossing was in plain view of the Germans. The French officers explained to me that so long as only small parties crossed by it the Germans paid no attention, but if columns of troops or trucks used it shelling started at once. In the same way the French did not shell, except under exceptional circumstances, the villages in the German forward area.
>
> On a high hill overlooking Pont-a-Mousson were the ruins of an old castle built by the De Guises. In old days it was the key to the ford where the bridge now stands. It was being used as an observation post by the French. I crawled up into its ivydraped, crumbling tower, and through a telescope looked far back of the German lines, where I saw the enemy troops training in open order and two German officers on horseback superintending.[14]

When the brief time in the observation post concluded, the American officers spent a day in the French trenches where they experienced the filth, vermin, rats, cooties, odors, and waist deep mud associated with trench warfare. That night Ted went on his first patrol into "no-man's-land." At their location the land between the opposing trenches extended from one-half to one mile. Barbed wire surrounded the trenches. The patrol ended without incident. Ted felt that the principal benefit he gained from his first front line experience was observing how the French went about feeding their troops in the trenches.[15]

Even though he was now in the war zone and away from his unintentionally dominating father, Ted still felt a compulsion to live up to his father's expectations. There were a number of letters back and forth between them that are revealing of this. In September he wrote his father, "We [referring to himself and Archie] are both trying to let it be seen that all the fiber did not go with the preceding generation." Teddy wrote birthday greetings to Ted and said, in part:

> Well until you are an old man you will never be able quite to understand the satisfaction I feel because each of my sons is doing and had done better than I was doing and had done at his age—and I had done well. And of course this is preeminently true of you. I don't mean that any of you will be President; as regards the extraordinary prizes the element of luck is the determing factor; but getting in the class of those who have to their credit worthy, and even distinguished, achievement—that's what I mean.[16]

Ted wrote Teddy a letter with an almost mystical paragraph near the end, saying:

> We five veterans, 'the lions brood' will have a fine time when we return.
> 'Twas in high vahalea* halls,
> The well tuned harps* begin,
> When the swords are out in the lower world,
> And the weary gods* come in.'
> *Sagamore *me and my four sons
> *The dinner gong with elephant tusks.

Ted was paraphrasing one of the many poems known by him, which he thought his father also knew. He was referring to a grand homecoming when the war was over, the five veterans being Ted, Kermit, Archie, Quentin, and Teddy.[17]

After training had continued for some weeks, General Pershing made a visit to the Gondrecourt area to observe the maneuvers the 1st Division was involved in. When the field exercises were concluded, Pershing was generally impressed with how well the officers of the Division handled their units, but he was especially impressed with Ted's performance and singled him out for special praise.[18].

At last the First Infantry Division received orders to the front. The 1st Battalion would be the first unit in the 26th Infantry Regiment to go into the front lines. Ted had all his unit's equipment checked and rechecked to make sure everything was in good order. Their truck convoy arrived early one morning as scheduled. The men loaded on and headed for the Lorraine front between Luneville and Nancy. By late afternoon, they began to pass through the devastated terrain that had been occupied by the Boche earlier in the war. At about 1700 hours the convoy stopped and the men piled out. They were at a little French village about fourteen miles behind the front lines. The Battalion bivouacked in the village for two days while reconnoitering details went forward to the trenches to familiarize themselves with the positions they would occupy. On the evening of the second day, in a driving rainstorm, Ted gave the order to move out and the White House Battalion began to foot slog toward the battlefront. As elements of the Battalion reached the trenches, they relieved the French soldiers there and occupied their positions. When dawn broke on October 21, 1917, the 1st Battalion was in its assigned trenches and facing the opposing Germans. One reinforced company would be on the line with the other three in support and reserve. This was an extremely quiet section of the Western front, and there was no action except for the five or ten artillery shells the Huns lobbed over each day. After only a day or two of being on line, Lt. Hardon, the 1st Battalion Signal Officer, received a very slight shrapnel wound. After Ted saw how minor the young officer's injury was, he congratulated him on being the first American wounded at the battlefront while serving with a United States unit.[19]

The plan for this initial combat experience called for each battalion to be on line for a ten day period. The companies within a battalion would alternate between being in the front line trenches and being in reserve. The sector of the front occupied by the 1st Battalion was so peaceful Ted didn't think they got much out of the ten days they were there. It rained so much the men occupied themselves mostly by repairing the cave-ins that constantly occurred in the trench system. There was at least one sure benefit though, the time in the trenches showed just how green the American troops were. In giving an example of this inexperience, Ted said that when his machinegun company came on line with all its guns and ammunition on the gun carts, the men uncased the guns and set them up but failed to unload the ammunition before sending the carts back to the rear.[20]

While the sector occupied by the 1st Battalion had been without incident, one of the other regiments in the Division had been hit by a German raiding party and three men were killed. The Americans wanted an immediate retaliation but the French, who were in overall command at the time, did not feel that the Big Red One was ready for such an undertaking. However, Ted went ahead and prepared a plan for an *embuscade* (raid) on the Germans and submitted it to higher authority. By the time the French command approved the plan, the 1st Battalion had already completed its ten days in the trenches and returned to the Gondrecourt area. One morning, Colonel George C. Marshall, by then the Chief of Staff of the 1st Division, drove up to Ted's headquarters to notify him of the approval of his plan and to introduce him to the French Lieutenant who was to assist in the raid. Ted was excited when given news that the raid would be conducted according to his plan, but was sorely disappointed when informed that he, personally, would not be allowed to participate. Lieutenant Archie Roosevelt was picked to head the small detachment of men selected to conduct the foray. The French officer would go along to assist. According to Ted's plan, the patrol would leave the trenches after dark and make its way to an old building in no-man's-land which the Germans were known to visit from time to time. The raiding party would surround the building and lay in ambush, hoping a Hun patrol would come by that night. Rehearsals went perfectly. When the night of the raid arrived, the doughboys crept out in the direction of the Germans but they got lost in the darkness and couldn't immediately find the building. The French officer wanted to go back to Allied lines, but Archie insisted that they continue on. A bitter argument developed between them before Archie ordered the Frenchman to go back. No enemy troops were encountered, but one member of the patrol got separated from the rest and experienced friendly fire in his direction when he tried to rejoin the group. This was the first raid into enemy territory conducted by the United States Army during World War I.[21]

Later, in remembering his World War I experiences, Ted recalled how things were done "the army way." He wrote that once, just as his battalion was about to be relieved and go in reserve, the American Army Medical Dept., which is on such a high level that it deals in theories rather than with troops, issued an order concerning Pediculi or lice. Immediately upon leaving the trenches, all the men were ordered to be inspected by a medical officer before going back to their billets. If any lice were found, all their clothes would be confiscated and new uniforms would be issued. The trouble was, there were no new clothes in the supply depots to give out. Another ridiculous aspect of the order was the fact that it required all one thousand men in the battalion to be inspected at the time of their relief, which was at 0200 hours. Another funny TRJr story about "army know-how" came about when Private Dan Edwards, a fellow member of the 26th Infantry Regiment, was on KP in the mess hall one day. The head cook told Dan to go to the food supply warehouse and pick up a batch of coffee. After being given the coffee, Dan looked at it and saw that it was full of worm holes. When Dan complained loudly and demanded that they take the coffee back, the food supply sergeant pulled out Cooks Manuel section 212, and showed it to him. It read: "worm holes in coffee need not necessarily be grounds for rejection, because they weigh nothing, they take up no space and they disappear when the coffee is ground." For his battle heroism later in the war Dan was awarded the Congressional Medal of Honor.[22]

When the 1st Battalion's tour in the trenches was completed, Ted was ordered to take his men back to their billets in Boviolles. He used this time to rest his troops, conduct training on his own, and catch up on some administrative details. Since it would be about a month before all of the Division's personnel had completed the trench duty and returned, Ted took a couple of days off to go to Paris and check on Eleanor.[23]

During the several months the Battalion was billeted at Boviolles, there were no major problems with the French civilians, but there were some amusing incidents that occurred. One time the owner of one of the barns in which some of the men were quartered came in and complained that the soldiers were laughing and talking in the barns at night and keeping her sheep and pigs from getting enough sleep. On more than one occasion, a French couple came in and inquired if Private John Doe was really a millionaire because, if he was, they thought it would be nice if he would marry their daughter. Usually this type of situation worked itself out. Ted would find that the soldier really had no intention of marrying their daughter and the French couple had no intention of letting her marry him when they found out Doe was not a rich American. It was also common for some civilian to come in and claim that some of his or her ducks, or chickens, or stove wood, or other such was missing and was sure some of the soldiers were responsible. Ted had no doubt that sometimes his men were responsible, but he had no way of knowing how many ducks or chickens, etc. the civilian had to start with. Almost every house in the rural French villages had a variety of small farm animals running around loose. There is no way to get an accurate count on the number any particular resident may have. Ted wanted to be fair with the locals, but he didn't have time to investigate each incident. As a way out, he appointed a subordinate officer named Barrett claims adjuster, and when any kind of problem came up with the locals, he would let young lieutenant Barrett worry with it.[24]

By the latter part of November, all the regiments comprising the 1st Division had completed the trench duty and returned to the Gondrecourt area for the final phase of training. The weather was miserable with some form of rain, snow, wind, mud, or ice constantly. This was an oppressing, dismal period which was referred to by the doughboys as the "Winter of Valley Forge." Training was as realistic as it could be made and was now conducted primarily on a division scale. There was a series of open warfare maneuvers requiring the troops to bivouac at night, and there were additional maneuvers in trench warfare tactics in and over the top of the practice trenches. In describing this phase of training, Ted said, "It was bitterly cold, and a high wind swept the hilltops. We were all soaked to the skin. The men either huddled against the side of a trench or stretched their ponchos from parapet to parapet, and sat beneath them in a foot-deep puddle of water." One time, a hole caved in on the CO, executive officer, and clerk of one of the companies in the 1st Battalion. Quick action was required in order to extricate them. It seemed to the men that the rain never let up. If they bailed the water and mud out of the bottom of a trench, it would rain again and fill the trench like a bathtub.[25]

While the open warfare maneuvers couldn't improve the weather conditions, at least the men were not stuck in a wretched trench. The high command used the 1st Division as a kind of guinea pig to experiment on with respect to new training methods. They set up practice reconnaissance patrols to see how close they could get to dummy trenches manned by aggressor forces. Practice raids were conducted and night problems were set up giving the men training in night vision, and an idea of what it's like in the trenches and on patrols in pitch black darkness. [26]

During these last weeks of training, Ted said he gained experience with respect to "getting supplies so they come through properly and contain the correct things, and getting our system worked out for care of the men in the trenches." He also got the Battalion in tip top physical condition. On one occasion, they had an eighteen-mile forced march with full field equipment. They covered the final ten miles in only $3^1/_2$ hours with no one falling out. [27]

As Christmas approached, it was clear that the Division was ready for combat. Certainly the 1st Battalion was, except for the fact that it was not up to full strength. There had been casualties from the weather and illnesses not related to the weather, and some men had been transferred to other units. Ted had been promised replacements, but so far none had arrived.

General Beaumont B. Buck, Commander of the 2nd Brigade, had had ample opportunity to observe Ted's performance as a battalion commander and when, just about Christmas time, he lost his Brigade Adjutant, he called Ted to Brigade Headquarters and offered him the job. On a brigade level, this was a cushy, safe job, and many officers would have jumped at the opportunity. Ted thanked the General but said he was sure his father would prefer that he remain with his battalion and to please let him stay with his men. Clearly, this shows that Ted continues to court his father's approval and wants to live up to his expectations. He still shared his father's romantic view of war. TRJr immediately wrote a letter to his father, saying that he turned the staff job down because, "when an amateur goes to war he does so for work and fighting, and not for advancement or profit." General Buck also wrote TR of his offer of a staff position to Ted, and of Ted's response. In his answer to the General's letter, Theodore expressed his approved of the Brigade Commander leaving Ted in charge of the 1st Battalion. [28]

The Battalion spent Christmas in Boviolles, the little French village where it had been billeted now for several months. The men created a fund for the purpose of erecting a Christmas tree in the square and giving the children of the village a nice Christmas. It was the first Christmas tree many of the children had ever seen and they were excited. The enlisted men conducted the festivities and took care of the children before turning their attention to the adults of the village. This was a small way the 1st Battalion had to thank these rural French civilians for putting up with and adjusting to the rowdy bunch of strangers who had been thrust into their midst. [29]

With the coming of the new year, the doughboys were aware that the time had come; they could be ordered to the front at any time. The 1st Battalion, though under strength, was ready to go. It had rated extremely high in two recent inspections. The Inspector General of the American Expeditionary Force reported that the Battalion's billets at Boviolles were clean and orderly, that the latrines were clean, that the streets were well and clean, and that the whole appearance of the village reflected credit upon the officers and men of the Battalion. Then came the important tactical and disciplinary inspection by G. H. Q. of the entire 26th Infantry Regiment. This inspection report was highly critical of the 26th Infantry in general, but very complimentary with respect to the 1st Battalion. [30]

General George B. Duncan had recently been promoted and given command of the 1st Brigade, after having been commander of the 26th Infantry Regiment for the previous six months. In January, he sent a communication to the Division Commander recommending Ted's promotion to Lieutenant Colonel and his transfer to the 18th Infantry Regiment. Duncan wrote: "I consider Major Theodore Roosevelt, Jr. to be an officer of unusual ability. He is most conscientious in the performance of every duty, never falters, has an excellent command of men, and is today probably the best battalion commander in the 1st Division." Neither the promotion nor the transfer was approved. Ted again was allowed to remain with the 1st Battalion. [31]

By the middle of January, the Battalion began receiving its promised replacements to bring each company up to full strength. The new men were raw recruits with no military training of any kind. They were mostly unshaven draftees from California and Wyoming and had not had a bath in over a month. Ted said, "They were the saddest looking hoboes when they arrived you could ever imagine." One man was partially paralyzed, another had an arm so stiff that he could hardly bend it at the elbow. Some of them could not speak English and one could not even understand English. These inexperienced, untrained men would be in combat within a short time. Those that managed to survive long enough would eventually make good soldiers. [32]

New orders finely came. The Division was to replace a French unit in the Toul sector of the front. While this was considered a quiet sector, it was much livelier than the area near Lorraine, where the Big Red One had gotten its first taste of war. In this new sector, no-man's-land was in places only fifty yards wide. Fighting had been going on in the area for three years, but the front had been stable with little movement one way or the other. Mud, wire entanglements, and abandoned trenches were everywhere. At one time, the sector had been held by a large number of troops, but the manpower had been reduced by both sides so that when the 1st Battalion took over its assigned section, one company would have to hold a trench line a full kilometer in length. From the point of view of the doughboy, the war primarily meant trying to maintain some degree of comfort in the wind-swept, cold, water-filled, miserable trenches and gun-pits. Occasionally one side or the other would conduct a night patrol. There were also random artillery and gas bombardments.[33]

At this point, Ted began to prove himself to be a top commander of mid-sized units in combat. He personally went on raids and patrols. He learned quickly that Napoleon was right, an army travels on its stomach. When troops are wet, or cold, or exhausted, a good commanding officer will do everything possible to get hot food to them. Ted wrote, "If you can get hot food forward to them, you have increased the fighting efficiency of your troops by thirty per cent." In a stable trench situation like the Toul section, safe movement could only be made at night, so Ted had the kitchens placed on the reverse slope of hills behind the trenches and hot food brought to the men at night by using connecting trenches. He had the cooks wrap the containers of food in blankets, place them on two-wheeled machine-gun carts, and bring them right up to the front line.[34]

Except when being attacked or under a bombardment, night is the scariest time for a front line soldier in combat. In describing the tricks darkness can play on a man's vision, Ted liked to tell the story of Sergeant Rose. Rose was an old-timer in the Big Red One and, in telling of being in a front line trench at night, once said to Ted, "I'm an old soldier, but when I stand and look out over this trench long enough, the first thing I know, those posts with the wire attached to them begin to do squads right and squads left, and if I ain't careful, I have to shoot them to keep them from charging this trench." One of the new men might shoot all his ammunition and throw all his grenades at the shadows of the night, and even report that he had several dead Germans lying in front of his position. When morning finally came, he would discover that an old stump out front had taken quite a beating. Knowing of the problems with night vision, TRJr normally placed himself in a position where he could personally see as much of the Battalion front as possible.[35]

The 1st Battalion was occasionally ordered into reserve, but most of the next three months were spent on the front lines. Ted, in writing of this period said,

> The division had fairly heavy casualties in this sector. The Germans staged a couple of raids, Also there were heavy artillery actions very frequently. Generally these would start around three o'clock in the morning. First would come the preliminary strafing. Then the shelling would commence in earnest and all communications would go out at once. From then on, runners were the only method of communication until everything was over. One could never be sure that each strafing was not the preliminary to an assault.

One time, the Division CO ordered an attack. The 1st Battalion was the initial assault unit and Ted's brother, Archie, who was now a captain and in command of a company, led the doughboys over the top. During the three month period at the front, the Battalion was ordered to conduct many night patrols. Some were for the purpose of capturing prisoners in order to gain intelligence information and others were to inflict casualties on the enemy. For a while, the patrols had no success, either because the Germans were not patrolling or because the doughboys just did not run into them. Ted decided that the only way to capture a prisoner was to pull one out of the Hun trenches, so he sent a patrol out one night to slip through the wire in no-man's-land, creep up on a German listening post, and grab a prisoner. The tactic worked and a prisoner was taken. Ted was so pleased with the Battalion having captured its first prisoner that he jokingly said, "We hardly wanted to let him go to the rear, as we had a distinct feeling more or less that we wanted to keep him to look at."[36]

While her husband was busy training the troops of his battalion, Eleanor was busy with her YMCA job. During the Great War, the French troops were given leave occasionally and could go to their homes. At first, the British soldiers were allowed to return to England for a few days leave. Since it was not possible for the Yanks to return home on leave, the YMCA developed leave centers in some twenty-three French towns. These centers would generally include sleeping and eating accommodations, a canteen, and recreational facilities. Eleanor worked primarily with the canteens and recreational facilities. Later in the war, she was put in charge of all the Y women working in the leave areas. When she was not away working at some leave center, she resided in her aunt's house in Paris.[37]

One evening Eleanor was invited to the home of some friends for dinner. General John Pershing was also a guest. In the course of conversing with Eleanor, the General said, "How do you happen to be here anyhow? No wives are allowed to come overseas. Where are your children? Your place is with them, not here. I think you ought to be sent home!" The next time Eleanor saw Pershing, he apologized, and after the war he gave her a citation commending her for her excellent work in the leave areas. Eleanor tells this story on pages 84–85 in her book, *Day Before Yesterday*. Other than what she wrote in her book, there was apparently no public criticism of her for leaving her three young children in the States while she went to the war zone to work and be near her husband. There were, however, some who agreed with the General and privately made disparaging comments. One of those deprecators was Mrs. Ray Walker, the mother of the author of *The Namesake*.

On March 11th, Captain Archie Roosevelt was outside his dugout repositioning his men, when he was severely injured in the leg and arm by an exploding German artillery shell. Ted immediately went to Archie, saw that he was in shock, and gave him coffee and brandy. Archie came around and was evacuated to an army hospital in Toul, and then to one in Paris. After several operations and several months in hospitals, he was classified as totally disabled and sent home. Years later, when World War II started, Archie was accepted into active duty even though he still had some residuals from his old injury. In 1943, while commanding a battalion of troops in the Pacific, Colonel Archibald Roosevelt was again seriously injured and again classified as totally disabled and sent home. He is the only American soldier to have ever been totally disabled, two different times, from two different injuries, received in two different wars. His military decorations include the Purple Heart and French Croix de Guerre from the Great War, and the Purple Heart and Silver Star from World War II. Perhaps, however, his most meaningful military honor was bestowed in 1943, when his men christened the New Guinea hill they were fighting on when he was hit, "Roosevelt Ridge."[38].

For many months, the Great War was close to a standstill with neither side able to gain any appreciable ground. By the spring of 1918, however, the Russians had gotten out of the war and were beginning their revolution. The German Army in France was re-enforced by several divisions that were released from the Eastern front when the Russians dropped out. On March 21st, the Boche began a great offensive, broke through the Allied front in a wide area and advanced in the direction of Paris. Before the advancement was quelled, several large bulges or penetrations were made in the Allied lines. The tip of one of these bulges was at the village of Cantigny, no more than sixty miles from Paris. At this distance the Germans could shell the suburbs of Paris with their long range Paris Gun. This situation was unacceptable to the Allied high command.[39]

On the morning of March 31st, Easter Sunday, the 1st Division got orders to prepare to move to another sector, and by April 3rd, it had been completely relieved in the Toul sector. The men were loaded onto troop trains and began to move in a northwestwardly direction. Ted, even at his relatively high level in the chain of command, was not told exactly where they were going, but they all knew they were headed to the big show. After traveling for several hours, an incident occurred that the 1st Battalion doughboys would remember and laugh and talk about for years. The Battalion's train stopped at a small station and Ted jumped off to pick up their orders and maps from the American Regulating Officer as he had been instructed to do. Before he could complete this business, the train started moving again and, said Ted, "my battalion was rapidly disappearing down the track." He ran after it as fast as he could and was shouting and cursing at the top of his lungs for the train to stop. Some of the battalion officers saw what was happening and forced the engineer to halt the train so the battalion commander could catch up and get back onboard.

After arriving at its destination, the 1st Battalion detrained at night and then marched two days through the beautiful French springtime countryside to the city of Chaumont-en-Vexin, where Division Headquarters were located. Mainly to keep the men busy, Ted had the officers and NCO's conduct various training exercises during the several days the battalion was in Chaumont.[40]

Leaving Chaumont, Ted led his Battalion on a four day march to the Montdidier section of the front. At first the doughboys enjoyed the warm sunshine and beautiful spring flowers with their clean, fresh scents, and the birds flying about calling to their mates. Then the scenery began to change and they began to pass caravans of refugees headed south, toward Paris. With a look of despair on their faces, displaced civilians led old wagons and carts, pulled by every kind of draft animal, and piled high with furniture, hay, farm produce, household belongings, the very old, the infirm, and the very young. As they got nearer the front, the troops passed through pulverized villages and fields, and orchards destroyed beyond recognition. Ted began to think of some of the men back home who were living "self-satisfied lives of ease," profiting from the war and the misery it was causing. He thought of politicians and other important men who were young enough to serve and said they wanted to be at the front, but did not think it would be proper to use their influence to get there. He thought of the men who had lost their lives, or eyes, or arms, or legs because they had no influence. Major Theodore Roosevelt, Jr. was beginning to lose his fanciful view of war.[41]

When the 1st Battalion took over its assigned sector at Montdidier in the later part of April, the troops found the front to be entirely different than that at Toul and Lorraine. In the area they had just left, there had been little movement, and, therefore, sufficient time to construct deep trenches and improve them with logs and other reinforcing materials. The front line at Montdidier had only been established since the German breakout and the trenches and dugouts were unimproved. Most of them were barely waist deep and offered far less protection. The ground was so hard that further digging was almost impossible. The very first morning on line, the Battalion was heavily shelled and hit with a platoon size raid. Casualties were taken in the bombardment, but the raid was repulsed and heavy losses were inflicted on the Boche.[42]

Captain Shipley Thomas, a staff officer under Ted who lived and worked with him on a daily basis during the Great War, had this to say about the early days in the Montdidier sector:

> ***** the front lines of both sides lay in a wheat field about one hundred yards apart, and holding more than a half mile of that front was Major Roosevelt. ***** During the day all but a few sentries slept, but as soon as dusk fell, the battalion went into feverish activity.

All night long Major Roosevelt walked along in front of his men encouraging them as they tried to dig fox-holes for themselves. Terrified staff officers disliked taking orders to him, for as one said, 'He spends his evenings walking up and down in no-man's-land.'

For two weeks this lasted amidst the most intense enemy artillery fire that can be imagined. There was never a moment of night or day when shells were not shrieking over head or bursting among the troop positions, for the Americans were facing an attacking German army all ready to continue the assault. Every night the paths back from the front were full of litter bearers. Rifle fire, artillery shells and gas were taking their toll, while raiding parties from both sides rushed sentry posts in the dark, where only the rattle of musketry gave the location. Major Roosevelt was everywhere. If there was a fight down on the right, he rushed down in the hope to be there in time.[43]

One of the captains that served in the 1st Battalion told of an unsuccessful raid he commanded one night. As the raiding party crept and crawled close to the German lines, a Hun machine gun was somehow alerted and started shooting. This commotion initiated an artillery duel, meaning that the artillery of both sides starts shelling the front lines of the other. Having been discovered and creating havoc on the front, the raid was called off and the men ordered back to the American lines. The raid commander crawled into a shell hole in no-man's-land near to the American trenches, and was counting off his men as they came in. He said, "There were several men missing, and as I waited a soldier came crawling up dragging a man I recognized as a Greek corporal named Bill Margues. Bill had been so close to the machine gun nest that had spoiled our party that his blouse was still smoldering over a painful bullet wound in his back. I asked the soldier helping him who he was. 'I guess this is the last that will be coming back, Mr. Ridgely', said Major Roosevelt for it was he, and he hoisted Margues to his shoulders and staggered through the wire." Later, Captain Ridgely told Ted that he intended to put him in for a citation. He did not follow through with the recommendation because Ted told him he would kill it if he did.[44]

In July of 1917, mustard gas was used on the battlefront for the first time. It was usually distributed on enemy positions by exploding gas shells fired by the artillery. There would always be a slight smell of mustard. Usually, a soldier could be exposed to the gas for two or three minutes without disastrous effects, but any longer than that was considered excessive. The only defense was prompt use of the gas mask and even that did not work in all cases. Four or five hours after excessive exposure, a man would experience a burning of the eyes, a dry and parched condition of the skin, respiratory problems, blindness and burns on exposed skin such as the hands and back of the neck. Even in mild cases, the affected soldier might be incapacitated for as long as three weeks. A gas shelling attack usually began in the still of the early morning. As the sky lightened, a thick gray mist might be seen spreading itself along the ground. For a commander in the front line, the practical problem was where to reposition the men so that they would not be in a heavily gassed area, but still be in a position to cover the assigned portion of the front if the gas attack was preliminary to an enemy ground attack. Consideration must also be given to whether the wind was likely to blow the gas away or into the new position the men had just been placed in. The gas had a mysterious way of getting into everything, such as the chow, and the dugouts and trenches.[45]

Even though the German offensive that began in March had been stopped before Paris fell, the French and British had been at war for four years and their morale was near bottom. The Americans had been in France for almost a year but, from ought that appeared, had done little to contribute to a final victory. In fact except for raids, the Americans had never conducted an offensive operation. The AEF high command felt that it was important for the American army to do something on its own, so they made plans for the Big Red One to attack and occupy the small village of Cantigny at the tip of a salient the Germans had made in the Allied lines. The attack would be led by the 28th Infantry Regiment. Ted's Battalion would be in support and was ordered to rush in and protect the right flank of the 28th Infantry as soon as the village was occupied. This mission must not fail for the eyes of America, and of France and the UK would be focused on the 1st Division's doughboys. May 28th, was set as the day of the attack.

A young, inexperienced lieutenant in the engineers was picked to lead a fifty-man digging party to make a jumping off trench for the 28th Infantry to go over the top from as the attack got under way. (This trench might also be called the line of departure or LD) A few nights prior to May 28th, the lieutenant led his men into no-man's-land to begin his digging mission. Somehow he got turned around and ended up leading his digging detail into the German trenches and they were captured. From interrogating their prisoners, the Huns learned of the American's attack plans and made some counter plans of their own. The German Command decided to beat the Americans to the punch and launch an attack of their own. Accordingly, in the early hours of May 27th, the Boche began an intense artillery and gas barrage followed by a ground attack on the 1st Division positions. Even though he had been exposed to the toxic fumes of mustard gas and the 1st Battalion trenches were being shelled, Major Roosevelt went from position to position to to relocate and encourage his men. At times, it was necessary for him to pull aside his gas mask to give orders. The brunt of the German ground attack fell against Company "A" of Ted's Battalion. Not affected by the gas to the full extent yet, Ted, under intense artillery and small arms fire, went forward to the "A" Company front and personally supervised its defense. The Germans took heavy loses and their attack was repulsed. By late morning Colonel Hamilton Smith, the CO of the 26th Infantry Regiment, had been informed that Ted had been gassed, was experiencing throat and respiratory problems, and could not see. The Colonel immediately sent the Regimental surgeon to Ted's command post with instructions to evacuate him. Ted was not in his CP though. The surgeon finally found him in a foxhole immediately behind the front lines. Ted was choking, coughing, and blind and refused to be evacuated. He said that he would be as good as new in a few hours. The surgeon pleaded in vain. Just at this time, Stuart A. Baxter, who had been picked to lead a patrol, reported to Ted to have the patrol route pointed out to him on a map. The Battalion Adjutant had to show Baxter the route, however; Ted still had no sight. Baxter said that when the surgeon arrived and suggested that Major Roosevelt be evacuated, he just laughed and continued to do his job. For his actions and injury of May 27th, Ted was awarded the Silver Star and the Purple Heart.[46]

The American attack began at 5:45 a.m. the next day with a heavy artillery barrage on the Boche trenches and Cantigny Village. When the 28th Infantry went over the top at 6:45 a.m., the artillery shifted to a rolling barrage. The infantry went forward in a line of skirmishers and was joined in the assault by French tanks. Cantigny fell with comparatively light losses to the 28th Infantry. Pursuant to the plans, Ted's 1st Battalion promptly went forward and took positions covering the right flank of the assault regiment. Later that afternoon while observing the German front, Ted spied a large enemy force moving into position behind a tract of woods. Realizing that the enemy was forming to counter-attack, Ted quickly gathered his men and led an assault against the flank of the German force. A terrific firefight ensued and a hand-to-hand struggle developed. Heavy losses were inflicted on the Germans and their counter-attack was not allowed to develop. The doughboys of the 1st Battalion were then ordered to return to their positions covering the right flank of the 28th Inf. In all, the Germans counter attacked Contigny seven times over the May 28th—30th period, all of which were repulsed. Contigny was secure. The Americans had passed the test. Twenty-two years would pass before Contigny would again fall into German hands. For his valor on May 28th, Ted was presented with the Distinguished Service Cross, and the French Croix de Guerre.[47]

The 1st Battalion was relieved and placed in reserve on the night of Saturday, June 1st. After seeing that his men were properly bedded down, Ted's thoughts turned to Eleanor and the scuttlebutt that had been circulating on the American front that the Germans had broken through in another sector and would soon occupy Paris. Feeling that he had to be certain of his wife's safety, Ted woke-up the Division Chief of Staff, Colonel George C. Marshall, and asked for a pass to go to Paris. Marshall turned down the request, but Ted, not to be deterred, contacted his Regimental Commander, and got permission to use the colonel's automobile to go check on his wife. Ted knew that it would be Sunday before he could get to Paris, and that his wife would be at home if she had not already fled the city. When he got to Paris and walked into Mrs. Hoffman's house, and saw that his wife was still there, he was excited and upset. Eleanor said, "His face was scorched and inflamed, the whites of his eyes an angry red. He was thickly covered with dust and shaken by a racking cough." Eleanor had not heard any rumor that Paris was in any imminent danger of falling and did not believe there was any problem in her remaining there. They immediately began to fuss about whether she should leave the City or not. To settle the argument, they called a friend on General Pershing's staff. The staff officer assured them that Paris was secure but he promised Ted that if it should fall, he would personally see that Eleanor got out. Ted then calmed down, took a hot bath, and put on a clean uniform. Quentin, who was training with an air squadron near Paris, dropped by, and the three of them went to the hospital to see Archie. After visiting with Archie a while, Quentin returned to his squadron and Ted and Eleanor went home. The effects of the gas caused Ted to choke when lying down, so Eleanor propped him up with pillows, hoping that he could get some sleep between spasms of coughing. He returned to his command early the morning of June 3rd.[48]

By now his Battalion had suffered many casualties, and Ted had experienced first-hand the unbelievable carnage of modern battle. The loss of so many of the regular army sergeants concerned him a great deal for he knew that they, more than anyone else, were the backbone of the 1st Battalion. One particular incident he witnessed during a period of incoming artillery haunted Ted for years. It had to do with the loss of a new replacement; no one even knew his name. Just as the new arrival got to his assigned platoon area a German artillery bombardment commenced and a dud struck the man in the legs, severing them both. The heat from the round cauterized the stumps so there was little bleeding. Right before he died, the young private looked up at his platoon leader and muttered, "Lieutenant, you have lost a hell of a good soldier." From his upbringing Ted was imbued with a sense of duty to serve the country in time of need. While this obligation would remain with him for the rest of his life, he was no longer enamored with war. He hated it.[49]

The Germans stabilized the front and over the next thirty days the war around Cantigny continued at a pace deadly to both sides. The 1st Battalion took part in a number of combat patrols and raids. Some were unsuccessful, like the one where the artillery concentration fell short and hit among the patrol detail, but some of the Battalion's forays went off like clock work. One particularly successful raid took place on June 29th. Ted's plan provided for a raiding party of sixty-nine men, broken down into four groups of sixteen to eighteen men each. The patrol order described the task of each group and gave all other pertinent information. The foray was carried off as designed, resulting in thirty-three prisoners being taken and about that same number of Germans being killed or wounded. 1st Battalion's losses were one killed and five wounded. The French added a Palm to Ted's previously awarded Croix de Guerre, citing, "On the 29th of June, 1918 he organized with great care and supervised closely, under enemy fire, the execution of a raid against hostile positions." After the war, the plan and execution of this raid were written up and lauded in the United States Army's *Infantry Journal* as an example of a plan that was sufficiently detailed, but simple to understand and follow.[50]

By this time the 1st Battalion was a crack outfit made up primarily of experienced combat veterans. It was probably as good, or better, than any other infantry battalion in existence. Just before being relieved and sent to the rear in the first days of July, one of the Battalion doughboys spied and shot a Hun carrier pigeon with a message in the container on its leg. The message was from a German regimental commander to his division commander, stating that he had broken through the Allied line and was then thirty kilometers south of the Chemin des Dames and continuing progress with little resistance. This was the first notice the Americans had of the extent of the German breakthrough, which would culminate in the Battalion's next battle, the Battle at Soissons.[51]

When the doughboys of the 1st Division were relieved in the Montdidier sector, they left, not as untrained, unproven, would-be soldiers, but as experienced combat troops, who just wanted to get the war over with and go back where they belonged. Cantigny itself was not a major battle in the Great War and cannot be compared to Verdun, or the Somme, or a number of other battles where the casualties ran into the hundreds of thousands. But it was a major battle to the 1st Division and to the American high command, and it was of major importance to the French people that lived in the area. As the men of the Division trudged by on their way out, the French civilians lined the streets and roads, and waved and smiled and cried. As far as they were concerned, the Big Red One had saved France. The Division had suffered nearly five thousand casualties during the battle. Learning of the Cantigny victory, TR wrote TRJr, "When the trumpet sounds for Armageddon, only those win the undying honor and glory who stand where the danger is sorest."[52]

Back in the rear, the Battalion was billeted in a little village near the town of Beauvais for what they hoped would be a nice rest with hot food served three times a day. Ted's attention now turned to getting his men and their uniforms cleaned up. They had not been able to bathe in months and their uniforms were filthy. Few homes in France had private bathing facilities, so most of the people in the small towns and villages simply bathed in the streams and rivers and thought nothing of it. Out of necessity, the doughboys quickly adopted this habit, but somehow, Ted just found it difficult to bathe in public. The entire time he was in France during World War I, he was never billeted in a house with a bathroom, so he would rig up some kind of vat, or something similar, to bathe in the privacy of his room. On one occasion he found a pipe about three feet high with one end sealed which would do as a tub. The pipe was narrow, and once in it he had to kind of double his body to get down into the water with just his head above the rim. Ted was down in his pipe enjoying his first bath in weeks, when the door to his room flew open and in came his landlady, upset about her disappearing chickens. With just his head showing, Ted assured her the matter would be properly investigated.[53]

While Ted and his unit were resting in their little village, his brother Quentin completed his flight training and was posted near the western front with the 5th Aero "Kicking Mule" Squadron. He went on his first combat mission on July 5th and made his first kill of an enemy plane on July 10th in the vicinity of Chateau-Thierry. Naturally excited over his first victory, as soon as he landed he went to Paris and celebrated by taking Eleanor to Ciro's for dinner. On another mission four days later, Quentin's squadron spied a flight of German Fokkers. True to the nickname his comrades gave him, "The Go and Get 'Em Man," Quentin peeled off and headed straight for the Krauts. Two Fokkers engaged him and a dog fight ensued. During the milieu Luftwaffe Sergeant Johannes Thom managed to get Quentin's plane in his sights for a clean shot. Quentin was hit in the head and died instantly. His plane crashed behind the enemy lines but did not burn or explode. The Germans marked his grave with the wheels and other parts from his aircraft and buried him with full military honors. Thom was one of Germany's top aces. It was his twenty-fifth kill. TR wrote a friend, "There is nothing to be said about Quentin. It is very dreadful that he should have been killed; it would have been worse if he had not gone." Even though the old politician had lost a son, he still had an infatuation with war.[54]

Four or five days after arriving near Beauvais, the Battalion was suddenly ordered to board a convoy of trucks for transportation to a secret destination. Ted had the men assembled and told them it was his opinion that they were headed for another big battle. They climbed on the trucks and moved out the same afternoon the order was received. The doughboys were in a gay mood as they rode along, joking and laughing, and singing what they called their anthem, "Hail! Hail! The Gang's All Here." As they drove by a cemetery, one of them pointed to a tomb and laughingly said, "Look there's Battalion Headquarters."

Part of the German offensive in March took place some miles distant from Contigny and had created a second big bulge in the Allied line pointed in the direction of Paris. Rather than attack the protuberance at its tip, as they had at Contigny, the high command decided to attack at its base. They hoped to force the

Boche to withdraw from the salient, or possibly even trap enemy forces by closing the escape routes as the bulge was lopped off The plan called for the assault to be made simultaneously by what were then considered to be the best three divisions in the Allied arsenal: the Big Red One, the American 2nd Division, and the French Foreign Legion. The attack would commence on July 18th near the town of Soissons. They wanted to catch the enemy by surprise.[55]

The convoy lumbered ahead until the wee hours of dawn, then stopped and the troops unloaded in a secluded woods near the front. The town of Palesne was close by. As quickly and quietly as possible the trucks were sent to the rear in hopes that the Huns had not been alerted. The 1st Battalion bivouacked in the woods for the rest of the day. A torrential rain started to fall after dark. Then, in the pitch-black night the troops gathered their arms and equipment and began to slog through the mud, toward the front. To add to the element of surprise, the doughboys would attack through the Allied unit occupying the front line trenches. The pre-attack artillery bombardment would be intense, but would be for only five minutes duration. The infantry was at the line of departure by 0400; the artillery commenced firing at 0430, and the doughboys went over the top promptly at 0435 hours. The Wehrmacht (German Army) was caught completely by surprise. The Americans moved ahead rapidly, catching many of the enemy half-dressed and still in their dugouts. Boche casualties were heavy. Before nightfall, a number of the forward German artillery batteries had been captured. The Huns rushed in reinforcements to stabilize the front. At dusk, two regiments of French horse cavalry made a senseless, headlong charge, but were mowed down by German machineguns. The top brass planned to commit Ted's unit when and where necessary, so the 1st Battalion was held in reserve the first day of the offensive. At the end of the day, Ted halted his men and had them dig-in. They were at the location of some German trenches, deep within what had once been the German lines. In describing that night one of Ted's officers wrote:

I am sitting on the parapet thinking how many places I should rather be than where I am and wondering when we would get our chow, which we hadn't had since the night before. There is heavy shell fire and my position is near a crossroad which is evidently a popular spot with the enemy artillery. To make it worse the German planes are in the air all about us and they are laying eggs all along the road which must be traversed by our chow detail.

Major Roosevelt comes up the road alone out of the darkness, calling to know what outfit we are. 'You shouldn't be alone, Major', I said. After I had told him, 'I wasn't when I started', he replied. 'Caruthers (Ted's adjutant) and the runners got it down the road. Has your chow come?' he asked. I told him not. 'Well, I'll see to that.' And he started back down the road again. 'Oh, Mr.

Ridgley,' he called, 'I want to tell you that D Company attacks at dawn in support of A Company. You won't like that, but a little farther on is a railroad. I am told it is in worse shape than the New Haven' (he knew I was from Boston), 'and I am saving D company to reorganize it.'[56]

The 1st Division attacked again at 0400 the next morning with 1st Battalion still in reserve. The reinforced Wehrmacht laid down withering artillery and machinegun fire. Some gain was made by the Americans, but at an extremely high cost. The attack bogged down. At 0530 the Division Commander decided it was time to throw his Sunday punch and ordered the 1st Battalion to leapfrog through the stalled unit and resume the attack. Personally at the point of the attack, Ted led his men through the hell of heavy German cannon and small arms fire for over a mile, until they captured the Division's objective, the town of Ploisy. During the assault, the doughboys of the 1st Battalion captured prisoners from four different German divisions and caused the enemy to suffer heavy casualties. As soon as the leading elements of his battalion entered the town, Ted started yelling orders and setting up defensive positions against an expected counterattack. Just at that moment, a Hun machinegun bullet tore through Ted's leg near the knee, and he went down. An aid man rushed over, tied a dressing around his leg, and helped him to his feet. Holding on to the aid man for support and still under heavy fire, Ted dragged himself along and supervised the setting up of a sound defensive line. Seeing what was happening and knowing that moving slowly in a hail of bullets meant certain death, two of the battalion officers grabbed Ted and held him down until an empty caisson came by. Stopping the caisson, they tied him on and instructed the driver to evacuate the Battalion CO to the nearest aid station. Major Roosevelt would be out of the war for a while and had earned an Oak Leaf Cluster to his Purple Heart. The battle raged on for three days after Ted was wounded. The 1st Division suffered over seven thousand casualties in the Saissons engagement. The counteroffensive conducted by the Allies beginning July 18th was the turning point in the war. Never again during the Great War would the Germans conduct a major offensive operation.[57]

The caisson driver hauled Ted to an aid station where the wounded were being accumulated for evacuation to a hospital. There the injured major received a tetanus shot, had a tag tied onto his shirt reading "Gunshot Wound Severe," and was laid aside to wait for an ambulance. Spotting a motorcycle with a sidecar, Ted hobbled into the sidecar and ordered the driver to take him away from the aid station. Not far down the road, Ted spied a colonel he knew who lent him his car and driver to go to Eleanor's residence in Paris. When they arrived, the driver helped him inside where Ted and Eleanor immediately got into a big argument. She wanted to take him to a hospital and he was demanding a bath, dinner, and a quart of champagne. Then, as if on order, the door opened and in walked Ted's brother-in-law, Doctor Dick Derby, the chief surgeon of the American 2nd Division. Derby examined the injury and realized that immediate surgery was necessary to prevent infection and save the leg. Dick and Eleanor put Ted in a taxi and accompanied him to an army hospital in Paris where he was operated on by Dr. Joseph Blake, a highly skilled trauma surgeon. Dick assisted. The bullet had gone clear through his leg just above the knee. Miraculously, there had been no bone damage or serious damage to the main nerve, but there was damage to tendons, minor nerves and veins. Eleanor said that she hoped the damage to Ted's leg would be bad enough to keep him out of combat forever. But that was not to be.

The hospital was packed with wounded, so Dr. Blake sent Ted home on crutches after only a few days. Shortly after Ted was injured, the 1st Division was taken out of the battle and sent to rest billets. Eleanor, who had been granted a thirty-day leave by the YMCA to look after Ted, answered the doorbell one day and there stood a half dozen officers from the 26th Infantry Regiment. Showing them in and to Ted's room, Eleanor went to the wine closet and picked out something extra-special for toasts. After their glasses were filled, Ted led his comrades in two traditional military toasts: "Gentlemen, the Regiment!" and then, "The dead of the Regiment!" The officers stayed a while, talking about what had happened, and who had made it, and who had not. They told Ted that by the time the Division had been relieved, the casualties were so heavy that the 1st Battalion was commanded by a second lieutenant. After this first group left, many others, including some of the enlisted men, came by to pay their respects. Richard Tobin, who at one time was U.S. Minister to the Hague, went to the house to visit while Ted was still prostrated. While Mr. Tobin was there, some of the regimental brass dropped by. Writing of the occasion later, Tobin said that the "admiration and affection the officers had for Ted was evident in their manner." One of them commented to Tobin that Ted never asked his men to do anything that he was not prepared to do himself.[58]

Among the other visitors to drop by was Ted's distant cousin, Franklin D. Roosevelt. FDR was Assistant Secretary of the Navy at the time and was on an official trip to the war zone. He enjoyed seeing Ted and Archie, and envied them their uniforms. He wrote that "they both have really splendid records."[59]

Even though Archie's arm was in a big cast, he was able to walk and as soon as Ted was able to get about on crutches, Eleanor and the two Roosevelt men would wander around the nooks and crannies of Paris, visiting antique shops, book stores, and enjoying a glass of wine at sidewalk cafes. They were young, living in the excitement of war, and in Paris. The three of them did some crazy, even childish, things, which fit Ted's personality more so than it did either Archie's or Eleanor's.

One of their favorite escapades was to go out in public somewhere and pretend Eleanor was a loose woman and that Ted and Archie were trying to pick her up. Another carefree activity was to act like they were mentally disturbed and laugh and dance around picking imaginary butterflies out of the air and then eating them.

Kermit had been fighting with the British in the Middle East and had earned the British War Cross. Desiring to get back with his countrymen, Kermit had been granted a transfer to the American Expeditionary Force. Unexpectedly, he showed up in Paris with Belle, his wife, in the latter part of July. With Quentin now gone, there was a feeling among the three brothers and two wives that either Ted or Kermit might not survive the war. Eleanor wrote, "We played around with the feverish high spirits felt only in the shadow of death." On one occasion they started marching down the street, Ted on his crutches and Archie in his cast, singing songs and motioning to onlookers to join in the celebration. Before it broke up, they had probably a hundred people in the throng. Eleanor claimed she and Belle were embarrassed by all the shenanigans.[60]

Except for the nearly two months Ted was recuperating from his leg wound, he and Eleanor managed to see each other on only four or five occasions during the 1 1/2 years they were in France.

By September, Ted had improved and was able to get around with the use of two canes. He had had all the sitting around he wanted and was anxious to get back to the war. He finally persuaded the medical people to give him a Class B rating, making him fit for limited duty. Then he wangled a posting to both the General Staff College as a student and the Army Line School as an instructor. On Sept. 13th, his thirty-first birthday, Ted departed Paris for Langres, where both of the schools were located. Three days later, the Army gave him a belated birthday present when his promotion to the rank of lieutenant colonel was approved. Ted now held the same rank his father held at the beginning of the Spanish-American War.[61]

With the silver leaves of a lieutenant colonel now on his shoulders, Ted began to work toward getting back to where he felt he belonged, with the Big Red One. He first got in touch with a staff officer in the Division and told him that he was able and anxious to go back to work. Then a few days later, the new Division Commander, General Frank Parker, called him up and told Ted he would be given command of the 26th Infantry Regiment if he could get a Class A medical rating and report for duty right away. Ted lied when he told the Division CO that getting the A rating would be no problem and that he would report for duty within a few days. Ted still walked with a cane and knew very well that getting an A medical rating to allow him to return to unlimited duty was impossible. Thinking the matter over briefly, he decided that to simply leave the schools and report for duty at 1st Division Headquarters was the practical way to proceed. So, with no orders and no medical authorization, he technically went A.W.O.L. when he simply left Langres and reported to General Parker for duty. Ted said he knew he wouldn't get into too much trouble because he was "going in the right direction." His plan worked. Orders were issued on October 18th making him the commanding officer of the 26th Infantry Regiment. With typical army efficiency, the official records give three different dates on which Ted was given command of the 26th Inf., Oct 18th, 20th, and 26th. The 18th seemed more likely to have been the day he actually reported to 1st Div. HQ and was, at least verbally, given command of the Regiment by General Parker.[62]

The 1st Division was in reserve, and the 26th Infantry had just received some eighteen hundred new replacements when Ted assumed command. The first thing he did was make up a training schedule and over the next week and a half the new men were given as intense a training regimen as possible. Orders came during the latter part of October, moving the Regiment toward the battle front, but at this stage in the war the Germans were retreating daily and there were no established trench lines. As the Boche pulled back, they would leave strong points to delay the pursuing allied armies. The front kept moving away. Over the next seven days, the 26th Infantry was ordered to move forward through the desolate regions that had been no-man's-land for four years, and attack and destroy any enemy strong points by-passed by the American 2nd Division, which was in front of the Big Red One. The regimental command post was constantly moving up from farmhouse to farmhouse. It rained almost continually and most of the troop movement was over the fields and through the woods because the roads were reserved for the motorized and horse-drawn vehicles. More often than not the doughboys would slosh along all day and most of the night; they got little sleep. Ted made sure hot food caught up with his men each day, so they could get some nourishment and rest.[63]

Ted's leg was hurting him so much and he limped so badly that he still used a cane, sometimes two canes. He rode in his staff car when it was practical to do so. Late in the afternoon of November 3rd, as the 26th Infantry was passing through the war-battered town of Landreville, Ted was astonished to run into his brother Kermit and his brother-in-law, Dick Derby. Kermit had been assigned to the 1st Division Artillery Regiment and Dr. Derby was chief surgeon with the 2nd Division. Ted said, "Seeing them so unexpectedly was one of the most delightful surprises." He halted his regiment for the night, supervised the setting up of defensive positions, and sent out patrols to make contact with the unit ahead. Then, according to Ted, he and Kermit, "sat in a ruined shed, used as regimental headquarters, surrounded by dead Germans and Americans, and talked over all kinds of family affairs."[64]

On November 5th, after marching practically all night for five nights in succession, plus two of the days, the Regiment went into position in a wooded area just south of Beaumont. Their orders were to take over from the regiment ahead and attack the Boche during the early morning hours of November 6th. By now everyone was totally exhausted. When Ted called in his battalion commanders to give them their attack orders, he got started but then was interrupted for a few minutes causing the battalion CO's to wait. When he got back to them, they were all asleep where they sat. As usual, it rained that night, but the doughboys got some rest and before daylight the next morning they went into position for the attack. With the precision of combat experienced warriors, the men went over the top under the concealment of a heavy mist. It was 0535 hours; they were right on schedule. The Regiment advanced seven or eight kilometers against light opposition to its objectives, Mouzon and Ville Montry. Many prisoners were taken in the advance; some of them were no more than boys. The Huns had been retreating for days and those that were captured were exhausted as much as, or more than, the doughboys. Some of Germans captured had been asleep until rudely awakened by the prod of an American bayonet.[65]

At 2000 hours, 8:00 p.m.) with the objectives secured and the advanced elements of the 26th Infantry fighting in Mouzon, the 1st Division was ordered to halt its attack, do a ninety degree turn to the left, pass laterally across the rear areas of a French division and the American 42nd Division presently occupying the front line to the left of the Big Red One, then do a turn to the right, pass vertically through another French unit, and attack Sedan the next day. The 1st Division troops had already fought and marched for twenty-four hours without stopping and were practically like the walking dead. Ted had them drop their backpacks, and then sent a detail to transport the packs to where the next bivouac area was to be located. He also managed to get the kitchens up to the front so his men could have a hot meal before beginning the thirty-mile forced march to the line of departure for the ordered attack. All night long the doughboys had to plow through mud and ruts, and take detours around minefields and blown-up bridges. Everyone moved as if in a dream. One officer fainted, lay unconscious for an hour, then came to and rejoined his outfit in time to make the attack. Another officer, who was riding a horse, nodded off to sleep and fell off his mount. By morning the regiment did its turn to the right, passed through the French unit at Omicourt and began the attack. Ted was at the head of the main body of troops. The disheartened Boche did not offer stiff resistance and good progress was made.

By afternoon the 26th Infantry was on the hills overlooking Sedan, and was on the verge of taking that city when orders were received to halt the attack, move to Chemery, and set up defensive positions for the night. The A.E.F. top brass had decided it would be proper to halt the 1st Division offensive and give the French the honor of liberating Sedan. In the early hours of November 8th, the Regiment attacked the town of Villemontry. The fighting was fierce, but was only on a platoon size scale. This was the last action for the 26th Infantry Regiment during World War I.

Later that day, after he had his bone weary regiment in bivouac, Ted reported to General Francis Marshall, his Brigade Commander. The staff car provided to Ted had broken down the night before causing him to walk on his bad leg for the last ten or twelve miles of the long forced march. General Marshall said Ted came limping up on two canes looking for the chow and packs for his unit. Seeing the exhaustion and pain on Ted's face, the General provided him with a horse to use to get back to his regiment. In assessing Ted's performance during the war, Francis Marshall wrote that he was "a magnificent soldier," that his men loved him, and that it had been "an honor to have commanded him."[66]

Colonel Douglas MacArthur arrived in France in October, 1917 with orders to assume the duties of Chief of Staff of the 42nd (Rainbow) Division. Later, he was promoted to Brigadier General and placed in command of one of the two brigades making up the 42nd Division. MacArthur was a fearless front line warrior during the Great War and earned the Distinguished Service Cross with one Oak Leaf Cluster, the Silver Star with six Oak Leaf Clusters, along with the French Croix de Guerre with Palm, and a host of other foreign decorations. His division commander recommended him for the Congressional Medal of Honor, but the awards board turned it down.

During the war, any of MacArthur's men caught without a gas mask would be severely punished, although the General never carried one himself. He was gassed twice and awarded the Purple Heart with one Oak Leaf Cluster for these gassing incidents. Had he availed himself of his mask, he might not have suffered any ill effects, in which case he would not have been entitled to the Purple Heart awards. Being rewarded for something he did not do is in a way similar to MacArthur's experience years before while he was on duty on the Mexican border. He claimed then that an enemy bullet passed through his clothing without touching his skin. Even though only in his thirties during the Great War, MacArthur was already showing some of the idiosyncratic traits for which he later would become famous. For instance, his manner of dress was different from that of the other high ranking officers. He wore an army hat with a visor, but it drooped on the sides like the kind worn by World War II aviators. He was always nattily clothed. Sometimes he wore a fur coat with a long flowing scarf. An incident, amusing to most everyone except General MacArthur, occurred on the night of November 6th, 1918, when some of the grimy doughboys of the 1st Division's 16th Infantry Regiment were moving, as had been ordered, laterally across the rear areas of the 42nd Division when they came upon young General MacArthur. He was fashionably dressed in his riding britches and highly polished boots. The doughboys, thinking he was a

Hun, captured him. How long MacArthur remained an American POW until recognized and freed is unknown. Some sources say a few minutes and some say a few hours, but the story was told over and over at the bars in officer's clubs for years. In his autobiography the General tries to make little of the occurrence, but he was humiliated, and privately blamed Colonel George C. Marshall, who had authorized the lateral movement of the 1st Division across the 42nd Division's boundaries. From MacArthur's own writings, and from the writings of biographer William Manchester and others, it is obvious that even as a young man MacArthur had a paranoid streak in his personality; he thought Marshall was one of those "out to get him." Consequently, George Marshall and Douglas MacArthur were never close friends.[67]

Ted's regiment bivouacked the nights of November 8th and 9th near the town of Bois de la Folie, but it was not until the night of November 10th that the men really began to feel that the war was over and they had survived. The mud-caked, battle weary doughboys began to light fires and cigarettes and gathered in groups to sing and tell stories, and talk of going home, and of those who wouldn't.

Early in the evening of November 11th, a soldier approached Ted and said, "Colonel, Mrs. Roosevelt is waiting in the car at the corner." At that instant it hit home to Ted that the war was over. Limping on his cane he went back to Eleanor, hugged the breath out of her and said, "How in the name of patience did you get here? Now I'm willing to believe the war's really over!" Then they just sat in the car for a while, neither of them able to speak. It was an exhilarating and emotional moment for them both. Eleanor later described their unspoken thoughts:[68]

Yes, the war was over. The world had been made safe for democracy and we could all go home and live happily ever after. At least we would never have to fight another war, nor would our children. People would have too much sense to fight wars. No doubt in our minds.

Ted accompanied his wife back a few miles to a little tent that had been made available for her use. There she told him how, on November 10th, the YMCA rewarded her for her good work by giving her a lift to the place where the front lines had been and where they thought the 1st Division was located. Eleanor wanted to let Ted know that she was leaving France and going home to their children as soon as possible. When the Division had not shown up by dusk on the 11th, a colonel in the 1st Engineers lent her his car and driver to go find her husband. The 26th Infantry was known to be nearby and the driver found Ted after a two-hour search. The couple ate a supper of canned bully beef, bread, strawberry jam, and hot chocolate. Still under the spell, they thought "nothing ever tasted better." Ted went back to his regiment that night, but the next day General Parker ordered Ted to Paris for two days. There Lt. Colonel and Mrs. Theodore Roosevelt, Jr. joined the wild Armistice celebration. Ted then returned to the 26th Infantry and Eleanor sailed for home.

Years later, just before the start of World War II, Eleanor was at a social function when a General came up to her and said, "Mrs. Roosevelt, I haven't seen you since 1918 in France. Of course you wouldn't remember it, but I once lent you a car. It was in the Argonne and you were looking for your husband." Forget a day she could never forget? The sentimental memories of those days of excitement, and youth, and intense living came flooding back, and she embraced him. The General turned out to be Francis Wilby, who rose to the rank of Major General and at one time was the Superintendent of West Point.[69]

Yes, the Great War was over. Nearly two million American doughboys were in France when the end came; over one hundred thousand of them would never go home. The total civilian and military deaths in that conflict have been estimated by various experts as fifteen million to twenty-five million. Military killed include: Britain $3/4$ million; France 1 million; Germany 2 million; Austro-Hungarian 1 million; Italy $1/2$ million; United States over 100,000. The 1st Division experienced a casualty rate (killed, wounded, and missing) of nearly 200%. Before the Armistice was signed halting the fighting, there had been a period of negotiations between the combating nations with respect to whether the Allies would accept only an unconditional surrender, or be satisfied with something less. President Woodrow Wilson was solidly in the camp of those willing to settle for a negotiated peace. And that is exactly what the Armistice was. Some historians today insist that had World War I continued to an unconditional surrender conclusion, World War II would have never occurred, at least not in Europe. In October, 1918 former President Theodore Roosevelt wrote:

> "During the last week Wilson has been adroitly endeavoring to get the Allies into the stage of note writing and peace discussions with an only partially beaten and entirely unconquered Germany. I have given utterance to the undoubtedly strong, but not necessarily steady, American demand for unconditional surrender. It is dreadful to have my sons face danger; but unless we put this war through, their sons may have to face worse danger—and their daughters also."[70]

History would refer to the final battle of World War I in which the First Infantry Division participated as the Second Battle of the Argonne. For Ted's heroics during that period, the United States awarded him an Oak Leaf Cluster to his Silver Star, and the Distinguished Service Medal. The Republic of France made him a Knight of the National Order of the Legion of Honor and Belgium conferred upon him its Croix de Guerre.

Accolades poured in from many of the top ranking officers under whom Ted had served. General George Duncan, who had commanded the 1st Division during part of the war, said that Ted had been the best officer in his command. General Beaumont Buck had been Ted's Brigade Commander and said, "He had always been among the leaders of his regiment in activity, enthusiasm, persistence and efficiency in the discharge of duty. He had won the love and devotion of the men of his battalion, and the confidence of the officers of his regiment." General Charles Summerall wrote that, "His courage, energy and leadership were a priceless asset to the command." George C. Marshall wrote, " My observation of most of the fighting in France led me to consider your record as a fighting man one of the most remarkable in the entire A.E.F."[71] There were many other tributes; however, the most poignant comment concerning Ted's Great War service, and almost assuredly the one that meant most to him, came from one of the officers serving under him during all those days at the front, who said:

To the men who fought with him he did not stand as the son and and namesake of a great president. He was the man who got them chow when other outfits were hungry; who never took rest himself until his troops had been put to rest; who did not make bullheaded errors that were paid for in human life in action; the man who was always ready to go where he sent them and more often than not was there ahead of them; the man who could raise more kinds of hell in a few minutes when things did not go right than anyone they had ever seen. If that great father of his had come to them then, he would have stood as I think it would have been his greatest pride in life to have stood at that moment, as the father of his son, and nothing else.[72]

The plan after the Armistice was for the A.E.F. to march a military force into Germany as some kind of psychological sign that the Allies had won the war. The 1st Division would lead the display and the 26th Infantry would lead the Division. The march began before dawn on November 17th, when the Regiment departed its bivouac area. By the time they made camp on the night of the first day, the unit had gone clear through the desolate no-man's-land, across what had been German trenches, and into previously occupied France. As the march was resumed early the next morning, they passed through French villages where starving French civilians watched the men go by through hollow, expressionless eyes. Little emotion was exhibited by these pitiful people because the Boche had told them that they were only temporarily leaving the area and would be back soon. On the third day the condition of the villagers improved, but then they encountered long lines of freed prisoners whom the Germans had working in the coalmines. Many of these dirty, ragged men from France, Italy, Russia or Rumania were nothing more than walking skeletons. Ted talked with some of these poor souls and they told him they were trying to get as far away from Germany as possible before the war resumed.

As the march continued, the fear that the Huns would return subsided and many of the towns the troops went through had some kind of ceremony in honor of their liberators. In one town, Ted was presented with an American flag with fifty stars on it, when there were only forty-eight states. When he asked for an explanation, he was told that the two extra stars were for Alsace and Lorraine. On December 5th, the Regiment crossed into Germany and began to see small children dressed in diminutive gray-blue uniforms identical to those of the Wehrmacht. The Germans referred to these youngsters as "little machine gunners." On December 11th, they reached the Rhine River. Ted wrote that that night he "formed the entire Regiment in line on the terraced water front facing the river and, with the band playing 'The Star Spangled Banner,' stood retreat." Crossing the Rhine the next day and continuing the march, the Regiment reached its final destination on December 14th. [73]

TR wrote TR Jr. a letter on December 3rd, which must have pleased his namesake immeasurably, saying, "Your triumph has been great. It is simply fine to think of you with your limp commanding your regiment during the last three weeks of the fighting, and now marching at the head of your division through Germany toward the Rhine. Heavens Ted, what experience you have had, and there isn't any family except the Garibaldis which, as a family, comes out of this war with the reputation that ours does." [74]

In writing about how the United States benefited from the war, Ted pointed out that the country was taught the consequences of being ill prepared, and he advocated a system of compulsory military training as a way to keep the country strong. Nearly half the American men of proper age had been turned down for military service because of some type of physical problem. Ted maintained that the rigors of compulsory training would help in keeping the young men of America, including at least some of the 4-Fs, in reasonably good physical condition. Referring to the fact that the country is made up of many classes and races, he had the opinion that required military training would help the racial, economic, and religious hodgepodge of our citizen's mix by teaching people to live together in harmony.

Surprisingly, Ted was critical of the high command in his later writings. Stating that few of the higher-ups had had experience with troops on a small unit level, he wrote that they "rested in blissful ignorance" when it came to the practical side of combat on the battalion and lower levels. As examples, he noted that when he was in combat those over him required him to spend time preparing diagrams showing where the "alternate gas positions" for his unit were. This was a foolish waist of time since where troops should go when under a gas attack depended on which way the wind was blowing and where the gas shells struck in relation to where the men were located. This was not something that could be predicted in advance. Ted also pointed out that they insisted that the small unit commander prepare and send to higher headquarters detailed maps showing the routes patrols had taken the night before. He thought this was a farce since men wandering and crawling around in no-man's-land in the pitch black of night, unsnarling themselves from wire and dodging enemy flares, didn't really know where they had been, much less being able to draw it out on a map. If the American officers in relatively high positions of authority had had the experience with troops on a lower level, as they should have, many of their unnecessary demands would never have been made and many casualties would have been averted.[75]

Former President Theodore Roosevelt had been in declining health during the fall of 1918 and was in the hospital in New York City when, shortly before Christmas, Eleanor's ship landed. She was home at last. She immediately went ashore and headed for her mother's home to reclaim her children, but, on her way, stopped by the hospital to briefly pay respects to her father-in-law. When she got to her mother's the two older children, Gracie and Teddy, remembered her and were glad to see her, but the youngest child, Cornelius (or Sonny), now age three, had no idea who she was and wanted to know how long she was going to stay. When Eleanor told the little boy that his father would be coming home soon, he wanted to know if he would be bringing home a stuffed German to put on the wall with the other mounted heads. Shortly after Christmas, TR, still gravely ill, was released from the hospital and went home to Sagamore Hill. A few days later, Eleanor spent the day with him. During her visit she told her father-in-law that Ted had never felt he was worthy of being his son. Teddy answered:

> "Worthy of me? Darling, I'm so very proud of him. He has won high honor not only for his children but, like the Chinese, he has ennobled his ancestors. I walk with my head higher because of him. I have always taken satisfaction from the fact that when there was a war in 1898 I fought in it and did my best to get into this one. But my war was a bowand-arrow affair compared to Ted's, and no one knows this better than I do."[76]

Touched by what her father-in-law had said, Eleanor wrote down his exact words as soon as she left. Many years later, in thinking about the occasion and Teddy's remark, Eleanor was sorry that TR would never know that before Ted died he would be awarded by the United States Government every decoration for combat valor authorized for infantry soldiers, including the Congressional Medal of Honor.[77]

A week after Eleanor's visit, Theodore Roosevelt died. Archie cabled Ted and Kermit, both still in Germany, "The Old Lion is Dead," but before they got Archie's message, General Frank Marshall heard the news on the radio and immediately drove to where the two Roosevelt brothers were and told them of their loss. Ted and Kermit stayed up all night reminiscing about their extraordinary father and their remarkable family. Ted sent a reply cablegram to Archie saying, "Dick sailing home immediately. Kermit and I will stay here for we suggest mother might wish to come over here with sister immediately to see about Quentin's grave and commemorative tablet. We would meet them. We are all together."[78]

On the long forced marches during the last days of the war, Ted had trudged through the mud and ruts for some ten or twelve miles and had aggravated his old leg wound. Hoping to avoid future medical treatment, he rode in a staff car or on a horse to keep pressure off of his leg on the march into Germany. It soon became obvious, however, that he needed more extensive medical care than he could get camped out in Germany, so a few days after receiving word of his father's death Ted said goodbye to his regiment and journeyed to Paris for some additional surgery. As with Teddy and the Rough Riders, the Big Red One and the 26th Infantry Regiment would always hold a special place in Ted's heart.[79]

The second surgery on Ted's leg was not extensive but did require hospitalization for a few days. During this confinement he was visited by his first cousin, Eleanor Roosevelt (Mrs. FDR). FDR was in France at the time, but was at another location with President Wilson, and did not accompany his wife to the hospital. Another patient in the same hospital was Mrs. FDR's uncle, David Gray. She gave both Ted and her uncle expensive gowns as gifts.[80]

Toward the last of January 1919, Ted had recovered enough from his recent surgery to invite to dinner three of his good friends, Lt. Col. George S. White, Lt. Col. William J. Donovan, and Major Eric Fisher Wood. Each of the four had commanded either a battalion or a regiment in the war and between them had received seven combat wounds. The officers talked informally about going home and post-war plans, and then Ted brought up the subject of forming a non-political organization made up of the soon-to-be ex-servicemen. Ted's idea was that the new association would not merely promote fellowship among its members but would further Americanism and champion veterans' welfare. There were already in existence associations from other wars, such as the Grand Army of the Republic, United Soldiers of the Confederacy, and the Spanish-American War Veterans, but none for the men of the Great War. Over the next few days, the group met on other occasions and details began to evolve. Membership would be open to all American Great War veterans, regardless of branch of service, rank, or whether or not they served overseas.[81]

One day in early February, Ted was visiting his friend George White, who was by then Chief Personnel Officer for the A.E.F. and worked out of General Headquarters. Just as they were discussing the proposed veterans' organization, General Pershing appeared and asked Ted to step into his office. In private, the A.E.F. Commanding General told him that there were reports of morale problems among the doughboys and he wondered if Ted had anything to suggest concerning that matter. The war had been over for three months now and the troops wanted to go home. They were beginning to grumble and make comments such as "Lafayette, we are still here!" Seizing the opportunity to perhaps help with the morale problem and at the same time take some concrete steps towards establishing the new ex-servicemen's organization, Ted suggested that Pershing set up a "morale conference" where selected, non-regular army citizen soldiers from the far-flung units of the American Expeditionary Force would be ordered to Paris to discuss troop morale and make suggestions for its improvement. Knowing that because of his job Colonel White had access to the personnel files of the entire A.E.F., Ted volunteered himself and White to make a list of suggested attendees. When the General agreed, Ted and the Colonel got orders telegraphed to Eric Fisher Wood to join them. As soon as Wood arrived, the three officers prepared a list of proposed conferees consisting of thirty citizen soldiers. Included on the list were ten company grade officers and several enlisted men. When they presented the list to Pershing, he eliminated all the enlisted men and all but one of the company grade officers, leaving only Captain Ogden D. Mills, Ted, Wood, White, Donovan and fifteen other field grade officers to attend. Orders were issued from General Headquarters requiring the selected officers to meet with several senior staff generals in Paris on the morning of February 15th for a three-day conference on the question of morale.[82]

By day, the conferees worked on the morale issue and made significant recommendations on how to best handle that problem. In the evenings, Capt. Mills and the field grade officers were Ted's guests for dinner at the Inter-Allied Officers Club. After dinner, Ted outlined the general concept of the new veterans' organization as he, Wood, Donovan, and White saw it, and said:[83]

> "It is a nervy thing for us, as a self-appointed committee, to set about such a thing. But someone has got to do it and it ought to be done as soon as possible for the good of the men and for the good of the country."[84]

Meeting again on the evenings of Feb. 16th and 17th, the group gave themselves a name, the "Temporary Committee of Twenty," elected Ted their chairman, and set a meeting in Paris for March 15th for as many servicemen as could attend. The Committee realized that almost everything done in Paris would be on only a temporary basis and that for the association to be set up properly, definitive steps would have to be taken back in the States. Knowing that Ted had a S.C.D. (Surgeons Certificate, Disabled) because of his injury and was, therefore, free to return to the States when he could arrange passage, the Committee suggested that he return to the U.S. as soon as possible and set up a meeting of all interested ex-servicemen for the purpose of adding permanency to whatever was accomplished at the March 15th Paris meeting.[85]

A day or two before the Feb. 15th Temporary Committee of Twenty meeting, Ted's mother Edith had arrived in Le Havre, France. She intended to visit Quentin's grave and make arrangements for an appropriate monument. Ted, Kermit and Belle met her ship and took her to Paris, where Edith's sister Emily Carow, who resided in Italy, met them. On February 18th, they all traveled to Quentin's burial site at the little village of Chamery. There Edith hired the villagers to construct and maintain a beautiful fountain beside the grave of her youngest son.[86]

Back in Paris and getting ready to sail for New York, Ted dropped by G.H.Q. once more. While there, he and George White prevailed upon a couple of generals on the staff to grant leaves to the delegates that planed to attend the March 15th veterans' organization caucus. Then they went public with the new group by sending out mimeographed announcements and running notices in newspapers telling of the purpose of the upcoming event. Within only a day or two after the publicity was initiated, General Pershing discovered what was going on and ordered Ted, White, Donovan, Wood, and a number of the other members of the Temporary Committee of Twenty to report to him immediately. When Pershing got the officers in his office, he read them the riot act as if they had in some way usurped his authority. Lt Col. Donovan calmed the General down, however, when he bluntly told him that the war was over, and that the membership in the new association would be made up of citizen-soldiers who had answered their country's call and now just wanted to go home and get about their lives. After Donovan's dressing down, Pershing gave unenthusiastic approval to the proposed organization and authorized an order issued to all division commanders to allow delegates to attend the up-coming meeting. Ted sailed for home before the March 15th Paris caucus began.[87]

Several hundred doughboys from nearly every state, and from nearly every army division, and staff organization in France were in attendance at No. 4 Avenue Gabriel on that cold March morning. By the end of the three-day conference, the number had swelled to almost a thousand. Eric Fisher Wood opened the meeting by explaining the concept of the new organization as envisioned by Ted Roosevelt and the Temporary Committee of Twenty. He told them that whatever was done in Paris would be subject to change by a later caucus to be held in the U.S. Then nominations and election of officers were called for. Lt. Col. Bennett C. Clark was elected Temporary Chairman of the caucus and Wood, as Temporary Secretary. Next, four committees were set up to work respectively toward: recommending a name for the new entity, setting up a national convention to be held in the U.S. in 1920, making the organization permanent, and drafting a constitution.

All four of the committees worked diligently on its assigned project, but the name recommendation committee had an inordinate amount of trouble. It seemed that each of the fifteen members favored a different name. They argued and discussed all the names proposed before finally agreeing on, "The American Legion."

One of the staunchest opponents of the name finally chosen was Sergeant Alexander Woollcott; he claimed the name "American Legion" had an "aura of the silk stocking" about it. To this, one of the other delegates responded that he hadn't noticed any of the doughboys with an aversion to silk stockings. In later years, Woollcott and Ted and Eleanor Roosevelt would develop a very close personal friendship. [88]

Back in the States, TRJr went to work arranging statewide meetings of Great War veterans for the purpose of selecting delegates from each state to attend the national caucus in Saint Louis set for May 8–10, 1919. He traveled the country, making speeches and calling on governors, mayors and others in positions of authority. When the caucus convened as planned, over one thousand delegates from every state were in attendance. Ted, as Chairman of the Temporary Committee of Twenty, rose to call the meeting to order and was instantly met with a tremendous ovation. When he finally was able to gain quiet, he made a brief opening statement outlining the purposes of the Legion and then called for nominations for a permanent chairman. While no formal nomination had yet been made, delegates began rising and expressing admiration for Ted. With this, Ted explained to the group that he was not available for nomination because the Legion was to be non-political, and he did not want it to appear that his nomination was a ruse to get support for any future political aspirations he may have. [89]

Against his expressed opposition, Ted was nominated. Again he stated his reasons and asked his name to be withdrawn. A raucous display from the floor transpired. "We want Roosevelt," "No, no,, no," "We want Teddy." TRJr again declined. Then almost every delegate stood up and shouted, "We won't take no. We won't take no." The display went on and on. It was reminiscent to the 1900 Republican National Convention when Teddy was nominated for vice-president. But, unlike his father, Ted was immutable; he would not change his mind. Finally, the veterans accepted Ted's decision and selected others to the positions of leadership. [90]

The American Legion came into being and in later years accepted into membership the veterans of World War II and the wars that followed. At its height, it boasted a membership of 3.3 million men and women. The Legion's impact on the country has been enormous. Millions of veterans have received their education, bought homes, and gone into business through the G. I. Bill, that was conceived by the Legion and became law primarily because of its influence. Many believe that the G.I Bill, more that any other single cause, is responsible for the development of the great American middle class. Veterans' hospitals and other health care benefits are pet projects of the organization. To promote Americanism, the Legion sponsors nationwide The American Legion School Awards, Boy's State, Girl's State, The American Legion Oratorical Contests, and American Legion Baseball. Additionally, many local Posts have projects applicable only to their community, such as local Government Day for school children to come into city halls and courthouses and observe how city and county governments work in their community. One post sponsored a cattle sale barn to provide local farmers with a good market for their livestock. There are many others[91]

TR Jr. was active in the American Legion for the rest of his life and served on its National Executive Committee, but he never served as an officer on a national level, except for the two months he was Chairman of the Temporary Committee of Twenty. As it turned out though, the reluctant decision the delegates made in May, 1919 to allow Ted's name to be withdrawn from nomination as Chairman was only a temporary reprieve. At its 1949 Annual National Convention, "In recognition of his proposing the organization, arranging for the Saint Louis caucus, maintaining a lifetime interest in the Legion and its principles, and giving his life for his country and the great principles of justice, freedom and democracy," Theodore Roosevelt, Jr. was, by unanimous vote, posthumously elected a Past National Commander of The American Legion.[92]

Before putting the Army and war related matters aside and turning his energies back to resuming life as a civilian, Ted answered the many letters he received requesting whatever details he could provide about loved ones who had lost their lives during the fighting in France. A typical letter of inquiry was sent by a Professor Gardner.

My Dear Sir:

My son, Second Lieutenant Charles T. Gardner, was a member of Company L, 26th Regiment, and was killed in action on July 22, 1918, not far from Soissons. I have been able to obtain very few reliable details as to his last experiences. Knowing that you were connected with that Regiment, I am writing to ask if you can tell me exactly where it was stationed that day, or tell me where I can secure the information. My purpose is to visit the scenes where he fought, and desire to locate the spot where he fell as nearly as possible. I know this is asking much of you, but know also that you can appreciate the sentiment which prompts me to trouble you thus.

Sincerely yours,

Ted promptly wrote back:

My dear Professor Gardner:

I remember your son perfectly. He was in Major McCloud's battalion. If you will go to Cuitry, which is just south of Soissons, you will be at the place from which the offensive started on July 18th. From Cuitry go to Misey-en-Bois, from there to Ploiey and thereafter to Berzy-le-Sec. This latter point is where it finished. I was hit myself between Ploisy and Misey-en-Bois. I presume your son was hit between Ploisy and Berzy-le-Sec. The last objective taken by the division was the railroad running from Soissons to Chateau Thierry.

I would suggest you write to Major Starling of the 26th Infantry, A.E.F. He is the only one of the officers of Major McCloud's battalion that I recall who is still alive and with the regiment. I will write myself to the regimental adjutant and see if he can tell us anything further. Please accept my deepest and most understanding sympathy.

Very truly yours,[93]

Ted Roosevelt

Lafayette We Are Here Source Notes

1. Roosevelt, T Jr., Average Americans, p.33–35; Roosevelt, Mrs.T Jr.. p. 74; Bosco p. 59.

2. Roosevelt, T. Jr., Average Americans, p. 40–43

3. Letter TRJr to Eleanor, 7/6/17, LOC C-8; Roosevelt, T. Jr., Average Americans, p. 20.

4. Roosevelt, T. Jr., p. 48–49, 73; Patch p. 50.

5. Statements of Charles Ridgely and Shipley Thomas, LOC C-39.

6. Roosevelt, T. Jr., Average Americans, p 44.

7. Stallings p 27; Lowell Thomas p 86; Patch p 46–47.

8. Roosevelt, Mrs. T., Jr. p 79; Roosevelt, T. Jr., Average Americans, p 101

9. Letter Stuart A. Baxter to N Y Herald Tribune, LOC C-56

10. Roosevelt, Mrs. T Jr., p 80; Letter TRJr to Eleanor 1/17/18 LOC C 61; Roosevelt, T Jr., Average Americans, p 100–101.

11. Roosevelt, Mrs. T Jr., p 80; Roosevelt, T Jr., Average Americans, p 101 and All In the Family p. 72; Letter TRJr to TR LOC C-8;

12. Letter TRJr to TR (no date) LOC C-8; Roosevelt, T Jr., Average Americans, p 57, 113.

13. Collier p 208; Letter TRJ to Ethel Derby 8/16/17 TR collection, Harvard U. 87M-100.

14. Roosevelt, T Jr., Average Americans, p 75–76

15. Ibid.

16. TR letter to TRJr, Morrison Vol. 8, p 1240.

17. Letter TRJr to TR 9/1/17, LOC C-8; Letter TRJr to TR (no date) LOC C-8.

18. Pershing Vol 1, p 192.

19. Andrus p 6; Miller p 6; Roosevelt, T Jr., Average Americans, p 85–86.

20. Roosevelt, T Jr., Average Americans, p 86.

21. Marshall, G., p 51–52.

22. Lowell Thomas p 103; Roosevelt, T Jr., Average Americans, p 88.

23. Letter TRJr to TR (no date) LOC C-8.

24. Roosevelt, T Jr., Average Americans, p 54, 71–72.

25. Marshall, G., p 52–53; Roosevelt, T Jr., Average Americans, p 84–85.

26. Marshall, G., p 53; Roosevelt, T Jr., Average Americans, p 105–107; Letter TRJr to TR (no date) LOC C-8.

27. Letter TRJr to TR (no date) LOC C-8.

28. Buck p 168–169; LOC C-61.

29. Roosevelt, T Jr., Average Americans, p 89

30. Inspector General Citation 1/2/18 LOC C-39; Letter TRJr to Eleanor 1/17/18 LOC C-61.

31. Statement of Shipley Thomas LOC C-39.

32. Letter TRJr to Eleanor 1/17/18 LOC C-61; Roosevelt, T Jr., Average Americans, p 93–97.

33. Roosevelt, T Jr., Average Americans, p 108; Miller p 6–7.

34. Roosevelt, T Jr., Average Americans, p 27–28, 82.

35. Roosevelt, T Jr., Average Americans, p 109–110.

36. Condolence sent by Major John Crutcher LOC C-32; Roosevelt, T Jr., Average Americans, p 110–113.

37. Roosevelt, Mrs. T Jr. p 87–96.

38. Roosevelt, Mrs. T Jr. p 95; Roosevelt, T Jr., Average Americans, p 119; Letter TRJr to Grace Lockwood Roosevelt, March 1918, TR Collection, Harvard U., bMs 1541.4³⁴; Letter Mrs. FDR to TRJr. LOC c-31.

39. Miller p 7–8; Reeder p 86.

40. Roosevelt, T Jr., Average Americans, p 124–126.

41. Ibid p 31, 125–127.

42. Roosevelt, T Jr., Average Americans, p 127; Miller p 9.

43. Statement of Shipley Thomas LOC C-39

44. Statement of Charles Ridgely LOC C-39

45. Pershing Vol 1, p 166–167; Roosevelt, T Jr., Average Americans p 148–150.

46. Buck p 171, 174; Statement of Shipley Thomas LOC C-39; Citation for Silver Star LOC C-39; Citation for Purple Heart LOC C-39; Letter Stuart A. Baxter to NY Herald Tribune LOC C-56.

47. Statement of Shipley Thomas LOC C-39; Buck 171–179; Marshall, G., p 94–95; Roosevelt, T Jr., Average Americans, p 133–135; Citation for DSC, LOC C-55; Citation for Croix de Guerre, LOC C-56.

48. Roosevelt, Mrs. T Jr. p 97–99.

49. Roosevelt, T Jr., Average Americans, p 140.

50. The Infantry Journal, March/ April 1934; Roosevelt, T Jr., Average Americans, p 136; Citation for Croix de Guerre with Palm, LOC C-56.

51. Marshall, G. p 98.

52. Miller p 18–19; Roosevelt, T Jr., p 32.

53. Roosevelt, T Jr., Rank and File p 230.

54. Roosevelt, Mrs. T Jr., p 200; Ward, 1st Class, p 388–389; Stallings p 118; Letter TR to Arthur Lee, Morrison Vol 8, p 1368.

55. Roosevelt, T Jr., Average Americans, p 166–167.

56. Statement of Charles Ridgely LOC C-39.

57. Statements of Charles Ridgely and Shipley Thomas LOC C-39; News Report, 7/24/18, The Evening Sun, LOC C-63; Roosevelt, T Jr., Average Americans, p 173; Welsh p 33; Reeder p 171–172.

58. Roosevelt, Mrs. T Jr. p 100–103; Letter Richard Tobin to Howard Braucher, 1/10/45, LOC C-56.

59. Freidel Vol 1, p 411–412; Ward, 1st Class, p 397.

60. Roosevelt, Mrs. T Jr. p 104–106.

61. Roosevelt, Mrs. T Jr., p 108; Official Army Records

62. Roosevelt, Mrs. T Jr., p 111; Roosevelt, T Jr., Average Americans, p 195–196; Official Army Records

63. Roosevelt, T. Jr., Average Americans, p 201–204; Stallings p 353.

64. Roosevelt, T Jr., Average Americans, p 204

65. Roosevelt, T Jr., Average Americans, p 206–207; Center for Military History, on line, 1st Div Record of Events.

66. Roosevelt, T Jr., Average Americans, p 210–211; CMH, on line, 1st Div Record of Events; Stallings p 362; Welsh p 57; Marshall, G., p 190–191; Letter Francis Marshall to TR 11/11/18 LOC C-77; Recommendation for Legion of Honor LOC C-39.

67. Manchester p 83–110; MacArthur p 68.

68. Roosevelt, T Jr., Average Americans, p 214; Roosevelt, Mrs. T Jr. p 114.

69. Roosevelt, Mrs. T Jr., p 113–116.

70. Roosevelt, T Jr., Average Americans,, Preface xvii.

71. Roosevelt, Nicholas, p 35; Letter Summerall to TR LOC C-77; Letter Buck to TR, LOC C-77; Letter G. Marshall to TRJ LOC C-29

72. Statement of Charles Ridgely LOC C-39.

73. Kenneth Roberts Article LOC C-55; Roosevelt, T Jr., Average Americans, p 217–231.

74. Letter TR to TRJ, Morrison Vol 8, p 1410.

75. Roosevelt, T Jr., Average Americans, p 152–157, 235–243

76. Roosevelt, Mrs. T Jr. p 118.

77. Ibid.

78. Collier p 241–243; Roosevelt, Mrs. T Jr., p 117–118; Morris, S. p 434.

79. Kenneth Roberts Article LOC C-55; Roosevelt, T Jr., Average Americans, p 217–231

80. Ward, 1st Class, p 424–425.

81. Rumer p 8–10; Moley p 43.

82. Rumer p 11–12.

83. Rumer p 13; Moley p 45–46.

84. Rumer p 13.

85. Rumer p 14.

86. Morris, S. p 442.

87. Rumer p 15.

88. Rumer p 16–31.

89. Moley p 64.

90. Rumer p 36–42.

91. Baker, Roscoe p 14

92. Resolution No. 348, Official Minutes, 31st Annual American Legion Convention.

93. Letter to Ted dated 7/5/1919, Ted's response dated 7/15/1919, also see Ted's letter to Mr. James Kerns dated 10/9/1919, both in LOC C-11.

6

THE POLITICAL YEARS

With the ending of the American Legion caucus in St. Louis, Ted set about on an extensive speaking tour to various cities around the country, orating in behalf of the Legion most of the time, with an occasional political speech for the Republican Party or for the benefit of the Liberty Loan drive. In Chicago, he told the audience that the Legion should get involved in every public movement having to do with Americanism, no matter how large or how small, that it should work toward legislation for a bonus system for discharged service men, and that it should encourage a system of universal military training.[1] In another city, he said:

It has been the policy of The American Legion, wherever I have come in contact with it, to play the game with all the cards on the table. The serviceman will not tolerate any other form of organization. He wishes, at all times, to be able not only to tell anyone what he is doing but equally to be able to find out anything that the organization, through some other branch, may be doing.[2]

Besides speaking engagements during the summer of 1919, TRJr was busy working on the details and arrangements for the first official Legion national convention to be held in Minneapolis on November 10–12. He also began work on his first book, *Average Americans,* which was an account of his activities during the Great War. In June he attended the commencement ceremonies at Harvard, where he and nine other graduates were awarded honorary Master of Arts degrees for their distinguished war service. On August 9th, he was promoted to full Colonel in the Army Reserve, inactive status.[3]

The media began to call Ted the "crown prince" back when Teddy was President. With the great man now gone, everyone in the immediate family recognized TRJr as the rightful heir to the Roosevelt political throne. Ted, himself, had had visions of following in his father's political footsteps ever since those years before the war, when he and Eleanor were skimping and saving and planning. Archie, Kermit, Ethel, and Edith were not political animals, and they were somewhat passive in their support of Ted's dreams. But Alice loved the excitement of politics; she was a fighter and was determined that Ted would be the next Roosevelt to be President of the United States.

After returning to the States from France, Ted and Eleanor rented an old home near Oyster Bay at Council Rock, resulting in the reestablishment of their residence in Nassau County. There was speculation by some that this was an intentional political move to better his chances of receiving his party's nomination for governor, but Ted realized he must start at the bottom and work up, just as Teddy had. Before the qualifying deadline in July, Ted took his first step up the political ladder when he sought and received the Republican nomination for his district's seat in the New York General Assembly for the upcoming 1920 term. Being the son and namesake of a man most Nassau County residents had worshipped, and with his own exemplary war record, the affable Roosevelt's election was a foregone conclusion.

The campaign got under way in earnest a month before election day when Ted made a speech before several hundred of his hometown constituents. In this, his very first oration as a candidate, he failed to speak to local issues, but bared his teeth and said "bully" a lot, as was a quirk of his father's, and discussed in general terms such subjects as "reactionary politics" and "constructive liberalism." He advised the recently franchised women voters to take seriously the right to vote. His Democratic opponent was a young attorney named Raff whose father was an old time Long Island tailor. Raff ran as his own man, saying, "My hat is in the ring, and it is not my father's hat." This strategy on the part of his opponent taught Ted an important political lesson: he should not imitate his father. Thereafter he avoided intentionally doing so. But the tendency to emphasize theory and general issues rather than specific practical issues would plague him to some extent for years to come.[4]

November 3rd 1919, was a very special day to the TRJr family. Signorina Maria Nam, an Italian friend of Ted's aunt Emily Carow, came to live with them. The family referred to her as simply Signorina. She nursed in an Italian military hospital during the war and immigrated to this country to be a nanny to the Roosevelt children. All the children, and later the grandchildren, loved her and cherished the time she spent with them. After the children left home to go to boarding school, she became Eleanor's personal secretary and took over management of the household. Eleanor thought the world of Signorina, saying that she was "as lovely a person as I have ever known." She stayed with the Roosevelt family for thirty years.

Since Quentin's death, there had been a tacit understanding within the family that the next male child born would bear his name. Besides Eleanor, Archie's wife Grace, and Kermit's wife Belle, were also pregnant and expecting to deliver soon.

Eleanor especially wanted to be the mother of her deceased brother-in-law's namesake. She felt she had been closer to Quentin than the other women, and she certainly had known him longer. Ted jokingly said that she wanted this so badly that she willed their new baby to be a male and to come prematurely. As it turned out, both of the other babies were girls. On November 9th, not only did Eleanor deliver Quentin, their fourth and last child, but Ted was elected to the New York Assembly by a two to one vote margin. Nassau County normally went Republican, but not in the overwhelming majority that it did for Ted. He was following right in Teddy's footsteps, and told a friend that he "was a man of destiny."[5]

Constantino Balocca had been born in Italy, but his family immigrated to New York before World War I. He was Ted's orderly during the war, and they shared many experiences while serving in France. Not long after baby Quentin's birth, Balocca was hired to work for the TRJrs as gardener, plumber, mechanic, electrician, and general handyman. The children, especially the boys, became attached to him and he taught them the various skills he had mastered. Balocca and his intelligent wife were like members of the family for the many years they were in the Roosevelt's employ.[6]

Ted was one of the rookie members of the General Assembly when it was called to order in early January 1920. Everything was normal; it appeared to be business as usual. Republicans held one hundred and ten seats, followed by thirty-five Democrats and five Socialists. All the Assembly members had been duly elected in their respective districts, and the election results were properly certified by the New York Secretary of State. After the roll was called, the body undertook the election of a speaker, and Republican Thaddeus Sweet easily won the honor. Next, the governor made a short address, and some routine business was transacted.[7]

At this point in history, the bloody Russian Revolution had just concluded successfully for the Bolshevists. In the United States, there was a widespread fear and distrust of anything considered Communist or Socialist, and a corresponding prejudice against any type of social, economic or political theory where most of the assets were owned or managed by the government. In the middle of the afternoon of that first legislative day, the speaker walked to the podium and ordered the sergeant-at-arms to bring the five Socialist members before the Assembly. When this was done, Speaker Sweet informed the assemblymen that the Socialists had been elected on a platform opposed to the best interests of America, and that the so-called Socialist Party was not actually a political party but was an organization whose allegiance lay with enemies of the State of New York and of the United States. Over the protests of the Socialists, the speaker then permitted a resolution to be introduced accusing the Socialist Party of seeking the violent overthrow of the government and also of violating the Federal Espionage Act. The resolution, which passed almost unanimously, went on to deny the Socialists their seats until their "qualifications and eligibility" were determined by the House Judiciary Committee.[8]

The House Judiciary Committee, in whose hands the matter now rested, began holding a public hearing on January 20th. Before any evidence was presented, Charles Evans Hughes, the former Governor of the State as well as a former Justice of the New York Supreme Court and Republican candidate for President, informed the Committee that he was there in the capacity as attorney for the New York Bar Association, and that his client requested that the assembly seats be restored to the Socialists until the charges against them had been proven by the evidence. Mr. Hughes then handed the Speaker some legal briefs and turned and left the chamber. The presentation of evidence then got under way. The documentation and oral testimony in support of making the expulsion of the five men permanent consisted of a number of books, pamphlets, and other written material, and a number of so-called expert witnesses, all of which were disparaging of socialism in general. Some of the evidence indicated that the doctrine sought the violent overthrow of any government that was not Communist or Socialist. No evidence was presented against any individual Socialist assemblyman, except for some vague and imprecise statements some of them had made in campaign speeches.

Some days later, when the unseated members were allowed to put on their evidence, something akin to a seminar took place. The Socialists attempted to educate the Assembly and the public on how law abiding and peaceful the Socialist doctrine really was, and how any changes it desired to make in government would be brought about under the law, and not by violence. Norman Thomas, who for decades was a world-renowned member of the Socialist Party, testified in behalf of the unseated five. At the conclusion of the hearing, which continued intermittently for nearly two months, the Judiciary Committee recommended that the five expelled Socialists not be reseated.[9]

Pursuant to legislative procedure, the matter then reverted to the full Assembly, but before a final vote was taken on whether or not to reseat the Socialists, every assemblyman was afforded an opportunity to speak to the issue. After the session had been going on for some ten hours, Ted, who staunchly believed that the failure to seat the duly elected men would be a disenfranchisement of the voters in their districts, finally was recognized by the Speaker and given the floor.[10] In this, his first official address as an assembly member, Ted said, in part:

We abhor the doctrines of the Socialist party. Many of us personally and through our families have suffered greatly from its actions and the actions of pacifists, for to them is attributed in large degree the unpreparedness of this country when war broke. Our actions, however, must have no reference to any except two things, justice and discretionary application. We must not let justifiable dislike force us to commit a crime against representative government. We must reseat these men and then, in our pleasure, take up and remedy by legislation such things in the party as may need correction. The Assembly, as sole judge of the qualifications of its members, has the right to expel anyone and its decision is final. As this power is subject to no external control it is doubly necessary for us to exercise it only with self-control, because the greater the power, the more dangerous the abuse.[11]

Ted went on to explain the situation as he saw it, stating that there were actually two issues involved. The first being whether the charges against the Socialists as a Party had been proven, and the second whether there was proof against any of the individuals which would justify their expulsion. With respect to the proof presented against the Socialist Party, he pointed out that while there was proof that it did not support the war effort, the Party's resistance to the effort was passive and confined to protests and failure to actively aid in the war. He further said that there was no proof of spying or any other conduct approaching espionage, nor was there creditable proof that the Party sought the overthrow of the government by force. As for the five individuals, his opinion was that everyone had the right of free speech, and since there was no proof that any of them had committed an overt or even covert act against the government, it would not be fair to refuse to reseat them because of what was assumed to be their state of mind.

The debate continued all night with speaker after speaker calling for expulsion. After the discussions concluded, Speaker Sweet went to the floor and publicly berated Ted for his un-American views, claiming that his father would have been appalled at what he had said. After Mr. Sweet had his say, the Assembly voted overwhelmingly to expel all five of the Socialists. Ted voted with the small minority to reseat them all.

Nothing similar to the expulsion of the five socialists had ever occurred in the New York General Assembly before. For that reason, and because of the "red scare" that prevailed at the time, the episode received wide press coverage, especially in New York. While Ted was only a freshman member, he had the Roosevelt name, and his remarks were extensively publicized. As a result of his unpopular stance and vote on the issue, he received a great deal of hate mail and public criticism, but he ignored the detractors and voted for what he thought was right, saying "the consequences be damned."[12]

In early fall of 1920, Governor Al Smith called a special session of the Assembly. This, under New York law, made necessary a special election in the applicable districts to fill the vacancies in the legislative body that had been created by the expulsion of the five Socialist members. All five expelled members were reelected by wider margins than in the previous year. When the Assembly went into its special session, the matter was again debated on the floor, and Ted again spoke in behalf of seating the outcasts, saying, in part:

> There is but one way to meet false ideas and that is with sound ideas. As you hate Socialism vote against expulsion.[13]

This time things had cooled down some. The Speaker and the Majority Leader had both dropped their opposition to seating the five duly elected men, and the number of legislators opposed to the Socialists had dwindled. When the votes were counted, the Assembly approved seating two and denied seating the other three. Thereupon, the two that had been granted their seats refused to accept them, stating that they would not be a part of such unconstitutional action.[14]

While the Judiciary Committee hearings were in progress, the proceedings would be interrupted from time to time so that the Assembly could continue its normal functions. Bills were passed, defeated, or referred to a committee; additionally, committee assignments were made. Ted was pleased to be appointed to the Labor and Industries Committee. He knew that being on that particular committee would give him an opportunity to introduce two bills which he considered to be important pieces of legislation.

For years Ted had felt that something should be done to bring capital and labor closer together for the betterment of both. As things were, employees, through unions, tried to get as much pay for as little work as they could, while employers tried to pay as little wage for as much work as possible. He thought there should be something like a partnership between these two forces. His theory was that the workers should have a voice in the management of the business they worked for and were entitled to receive a share of the profits. In this way, the employees would work hard to make the business a success because they would participate in the profits. This arrangement would create a less antagonistic relationship between labor and management. In turn, the workers would buy permanent homes, save their money, and the community would be stable and peaceful. With this in mind, the first bill he introduced in the Assembly authorized the stockholders of a corporation to adopt a bylaw allowing company employees to be elected to the board of directors by secret ballot. Labor, management, Democrats, and Republicans were all critical of Ted's bill. It was said to be Socialistic by some Assembly members, and unrealistic by others because of the fundamental divergence of interests between capital and labor. When put to the vote, Ted's proposed law was overwhelmingly defeated.[15]

Not giving up, Ted introduced other social welfare type bills. One provided for a Minimum Wage Board to protect women and children from wage discrimination and certain other abuses. Under this proposed legislation, the governor would appoint a three-person commission, made up of one representative from employees, one from employers, and a third from the general public. At least one member had to be a woman. The duty of the commission would be to conduct administrative hearings and remedy cases where a woman or a child had received less than the specified minimum wage. Another of Ted's proposals would require local school boards to establish and maintain kindergartens in their districts if petitioned to do so by at least 25 parents of pre-school children. Again, the cry went up from conservatives that the bills were Socialistic. Ted responded by telling his legislative constituents that similar bills were already the law in a number of states and that they should not be spooked from voting in favor of good legislation just because someone claimed it to be Socialistic. Both of these bills were referred to committee, but there they died.[16]

To the average citizen at that time, the most important issue was the 18th Amendment, which had been ratified and made into law by Congress early in the year. Commonly known as the "Prohibition Law," it made it illegal to manufacture, transport and/or sell alcoholic beverages anywhere in the United States. Until this amendment was repealed, the country ran amuck with whiskey stills, rumrunners, bootleggers, and illegal shot houses. For a brief period earlier in his life, it appeared that Ted may have a serious drinking problem, but he handled it well and thereafter was what is termed a "social drinker." The truth was, though, that no one liked to take a good, stiff drink, or two, or three more than TRJr Being in the state legislature, as opposed to Congress, he had no chance to vote on the prohibition issue, but Ted said publicly that he thought the real evil in intoxicating liquor lay with saloons and hard whiskey, and not with beer and wine. He added that no matter if you personally disagree with the law, it should be obeyed. Most certainly though, Ted, like most Americans, continued to enjoy a good drink in spite of prohibition.[17]

Throughout both the regular session and special session, Ted voted the Republican Party line on most issues, like increasing teacher's salaries, training teachers in adult education, and maintaining a state farmer's council. But when he introduced his minimum wage commission bill, the corporate secret ballot bill and voted against the party old guard's wishes on a few other matters, Ted served notice on the conservative wing of the Republican Party that he thought for himself and was not afraid to buck the party line when he was convinced that justice and good government so required. Many of Ted's fellow Republican legislators looked on him as a rebel.[18]

The year 1920 was a presidential election year, and Teddy Roosevelt's old friend from the Spanish-American war days, General Leonard Wood, was campaigning for the Republican nomination. Ted knew Gen. Wood well, having known him from when his father was President, and he had previously called on him to assist in setting up the Plattsburg Training Camps. All of the Oyster Bay Roosevelts thought that Wood would make an outstanding president, and were working in his behalf.

Prior to the Republican Convention in June, General Wood entered the Republican primary in every state that had one, and went into the convention with a slight lead over the other candidates in committed delegates. Wood had had some problems during the course of the campaign with his campaign manager, Frank King. King was a highly thought of professional political advisor and had managed Teddy's campaign for president in 1904. However, Wood and King did not see eye to eye on what the best campaign strategy was, and King resigned. Wood replaced him with William Proctor and Frank Hitchcock. Proctor was a millionaire but had no appreciable political experience, and Ted had questions about Hitchcock's character. When the convention got underway, Wood and his backers hoped they could get a steamroller going behind him and sweep the convention. Ted attended the convention and helped his father's old friend by talking to delegates and influential Republicans behind the scenes in the "smoke filled rooms," encouraging them to get behind the General's candidacy. All the tactics employed by Wood and his supporters failed, however, and the convention deadlocked when the delegates' votes were cast for the presidential nomination. Finally, on the tenth ballot the deadlock was broken when Warren G. Harding, a compromise candidate, received the nomination. Ted and the Sagamore Roosevelts were disappointed that General Wood faltered, and were not pleased with the selection of Harding. They adopted a positive attitude though, saying that maybe Harding was a better man than they thought, and speculated that a Republican Congress, if elected, could overcome Harding's shortcomings. Alice, probably the most politically astute of Teddy's children, best expressed the family's feelings about Harding, saying, "To call him second rate would be to pay him a compliment." The Republican ticket was completed with the nomination of Calvin Coolidge as the Vice Presidential candidate.[19]

The Democrats held their convention shortly before that of the Republicans. The Democratic presidential nominee, James Cox, selected Ted's cousin, Franklin Delano Roosevelt, as his running mate. At the time FDR was only thirty-eight years old, and was not politically well known on a national level, even though he had served as Assistant Secretary of the Navy during the Wilson administration. Cox's idea was that the magical Roosevelt name would attract some of the swing vote and also garner votes from liberal Republicans.

When the campaign got underway Cox's strategy began to work like a charm.

In his speeches, FDR helped the charade along by often quoting Teddy and referring to him, and calling himself a "progressive" Democrat. The news media helped the Democratic cause by pointing out that both TR and FDR had gone to Harvard, been in the New York legislature, and had been the Assistant Secretary of the Navy. Along the campaign trail, people, thinking FDR was TR's son, would shout phrases like, "I voted for your father," and "You're just like the old man." To counter FDR's favorable effect on the voters, Harding and his advisors approached Ted with the request that he travel the country during the campaign, speaking in behalf of Harding and emphasizing that FDR was not of the Teddy Roosevelt clan. Alice made a side deal with Harding that in return for Ted's help, he would support her brother if he ran for Governor of New York in 1924. Ted, eager to help, began campaigning for Harding.

FDR had always been a little too polished for the Oyster Bay bunch and they remembered that Franklin had remained safely in the Democratic Party in 1912, rather than join Teddy as a Progressive. They also resented the fact that during the war he held smugly and safely to his position as Assistant Secretary of the Navy, rather than take Teddy's advice to resign and get into the fighting in France. Ted was especially antagonized when FDR begun to claim that he had "known war." He knew very well that the closest FDR had been to the front lines during the Great War was back with the long range artillery for a couple of hours when he was in France on an official tour as the naval Assistant Secretary. Alice and Ted, and probably others in the family, recognized the threat FDR posed to Ted's political ambitions. Whether Democrat or Republican, there was room for only one Roosevelt as a major player in the national political game. They could not allow FDR to become Vice President. They had to beat him.[20]

In early fall, before leaving home to cover large areas of the country and speak in behalf of the Warren Harding/Calvin Coolidge ticket, Ted qualified to run for the 1921 term in the New York General Assembly. Just as he was leaving on his tour, he shocked Eleanor, by telling her that since he would be gone, she would have to deliver campaign speeches in his stead during the local campaign. Eleanor was aghast, as she had never done anything like that in her life. However, during the five or six weeks that the campaign lasted, she, accompanied by their war trophy dog, Caesar, gave twenty-six speeches (or as she put it, varied the same speech twenty-six times). Eleanor did an excellent job. Ted won reelection, and by a larger majority than the previous year.[21]

While his wife was attending to politics locally, Ted was off on his extended tour in behalf of the Republican Party and its presidential nominee. His first stop was in Maine, where the election was in September rather than in November like the rest of the country. There he hit hard at the Democrats, claiming that the Wilson administration had usurped the power of Congress like a dictatorship, and that the Republicans would restore to Congress its constitutional powers and return representative government to the people. Hitting at FDR, he claimed the Republicans had won the war, and lashed out at the personal war records of the leaders of the opposing party, stating that there was not a single member of the immediate family of any nationally known Democrat who had been in harm's way during the war. In his usual calm, reassuring way, FDR parried Ted's verbal blows, explaining that the war was not won by Democrats or Republicans, but by the men of both parties. As charming and impressive as he was, Franklin could not switch the normally Republican Maine vote, which went for Harding by a large majority.[22]

Ted's participation in the campaign then shifted to the west where he covered over four thousand miles, partially by airplane, and spoke in twenty states. There he attacked FDR for trying to cover himself with the mantle of Teddy Roosevelt, telling his audiences that Franklin "is a maverick," and "he does not carry the brand of our family." In defending himself, FDR praised former President Roosevelt for having definite convictions about issues and fighting fair while others, meaning Ted without actually naming him, made misrepresentations and used unfair political methods.[23]

TRJr's oratory was not confined to denouncing FDR's claimed tie-in with Teddy; he attacked the Democratic Party as being the party of big government, pointing out that the Wilson administration had hired sixty thousand useless government employees. He also brought up the League of Nations issue. James Cox and FDR were in favor of the Unites States joining the League, while the Republicans were opposed to the wording in the League's charter, which they thought would give foreign countries the power to cause the United States to enter a war without the expressed consent of the United States Government. The Republicans were not so much opposed to some type of organization of the various countries, but they did object to turning over important issues of government to what a majority of the other League members might decide to do.[24]

On election day, Warren Harding was swept into office by one of the largest majorities in history. The 1920 election created a giant cleft in the extended Roosevelt clan with the Sagamore Hill group on one side and the Hyde Park (FDR's home, Hyde Park, New York) wing on the other. As time passed, the split widened, and, with the exception of one or two individual defectors, would not heal until all the major participants were dead.

With the coming of 1921, the New York General Assembly went back into session. There had been rumors that Ted would be elected speaker, but this did not come about, nor did any important committee assignments materialize. Early in the session, Ted again confounded and irritated the old guard conservative Republicans by introducing what, in their opinion, were radical, left wing bills.

One of Ted's proposals was to increase the state income tax exemption from $200 per child to $500 per child. Another of his bills would make a landlord criminally liable for discriminating against a tenant or prospective tenant because there were children in the household. None of Ted's proposed legislation became law.[25]

The keen sense of humor that Ted had been blessed with did not desert him on the day he was accosted in the Assembly Hall by an irate constituent. The lady berated him for not staying in the army after the war. He responded that the reason he got out of the army and entered politics was that politics was more exciting. "Politics? More exciting than war?" asked the woman. "Yes, indeed," said Ted. "In war you can be killed only once, but think how many times you can be killed in politics."

Throughout his life Ted kept his body in excellent condition with exercise and various other physical activities. One of his favorite pastimes was squash. He loved to play, and participated in the sport as often as he could. The only trouble was that he was so competitive he was always getting bunged up by running hard into the wall. Another thing Ted enjoyed doing in Albany that was not related to being an assemblyman, was getting together with a gang of his old classmates from Albany Academy. Even though it had been twenty-five years, the bond between childhood friends runs deep, and they all loved to have lunch together and embellish their old-time stories.[26]

In March, 1921, President Harding, out of appreciation for TRJr's great help in November, appointed him Assistant Secretary of the Navy. On his last day as a member of the Assembly, many of the members rose to the floor and complimented Ted on his conduct while there. In response, Ted said that the gentlemen in the Assembly had taught him many things in the last two years, but of all the things he would carry away with him, the one that meant the most was the fact that he had made many warm and lasting friendships. "I am not saying Democratic friends or Republican friends, just friends." The applause given him was prolonged.

Ted, Eleanor, Alice, and the rest of the family were exuberant over the appointment. Some of the press were writing that this was a stepping-stone to the White House. Again Ted was following right along in Teddy's footsteps. The only difference was that Ted had already had his war while Teddy had resigned as Assistant Secretary of the Navy to go off and fight in his. Not long after his appointment, Ted's distant cousin, Franklin Delano Roosevelt, who had served as Assistant Secretary of the Navy during World War I, was stricken with a severe case of polio. Ted promptly sent Franklin a short note of condolence, but the damage from the 1920 election was deep. FDR did not believe Ted was sincere and resented the gesture. (In later years two other members of the extended Roosevelt family would hold down the job of Assistant Secretary of the Navy. FDR, when

President, appointed Henry L. Roosevelt, and Calvin Coolidge appointed Theodore Douglas Robinson, a cousin.)[27]

With his appointment, Ted, along with Eleanor, Gracie, Teddy III, Cornelius, baby Quentin, and Signorina packed up their personal belongings and moved into a furnished house they rented in Washington D.C. Gracie, Teddy III and Cornelius got settled in local schools. The family remained in the nation's capital for over three years and, until the last few months, thoroughly enjoyed their time there. Eleanor and Ted's sister, Alice, had been friends from their first meeting. Since Alice and her husband, congressman Nick Longworth, already lived in Washington, Eleanor and Alice went places together and came to be like sisters.

The Washington cocktail party scene was not something that really appealed to Eleanor and Ted, and they avoided this brand of social activity when they could. Their idea of a good time was to have a few friends over for dinner and a game of bridge or poker. President Harding and the First Lady were frequent guests. Secretary of Interior Albert Fall played occasionally. Ted and Alice can be visualized playing poker, but Eleanor learned to play and no one enjoyed this game of chance more than she did. In her book *Day Before Yesterday* Eleanor writes of one poker hand in which the players were the Longworths, Senator Charles Curtis (later Vice-President), Secretary of the Treasury Andrew Mellon, Secretary of War John Weeks, Shipping Board CEO Albert Lasker, and Ted. On the deal Mellon had four queens, someone else had a full house, and Curtis had four kings. After a number of raises Curtis won a big pot.[28]

As was his custom, Ted jumped into his new job, entailing new responsibilities, with great energy and enthusiasm. Secretary of the Navy Edwin Denby delegated to him the oversight of the naval yards and naval stations. After a short time to analyze the situation, Ted modified the management procedure used by the Navy for these facilities by providing each yard and station with an additional officer called, "Yard Manager." The Yard Managers were placed in charge of the equipment, repair, buildings, and supervision of civilian employees. This freed the yard or station commandant to handle the military functions of the facility. Secretary Denby also made Ted responsible for the Navy budget. This necessitated him keeping abreast of the Navy's financial requirements and being prepared to go before congressional committees, with little advance notice, to answer questions regarding revenue requests.

Into Ted's hands also fell the task of disposing of the immense amount of surplus naval equipment accumulated during the recent war. His job was to see that the surplus material was liquidated efficiently and for the best price possible. Ted set up a system of selling the material at auctions with sealed bids. This method proved highly successful. One trade publication reported that the method of sale set up by Col..Roosevelt "met with the universal approval of businessmen, besides netting the Government an immense increase in revenue."[29]

Another duty of the Assistant Secretary was to be the surrogate of the Secretary in his absence. Not long after Ted was appointed, Secretary Denby was called away from Washington and Ted had to take his place at a cabinet meeting. The meeting took place in the Cabinet Room of the White House, and was a first for the new Assistant Secretary. The Navy had requested that the censorship requirements for messages dispatched over naval radios be lifted if the message was purely of a commercial nature. A change of procedure involving a security matter required cabinet approval. Ted's argument to lift the official scrutiny impressed the cabinet enough that authorization for the change was given. It was just thirty-three years previously that Teddy, as Assistant Secretary of the Navy, had attended his first cabinet meeting.[30]

Mrs. Theodore Roosevelt, Jr. was a very special woman, and her husband knew it. Like Ted, she was energetic and opinionated about some things, and at times stubborn, but she was very intelligent and completely loyal to Ted and the Sagamore Hill branch of the extended family. Having complete confidence in her judgment, on July 19, 1921, Ted signed a document transferring to her all of his assets, thereby turning over to his wife the job of handling the family investments. Eleanor felt that with her limited financial experience she was not competent to handle the job on her own, so she sought the advice of Walter Janney, an old family friend and former partner of Ted's in the investment banking business. Placing Eleanor in charge of the family finances did not seem of much consequence to Ted at the time, but as events unfolded it was one of the smartest and luckiest things he ever did.[31]

While the Great War was over and most countries were reducing the size of their military, there was a warship building race going on between the United States, Britain, Japan, and, to a lesser extent, France and Italy. It was like "keeping up with the Jones'" when it came to battleships (a.k.a. capital ships) and other large combat types, such as battle cruisers and aircraft carriers. In the early '20s the world was not yet suffering from the coming economic depression, but the cost of World War I had been enormous and there was a widespread clamor within the United States to reduce government spending. None of the nations involved in the arms race fiasco had sufficient funds to engage in such a costly game. The British had previously made some vague overtures to the US concerning some type of naval reduction, but nothing came of it. Then, in December of 1920, Senator William Borah, "The Lion of Idaho," with the encouragement of some of the other senators, got a resolution through Congress encouraging the President to call a conference aimed at ending the naval arms race.[32]

Early in July 1921, the United States notified Great Britain through diplomatic channels that it was interested in arranging an international conference in the fall to work toward the reduction of naval arms. The U.S. Navy would of necessity be central to any such conference. Before being officially notified that the conference was to be held, TRJr, in a precept to the General Board of the Navy, asked for a study and corresponding report to be made concerning the naval strength required to maintain the current diplomatic policies of the United States. In making the study and report, Ted instructed the board to be guided by five general principles:

1. The United States will not consent to the limitation of its sovereign power.

2. The United States will continue to maintain the Monroe Doctrine.

3. The United States will not consent to any limitations of its Navy that might imperil any part of its territory or the citizens thereof.

4. The United States must have at all times a sufficient force to insure unimpeded lanes of communication for its commerce.

5. The United States must be in a position to maintain its policies and the rights of its citizens in any country where they may be jeopardized.[33]

In complying with Ted's request, the Board concluded that Japan was an aggressor nation whose goal was the eventual economic and political domination of the Far East, and recommended that the U.S. Navy maintain a strength equal to that of Britain and twice that of Japan.

Responding to the congressional resolution, President Harding instructed Secretary of State Charles Evans Hughes to proceed with setting up the conference and to personally act as chief negotiator in behalf of the Unites States. Secretary of the Navy Denby told Ted Roosevelt to assist Hughes in any way he could. Secretary Hughes formulated a plan that, at the very opening of the conference, he would show the good faith of the U.S. by committing the country to making drastic and specific reductions in its naval strength, provided the other participating nations were willing to make similar reductions. With this in mind, Hughes and Ted kept pressing the General Board for specific reduction proposals in terms of tonnage and/or number and types of ships. Over the period of the next several weeks, the Board made a number of reports that were rejected by Secretary Hughes because the cuts proposed were not drastic enough to convince the other nations that the U.S. was sincere in wanting a reduction in naval arms.

By October, Hughes had worked so much with Ted on the upcoming conference and on reducing the size of the Navy that he considered the Assistant Secretary to be indispensable to the project. President Harding had a committee of technical experts formed to advise the U.S. Delegates, and then chose Ted to chair the committee. Secretary Hughes protested, telling the President that TRJr had irreplaceable knowledge of what they were trying to accomplish and must be available to assist the Secretary of State. Harding replied that Ted would just have to serve in both capacities.[34]

With Ted's help, and with the aid of Admiral Robert Coontz, the Chief of Naval Operations, and Coontz's assistant, Captain William Pratt, the final proposal to present to the conferees was drafted. Hughes ordered the contents of the proposition, and even the fact that the U.S. had a proposal to present, to remain top secret. The conference got underway in Washington D.C. on November 12th. Delegates from the five major participants, as well as delegates from Portugal, China, Holland, and Belgium were in attendance. The proceedings began normally, with a minister leading prayer followed by a brief welcome by President Harding. Then Secretary of State Hughes went to the podium and reminded the delegates of the failures of previous arms limitation conferences and told them that the way to accomplish the purpose of the meeting was to do it "now!" Then he outlined the U.S. plan, which essentially was:

- That all warship construction would immediately cease, and that no replacement tonnage shall be laid down for ten years.

- That with respect to capital ship tonnage, the U.S. be limited to 500,000 tons, Britain to 500,000 tons and Japan to 300,000 tons.

- Subject to the ten-year moratorium and the tonnage limit, capital ships may be replaced when they are twenty years old.

- No replacement capital ship shall have a tonnage in excess of 35,000 tons.

- The U.S. would immediately scrap 845,000 tons of warships to consist of fifteen battleships presently under construction, and fifteen older battleships, provided the other counties did likewise.

The U. S. proposal also included limits on auxiliary vessels, including cruisers, destroyers, and submarines

The onlookers in the galleries were on their feet cheering and clapping before Mr. Hughes finished. The extensive specific proposals made by Hughes caught the delegates from the other countries completely by surprise. They had expected generalities followed by long weeks of negotiations. It was now obvious to all that the United States was very serious about naval arms reduction. There was real hope the arms race would end and a lasting peace would come about. Ted said it was one of the most dramatic moments he had ever witnessed. The British turned red and then pale. The Japanese just sat there expressionless.[35]

One of the first things the conferees did was to form a joint committee of technical experts from the various countries to discuss purely technical matters among themselves. It was the thought that each country's experts on the committee would consult with his respective delegates, and thus help each participant better understand the points of view of the other participating nations on technical, as opposed to a political, matters. Ted was chosen to chair the joint committee.

It soon became obvious to all that no agreement could be reached on auxiliary ships (cruisers, destroyers, and submarines) because of the extremely divergent views of France and Great Britain. Even though the French could not afford the naval arms race, they spoke with their heart rather than their head, as they are prone to do, maintaining that their national honor was at stake and they could never agree to limit these types of vessels when they didn't have enough at the time to properly defend themselves. Because of her bad experience with German submarines during the war, Britain wanted to severely limit the allowable tonnage for submarines, or even prohibit them altogether. The main focus of the conference was, therefore, on battleships and aircraft carriers.[36]

The Japanese suggested the same ratio apply to both carriers and battleships, but demanded a 10–10–7 ratio (meaning that for every 10 tons of weight for this ship type the U.S. and the UK had, the Japanese could have 7 tons) rather than the 5–5–3 ratio proposed by Secretary Hughes. They also wanted to retain the battleship Mutsu, which was practically completed. In fact, it already had about five hundred sea miles on its hull. The money for building the Mutsu had been donated by the working people and school children of Japan. To allow Japan to complete and retain this ship would increase its total capital ship tonnage by 25,000 tons. The British disagreed with the 35,000-ton limitation on battleships, claiming that a capital ship with sixteen-inch guns could not be constructed in a manner in which it could properly defend itself against submarines, mines, and aircraft with such a small weight limitation. The minimum weight required should be 37,000 to 38,000 tons the British said.

After weeks of back and forth negotiations and proposals and counter-proposals, Ted suggested to Secretary Hughes that the U.S. agree to let Japan complete and retain the Mutsu, provided they would scrap the Settsu. This would increase the Japanese capital ship tonnage to a total of 315,000 tons. In return the U.S. would complete the battleships Colorado and Washington and retain them in the fleet. Both ships were already in advanced stages of construction. After the two new battleships were completed, the U.S. would then scrap two of its older battleships, thus bringing its total capital ship tonnage to 525,000 tons. In this way the five to three ratio with Japan would be maintained. Ted personally met with the Japanese delegation and they agreed to his proposal.[37]

After considering the matter further, the British proposed to construct two new battleships of the 37,000-ton class and scrap four older battleships, provided the weight limit for future construction was raised to 37,000 tons. Ted met with the American technical experts to discuss the British suggestion. They saw no problem with this, and the U.S. agreed to the British counter proposal.

When the subject of tonnage limits on capital ships in the French and Italian fleets came up, it looked for a while like the French would take such an unreasonable position that the conference would break up. Finally, though, the conferees, including the French, agreed to a 175,000-ton limit for France and Italy.[38]

In the early twenties, there was much disagreement among navy men as to whether the aircraft carrier had or would replace the battleship as the most important class of combat vessels. At that time aircraft were able to fly only relatively short distances, the bomb load planes could carry was light, and bomb sights were poor to non-existent. However, in the summer of 1921, aircraft bombs dropped in tests proved that airplanes could sink anchored and undefended old battleships. Ted Roosevelt had a definite opinion on the matter. Testifying before a congressional committee he said:

> The capital ship forms the body of the Navy in the same way that the Infantry forms the body of the Army. In order to function properly both capital ship and Infantry have to have vitally necessary auxiliary or complementary arms, but nevertheless, both remain the body of our respective services, and in final analysis, the old maxim about the Infantry that I think was put forward by Napoleon and other numerous gentlemen in the past, holds true of the capital ship ****The Infantry is the Army *** when the Infantry is defeated the Army is defeated. ****That, in my opinion, holds good of the capital ship in the Navy.[39].

Most of the top navy brass agreed with Ted's view.

When the delegates got around to the issue of aircraft carrier tonnage, they were aware that a normal size carrier would weigh from 25,000 to 30,000 tons, and they fixed the maximum allowances at 135,000 tons for the U.S. and Britain, 81,000 tons for Japan, and 60,000 tons for France and Italy. The maximum weight of any individual carrier was fixed at 27,000 tons.

At that particular time, the United States had under construction two battle cruisers which, if completed, would weigh about 43,000 tons each, way over the tonnage limit. These ships could, however, be converted to aircraft carriers with each one weighing only 33,000 tons. Ted and the U.S. Technical Advisors recommended to Secretary Hughes and the other American Delegates that an exception be requested to allow the conversion of these two battle cruiser hulls to carriers. Britain responded to this by saying that if the U.S. converted two hulls, they also wanted to convert two. Secretary Hughes, Senators Underwood and Root, and the other U.S. delegates decided to forget the whole thing and just scrap the hulls. When TR Jr learned what the delegates planned to do, he met with them and, with fire in his eyes, told them we would be foolish to scrap these two ships when they could easily be converted to aircraft carriers, and that "we might just as well make up our mind that we will be without these all important craft for the next decade." After Ted's impassioned plea, Mr. Hughes and the other U.S. delegates relented, and it was written into the final treaty that any of the parties could construct two carriers weighing as much as 33,000 tons, but that all others were limited to 27,000 tons.[40]

Thanks to Ted Roosevelt, these two carriers were saved from the scrap heap. After construction was completed they were commissioned in 1927 as the USS Lexington (CV-2) and the USS Saratoga (CV-3). Fourteen years later, when Pearl Harbor was attacked, both vessels were still a part of the U.S. Navy's very limited aircraft carrier force. After participating in raids against Japanese held island installations early in World War II, the Lexington was sunk by Japanese bombs and torpedoes in May 1942 during the Battle of the Coral Sea, but not before her planes sank a Japanese flattop and severely damaged two others. During the war the Saratoga took part in numerous raids against Japanese installations. Her aviators sank one enemy carrier, and severely damaged a number of cruisers and other warships. She was herself extensively damaged in three different engagements. After V-J Day, the Saratoga, proudly displaying her seven Battle Stars, performed her last war-related service, bringing home nearly thirty thousand servicemen from the Pacific Theater. Today she rests at the bottom of Bikini Lagoon.

What motivated Ted to fight so hard for the two hulls to be completed as carriers is a mystery, particularly in view of his personal opinion that the battleship was still king. Of course he saw firsthand the advantages of aircraft during his service in the Great War, and he may have been influenced by some of the young carrier advocates he was associated with in the Navy Department. At the time of the Japanese attack on Pearl Harbor, there were only seven fleet carriers in the entire U.S. arsenal of warships. One can only speculate as to what course World War II would have taken in the Pacific had the United States begun that conflict without the services of "Lady Lex," and "Sara."

Later in the conference, after the matter of aircraft carriers was agreed upon, the Big Three took up the issue of fortification of island possessions in the Pacific area. The delegates quickly agreed that the status quo would be maintained. The United States agreed not to fortify any possession west of Hawaii, including the Philippine Islands and Guam. The British were not to fortify anything north of Australia and east of Singapore. In thinking over the proposed agreement with respect to island fortifications, Ted realized that under the terms of the tentative agreement that had been made, Japan would be free to fortify any Pacific Island she might acquire in the future. When he brought this to the attention of the Secretary of State, Mr. Hughes in turn met with the Japanese and an understanding was reached that no future Japanese island acquisitions would be fortified.[41]

After the delegates had finished their work and made informal agreements on the number and tonnage of battleships and carriers, and on fortification of the Pacific Islands, the next order of business was the drawing up of a document accurately expressing the understandings arrived at by the participants. TRJr was appointed Chairman of the committee that was assigned the job of drafting the treaty. Naturally, there were many lawyers and technical experts on the committee, but Ted, with the assistance of Admiral William Pratt and Dr. George Grafton Wilson, an international law professor at Harvard, authored most of the document. They strove to write the agreement in plain, understandable English, and to make it as compact as possible. After the agreement was completed, it was executed by the participants, then ratified by the U.S. Senate, and in March, 1922, it became a binding pact between the participating nations. In later years, the Treaty was renounced by Japan and became naught to all parties, but it was an important diplomatic and foreign policy agreement for the decade following its enactment.[42]

Relations between the United States and Japan improved immediately after the Treaty was signed, but with the U.S. passage of the Immigration Act of 1924, excluding Orientals from immigrating to the States, relations began to sour and continued to deteriorate until the conclusion of World War II.

In 1927, Great Britain, the United States, and Japan met in Geneva in hopes of further agreements limiting warships. The U.S. and Britain could not agree on cruiser numbers and the conference was a total failure. In '29 the same powers met in the London Conference. This time the participants did agree on a 10–10–7 ratio with respect to cruisers and other smaller warships, even though practically all U.S. Naval Officers opposed raising the ratio for the Japanese with respect to these ship types. The 1929 Treaty was said by many to have been strictly a political ploy and was, therefore, very controversial within the United States. The weakness of the United States Navy at the time of the Japanese attack on Pearl Harbor was to some extent attributable to the Washington and London Conferences.[43]

With the Arms Limitation Treaty in place, there was great contentment in the United States. It appeared there was no chance of a major armed conflict for years to come. Congress had its mind on other matters, and was in no mood to appropriate money to the military. TRJr said that Congress was plagued by "soft-headed pacifists" with an "Alice in Wonderland" mentality." At least Will Rogers, the great American humorist, wasn't fooled, he said that the purpose of the Arms Limitation Conference was to make war less expensive.

In the remaining $2\frac{1}{2}$ years he served as Assistant Secretary of the Navy, Ted spent a great deal of his time encouraging Congress to keep the Navy strong and at full treaty strength. He lobbied congressmen, made speeches, and wrote magazine articles advocating a Navy adequate for the defense of the nation. He was instrumental in the holding of the first "Navy Day," in an effort to aid the Navy's public image. In a letter he wrote concerning Navy Day, Ted stated:

> The people of the seaboard are reasonably familiar with the Navy. They see the great ships. They know the Navy men. In the interior of our country, it is, however, a different story. The people of Kansas and Oklahoma do not get the opportunity for first hand information that their fellow-countrymen of California and New York do. They do not realize that the Navy serves them equally with the people of the seaboard.[44]

Later in 1922 there was a serious move in Congress to reduce the total Naval enlisted personnel from the requested 96,000 down to 65,000. Ted, like his father, believed that the best way to maintain peace was to be militarily strong. An aggressor nation was not likely to attack a country well prepared to defend itself. He said that to cut the naval manpower to that extent would reduce our world status and "would be a national disaster." To counter the proponents of reduction in naval personnel, Ted testified before the House Naval Affairs Committee, and lined up two congressmen favorable to a strong Navy to address the full House of Representatives. Additionally, he spoke before the National Press Club, and got President Harding to write a letter to the Speaker of the House, stating that the naval enlisted personnel should not be reduced below 86,000. When the naval funding bill was finally passed by Congress, the President's 86,000-man recommendation was approved. While Ted was not happy with a 10,000-man cut, he knew that the manpower approved was at least sufficient to maintain a reasonably strong Navy.[45]

In the fall of 1922 tragedy struck the Oyster Bay Roosevelts with the death of Richard Derby Jr., the son of Ted's sister and brother-in-law, Ethel and Dick Derby. The whole family was deeply saddened. Ted wrote a touching letter to Ethel and Dick, telling them that their boy was now safe with TR and Quentin, and that one day they would all be together again.[46]

As if gazing into a crystal ball, in the early '20s Ted predicted that one day Japan would attack the United States. Based on this forecast, he ordered the General Board of the Navy to study the Pacific area and make a recommendation as to what the general strategy of the United States should be in the event of a war in the

Pacific at some future date. In 1923, after completing its work, the Board again reported that any war in the Pacific would almost certainly be with Japan. As a peacetime strategy, the Board advised that: the base facilities in and around Pearl Harbor should be expanded, all new warships should be built with the ability to operate trans-Pacifically; Manila and Guam should be fortified as much as the naval arms treaty permits so that these bases could hold out until reinforcements arrived; an expeditionary force should be kept ready to reinforce Manila and Guam as soon as war broke out; mobile docking and repair equipment should be kept ready for distant operations; and good relations with other nations in the Pacific area, such as Australia, China, Holland and Russia, should be maintained. If a war with Japan did in fact break out, the Board recommended that U.S. tactics should include the immediate reinforcement or re-taking of Manila, a complete blockade of the Japanese mainland, and any other action indicated should be taken, such as bombing Japan, or engaging the enemy fleet.[47] In a letter Ted wrote to the General Board, he stated:

> After the fall of the Philippines, there will unquestionably be an almost irresistible demand from the people of the United States to have our Fleet, numerically superior, proceed at once to Asiatic waters and force an engagement. It is more than probable that this demand will have to be acceded to *****.[48]

As history actually unfolded, at the outbreak of World War II the U. S. Pacific fleet was not superior to the Japanese fleet. Neither Ted nor the General Board foresaw in 1923 that World War II would immediately involve the United States in two different theaters of operation, Pacific and European, on two different oceans, Pacific and Atlantic. While the American public was not immediately informed of the full extent of the losses from the Japanese attacks at Pearl Harbor and in the Philippines, it was told that the losses were severe. Most Americans realized that an immediate counter blow against Japan was not practical. Ted's prediction as to a public clamor for an immediate, devastating retaliation against Japan did not materialize. What public demand that did arise was satisfied by the 1942 Doolittle bombing raid against the Japanese homeland.

In 1912, President William Howard Taft signed an executive order setting aside two large tracts of public lands as oil reserves for the Navy, to be drilled only in case of an emergency. Both of these oil reserve properties lay in California and were designated as Naval Petroleum Reserve No. 1, which consisted of about 39,000 acres, and Naval Petroleum Reserve No. 2, which was of about 30,000 acres. Naval Petroleum Reserve No. 3, of approximately 10,000 acres, at Teapot

Dome, Wyoming, was created under the administration of President Woodrow Wilson in 1915.

Geological tests and reports done in 1920 indicated that the pressure in the underground oil reserve was dropping because wells on adjoining property were pumping out some of the Navy's emergency oil supply.

During the last year of the Wilson presidency, a federal law was passed placing the complete control of the Naval Oil Reserves into the hands of the Secretary of the Navy. The administrations of Teddy Roosevelt (1901–1908), William Howard Taft (1909–1912), and Woodrow Wilson (1913–1920), that immediately preceded the Warren Harding presidency, were all very supportive of the conservation of the country's natural resources. When Warren Harding ran for President, he campaigned on a promise to take the government out of private business and put good business practices back into government. When he was elected, things changed drastically with respect to conservation of natural resources. One of the first things he did after taking office was to appoint Albert Fall Secretary of the Interior. Fall was from New Mexico and, prior to his appointment, had been in the U.S. Senate. He had vast mining and land interests, and an abysmal record on conservation-related matters. No more than a month after Harding's inauguration, Fall and Secretary of the Navy Denby met and agreed that the best way to handle the depleting naval oil reserves was to lease the lands to private oil interests for drilling. The Navy would then benefit by receiving a landowner's share of the oil pumped out. Denby decided that since the Navy Department did not ordinarily deal in oil leases, it would be appropriate to first transfer the naval petroleum reserve properties to the Department of the Interior, since that department was accustomed to handling all types of leases. Secretary Fall drew up a proposed executive order for President Harding to sign transferring the oil properties to the Interior Department. Secretary Denby routinely sent a copy of the document to Assistant Naval Secretary Roosevelt. This was the first knowledge Ted had of the imminent transfer and leasing of the oil reserves. Not being well versed on the oil situation, Roosevelt consulted with Admiral Robert Griffin, the Chief of Engineering of the Navy, for advice about the matter. Griffin convinced Ted that the transfer and leasing would be a mistake.[49]

After his talk with the Admiral, Ted met with Secretary Denby and advised him against the transfer. Denby responded that, even though the executive order had not actually been signed by the President, it was a done deal, and it was too late to back out. Consulting again with the Admiral, and a number of other knowledgeable naval officers, Ted decided that if the Navy Department could get the proposed executive order amended to the extent that the Navy's consent must be obtained before any leasing or drilling could occur, the oil reserves would be sufficiently protected from exploitation by private oil interests. Denby agreed to

Ted's proposed change provided Secretary Fall also agreed. When the Interior Secretary consented to the charge, Ted delivered the amended executive order to President Harding, who, finding nothing objectionable, promptly affixed his signature. Ted heard no more about the matter for about a year.[50]

Before World War I, when Ted was a partner in Montgomery, Clothier & Tyler investment bankers, the firm had aided in the financing of Sinclair Oil Co. At that time Ted acquired some stock in the Sinclair Company and was elected to its Board of Directors. When he went off to the army, he sold his stock and resigned his directorship. In the spring of 1919, after his release from active military service, TRJr was promptly re-appointed to the Sinclair Oil Co. Board, and wasted no time in using his influence as a board member to get his brother Archie a job with the company. Ted resigned his position as a director in August, '19, prior to entering the race for a seat in the New York General Assembly. A short time after the November election, Ted and Eleanor bought a thousand shares of Sinclair Oil stock at a price of $25.00 per share but he did not seek, nor was he re-appointed to the Board of Directors.

In late spring of '22, after managing the Navy's battle with Congress to prevent the reduction in its enlisted strength, Ted took a week off and went out of town for some fishing. When he returned, the newspapers were full of a story about how the Navy's oil reserve land at Teapot Dome, Wyoming, had been leased to Mammoth Oil Co., a subsidiary of Harry Sinclair's, Sinclair Oil Company. When news of the leasing arrangement became public, Sinclair Oil stock immediately jumped $10 per share. When TRJr read about the leasing of the naval oil reserve land and of the increase in the value of Sinclair stock, he was extremely upset, telling his wife:

> My political career is over and done with. That land has been leased to Sinclair and I didn't know about it. The Sinclair Oil Company stock has jumped ten points on the strength of the lease, and we own a thousand shares. I can never explain it. People will think my price is ten thousand dollars and will never believe the truth.[51]

When Eleanor got him calmed down, she reminded him that in July, 1921, he had legally transferred all his assets to her and placed her in sole charge of managing the family finances. She then gave him the wonderful news that she had sold all their Sinclair Oil stock several months before the oil reserve land had been leased, at a loss of four dollars per share and that she still had the sales slip to prove it. Ted's face lit up like a light, and he exclaimed, "Thank God, thank God!" While the oil reserve leasing scandal remained in the news, Ted did not feel it involved him because all their stock in Sinclair Oil had been previously sold. He had no more personal concerns about it for nearly two years.[52]

As the full story came out, the public learned that in July 1921, a portion of the Naval Oil Reserve property in California had been leased to Pan American Oil Company; a business owned by oil tycoon, Edward L. Doheny. The government's decision to lease this particular property had been made during the administration of Woodrow Wilson. The offer to lease the tract had been publicly advertised and competitive bids were required. Pan American Oil had simply been the highest bidder. The Navy Department benefited monetarily from the transaction, and there was little criticism from the general public or the press.

In April, a short time after the inauguration of Warren Harding, the Department of Interior, under Secretary Fall, leased the entire Teapot Dome reserve to Harry Sinclair's company, and also leased some additional acreage in the California reserve to Doheny. Secretary of the Navy Denby consented to both of these new leases, even though there had been no pre-lease publicity, nor had there been any competitive bids required or received. *The Denver Post* originally broke the story, claiming that Sinclair had received a "gift" of the valuable oil reserve property. Many other newspapers, including the *Wall Street Journal, Rocky Mountain News, Denver Times,* and *New Mexico State Tribune,* soon took up the outcry.[53]

Even though Sinclair's Mammoth Oil Co. had a government lease on the Teapot Dome reserve, there was a complication. Lee Darden, one of Warren Harding's friends and supporters, was trespassing on the property and illegally pumping out oil. President Harding met with the man and advised him to stop pumping and vacate the property, but Darden reasoned that he had paid for the right to pump the oil by his campaign contributions to Harding and continued his illegal activities. At this point, Secretary Fall contacted Ted and told him President Harding wanted him to send a detachment of Marines to Teapot Dome and forcibly evict Mr. Darden. Ted met with General John Lejeune, the Marine Corps Commandant, and asked him to send a small detail to Wyoming and place Mr. Darden and his drilling crew off of the oil reserve property. In early August, 1921, a detachment of five armed Marines accompanied by several Department of Interior officials and two newsmen, peacefully evicted. Darden and his crew, and then placed "No Trespassing" signs on the property.[54]

About a month after the public gained knowledge of the Sinclair lease and the second Doheny lease, a Washington D.C. attorney named Harry Slattery made an appointment to see Assistant Secretary Roosevelt. Slattery, a staunch conservationist, had worked in a low-level job for the Inland Waterway Commission during Teddy Roosevelt's administration. When, during their conversation, Slattery brought up Secretary Fall's poor conservation record, Ted became very defensive and told Slattery that Fall had been one of his father's

Rough Riders, had made his father's nominating speech at the 1916 Republican convention, and was a good friend of the Roosevelt family. The conversation became more heated when Slattery let Ted know he disapproved of Ted's having presented the amended executive order to Harding for his signature, and also told Ted that Fall "would turn over the naval oil reserves to private interests in the oil industry." At this point, Ted became very angry and ordered the man to get out of his office.[55]

Mr. Slattery, over the years, was closely aligned with Gifford Pinchot, the famous early twentieth century environmental conservationist, who also deplored the oil reserve leases. Working with Slattery, Robert M. La Follette, a conservation minded, Progressive-Republican Senator, got Senate approval of a resolution calling for the Senate Public Lands Committee to investigate all aspects of the naval oil leases. Within a few weeks after La Follette's resolution passed, Albert Fall resigned as Secretary of the Interior.

Herbert Hoover and Theodore Roosevelt, Jr. had at least three things in common. Hoover was Secretary of Commerce, so they were both cabinet officials. They were both young and in a sense carried the Republican Party's hope for the future. And they both felt that their political party was stagnating under the immoral and ineffective Harding. As proof of the decline of the Grand Old Party, they only had to look at the losses suffered in the 1922 off-year elections. Ted and Hoover met privately in '23, and they came to the conclusion that to recover its losses the Party needed a constructive, more progressive program for the 1924 elections. Working together, they put their thoughts and suggestions for such an agenda in the form of a memo, which Ted promptly sent to the President for his consideration. Harding wasted no time in rejecting the proposals and letting Ted know that, in his opinion, such revisions in the Party's goals and strategy were not warranted. The young assistant secretary did not take the President's denial well, writing in his private journal:

> The President is fooling himself. He thinks that the last autumnal elections were not a repudiation of the national administration . . . he plans to make about fifteen speeches this summer and expects that to arouse interest and support for the party. He can't possibly do this unless he can change his entire method of expression, for no one knows when he is through with a speech what he means.[56]

By the spring of 1923, Ted was considering his political options. What he really wanted to do was continue along in his father's footsteps and become Governor of New York, but at that time some progressive Republicans in the West were encouraging President Harding to place Ted on the 1924 Republican ticket as the

Vice Presidential nominee in lieu of Calvin Coolidge, the incumbent Vice President. Besides the westerners, many of the old line conservative Republicans from New York were also prodding the President to put Ted on the ticket. It wasn't because his fellow New Yorkers were progressive, or because they were Ted Roosevelt fans that they wanted him on the national ticket, but because he had alienated them with his independent, somewhat liberal philosophy that first surfaced when he was in the General Assembly. They still considered him to be a mutineer and did not want to have to deal with him as Governor. If he was on the national ticket, he could not run for governor. Although still undecided, Ted began to make frequent appearances in New York City as a speaker at various events and political rallies, and to travel to Albany to meet with influential Republicans in hopes of gaining their support if he chose to seek the gubernatorial nomination.[57]

In mid-summer, President Harding, accompanied by Secretary of Commerce Herbert Hoover, made an extended visit to the Western States. While on their trip, the President startled Secretary Hoover by asking him:

If you knew of a great scandal in our administration would you for the good of the country and the party expose it publicly or would you bury it?

Hoover answered that something of this nature should be revealed to the public. Whether Harding was referring to the Teapot Dome ignominy that was developing or some other disgraceful happening during his term is unknown. In August, while still in the West, President Harding suddenly and unexpectedly died, apparently of a stroke or a heart attack. The dour, taciturn Calvin Coolidge was now President of the United States.

Ted traveled to Albany in the latter part of September and conferred with Eddie Machold, then the Speaker of the New York General Assembly. Machold had earlier been a probable candidate for the Republican nomination for governor, but in this meeting he told Ted that he had about decided not to run. The Speaker and the Assistant Secretary then had a serious "what if" discussion about their political ambitions and possibilities. Their talk went along the line of: what if they joined forces and essentially took political control of the State of New York? If Ted was elected governor in 1924 and then re-elected in '26, they would certainly be a dominating force at the 1928 Republican National Convention should Ted decide to make a bid for the Republican presidential nomination. While no definite commitments were made, quite naturally Ted was intrigued with the idea. He returned to Washington thinking that the supposition he and Machold talked about just might materialize, and probably also thinking about his dad and the father-son presidents, John Adams and John Quincy Adams.[58]

A great deal of preliminary work had been done by the Senate Public Lands

Committee before October 1923 when the hearings on the oil reserve leases finally began. While not the committee chairman, Senator Thomas Walsh, a Democrat from Montana, was a member of the Committee and took the part of lead dog during the hearings. Ted was one of the first witnesses called to testify. Knowing that his boss, Navy Secretary Denby, was very much involved in the oil leases, and not wanting to run out on him, Ted was truthful but very reserved in what he said. He briefly answered the questions asked of him, but he did not volunteer any information. When he read an account of his testimony in the newspapers the next day, he realized he should have been more forthcoming, and voluntarily went back before the Committee to give a more detailed account of what he knew about the matter. As far as Ted was concerned, he had now done his duty and the matter was finished. [59]

During the first three months of hearings, the committee uncovered nothing of major consequence. The witnesses that testified essentially said that in the event of an emergency, the Navy's oil supply was better assured by the private interest leases than by doing nothing and allowing the oil to be drained away by wells located just outside the boundaries of the reserve property. It appeared that the decision to lease the oil reserves made by Secretary of the Interior Albert Fall and Secretary of the Navy Edwin Denby, while unpopular with conservationists, was simply a judgment call on their part, which they were authorized by law to make.

By late '23, Archie Roosevelt had been working with Sinclair Oil Company for nearly five years and had done very well for himself. His job involved him with his employer's overseas interests, and he had made a number of trips to the Near East on company business. Mr. Sinclair was so pleased with Archie's job performance that he had made him a vice president of the company and raised his salary to $15,000 per year.

As the new year approached, Archie became suspicious of some of Harry Sinclair's business dealings in general and with the Teapot Dome oil lease in particular. In the middle of January, Sinclair told Archie that he was worried about the Senate Investigating Committee and instructed Archie to book him (Sinclair) passage to Europe on the next available ship, but to make the reservation under an assumed name. After Sinclair departed, Archie got up the nerve to talk with G. D. Wahlberg, Mr. Sinclair's confidential secretary, and point blank asked him if their boss had bribed Secretary of the Interior Fall in order to procure the Teapot Dome oil lease. Wahlberg replied that there was crooked business going on, that he thought someone had lent Mr. Fall some money, and that he was especially concerned about payments totaling $68,000 that Sinclair made to the foreman of Albert Fall's ranch. Wahlberg added that he had the cancelled checks to prove it. On Friday, January 17th, immediately after talking to Wahlberg, an excited Archie called up Ted in Washington from the Sinclair Oil headquarters in New York, and told him he needed to see him right away about a matter that he could not discuss on the phone. Ted was scheduled to speak in New York that very night, so the brothers arranged to meet privately after Ted finished his address. As soon as they got together, Archie told his brother that his suspicions of the Teapot Dome lease had been confirmed by his conversation with the confidential secretary and that Harry Sinclair had fled the country under an assumed name.[60]

Involved with Sinclair Oil as he was, Archie would at some point be called on to testify before the Senate Committee investigating the oil leases, but he had not yet even received a subpoena. There was no question that Archie would testify truthfully. The question was, should he wait to be subpoenaed or voluntarily appear before the committee as soon as possible? Archie planned to resign his job, but he had a family to support and physical disabilities from his war injury. Prospective employers might consider him to be a whistle blower for testifying against his employer and be hesitant to hire him. Realizing the serious consequences to Archie, Ted sought the advice of Alice's husband, Representative Nick Longworth, and her friend and alleged lover, Senator William Borah, as well as Senator Frank Brandegee. Ted then told Archie that if he failed to come forward voluntarily, his honesty and integrity would be impugned. Archie agreed, and he and his wife Grace went back to Washington with Ted on Sunday. That afternoon, TRJr called Senator Walsh, the workhorse of the committee, and arranged for Archie to appear as a witness the very next morning.[61]

Having gotten Archie scheduled to testify, Ted's thoughts turned to Mr. Wahlberg and getting him to testify as soon as possible to substantiate Archie's testimony. Ted was concerned that Sinclair, or someone acting on his behalf, might get to Wahlberg with some kind of threat, bribe, or intimidation. Archie knew Wahlberg's telephone number and the name of the street he lived on in New York, but he did not know his house number or apartment number. After calling Wahlberg's telephone number several times and getting no answer, Ted called an acquaintance, William J. Burns, Director of the Bureau of Investigation (predecessor of the FBI) and owner of Burns International Detective Agency. After telling Burns what Archie had said, Ted asked him if he could find Wahlberg and have him call Ted's home. Burns assured Ted he would find the man and have him phone. A couple of hours later, Ted's phone rang and it was Mr. Wahlberg. He spoke first with Archie. Archie told him that he should come to Washington and testify before the Senate Committee the next day, but the Confidential Secretary refused, saying that he had a family to support and would lose his job. Ted then got on the line and told him that he was setting a poor example for his children, and anyway the Committee was bound to subpoena him after they heard what Archie had to say. In a quivering voice, Wahlberg finally agreed to catch the early train to Washington the next morning and come before the Senate Committee.[62]

After Mr. Wahlberg hung up, Ted, Eleanor, Archie and Grace discussed how scared and hesitant the man was. They speculated that when Wahlberg didn't show up for work Monday morning someone at Sinclair Oil might figure out where he was and try to intercept him when his train stopped in Baltimore. Grace knew Wahlberg and volunteered to travel to Baltimore very early the next morning, find him on the train, and stay with him until he arrived at the Senate Office Building, where the hearings were being held.[63]

Grace managed to find Mr. Wahlberg on the train and accompanied him to the hearing room. He was called to the stand immediately after Archie finished his testimony. Right in front of Wahlberg sat Mr. Stanchfield, one of Harry Sinclair's attorneys. Stanchfield never smiled or nodded to the witness but coldly stared directly into his eyes. Wahlberg's face had lost its color and his hands were quivering as he took the witness chair. After placing him under oath, Mr. Walsh asked him if he had knowledge of the check sent by Harry Sinclair to Albert Fall. Wahlberg turned red and was speechless for what seemed like an eternity, but was actually more like thirty seconds. There was no sound in the hearing room in anticipation of the answer. Finally Wahlberg shook his head no, and in almost a whisper said:

No, Senator, Mr. Roosevelt is mistaken, I never mentioned a check for sixty-eight thousand dollars. What I said was that Mr. Sinclair had sent Secretary Fall a present of six or eight cows and bulls.[64]

With this, the hearing room erupted. Committee members, reporters, spectators, attorneys, and senate pages were all talking at once. Everyone heard what the man said, but no one believed him. They all knew a scandal of major proportions was about to erupt. When order was restored, Archie was recalled to the stand and asked if he was sure he had heard Mr. Wahlberg correctly concerning the $68,000. His answer was,

Dead sure.[65]

At this point it was obvious to Ted that, even though he was innocent of any wrongdoing, he would be drawn into the middle of the controversy simply because his name was Roosevelt and he, as Assistant Secretary of the Navy, had been at the wrong place at the wrong time. He knew the matter would receive worldwide news coverage, and that his political plans had been dealt a serious blow. Even though the Teapot Dome matter was hanging over his head, TRJr was not completely politically dead. He continued to be in demand as a speaker. Over the spring and summer he appeared before numerous groups, including the Jewish

Philanthropic Society and the National Security League. Until, however, additional facts were disclosed by the committee, neither Ted nor the general public had any way of knowing the full extent of the Teapot Dome scandal.

When the full oil reserve leasing story came out, it developed that Harry Sinclair had made what he claimed to be a loan to Albert Fall in the amount of $25,000 and that he had paid Fall an additional $10,000 as expenses for a trip to Europe. Sinclair also purchased an interest in a ranch Fall owned for the exorbitant price of $233,000. In addition to Sinclair's "loan," expense advance, and purchase, Edward Doheny had made an alleged "loan" to Mr. Fall in the sum of $100,000.[66]

No creditable evidence was ever developed concerning the $68,000 Wahlberg told Archie about. What the truth is about this aspect of the case remains a mystery.

FDR and the Hyde Park camp were jumping with joy. Louis Howe, one of Franklin's most loyal and trusted advisors, wrote him a memo saying, "I am sending you clippings from which you will see that little Ted appears to be down and out as a candidate for governor." A few days later, in another note, he said, "This will amuse you, I hear sub rosa that Mrs. Ted has a fine bunch of Sinclair stock, and that knowledge led to the extreme haste in putting brother Archie on the stand. The general position of the newspaper boys is that politically he is as dead as King Tut, for the moment at least."[67]

As epilogue to Teapot Dome scandal, when Harry Sinclair returned from Europe he was subpoenaed before the committee, but refused to fully answer the questions posed to him. As a result, he was cited for contempt of the Senate and had to serve a ninety day jail sentence. He was, however, more forthcoming in a second appearance before the Committee. During a later criminal trial, Sinclair was again found guilty of contempt of court. A mistrial was declared in the case, however, when it came out that he had hired William Burns to have his detectives follow the jury members after they were released to go home at the completion of each day of the trial. Sinclair apparently hoped the detectives might see one or more of the jurors in some act of indiscretion to use on appeal, or perhaps even blackmail. In all, Sinclair served a total of six months in jail for the two contempt citations. After learning of Sinclair's hiring of Burns, Ted speculated that after he and Archie asked Burns to find Mr. Wahlberg, Burns did as they asked, but then pressured the terrified secretary to lie about the $68,000.

In a civil action, the federal government had the oil leases to Sinclair and Doheny set aside. While no criminal conduct was ever proven against Navy Secretary Denby, a demand for his resignation went up in Congress. Even though President Coolidge never asked for it, Denby bowed to the pressure and submitted his resignation. He returned to his home in Detroit where he was an admired and respected citizen, and where he died a few years later.

Several years after the scandal broke, Fall, Sinclair, and Doheny were tried and acquitted of criminal conspiracy. In a final trial held in 1929, Albert Fall was found guilty of accepting a bribe, was sentenced to a one-year term in the penitentiary, and ordered to pay a fine of $100,000. He thus became the first person convicted of a felony committed while sitting as a member of the President's Cabinet.

It is impossible to understand why Doheny and Sinclair were never charged with bribing a public official. If Albert Fall was guilty, Sinclair and/or Doheny had to be guilty. Teapot Dome remained the worst political disgrace in American history until replaced by the Watergate scandal that occurred during the Richard Nixon administration. The Democrats tried to use Teapot Dome against the Republicans for years to come, referring to the Grand Old Party as the Grand Oil Party. But it was the "roaring twenties," times were good in the U.S., and it did them little good. The Republicans remained in control of the White House until FDR and the Democrats took over after the 1932 elections.[68]

In early summer, the Senate Investigating Committee made a report that exonerated Ted Roosevelt of any wrongdoing in the Teapot Dome fiasco. But he had already been maligned by the national press and by some members of Congress because of the fact that he had formally been a shareholder and board member of Sinclair Oil, and had gotten his brother a job with that company. He was also criticized for having ordered the Marines to evict the trespasser from the Wyoming oil reserve land and for personally delivering the amended executive order to the President. There had even been a resolution introduced in the Senate asking him to resign; however, when voted on, it was overwhelmingly defeated. After being disparaged over and over for things he had innocently done, Ted was fed up. When he heard that Congressman William F. Stevenson of South Carolina had attacked him on the house floor for owning Sinclair Oil Co. stock at the time the Teapot Dome reserve was leased to Sinclair, he was ready to fight. This accusation was not true. Eleanor had sold all their Sinclair stock at a loss before the lease came about. Ted was very upset about this outright lie. Just as he was about to leave the house one morning, Ted told his spouse that the first thing he was going to do that day was find Representative Stevenson and beat the hell out of him. Eleanor could tell he was serious, and tried to talk him out of it by telling him that it would do no good and would only cause him to receive more bad publicity. Ted answered that he was still going to do it, "and to bloody hell with the consequences." Knowing her husband was about to make a big mistake that he would end up regretting, Eleanor called her sister-in-law, Alice Longworth. After Alice heard what was about to happen, she got her brother on the phone and told him that she knew Stevenson was a rat and deserved to be whipped, but she hoped Ted would take the man's glasses off before he hit him because the Congressman was very small and quite elderly. Disappointed, Ted said, "Oh, damn, then I suppose I can't do it." He did, however, issue a statement to the press explaining his former association with Sinclair Oil, and when and why he got Archie a job. His press release also stated:

Every crook should be punished regardless of politics or position. Equally crooked, however, with those who take bribes is he who, cloaking himself in Congressional immunity, willfully misrepresents facts in an endeavor to injure an innocent man. Regardless of politics, such a man should be held in strict account, and such a man is Congressman Stevenson of South Carolina.

In conclusion, Ted said in the article that fair play dictated that men such as Stevenson should be driven from public office. Nearly two thousand letters came in favorably responding to Ted's published statement, many of them from South Carolinians.[69]

TRJr was a delegate at the Republican National Convention held in the early summer of 1924. As Calvin Coolidge was receiving the GOP's nomination for President, Ted must have thought back a couple of years to the plans he and Eddie Machold made, and how he and Herbert Hoover had drawn up a proposed new platform for the Republican Party to make it more liberal and, hopefully, more attractive to the average voter, and how there had been a move on to replace Calvin Coolidge with him as Warren Harding's running mate. What if there had been no Teapot Dome scandal and Warren Harding was still alive? Things had certainly changed.[70]

Still undecided as to his future, Ted knew that Al Smith, the current New York Governor, was a candidate for the Democratic nomination for President. Smith was an extremely popular governor, but if he was his party's presidential nominee, he would no longer be a factor in the governor's race. In that scenario, the GOP candidate would have a much better chance to be elected. Ted had his fingers crossed as the Democratic National Convention got under way in midsummer. He was hopeful that Smith would be the presidential or vice presidential nominee.

Ted's wish was not to be. By this time the polio that had ravaged Franklin D. Roosevelt earlier had stabilized, and he had recovered as much as he would ever recover. At the Democrat Party's convention, FDR made his first major speech since his illness. Managing to stand at the podium with the help of braces and a crutch, he called for party unity and said, in part:

You equally who come from the great cities of the East and the plains and hills of the West, from the slopes of the Pacific and from the homes and fields of the Southland, I ask you *** to keep first in your hearts and minds the words of Abraham Lincoln *** 'With malice toward none, and charity for all.'

He then nominated Al Smith, "the Happy Warrior of the political battlefield," for President of the United States. The delegates were mesmerized by FDR's inspiring eloquence. When he finished his nominating speech, the clapping and cheering went on for over an hour. While Smith did not receive his party's nomination for either President or Vice-President, FDR emerged from the convention as the Democrat Party's bright young star for the future. With the incumbent governor now certain to run for re-election, Ted knew his chances to become the next Governor of New York were poor.[71]

With Smith back in the governor's race, Ted was convinced he should forget about being governor and stay in Washington if Coolidge would promise him a cabinet position, such as Secretary of War, or even keep him on as Assistant Secretary of the Navy. With this in mind, shortly after the Democrats ended their convention, Ted made an appointment to meet with the President for what he thought would be a serious discussion about his future with the administration. Writing about their meeting later, Ted stated:

> I said both administratively and politically I felt I ranked a cabinet position, if I was not going back to run for Governor of New York. He nodded his head and said he agreed with me.[72]

Coolidge, however, gave no indication that he would offer Ted a cabinet job, or even keep him on as an assistant secretary. Like Ted, no doubt the President was thinking back two years and the move to replace him with Ted as Harding's running mate. Coolidge may also have had a more sinister motive. He may have thought that if Ted was a candidate for governor of New York, even if he was defeated, it might help carry the State of New York into the Republican camp in the presidential election. Failing to get a positive response, Ted took the vague reply Coolidge gave him to be negative, and therefore felt his only chance to remain in the political forefront was to seek the Republican nomination for Governor of New York.[73]

Resuming his lobbying activities toward getting the GOP gubernatorial nomination, the discouraged, thirty-six year old Assistant Navy Secretary began traveling to Albany and other New York municipalities as often as possible, contacting as many business and political leaders as he could. A "Teddy for Governor Club" was formed. Alice assisted by using her considerable influence with well-connected New Yorkers. She successfully recruited a number of important people into her brother's camp, including Senator James Wadsworth,[74]

The New York State Republican Convention was scheduled to convene in early September. At first, it looked as if the gubernatorial nomination would boil down to a three- man race between Ted, Eddie Machold, who was Speaker of the

General Assembly, and William Haywood, the U.S. Attorney. All the Party old guard, except Senator Wadsworth, wanted Machold to be the candidate. Most of Ted's supporters encouraged him to go ahead and make an early announcement of his candidacy, but on the advice of Wadsworth he held back, and instead placed an open letter in the newspapers, stating, in part:

> It would be foolish for me or any other man to say he did not wish to be Governor of the great Empire State of New York. Next to the Presidency there is no greater office in the United States. What I do feel, however, even more that this, is that it is necessary to elect a Republican Governor this autumn.[75]

Ted and Eddie Machold were very good friends, and when they met three days before the convention, Ted reminded him of his 1922 promise that he would not oppose Ted in a campaign for governor. Shortly thereafter, Machold dropped out of the race, either because of his previous commitment to Ted or because he realized there was little to no chance of a Republican defeating Al Smith. Many of the party leaders felt that the only way to beat the popular Smith was to select a candidate that could cut into the predominately Democratic New York City vote, but they did not believe there was anyone in the GOP stable who could do that, including Ted. The party leaders feigned enthusiasm when Ted was nominated by Speaker Machold and then selected as the Republican candidate for Governor on the first ballot.

In his acceptance speech, Ted blasted the Democrats for making misleading promises and for their stand on the League of Nations. He also bragged on the Republicans for reducing taxes and aiding farmers, defended the GOP for its support of a protective tariff, promised sweeping reforms that would eliminate governmental extravagance, and vowed to further reduce taxes. He said he would work toward getting a bonus for the heirs of deceased veterans, work toward getting a forty-eight hour work week for women, and see that the Volstead Act (Prohibition Law) was strictly enforced.[76]

TRJr resigned his position as Assistant Secretary of the Navy and left Washington. Even though the family had actually resided in the nation's capital for the past $3\frac{1}{2}$ years, they had continued to pay rent on the house in Oyster Bay, so technically their legal residence was still in New York. Needing the peace and quiet to make plans for the upcoming campaign, Ted went back Oyster Bay.

How would history rate his performance as Assistant Secretary of the Navy? Obviously, he did an outstanding job on the Arms Limitation Treaty, and at least a good job in disposing of war surplus equipment, in maintaining adequate naval funding, and in preventing a drastic reduction in enlisted personnel. The gray-haired admirals and other officers he came in contact with at the Navy Department called him "Ted" and thought he did a good job. Ted was in his mid-thirties at the time of the Teapot Dome disgrace. Other than what he actually did with respect to Teapot Dome, the only two other actions he could have taken to head off the scandal would have been to protest the leases forcefully to President Harding or go public in the press. From Harding's terrible performance as Chief Executive, it's almost certain appealing to Harding would not have prevented the scandal. Ted had no way to know of the bribery of Secretary of Interior Fall until the time of the Senate hearings. Before that, he must have thought the matter not serious enough to ruin his political career by going public. If the way he handled the oil reserve matter can be accepted as reasonable at the time and under the circumstances, or even excused, his overall performance as Assistant Navy Secretary was very good.[77]

Eleanor went back to the nation's capital as soon as the state convention was over. Her job was to vacate their rented house and get the family moved back to Oyster Bay. She withdrew the children from school and got all the family belongings packed and shipped back. Even though Prohibition was in effect, being cautious she asked for and received permission to move their pre-prohibition supply of liquor back with their personal belongings. She packed a couple of bottles in each item of luggage, box, and crate, and managed to save their entire supply.[78]

The Democrat Party's State Convention was held a few days after that of the Republicans. As expected, their big gun, Al Smith, was nominated by acclamation as their gubernatorial candidate. Ted's first cousin, Mrs. Franklin Delano Roosevelt (Eleanor) seconded his nomination and then took a verbal poke at her kinsman. This would actually be incumbent Smith's forth campaign for governor. In 1918, while Ted was in France fighting in the final days of the Great War, Smith was elected the New York chief executive by fifteen thousand votes. In '20 he lost to Republican Nathan Miller, but he won the office back by 400,000 votes in '22. Besides being an experienced campaigner, Smith was a quick-witted Irish Catholic, was extremely popular with the voters, and had a tremendous knowledge of state government.[79]

Besides opposing a very popular incumbent with a good record, Ted had at least three other major problems to overcome. First, and certainly the most serious, was the terrible publicity he received from the Teapot Dome scandal. Being the eldest son and namesake of a very famous man, everything Ted did was overly publicized. The news media had blown his innocent involvement in the Teapot Dome affair way out of proportion. Even though the Senate Investigating Committee had cleared him of any wrong, many voters had the attitude with respect to politicians that where there is smoke, there is fire. Other than to simply proclaim his innocence and refer to the fact that the investigating committee had exonerated him, Ted had no practical way to prove to those skeptical voters that he was not guilty. Some of the voters who did not think he was actually involved in the bribery, said he was too trusting and that he was stupid to have been duped that way by the unsavory characters around him.

Another major hurdle Ted faced was the fact that, because of his absence from the State of the past $3\frac{1}{2}$ years, he had lost touch with the political issues in New York. Many voters associated him with Washington rather than New York.

Finally, there was a question as to whether Ted's personality was really suited for the political arena. He was certainly extroverted, polite, and amiable, and he was a gifted public speaker, but he was opinionated and naive, especially when it came to politics. As far as Ted was concerned, the Republican beliefs were close to God, while the Democrat's philosophy would lead to the ruination of the country. There was no in-between. Speaking on the subject, he said:

> We Republicans have married decency and idealism. Our heads may be in the clouds, but our feet are on the ground. Democrats use words to cloak their meaning and simply for the purpose of capturing votes. We Republicans do not.[80]

While Teddy Roosevelt had been a Republican, he was not adamant about it. For example, in 1912, when he bolted the Republican Party and ran on a third party ticket. Even Ted's immediate family recognized that he lacked subtlety, and he said himself that he may not have the patience to be a politician.[81]

In the 1920s the Ku Klux Klan was a political factor in most states, including New York. Al Smith had long publicly condemned the Klan. While Ted had often privately denounced the organization, he had never had the occasion to do so in a public way. As the campaign was about to get under way, the Klan made some overtures to TR Jr, but he wasted no time in rejecting them and publicly expressed his hatred of the Klan and what it stood for, saying:[82]

> At this time intolerance in many forms is strong in the country. . . The word Americanism is soiled when used by a group for furthering intolerance. Such a group is the Ku Klux Klan.[83]

Ted's remarks took the Klan out of the race. It didn't support either candidate.

Over the course of the four-week campaign a number of issues were raised. Ted reminded the voters again and again that Smith was a product of the corrupt Tammany Hall political machine, and that the Democrats were the party of big government inefficiency. Al, to his credit, personally had little to say about Ted's connection with Teapot Dome, leaving remarks on that subject to others. He told some of his supporters:

I'd win sympathy for him if I went after him too hard. He's having a swell time. The big bosses are telling him he's in, that it's all over. They always do that. Pretty soon he'll make a mistake and then I'll smash him. [84]

Al Smith was exactly right; the mistakes would come and he would smash Ted.

On the issue of labor legislation, Smith had a proven record of minimum wage and hour accomplishments. Ted's labor plank was similar to Smith's, but he had no proven record to show except for the defeated labor bills he had introduced in the New York General Assembly in 1920–21. Labor unions applauded his unconventional theory that there should be a partnership between capital and labor and that company employees should participate in any profits made by the employer, but business investors and top management officials were opposed. Part of TR Jr.'s program included the enactment of a protective tariff on some goods and a reduction in corporate taxes, but he had a hard time explaining to the working people how in any direct or indirect way this would benefit the average New York citizen. [85]

Another matter important to the voters was the water supply and whether the water generating facilities and the water distribution facilities should be owned and/or operated by private companies, or by the government or some government agency. The Democrat's stand on this subject was simple, government ownership and operation of both. In explaining where he stood on this question, Ted said that he was in favor of public generation because few employees are required for that operation, but that many are required to distribute the water to consumers, making private ownership of the distribution facilities more desirable. Ted and the GOP were obviously trying to please everybody. In responding to his opponent's stance on the water issue, Al Smith said, "The man that wrote the water power plank in the Republican platform knows as much about water power development in this State as I know about the rise and fall of the tide in the China Sea." Tying in the water supply issue with Ted's claim that he was a conservationist, Governor Smith, referring to Teapot Dome for one of the few times, said that his Republican adversary did not practice proper conservation when he was involved in turning over the naval oil reserve to private interests. [86]

For the first three weeks of the campaign, Ted and Eleanor were aboard a train traveling around the state, making brief whistle stops at every town and village along the line. Major speeches were sandwiched in between in the large cities such as Buffalo, Syracuse, and Rochester. Sometimes they made as many as twenty stops a day. There was always an advanced notice as to the time Ted's train would arrive, and large crowds gathered to hear and see him. Knowing that voters were waiting on him at the next stop, keeping on schedule was absolutely necessary. Typically, as the train pulled in and came to a halt, Ted would stand on the rear platform and greet the mayor and other dignitaries present and invite them aboard. Then, looking out in the audience, he would spot an old army buddy or some friend prearranged to be there. Ted and his friend would then exchange a few words about the war, or hunting, or whatever they had in common. Then, he would begin to talk about the issues. The train engineer had been instructed to start the train rolling after a five-minute stay, but in that brief time Ted would not have finished his talk. As the train began to move, he would shout, "Wait! Wait! I haven't finished! Stop the train!" As prearranged, the train would continue down the track as the crowd roared with laughter. The dignitaries aboard would go on to the next stop, where transportation was waiting to take them back home. The final week of the campaign was reserved for speeches and appearances in New York City.[87]

Al Smith was not at all worried about the election outcome and didn't even start campaigning until two weeks before election day. Referring to Ted as a "myth in Washington and a name in New York," he made one speech a day, thoroughly covering only one issue in each, rather than trying to cover several issues in a brief whistle stop as TR Jr did.

The New York State Republican Party did not offer any advice or assistance to Ted on what issues to discuss, but then apparently Ted did not request any help from them. Traveling on the train with him were a number of newspaper reporters who became friends with the unprepared candidate. The newsmen liked Ted and would frequently give him advice on some topic to focus on. While the reporters meant well, they were not professional political advisors, and they could not offer the sound guidance that the state party might have provided.

Who planted the seed in his mind for Ted to bring up the fact that Smith had encouraged the state legislature to pass a law establishing an "executive budget" is unknown. Ted lit into the incumbent on that subject, however, stating that to create such a budget would take fiscal powers away from the people and their elected legislative officials and place it into the hands of the Governor and Tammany Hall. He added that similar action on the part of the British was one of the reasons the Revolutionary War was fought. Laughing at the suggestion that an executive budget was the cause of the American Revolution, Smith reminded the voters that the passage of a law authorizing this budget had been the recommendation of a non-partisan commission he had appointed to study ways to improve state government, and that it had been approved by "such eminent members of Tammany Hall as Elihu Root, General Wickersham, Henry L. Stimson, and Charles Evens Hughes."(Elihu Root, Republican U.S. Senator and U.S. Secretary of State; George Woodward Wickersham, Republican U.S. Attorney General; Henry L. Stimson, Republican U.S. Secretary of State and Secretary of War.)[88]

In another claim based on misinformation, Ted said that Governor Smith was attempting to take the control of education out of the hands of the New York State Department of Education and place it into the hands of the Chief Executive. This accusation was based on a misprint in a proposed constitutional amendment that

Smith had endorsed several years before. In answering the charge, Al Smith explained about the typo error and then said:

> I presume that Colonel Roosevelt made the statement to which I refer, not of his own knowledge, but as a result of misinformation handed to him by somebody in the Republican Press Bureau. ***** It is unfortunate that he has made it so far without having looked up all the facts.[89]

During the course of the campaign, Ted made many statements and charges based on bad information, and/or his lack of knowledge of the political issues, and/or his lack of political acumen. In one speech, he bragged on the Republicans, saying, "We put up men who can deliver the goods." Even though the incumbent governor had vowed not to personally refer to Teapot Dome, he just couldn't help it in this instance, and promptly responded to the effect that the GOP had certainly put up men who delivered the goods at Teapot Dome.

One of Ted's whistle stops was in the town of Hamilton, the home of Colgate University. In the crowd waiting to hear him were a large number of Colgate students. Smiling at the impressive group of young people, Ted said:

> I hear you played a football game against Cornell last Saturday. It must have been—(someone in the crowd shouted 'It was against Nebraska') Oh, well it was a great game. I congrat—(several Colgate students bellowed 'We lost!')[90]

Ted then wheeled around, glared at the supporters behind him and asked, "Who told me that?" A few days later, Gov. Smith, speaking before a large crowd, mentioned one of the erroneous statements his opponent made and then asked, "Who told me that?" He then cited another and asked, "Who told me that?" As Al went down the list of twelve mistakes, the crowd soon joined in the chorus with him, shouting, "Who told me that." Without really trying, the incumbent was having fun and was winning the election.[91]

From the standpoint of the Oyster Bay Roosevelts, the bitterness between them and the Hyde Park wing of the family started when FDR remained a loyal Democrat rather than joining Teddy Roosevelt when he bolted the Republican Party and ran as a Progressive (Bull Moose) Party candidate in 1912. The problems intensified when Franklin held onto his safe job as Assistant Secretary of the Navy during World War I rather than take Teddy's advice and join the army for active service at the battlefront. From the Hyde Park standpoint, the split came about in the 1920 presidential campaign when Ted toured the country for the Republicans, denouncing FDR's claim of close ties with former president Theodore Roosevelt. No matter who was responsible for the split, FDR, his wife Eleanor, and their trusted advisor, Louis Howe, were all aware that FDR's political career might well be at an end if Ted was elected governor. The Hyde Park bunch was as cognizant as Ted and Alice were that even though they were members of different political parties, as a practical matter there could be only one Roosevelt on the ballot for President. Hyde Park had to pull out all the stops to see that Ted was defeated.

While Al Smith had little to say about Teapot Dome during the campaign, Ted's first cousin, Eleanor Roosevelt (Mrs. Franklin Delano Roosevelt) did. In describing her campaign activities, Mrs. FDR said:

> We had a framework resembling a teapot, which spouted steam, built on top of an automobile; and it led the procession of cars which toured the state, following the Republican candidate . . . wherever he went![92]

On one occasion during this political escapade, FDR's wife and the ladies who were with her made a side trip in their political float automobile to the nearby home of her aunt, Bamie Roosevelt Cowles. Bamie, who was also Ted's aunt, must have thought her niece was trying to bring her into the middle of the family dispute, for she did not appreciate the visit.[93]

The Volstead Act (Prohibition Law) was in effect in 1924, and there were a substantial number of citizens whose votes would be influenced by the candidate's stand on the liquor issue. Al Smith was an Irish Catholic, and during the campaign gave only weak lip service to the enforcement of the Volstead Act. Anyway, he wasn't going to get any appreciable number of votes from the part of the electorate who were staunchly dry. Ted, on the other hand, wanted the endorsement of the Anti Saloon League and the Women's Christian Temperance Union. To get the approval of these two organizations, he had to make it appear that he was at least more anti-liquor than Smith. In actuality, however, nobody liked a good drink of whiskey more than Theodore Roosevelt, Jr. He even had his own private stash of pre-prohibition booze that his wife brought back from Washington. Edith, Ted's mother, was so opposed to prohibition that she, for the first time, began serving cocktails to social guests at Sagamore Hill.

One of Ted's strong character traits was his innate honesty. He almost always spoke from the heart, which sometimes got him into trouble. One of the few times in his life when he compromised his true convictions was the manner in which he courted the dry vote during the campaign. In speeches, he was less than completely honest. He said that even though he was opposed to hard liquor and saloons, and personally favored the public sale of only beer and wines, the law was the law and Prohibition would be strictly enforced if he were elected governor. Both the League and the WCTU were impressed and gave Ted their endorsements.[94]

TRJr said all along that his only chance to win the election was to keep the vote fairly close in New York City. After the rousing response he received on his upstate whistle stop tour, he had hopes that this success would carry over into the city. In his plan for the campaign, Ted reserved the last week for appearances and speeches in New York City, with a big campaign-ending rally in Madison Square

Garden. After the second day of speaking, kissing babies, and shaking hands in the Big Apple, he was discouraged and told Eleanor he thought he was going to lose.[95]

In the national election against Calvin Coolidge, the Democrats put up John Davis of West Virginia. Almost a political unknown, the Democratic candidate was a compromise nominee, selected after over one hundred failed ballots. Davis was an attorney by profession and represented many wealthy individuals and large corporations, including J. P. Morgan and Company. Even though he was an impressive and intelligent man, Mr. Davis gave the voters no convincing reason to vote for him rather than to "Keep Cool With Coolidge", (the Republican incumbent President's campaign slogan). In the final count, Coolidge received 54% of the national vote, Davis 28.5%, and Robert La Follete, the Progressive Party candidate, 16.6%. Coolidge carried the State of New York by 700,000 votes, a landslide victory for the Republicans.[96]

Normally, when a presidential candidate wins a state by a wide margin, he will carry his party's candidates in other races to victory on his "coat tails." This dictum did not hold true in the 1924 New York governor's race. Even though Ted Roosevelt won fifty-six out of the sixty-two of the New York counties, Smith took the five large New York City counties and Albany County and won the election by 108,589 votes. The state totals were 1,627,111 for Smith and 1,518,522 for Ted. Offhand, this appears to be a fairly close election, but in actuality over 800,000 New Yorkers had to switch parties on their ballot to vote for the Republican Coolidge and the Democrat Smith rather than vote a straight ticket, it was not close at all. Al Smith later said that it was his easiest election.[97]

Ted was disappointed, but knew from the beginning that he had an uphill struggle against the extremely popular and crafty incumbent governor. Thousands of heart-warming notes and letters came in expressing condolence and congratulating him on his effort. After making a public announcement thanking the people that helped and supported him, Ted and Eleanor took a train pointed south, and spent a couple of relaxing weeks with Governor and Mrs. John Parker of Louisiana.[98]

In retrospect, Ted must have asked himself what could or should he have done to reverse the election outcome. Even though it may have cost him his job and ruined his political career, he could have attempted to prevent, or at least refused to have been any part of the oil leases. When Secretary of Interior Fall told him to send a military force to evict squatters from the Teapot Dome oil reserve, Ted could have told him that it was tenant Sinclair's obligation to seek eviction of trespassers through the courts rather than the government's obligation to evict someone off of land leased to a private interest. But to refuse the orders of the President and the Secretary of the Navy was too much to expect. He certainly, though, should have insisted that the New York Republican Party furnish him expert advice with respect to campaign issues and strategy, especially since he was not current on New York politics. Even if Ted had done all these things, the election may have been closer, but the outcome would have been the same against the popular Al Smith.

To have improved his chances of one day being elected New York Governor, Ted should have accepted the chance to become the first National Commander of the American Legion. It was only a one-year job, and would have given him a foundation upon which to build a political power base national in scope. Instead, he took the high road and refused the nomination because it might seem he was using the Legion for personal gain. The American Legion in 1924 was composed exclusively of ex-servicemen from the Great War. The World War I generation was then assuming its rightful place at the helm of America. A great majority of its members would have favored and supported Ted's political ambitions rather than have been resentful of him for using the organization as a vehicle for political gain. If there is one thing the Legion understands, it's politics.

Secondly, he should never have followed in his father's footsteps by accepting the job as Assistant Secretary of the Navy. While he would have had no way of knowing that in refusing the position he would have avoided the Teapot Dome mess, still, there was no reasonable way working with the Navy would lead to anything politically. He should have stayed where he was and made a name for himself in the New York Legislature. Teddy had profited politically from being the Navy Assistant Secretary because of the occurrence of the Spanish American War, but Ted had already had his war and there was no real prospect that another one would take place any time soon. Had he stayed put in New York and bided his time until 1928, when Al Smith was the Democratic nominee for President and could, therefore, not seek re-election as governor, Ted, with a strong Jewish candidate as his lieutenant governor running mate to get at least some of the traditional Democratic Jewish vote (Albert Ottinger, the NY Attorney General as an example), just might have won the race. His opponent would have been his archrival, Franklin Delano Roosevelt. While Ted lacked his cousin's suavity, in the mid 20's he was every bit as well known to the public as FDR, and the Great Depression, which millions of voters blamed on the Republicans, was still a year away. The Republicans were still in vogue. As the '28 election actually unfolded, Democrat FDR was elected NY governor by a close vote, while Republican Herbert Hoover was elected President by a landslide, so there was a long Hoover "coat-tail" for other Republican candidates to ride on. Had this argured scenario occurred, and had Ted prevailed in the gubernatorial election, it is highly unlikely that FDR would have gotten the Democratic nod for President in 1932, even if he had been elected governor in the 1930 race. The history of the United States would have been drastically changed.

As a brief election epilogue, Al Smith was re-elected governor in 1926, and was the Democratic candidate for President in 1928. The depression did not come about until 1929, so the Republicans remained in power after the '28 elections, with Herbert Hoover being elected President by a large majority. In a close race, FDR was elected New York Governor in 1928, and was overwhelmingly re-elected in '30. Two years later he was elected President of the United States, and then re-elected three times. Franklin Delano Roosevelt was still sitting as President when he died in 1945, thus ending an almost half century of major influence on American politics by a member of the extended Roosevelt family.

Mrs. FDR later admitted that she knew Ted had nothing to do with the Teapot Dome scandal and that her teapot car was a "rough stunt," but she gave herself an excuse by saying that in politics and war, all is fair. Some believe that her display during the campaign so unnerved Ted that it caused him to make some of his many mistakes.[99]

Even though Ted stayed on speaking terms with FDR, who was his distant cousin, and with Mrs. FDR, his first cousin, they remained bitter political enemies for the rest of their lives. Ted's wife Eleanor never forgave Mrs. FDR for her antics during the 1924 campaign and avoided contact with FDR and his Eleanor when at all possible. Some believed that Mrs. Ted's real problem with the Hyde Park branch was that she felt FDR and his Eleanor had somehow robbed her and her husband of their rightful place in the White House. However, there was no reasonable way Theodore Roosevelt, Jr. would have ever followed in his father's footsteps and been elected President of the United States. He possibly could have been elected governor in 1928 and thereby may have prevented FDR from ever becoming president, but with the onset of the depression in '29, no Republican had a chance of being elected Chief Executive of the country until after World War II.

Fifty years later, long after the deaths of Ted, FDR, and both Eleanors, when their surviving children were elderly, the family wounds began to heal. Still, it was not until 1989 that the two political wings of the Roosevelt family got together for a true reunion weekend.[100]

The Political Years Source Notes

1. NY Times, 8/31/19 p 7.

2. Moley p 74.

3. Roosevelt, Mrs. T Jr. p 123; Official Army Records

4. Collier p 258–259; Article in Providence Bulletin, LOC c-64; MacLennon letter to TRJr. 7/17/1919 and Martin letter to TRJr. of 10/25/1919, LOC c-11; LOC c—56 & c-63; Boston Enterprise article, LOC C-64.

5. Roosevelt, Mrs. T Jr., p 123–124; Pringle p 240; Article in the NY Evening Sun 11/5/1919, LOC C-64.

6. Roosevelt, Mrs. T. Jr., p 124–125.

7. Madaras p 94–97; Waldman, Crisis p 2–3

8. Waldman, Crisis p 4–12.

9. Madaras p 98–99; Waldman, Crisis p 29, 50–61; Waldman, Labor p 101–102.

10. Cook, Vol 1, p 242.

11. Roosevelt, Mrs. T Jr., p 125–126; Copy of speech, LOC C-48. Newspaper clipping, LOC C-64; Socialists Trial Folder, LOC C-38.

12. Madaras p 106–108; LOC C-63.

13. Madaras p 110–111.

14. Socialists Trial Folder, LOC C-38; TRJr. letter to Albert Beveridge of 9/30/1920, LOC C-11.

15. Roosevelt, Mrs. T Jr., p 127–129; Clipping from NY Tribune, July 1920, LOC C-64; TRJr. letter to J. H. Mitchell of 7/5/1920, LOC C-11; Copy of Ted's bill, LOC C-63.

16. Madaras p 113–114; Copy of bills and Ted's speeches in support thereof, LOC C-37.

17. Ibid p 118–119.

18. Ibid p 114–116.

19. Bagby p 27–31, 50; Collier p 259; Madaras p 123–126; In the bound volume of TRJr. speeches 1920–1924 there is a summary and analysis of the Leonard Wood Presidential Campaign, LOC C-45; Leonard Wood Campaign folder, LOC C-36.

20. Burns p 76; Collier p 257; Felsenthal p 142.

21. Roosevelt, Mrs. T. Jr., p 126–127.

22. Bagby p 142; Madaras p 130–131; Ward, 1st Class, p 540.

23. Freidel, Vol 2, p 85; LOC C-36, Many speeches TRJr. made in support of Harding are at the LOC C-45.

24. Madaras p 132; Morgan, Ted, FDR p ????.

25. Madaras p 135–136; TRJr. letter to J. F. Flugarth of 2/3/1921, LOC C-12.

26. Newspaper clipping in LOC C-63; LOC C-55 & C-56.

27. Gunther, Roos. In Retro, p 7 and note; Collier p 262, 280; Ted's departing from the Assembly, LOC C-12. Official date of resignation is 3/10/1921.

28. Roosevelt, Mrs. T Jr., p 134–135; Felsenthal p 143; Ward, 1st Class, p 556.

29. Roosevelt, Mrs. T Jr., p 132–133.

30. LOC C-63.

31. Roosevelt, Mrs. T Jr. p 141.

32. Hoag p 1; Morrison, S E, p 5–6; Wheeler p 53.

33. Sprout p 145n 88; Wheeler p 54.

34. Madaras p 142–147; Pusey Vol. 1 p 458; Sprout p 166n 15.

35. Madaras p 148–153; Pusey p 468–472; Sprout p 154–155; Sullivan p. 22–23; Much material on the arms conference is at LOC C-39.

36. Madaras p 154–155; Pusey p 468–472; Sprout p 166n 15 and p. 207–211.

37. Madaras p 158–164; Pusey p 473–480; Sprout p. 167–180; Ted's diary entries of 12/1/21, 12/2/21, and 12/14/21, LOC C-1.

38. Madaras p 166–169; Pusey p 473–480; Sprout p. 165 and 168.

39. Wheeler p 113.

40. Madaras p 178–180; Pusey p 485–486; Sprout 236–237; Diary entries of 1/11/22, 2/18/22, 2/21/22, LOC C-1.

41. Madaras p 187; Morison, S E, p 5 -6; Pusey p 485–487; Sprout p. 243–251.

42. Madaras p 182 -183; Sprout p. 241–242; Diary entry of 1/23/22, LOC C-1.

43. Hoag p 6; Wheeler p 138, 189.

44. Hoag p 177; Diary entry of 2/9/22, LOC C-1.

45. Hoag p 163; Madaras p 196–199; Wheeler p 137; Ted's diary entry of 4/4/22, LOC C-1.

46. TRJr. letter to Ethel and Dick Derby of 10/5/22, TR Collection, Harvard U 87–100.

47. Wheeler p 80–81; Diary entry of 2/8/22, LOC C-1.

48. Wheeler p 82n.

49. Noogle p 16–20; Roosevelt, Mrs. T. Jr. p 149; Sullivan and Rather p 638–639; Werner and Starr p 40–41.

50. Madaras p 209–210; Roosevelt, Mrs. T Jr. p 150; Werner and Starr p 45–46; An explanation of the executive orders and a copy of the amended order is in LOC C-39.

51. TRJr. letter to Senator Wadsworth dated 6/9/1922, LOC C-12, also 2 folders in C-39 and TRJr. letter to George Tichner in C-11.

52. Roosevelt, Mrs. T. Jr., p 147–148.

53. Stratton p 241, 247–248.

54. Noggle p 18–20; Stratton p 251; Sullivan and Rather p 639; Memo of 4/1/1923, LOC C-39.

55. Madaras p 210; Noggle p 18–19; Werner and Starr p 46.

56. Collier p 284–285.

57. Ibid p 285.

58. Ibid p 286.

59. Collier p 287; Noggle p 46–47; Stratton p 253; TRJr. diary entry of 11/14/1923 (page 578 LOC C-1.

60. Roosevelt, Mrs. T Jr., p 152–153; Stratton p 294; Sullivan and Rather p 641–642; Article in Tribune 1/22/1924, LOC C-71 and TRJr. Letter to Senator Wm. Campbell dated 2/15/1924, LOC C-39.

61. Roosevelt, Mrs. T Jr., p 152–153, Ward, 1st Class, p 684n.

62. Roosevelt, Mrs. T. Jr. p 153–154; Werner and Starr p 128–133

63. Roosevelt, Mrs. T. Jr., p 154.

64. Noggle p 79–81; Roosevelt, Mrs. T. Jr., p 154.

65. Collier p 289.

66. Stratton p 294–295; NY Times 4/13/1924, 5/5/24, 5/9/24, 5/25/24.

67. Ward, 1st Class, p 684.

68. Noggle p 117, 185. Stratton p 311–327.

69. Roosevelt, Mrs. T. Jr., p 157–158

70. Collier p 292–295.

71. Cook, Vol 1, p 351.

72. Collier p 295

73. Collier p 295–296.

74. Madaras p 374; LOC C-13.

75. Madaras p 377.

76. Collier p 296; Madaras p 379–380.

77. Roosevelt, Mrs. T. Jr., p 161; Kenneth Roberts's statement, LOC c—55.

78. Roosevelt, Mrs. T. Jr., p 162.

79. Handlin p 72; Cook, p 352.

80. Pringle p 244–245.

81. Collier p 278, Josephson p 316; Madaras p 375; Pringle p 243.

82. Roosevelt, Mrs. T. Jr., p 165; Madaras p 385.

83. Roosevelt, Mrs. T. Jr., p 165.

84. Pringle p 247.

85. Eldot p 222; Mararas article p 383–384.

86. Eldot p 250; Many of the speeches Ted made during the campaign are in LOC C-45 & C-46.

87. Roosevelt, Mrs. T. Jr., p 162–163.

88. Madaras p 382; NY Times 10/18/24

89. Hapwood & Moskowitz p 323.

90. Pringle p 247.

91. Hapwood & Moskowitz p 216; Josephson p 317; Pringle p 247.

92. Davis, Kenneth p 772.

93. Cook p 352; Davis, K., p 772; Ward, 1 Class, p 701n.

94. Eldot p 369–370; Madaras article p 384–385.

95. Roosevelt, Mrs. T. Jr., p 165; NY Times, 11/2/24, p 15.

96. Davis, K., p 770; Josephson p 317.

97. Roosevelt, Mrs. T. Jr., p 165.

98. Roosevelt, Mrs. T. Jr., p 166; NY Times 11/6/1924

99. Cook p 352; Davis, K, p 772; Ward, 1st Class, p 701n.

100. Collier p 481.

Ted on platform of a troop train in 1941.

TRJr. shaking hands with President Calvin Coolidge, September 26, 1924.

Theodore Roosevelt Jr.'s grave marker at the American WWII cemetery in Normandy, France.

Lt. Colonel TRJr., his wife, Eleanor, and General Frank Parker in France, 1918.

Ted standing in his personal jeep "Rough Rider." (Note bullet hole in windshield.)

Roosevelt Family in 1903.
From left: Quentin, TR, TRJr., "Archie,"
Alice, Kermit, Edith, and Ethel

TRJr, Major General Terry Allen, and Lt. General
George Patton in Sicily, 1943.

Ted and son Quentin in 1942.

7
THE YEARS ABROAD

Now what to do? After Archie resigned his position with Sinclair Oil, cousin Emlin Roosevelt gave him a job with Roosevelt and Co. and Kermit had his own shipping business. Ted was the only one of the brothers who was without gainful employment. This bothered him, not because he and Eleanor especially needed the money, but because he could not handle idleness well. In the back of Ted's mind was the idea to again run for public office, so he really didn't want to return to investment banking and then in a year or two have to give it up to get back in politics.

Kermit had established his business while Ted was still the Assistant Secretary of the Navy, and soon began to ask his brother to do favors to help him with customers. At first they were harmless enough, like simply meeting with various of his clients and being nice to him. But when the requests got to the point that he wanted his brother to use his political influence to get him business, Ted considered that to be unethical and he refused. This created hard feelings between them and they had some harsh words. The closeness they had felt all of their lives began to wane. Ted and Kermit had in past years talked a number of times about making some type of serious hunting trip together. When they heard that the Field Museum of Natural History in Chicago was desirous of acquiring specimens of rare fauna from Central Asia, they thought a hunting trip of this nature would be fun and also a way for them to become friends again. They promptly contacted the museum.

The Field Museum was interested in setting up habitat group displays of unusual animals from the Far East, such as the ibex, brown bear, and especially the Ovis poli, an extremely rare specie of wild sheep with spectacular horns. This almost mystical animal was first made known to the Western world by the thirteenth-century writings of Marco Polo. Some scholars questioned the accuracy of Polo's claims and wondered if he had really made the extensive journey to strange places as he said. For instance, why did he never mention the Great Wall of China, and why had no one in the West ever seen this king of sheep with enormous horns? The Ovis poli was thought to exist in the Pamirs Mountains in Chinese and Russian Turkestan, and was so scarce that no museum in the world had a display of the animals. The museum's wish list also included a number of animals found in India and Nepal. After Mr. James Simpson, President of Marshall Field and Co., agreed to finance this very expensive zoological expedition the Roosevelt brothers proposed to lead, Ted and Kermit began to make final plans and preparations.[1]

The undertaking was officially christened the "James Simpson—Roosevelts—Field Museum Expedition." Extensive coverage was given to it by the press, and there was immediately a worldwide interest in the project. Until then, few people had ever heard of the Ovis poli. Someone asked Will Rogers what an Ovis poli was, and he quipped that it "was a political sheep you hunt between elections." Hundreds of men and women from all over the world sent in requests to go along. Some of the applicants were scientist, some were hunters, and some were simply adventurers. Some even offered to pay their own way.

The plan was to hire guides that lived in the area where they intended to hunt and to pick up coolies as needed along the way to handle the supplies and equipment. George Cherrie, a scientist who had accompanied Teddy Roosevelt on one of his South American expeditions, and Suydam Cutting, a photographer and world-class tennis player, who was an old friend of Ted's, were included in the party.[2]

Ted, Kermit, George, and Suydam got busy rounding up the supplies and equipment that would be needed as well as getting the necessary permits from the governments of Britain, China and Russia. The expedition would take them to India, then across the Himalayas into Chinese and Russian territory, and finally back to India and into Nepal.

Besides proper hunting and cold weather clothing and equipment, they took two cougar hounds from Mississippi and two others from Montana to help in hunting big cats. Realizing Westerners with formal government permits traveling along old caravan routes and trails from one remote village to another might be considered dignitaries by some of the local officials they met, dinner jackets and collapsible hats were packed just in case the occasion arose to wear formal attire. Following a habit he had developed as a boy, Ted made sure he included with his personal gear some of his favorite literature, including Shakespeare, *Pilgrim's Progress,* the *Bible,* Kipling and some other poetry and several other books. Before leaving, Ted contracted with *Cosmopolitan Magazine* to write several articles about the venture when he returned.[3]

Eleanor and Kermit's wife Belle were excited about the trip because it was arranged for them to meet their husbands in India in November after the most arduous part of the expedition was over. Then they and their husbands would do some sightseeing and hunting of their own. Eleanor would leave the children with Signorina, and both grandmothers were ready, willing, and able to assist.[4]

Saying goodbye to their wives and children, the men sailed aboard the Leviathan in mid-April, 1925. First, they stopped for a few days in London for meetings with travelers and adventurers with experience in the Pamirs Mountains area. They next went to Paris to gather the last of their necessary supplies and equipment. While in France, they took time to visit Quentin's grave. Then after traveling by train to Marseilles, they boarded a ship bound for Bombay, India, landing there on May 11th. From Bombay they went by train to Srinagar, the summer capital of Kashmir, where coolies and pack animals were acquired. Here they met up with Rahima Loon and his brother, Khalil, the experienced guides hired to accompany them on the expedition.

The hunting actually began on May 19th, when they departed from Srinagar on horseback, with coolies walking along leading the pack train. Over the next five months they trekked some 3,700 miles, usually on horses, but sometimes riding yaks or walking. The centuries-old caravan routes on which they traveled took them over high Himalayan passes, across deserts, and through beautiful valleys, including the Vale of Kashmir. They experienced baking heat and bitter cold, rain, snow and ice, and howling mountain winds. At night, when they were at places like the foot of the Saser Glacier or the Jilgalong Valley, they would pitch tents and use their sleeping bags. But when near a town or village, all having strange names like Khan Ayalak at the Muzart Pass and Tashmalik, they slept in *serais* (inns) where heat was provided by burning yak dung. Meals consisted mainly of what game they killed and whatever food they were able to acquire from the locals. They ate a lot of leathery mutton and unleavened chepatis. Sometimes they didn't know what they were eating and were afraid to ask. Ted had what he described as the most unusual thing he ever ate, rat embryos dipped in honey. During the long nights, Ted and Kermit would pass the time by talking about what they were going to eat when the expedition was over and they were back in civilization. When in the terrible heat of the dry plains, they discussed icy drinks and cool salads; in the freezing mountain weather, they talked of the kind of food that would warm your insides, like plates piled high with hot and tender roast beef. Most days, they would do some hunting and then pack up and move along the ancient pathways some fifteen or twenty miles before stopping for the night. Occasionally however, they would remain at a good hunting location for three or four days. During the first months of the hunt, a number of the large mammals desired by the museum were killed and the hides properly preserved.[5]

With the time allotted for the project over half gone, the expedition reached the Pamirs Mountains and the hunt for the elusive Ovis poli began. During the first days, only a few of the animals had been seen, and all were at extreme distances. One day when Ted and Kermit were hunting together on foot, slipping and sliding on the snow covered rocks, they struggled to the summit of a sixteen thousand foot mountain and spotted a nice group of poli some eight hundred yards away. Observing the animals through binoculars, they could plainly see them jumping from rock to rock and nibbling on vegetation as they ambled along. There were eight poli in the flock and all of them had horns judged to be forty-five to fifty inches in length. By now it was late, and the brothers had to temporarily abandon the hunt and return to camp before it got too dark to see.

Up before dawn, they were back on top of the mountain by 6:00 a.m., and almost immediately they spotted the same group off in the distance. As Ted and Kermit would creep toward the poli, the animals would retreat and keep the range too great for a shot to be taken. Trailing the flock higher and higher to a seventeen thousand foot elevation, the hunters were gasping for air and lost sight of their quarry. Finally locating them again, the brothers made an end-around movement to place themselves ahead of their prey and at a spot where they expected the poli to go by. The maneuver worked as they wanted, for soon the animals appeared in single file and were only about 250 yards away, within easy shooting range. Selecting the two biggest rams as targets, Ted and Kermit fired simultaneously, hitting both rams but neither fell. They trailed the wounded animals in the snow until almost dark, but then had to abandon the search and go back to camp. Up again before dawn and back up on the mountain at early daylight, they found both of the big males dead, but they had been partially eaten by wolves. In their damaged condition the rams were not suitable for display purposes. It was a shame for one had horns measuring forty-nine inches in length, and the other fifty-one and one half.[6]

Still on the hunt for poli, the next day the party moved into the Russian Pamirs and almost immediately they bagged an adult female in excellent condition. Back in camp for the night, the animal was measured for mounting purposes, skinned, and proper steps were taken to preserve the hide. Again up before dawn and back on the hunt at first light, Ted and Kermit each killed an adult ram, but neither of them was as large as the ones the wolves had eaten. During the final days of the hunt for the political sheep, the party had luck on their side and were able to harvest five more good specimens. The Field Museum would now be able to display to the public an excellent family group of the rare Ovis poli.[7]

Back home, Eleanor and Belle had been preparing to leave the States and join their husbands in India. Eleanor took target practice with her new .303 Mauser and she did a lot of hiking up and down hills to improve her stamina. When time came to depart, the ladies packed not only hunting clothes for all seasons, but also dresses and clothing to wear on formal occasions. While Eleanor and Belle took a somewhat different route than their husbands to reach Srinagar, they arrived safely and joined the men on November 9th, the appointed date. The journey took them a month.

When their wives saw them for the first time in seven months, Ted and Kermit looked like bears in their heavy, dirty, smelly clothes and long beards. They first thought the rough looking men they were gazing at might be outlaws. Eleanor had never seen Ted with a beard before, and she was surprised to see that his facial hair was dark red. Naturally, the first order of business was a good, clean shave. As soon as Ted got cleaned up and out of his tattered hunting clothes, he presented Eleanor with the exquisite satin Chinese robe he bought for her during the journey. The garment was scarlet and heavily embroidered with colorful birds and flowers. The couples spent about a month in Kashmir, living on a houseboat on the Jhelum River, and continuing to hunt exotic animals for the museum's collection. Rahima Loon and Khalid were still with them, as was a cook, a butler, and a number of coolies.

With the houseboat substituting as a hunting lodge, each of the four Roosevelts killed a barasingha stag (swamp deer), two of them being on the private game preserve of the Maharajah of Kashmir. Then, looking for better hunting grounds, the guides had the houseboat muscled upstream by using four coolies to walk along the river bank pulling tow ropes and other coolies to push the boat along by digging long poles into the river bed. As the boat was slowly pushed and pulled along, the two couples sat on the roof, leisurely playing bridge and enjoying the spectacular views of the snow covered mountains, and quaint little temples and villages they passed.

After stopping at night for the coolies to rest, the next day they reached the home of Rahima Loon near the village of Bandipur. Here their guide gave them a sumptuous Kashmirian meal prepared by the women of his household. After being seated in the dining room, they were served an appetizer of hard biscuits and tea followed by a soup course. Then came lamb, chicken, goat sausage with rice, and another kind of rice with curried mutton balls. Last were sweetmeats and wonderful aromatic coffee. In return for the delicious food, Eleanor and Belle gave Rahima's two young sons wrist watches with luminous dials.

Leaving Belle and Kermit in Bandipur, early the next morning Ted, Eleanor and Rahima mounted horses and, with a cook, coolies, and pack train, began climbing up an old mountain trail to a temporary hunting camp their guide had prepared well in advance. Pausing for only one night, the group continued climbing the next morning, but now on foot because the trail became too steep for the pack animals and riding horses to negotiate. The going was slow as they climbed. It was difficult to maintain their footing on the narrow ledges and to balance themselves on the shaky log bridges placed across the deep mountain gullies with whitewater rapids far below. Ascending to an altitude of nearly nine thousand feet, the party finally arrived at the permanent camp from which they would hunt. Taking into account where they were, Ted and Eleanor were surprised at how elaborate the facilities Rahima had prepared for them were. While their sleeping tent was not heated in the below-freezing cold, their sleeping bags were warm and comfortable, and there was a separate tent off to the side to serve as a bathroom. They had hot baths every night. There was a lean-to used as a kitchen with a charcoal brazier for cooking. Meals were served in the dining tent. The savory dinner the first night they were there consisted of delicious soup with vermicelli, chicken, mashed potatoes, roast lamb with browned potatoes, creamed cauliflower, carrots, and pudding for desert.

Over the past seven months Ted had been at high altitudes often and had no problems handling the rarified air on the mountain; Eleanor on the other hand was not acclimated to the atmospheric conditions at such a high elevation. The first two days in camp Ted, Rahima, and a party of coolies climbed to a higher altitude to hunt, and Ted added to the mammal collection with a seven-foot bear and a nice barasingha. Eleanor chose to stay in camp, writing letters, hiking in the immediate area, and enjoying the beautiful snowcapped mountains all around them.

The third night in camp Rahima promised Eleanor he would lead her to a bear if she would go out with them. She reluctantly agreed, and early the next day the hunting party started for where the guide believed they would find game. Before long, they were climbing almost straight up and Eleanor began to huff and puff. To help her, Ted looped his scarf through his belt and had her hang on to it as he pulled her higher. Just as they reached the steepest part of the route, Eleanor got dizzy and fainted. This had never happened to her before and Ted was petrified. He took her hands in his and began to gently massage them while Rahima held onto her feet to keep her from falling off of the mountain. When Eleanor had not regained consciousness after a few minutes, Ted reasoned that a sip of whiskey might revive her and told one of the coolies to hurry back to camp and bring him his flask. Before the coolie had time to return, Eleanor came to and they reversed course and started slowly descending. When they got back to camp, they discovered that the coolie Ted sent back had rushed into camp excitedly exclaiming, "Lady Sahib dead! Sahib wants his whiskey." Ted and Eleanor enjoyed many a laugh over the years telling and retelling this story to friends and family.

Before returning to Bandipur to rejoin Kermit and Belle, Eleanor and Ted hunted in the mountains for several more days but at a lower altitude. No noteworthy kills were made. Back together, the four Roosevelts returned to Srinagar for a couple of days. Next, they went by automobile to Rawalpindi for a day, and then drove to a British Army camp at Mardan in the North-West Frontier Province where they had been invited to have dinner with the officers of the historic Queen Victoria's Own Corps of Guides. Sixty officers and guests in formal dress were seated at a long table on which silver pieces commemorating battles in which the Regiment had participated and awards it had received were lined down the center. The formalities included a toast to the King-Emperor. Two hours of spirited dancing followed dinner. The festivities were concluded with a detachment of pipers and drummers marching into the banquet hall playing the "March of the Black Watch." The officers and guests fell in behind and all marched around and around the table. Needless to say, Ted, Eleanor, Belle and Kermit had a wonderful time.

The next day the couples split up again, with Kermit and his spouse going to Delhi while Ted and Eleanor went to the great walled city of Peshawar in what is now Pakistan. Prior to 1947, Pakistan was ruled by the British as a part of India. Dating back to before recorded history, the origins of Peshawar are lost in antiquity. The city is within a few miles of the Khyber Pass, which was the only overland caravan route between China and the Middle East. For centuries Peshawar had been a favorite stopping place for travelers because of the luxurious silks, fine porcelain, and other exquisite merchandise found in its bazaars. Ted and Eleanor had a great time wandering the shops and admiring the beautiful and unusual items offered for sale. From one shop, Ted bought his wife a pair of "bright-colored leather slippers with turned-up toes and embroidered in gold and silver," that she had particularly admired.

The Khyber Pass varies in width from about twelve feet to well over two miles, and it is walled on each side by high precipitous cliffs. It winds for about twenty miles through the mountains to near Kabul, Afghanistan. Through the sometimes-violent history of the Pass marched the Aryans in 1500 BC, the armies of Alexander the Great, Genghis Khan, and many others including in more recent history the regiments of the British Empire. In an adventurous mood, Ted and Eleanor actually drove through the famous Pass, but when they reached the Afghanistan border, they found it closed and guarded by armed soldiers. Disappointed at having to turn back, Eleanor told Ted she wanted them to come back someday and go all the way into Afghanistan and see some of that mysterious Islamic country. Ted replied, "I'm taking no chances with you. We might do it when you're old and ugly," but he didn't say no.

The Roosevelts found riding on an Indian train to be an adventure within itself. The passenger cars were always crowded with people and all sorts of their possessions. Back in Peshawar, Ted and Eleanor boarded a train at the station and made the long overnight trip to Delhi. Besides looking at the people with dress and customs far different from their own, they were entertained by the antics of the Rhesus monkeys at every stop along the way. Passengers would toss the animals bits of food just to watch them scramble to get it and then eat it as fast as possible before another simian could steal the morsel. Ted picked up Eleanor's camera and began snapping the shutter, thinking he was taking pictures of the monkeys.

Eleanor didn't tell him there was no film in the camera; she didn't want to hear him fuss.

After arriving at their hotel in Delhi, the first thing Ted did was to head for the bathroom to enjoy his first bath in months in a real porcelain tub with hot running water. After joining Kermit and Belle, the four of them made a social call on the American wife of one of the members of the Governor General's Executive Council. As they approached the residence, the lady they intended to visit ran outside and exclaimed that Eleanor and Belle were welcome to come in, but that Ted and Kermit had to leave at once. She explained that other guests in her home included some Indian ladies in seclusion, and custom forbade them to be seen by any man other than their husbands, brothers, and fathers. Ted and Kermit immediately departed.

A day or two later, Eleanor and Belle decided to do some shopping on their own in downtown Delhi. Ted and Kermit were to meet them at Imre Schweiger's, the most exclusive shop in the City. Just as the men walked into the shop, Mr. Schweiger was showing Eleanor an expensive emerald necklace with stones as large as marbles. Seeing the admiring look in his wife's eyes, Ted asked how much it was. After hearing the price, he told the merchant he would let him know the next day whether he would buy it or not. Eleanor was shocked. After they left the shop she protested that they couldn't afford such an expensive piece of jewelry without dipping into their savings. After they argued about it for a while, Ted ended the conversation when he emphatically told her that it was a bargain and that they would not have to go into any of their savings because the price just happened to be the exact amount *Cosmopolitan Magazine* was paying him for the articles he was to write about the expedition. He added, "You are going to be young only once. That necklace would mean a lot more to you now than it would when you are seventy." His mind was made up and he bought his spouse the dazzling piece of jewelry. Eleanor treasured her beautiful emerald necklace for many years. After Ted's death, she passed it on to Anne, their oldest son's wife.

From Delhi the group traveled to the Central Province of India where they met Mr. Baptista, a renowned scientist from the Bombay Natural History Society. Then they motored into the famous Allapilli Forest, where they set up camp. There, with Mr. Baptista's help, they successfully trapped and preserved a myriad of small specimens, including parrots, kites, heron, dickey-birds, crow-pheasants, woodpeckers, snakes, and owls. Besides the small fauna, Kermit managed to kill a tiger and Eleanor shot a jackal to add to the museum's collection. All in all, on this segment of the expedition they collected ninety-six animals, including a rat that slipped into a table drawer and ate some of Eleanor's money.

Even though hunting privileges were rarely given, Ted, Eleanor, Kermit, and Belle were all granted special permission by the Maharajah to hunt in Nepal.

Learning of the Roosevelts' approval, the British envoy to Nepal extended to them an invitation to spend a week at his lodge and hunt the wild mammals found in the area, particularly tigers. Excited at the opportunity, the hunters packed enough gear for a week's stay and boarded a train for the twenty-four hour trip to Bikna Thori, Nepal. After they had traveled for many hours and were over half way to their destination, an English passenger sitting nearby overheard them talking about going to Nepal and informed them that the railroad bridge up ahead was out. He said that they would have to detrain at the river, get a boat to cross, and then catch another train on the other side. When their train stopped for the passengers to get supper, Ted sent telegrams ahead asking for coolies and a boat to meet them at the washed out bridge, and requested the trainmaster to please hold up the train on the other side until they got there. As luck would have it, their train stopped and put its passengers off about three miles before reaching the river. It was raining hard, and there were no coolies. Thinking fast, before the passengers got away, Ted hired some of them to help carry their baggage to the riverbank. But when they got there, there was no boat, and it was pitch-black dark and still raining.

Not really knowing what to do, the Roosevelts shouted toward the other side of the river. Shortly, they received a reply to the effect that it was late, dark, raining, and the boat would come in the morning. Visualizing some of their precious hunting time was being lost, Ted bellowed back some unpleasant remarks. Surprisingly, a boat soon appeared out of the night. After crossing the river, they were told that the train station was a half-mile up the trail. They finally got to the station, lugging all their gear, but were then informed that the train had already left and would not be back for twenty-four hours. By now all of them were soaking wet and discouraged. Eleanor and Belle unrolled their sleeping bags and lay down under the roof of the station platform while Ted and Kermit went off trying to find a car to hire. Instead of an automobile, the brothers managed to wake up an English planter living nearby and told him of their plight. The farmer said that there was another train to Bikna Thori leaving from another station about forty miles away. The Englishman volunteered to drive them to that station and called ahead for the stationmaster to hold the train until they arrived. Very appreciative of this stranger's courtesy, the four exhausted and exasperated travelers piled themselves and all their baggage into the good man's vehicle and sped away as fast as the bumpy road would permit. Finally reaching the new station, the stationmaster explained that he held up the train as long as he could, but had to release it when they did not arrived as soon as he had expected. All the Roosevelt's were now totally drained, dirty, wet, and ready to throw up their hands and cry. Just then lady luck changed; the stationmaster surprised them by saying that he had a special supply train already made up to go to their destination and that he might as well send it on. He would allow the Americans to ride this train if they wished. They did. They finally arrived in Bikna Thori, and only about six hours later than originally planned.

Mr. Hugh Wilkinson, their host, was waiting with a car to take them to his hunting lodge. He also had an elephant there to transport their equipment. The Roosevelts found their accommodations at the camp to be comfortable and the scenery to be spectacular. Winding along on a scenic jungle the road, they came to an open area and saw the lodge building on a hill overlooking a picturesque river. On the other side was a grassy plain with tall snowcapped mountains off in the distance. After getting organized and resting a while, all were anxious to begin hunting the next morning.

Their host-envoy had developed tiger hunting into an organized team effort almost like an organized game. The night before a hunt he would have a number of live steer calves tied at various spots in the jungle as bait for the tigers. When morning came, large wooden shooting platforms called howdahs would be strapped on the backs of five elephants and a number of other elephants would be saddled with pads on their backs. The bait would be checked to see which calves had been killed by a tiger. Habitually, a tiger would kill an animal and partially consume it on the spot, then leave the meal and lie hidden nearby for several hours until it was ready to return to the kill and feast some more. After selecting a kill site with an area of jungle, brush, or other cover nearby where Mr. Wilkinson believed the predator was probably hiding, he would have the hunters mount the elephants with pads. The entire pachyderm herd would then be led by the mahouts to the vicinity of the partially eaten calf. The elephants would be placed in a crude circle several hundred yards in diameter around the area where the tiger was thought to be hiding. The animals that had "howdahs" on their backs would be interspersed among the others. Each hunter would then climb onto one of the shooting platforms and all the behemoths would be ridden toward the center of the ever-decreasing circle. All the while the mahouts were shouting and the elephants were bellowing. The commotion would drive any resting tiger into the middle of the cover. As the circle tightened, the mahouts would cause the elephants to trample down a strip of grass and brush several yards wide in a ring around the tiger's hiding place, like a firebreak around a woods or a racetrack around the infield. The shooters would then have a clear field of fire. Two of the most experienced mahouts, mounted on two of the best trained tuskers, would then enter the small area remaining in the center of the circle and drive out any concealed tiger. As the tiger tried to escape across the trampled ring, at least one shooter would likely get a clear shot. During their week of tiger hunting, the four Roosevelts accounted for seven of the big cats. Ted got two, one of them by making a fast shot from the hip.

Once during the tiger hunt, the party stumbled across a group of rare Indian rhinoceros. The rhinos were infuriated at being disturbed by the group and charged toward the elephants. The elephant Eleanor was riding spooked and ran away. Ted's spouse was bounced and jostled along until the behemoth reached a swamp area and the mahout managed to get it under control. Both Ted and Belle brought down one of the rhinos during the melee.

When the tiger hunt was over, the hunters retraced their steps back to Lucknow. The schedule next called for the Roosevelts to hunt in the marshes and swamps near Kheri in the Oudh for swamp deer, tiny hog deer, and any other game on the Field Museum's list that they encountered. Departing again by train from Lucknow, they got off at Palia, where they were met by Colonel J. C. Faunthrope, a noted local hunter. The Colonel drove them to the splendorous hunting camp of their hostess, Her Highness, the Maharanee Saheba. As soon as they could organize their gear and get into their hunting clothes, they wasted no time in climbing aboard the waiting elephants and heading for the hunting area. The enormous beasts were well trained and would feel their way as they trudged through the murky swamp water and mud. At noon the hunting would temporarily cease and a sumptuous lunch would be served in the field by the Head Chef of the Carlton Hotel in Lucknow. Shooting a scampering swamp deer from the back of a moving elephant is very difficult, especially so if the target is a little hog deer. Still, they managed to get good family groups of both swamp deer and hog deer in three days of hunting.

Having quickly satisfied the primary reason for hunting in the swamp, and with several days remaining on this segment of the trip, the Roosevelts turned their attention to hunting other game. Ted knew that the wild animals in the area were accustomed to seeing the local populace riding ox carts and did not associate the carts with danger, so one day he went out in an ox cart in hopes of getting a shot at a black buck. He didn't see a buck, but he did add a beautiful leopard to the museum's collection. The final hunting days of the "James Simpson—Roosevelts—Field Museum Expedition" were spent successfully hunting for game further down on the museum's wish list and a number of different species were taken, including wild pigs, swamp partridges, peacocks, wildcats, and an axis deer doe and fawn.[8]

All in all, the expedition brought back over eighty large animals of twenty different species, and over fifteen hundred small mammals, reptiles and birds, many of which were mounted and displayed by the museum for years. While it has never been satisfactorily explained why Marco Polo never wrote of the Great Wall of China, Ted, Kermit, and the Field Museum at least corroborated his description of the Ovis poli. The expedition had been a great success.[9]

With the business side of the trip concluded, the brothers and wives started thinking about a leisurely journey home, and while on the way seeing some sights and meeting some interesting people. First, they drove in a loaned convertible automobile some sixty miles on an unpaved, extremely dusty road to the palace of the Maharanee Saheba to express to her their gratitude for allowing them to hunt. When they arrived all covered with road dust, the Maharanee met them at the front steps and insisted that they come right in and meet her relatives. She gave them a few minutes to freshen up and then served them tea and sweets of all kinds. The Roosevelts enjoyed the refreshments, but they noticed that neither the Maharanee nor any of her relatives ate with them; they surmised this was because of the caste system that prevailed in India.

After returning to Lucknow for a day, the family took a train to Delhi for a five-day visit at the Viceregal Lodge at the invitation of the Viceroy and Vicereine of India. Besides the Roosevelts, two of the seven other guests were Lord and Lady Arthur Lee of Fareham. To bump into the Lees in India was a delightful surprise for the four Americans and was, they said, an example of how the world was growing smaller with the improved transportation systems that were being developed. As a young man, Lord Lee was a British observer attached to the Rough Riders, and he had been a special friend of the Roosevelt family ever since. In his long and distinguished career, he had held many important posts with the British Government, including First Lord of the Admiralty, and he wore many impressive orders and decorations on his uniform. When he was dressed in his formal attire with all his regalia, prominently displayed over his heart he always wore the award he treasured most, the small badge depicting him as a Rough Rider.[10]

The night before the Roosevelts left Delhi they attended an investiture dinner. A very formal affair where orders and decorations are bestowed on deserving recipients. It was held in the grand ballroom of the Viceregal Lodge and all the guests were in their finest formal wear. The Indian Maharaj and other Indian royalty and dignitaries were in brightly colored costumes made of silk and other fine fabrics and wore their most exquisite jewels. The military aides and guards were in full dress uniform and the Viceroy was in robes of velvet trimmed with ermine. Ted and Kermit were in tuxedos and Eleanor and Belle wore formal gowns. The ceremony began with the sounding of trumpets and the Color Guard marching in to music played by a Military Band. From his place on the throne, the Viceroy would announce the name of a recipient of an award. The man would stand and remain standing while the Viceroy read a list of his previous honors. Then he would walk up to the throne, receive his new award, and return to his seat. Some of the honorees were knighted and knelt while the Viceroy tapped them on the shoulder with his sword. Ted and Eleanor were impressed and moved at seeing English pageantry and ceremony at its finest, but at the same time they had to smile, for they found it something like the Elks, the Shriners and the Arabian Nights.[11]

Early the next morning, they caught a train to Bombay, and there boarded a ship that eventually took then to England. After visiting in London a few days, they boarded another ship for home. It was well into 1926 when the Roosevelts disembarked in New York.

Home again in Oyster Bay, Ted had not seen his children in nearly a year. Gracie was now fourteen, Teddy eleven, Cornelius ten, and Quentin six. He spent some time with them before beginning another project. The TR Jrs were fortunate that all their children were bright, healthy and normal kids.

When he resigned his job as Assistant Secretary of the Navy, Ted hired his very efficient secretary, Miss Margaret Hensey, to move to New York and work for him. She remained with him for the next twenty years.

Ted was a prolific writer, especially during the $2^{1}/_{2}$ years following the completion of James Simpson—Roosevelts—Field Museum Expedition. In 1926, he and Kermit co-authored a book entitled *East of the Sun and West of the Moon,* which told of their experiences on their Field Museum adventure. In addition, with Miss Hensey's help Ted began work on the articles he contracted to write for *Cosmopolitan* Magazine. He also wrote articles for several other magazines, including *Field and Stream,* and started to work on two new books, *Rank and File,* and *All in the Family.*[12]

Rank and File is a series of true short stories about ordinary citizens who served the United States with distinction during the Great War. The book was dedicated to the memory of Ted's deceased brother Quentin, who was a casualty of that conflict. In the foreword, Ted writes:

> I believe that a nation is mirrored in war by the rank and file of its soldiers, not by any individual strategist; just as I believe that it is mirrored in peace by its ordinary every day citizens rather than by some brilliant statesman *****.
>
>   These men took the war as a duty of citizenship. They did their turn at the wheel, came back to this country, and took up the work they had left.

Ted points out in the book that many times in war gallant acts are either not reported, or not recorded, or there are no surviving witnesses to tell of the event. He states that the stories told in the book are not necessarily the most heroic ones that occurred during the Great War, but are simply examples of brave acts that were performed by every-day American citizens.[13]

One chapter in *Rank and File* stresses the value of the regular army enlisted man. It points out that the old-time army sergeant often got drunk and thrown in jail, but that during war he was in the front lines and was the backbone of the Army. In a chapter entitled "The Battle of Henry Johnson," the brave acts of a black soldier in the all-black, except for white officers, 15th Infantry Regiment are described. "Anchors Away" tells of how the crew of a naval seaplane ran out of gas and had to land many miles out in the open sea. The men rigged a makeshift sail and managed to keep the plane afloat for days, until they were able to sail their improvised craft to safety. Other tales in the book include that of a college professor who, as a forty-four year old infantry lieutenant, continued to lead his platoon after he had been critically wounded. He had himself hoisted onto the back of a stout private so he could be moved around among his men during the remainder of the battle. Another chapter tells of the valor of another lieutenant, who in one day had seven horses shot out from under him while he was delivering messages between the artillery and the infantry.

"The Sword of the Lord and of Gideon" is a chapter devoted to the exploits of Sergeant Alvin York of Pall Mall, Tennessee, who was the most decorated U.S. soldier in World War I. Many years after Ted's death, Earnest Hemingway compiled a group of war stories which he published in book form as *The Best War Stories of all Time*. Hemingway's book includes tales written by such authors as, Stephen Crain, T. E. Lawrence, William Faulkner, and Victor Hugo. The stories tell of particular incidents that occurred in various wars, including The Battle of Hastings, World Wars I and II, the French Revolution, David's slaying of Goliath, and others. Ted's "The Sword of the Lord and of Gideon" was chosen by Hemingway as worthy of the distinction and was included in the book.[14]

While Theodore Roosevelt, Jr. was certainly not an ordinary man in either his birth, education, intelligence, or physical stamina, he nevertheless loved and was loved by the common people he came in contact with. These warm and compassionate feelings are revealed in his words and actions throughout his life. The forward and vignettes in *Rank and File* are indicative of his admiration for ordinary Americans.[15]

Copyrighted in 1929, *All in the Family* describes growing up in the Teddy and Edith Roosevelt household. Ted writes of Sagamore Hill, its furnishings and the land around it, meal times in his boyhood home and the toys and other articles he and his brothers and sisters thought of as treasures. Other chapters include his memories of the various pets and other animals in the household, the sports and games the family played, and what his parents taught their children with respect to ethics, religion, history, and the importance of education.[16]

In the summer of 1926 and again in '28, Ted spent several weeks in Plattsburg New York participating in military training. Cornelius went to the camp with his dad for two weeks in 1928 and he had a swell time watching the training, riding post horses, and playing with the children of the regular army officers stationed there.

On the last day of training, Ted was selected as reviewing officer for the entire regiment of some two thousand trainees. He was touched by the honor and tears swelled in his eyes as he went down the ranks of his old comrades. He wrote his sister:

On the extreme right of the review were formed the few remaining old-timers who had served with me in the 26th Infantry. There were some thirty-five in all. They were dressed in their tailor-made uniforms, spick and span, buttons shining, with their medals and wound stripes. They marched by me first. Many of the old non-coms had not carried a rifle for ten years, but they dressed as straight as a hem and their pieces were in perfect alignment. After they passed me they wheeled out of the line and formed on my right, standing rigidly at attention while the rest of the troops moved by.

The C.M.T.C. boys were assembled by the grandstand at the other end of the field so that I could talk to them. While this was being done I turned to the contingent of old-timers. The senior N.C.O. presented them to me, brought them to the order and gave "open ranks." Then I walked down their line inspecting them, and the massed band suddenly struck up "Auld Lang Syne." I almost bellowed. As I walked down the line looking at one hard-bitten old face after the other the picture would rise before me of Murphy bringing in the first prisoner; of the time when Krapahousky and I stilled a panic that had broken out in the lead platoon of A. Company; of when Tubbs had taken the machine-gun that was holding us up. Immediately after I had inspected them they closed ranks, formed squad columns and marched ahead of me to the grandstand. When the boys saw them coming they burst into roars of applause. They wheeled into the line behind the grandstand and came to the order with machine-like precision, and again the C.M.T.C. Regiment cheered.[17]

Edith, Ted's mother, had warned him that the old guard Republicans would try to use him as their hatchet man against the Democrats in general and Al Smith in particular. She said that after he cut Smith and the Democrats up in speeches, they would act as if he was speaking without Republican Party authorization. She didn't think he would want to get himself into that kind of situation. Some of the newspapers were speculating that Ted would be a candidate for Governor in 1926, and he did still have political aspirations. Not wanting to disappoint the GOP leaders, he did not heed his mother's advice, and soon began making speeches attacking the Democratic Party as the party of big government and as an usurper of the rights reserved to the states by the U. S. Constitution. Ted sincerely believed and said publicly many times that the Democrats would destroy the individual citizen's initiative and self-reliance by causing them to rely on big brother government for their needs.[18]

While he did not get his party's nomination for Governor in 1926, Ted continued his denouncements of the New York Democratic Party at every opportunity. At the request of the Republican leaders, he spoke on Oct. 1, 1927 at the Republican State Convention. There he viciously attacked the Tammany Hall control of vice-ridden New York City and Albany, declaring that "the red light district has crawled to the very steps of the State Capitol." Later that month in a speech in New York City, he said that Governor Smith was "bred in the Tammany fold and is the bellwether of their flock," and went on to make other charges of Democratic managed vice in New York City and Albany, specifically claiming that:[19]

> We do not question the personal integrity of Governor Smith, but he is sponsored and backed by Tammany Hall, and a man must be judged by the company he keeps.
>
> For years Tammany has sat astride the City of New York. That great corrupt political machine holds the metropolis in its grasp. From Tweed to Olvany the dynasty stretches in an unbroken line. Methods have changed, but fundamentals remain unchanged.
>
> There is one conclusion and only one that fair minded citizens of this state and nation can draw—Governor Smith is a Tammany man, and there is no such thing as a new Tammany.
>
> Under indictment now for running a gambling pool are John and Daniel O'Connell, two of the principal Democratic leaders of Albany and brothers of the Democratic county chairman ****.
>
> Among others that are being tried at the same time for the same offense are John Boyl, Democratic ex-Assemblyman and one of the leaders of the third ward; Arthur G. Malloy, Democratic leader; Robert H. Burns, captain of the watch in the Capitol and brother of the Democratic candidate for sheriff in the last election.
>
> The tickets for this gambling pool were peddled not only throughout the city, but within the State Capitol. There were paid agents of the pool with order books in the Assembly chamber and elsewhere.[20]

The leaders of the Democratic Party, the newspapers, and even many of the Republican old guard derided Ted's efforts to again link the popular Al Smith with vice. A few of the Republican hierarchy even claimed they had attempted to talk him out of doing it. Edith was right; they hung him out to dry. Governor Smith was the odds on favorite to be the Democratic nominee for President in 1928, so the GOP strategists had copies of Ted's charges printed up and distributed throughout the Midwest and South, where Smith was thought to be the most vulnerable.

Soon afterwards, TRJr went on a speaking tour in a number of midwestern states, and repeated his accusations to the thousands that came to hear him. Many of the charges he made were later supported by guilty pleas entered by some of the individuals he alluded to. During his travels, Ted received an enthusiastic reception everywhere he went. There was talk, and even some media speculation, that he was not politically dead and would be a good candidate for Vice President. Ted was, however, facing reality. He well knew that the influential Republicans would never consent to him having the nomination for Governor in 1928. He was further convinced that his old friend Herbert Hoover would receive the Republican nomination for President, and would balance the ticket by selecting a mid-westerner as his running mate. (Ted was right. Hoover was nominated and picked Charles Curtis, a U.S. Senator from Kansas, as his running mate.)[21]

In the mid-twenties, even though prohibition was still in effect, a number of prominent New Yorkers, including Vincent Astor, Nelson Doubleday, Marshall Field, and Ted and Kermit Roosevelt, rented the whole floor in a building in downtown Manhattan and formed a private, for men-only, social club where they could meet, enjoy a good drink of illegal liquor, and relax. They elaborately furnished "The Room," as it was called, with antiques and lined the walls with animal heads, trophies, and other macho objects donated by the members. The Roosevelt brothers contributed German flags they brought back from the war and a Remington Bronze from their father's collection. Ted was never a light drinker, but he knew when to quit. Kermit was beginning to drink too much.[22]

By early 1928, Ted and Kermit began talking about making another expedition to some far-off land to hunt and bring back the hides of rare, or even unknown, animals for scientific study and display. They got out maps of the most remote corners of the earth and discussed several likely sites, including Borneo and Angola, before finally settling on a trek to the area of China northwest of Indo-China where the Himalayas descend into the coastal plains. The area selected was centered approximately one thousand miles east of where they had hunted two years before.

Several factors influenced the brothers in picking that particular spot. The area was so remote that it had never been properly mapped, and it was almost unknown to the Western world. But the thing that sold them on the area more than anything else, was the fact that the region was habitat for a number of rare mammals, including the giant panda. While a few panda skins obtained from native hunters existed in museums, no Westerner had ever shot one, and it had never been studied scientifically. The animal was thought to exist in the dense bamboo jungles in the Szechwan (Sichuan) Province of western China near the Tibetan border, but zoologists knew so little about it that they were not sure whether it was a bear, a raccoon, or some previously unknown species. By summer, the Roosevelt brothers had aroused the interest of their old standby, the Field Museum in Chicago. In turn, Mr. Stanley Field, the museum President, prevailed upon William V. Kelly, the President of the Miehle Printing Press and Manufacturing Co., to finance the project. It was officially titled "The Kelley—Roosevelts—Expedition of the Field Museum of Chicago."[23]

As plans developed, the undertaking would be in three divisions. Two of them would be led by the Roosevelts, first into the Yunnan and Szechwan provinces of China and later into French Indo-China (now the country of Vietnam). In addition to the giant panda, they would hunt other rare mammals, including the takin (Takin is a mammal with impressive horns and in appearance is similar to what a half goat-half antelope would be. Its nearest relative is the arctic musk ox.), the golden monkey, the McNeill's stag (a type of deer), water buffalo, seladang, and banteng. In addition to hunting, they would do rough mapping as they traveled through any uncharted territory. The third part of the expedition would be led by Harold J. Coolidge, Jr. of Harvard University. Besides Coolidge, three other scientists were included. Their purpose was to collect and study the birds, mammals and reptiles that were native to northwestern French Indo-China.[24]

This adventure would be far more elaborate than the previous Simpson—Roosevelts—Field Museum hunt, as they would take with them a coterie of naturalists to collect birds and small animals of the region, interpreters, skinners, and hide preservers. Suydam Cutting, who had been a member of the previous expedition, would go along as an extra hunter. Needed supplies and equipment were acquired, including a supply of knives, flashlights, and pocket tool kits to present as gifts to village headmen and others when the occasion arose. Necessary permits were obtained from the countries involved. To prepare themselves to do the promised mapping, the Roosevelt brothers studied map-making under the renowned Dr. Isaiah Bowman of the American Geographical Society. Ted had previously committed himself to make a speaking tour on behalf of the Republican Party, so they could not depart the U.S. until after the fall elections.[25]

As expected, Al Smith got the '28 Democratic nomination for President, and Herbert Hoover was the Republican candidate. Ted traveled the country the month before the election speaking in person at rallies and over the radio on behalf of his party's candidates. He pointed out that Hoover was a self made man and a humanitarian, while all Al Smith had ever done was hold political office. He said that Smith was a personable fellow and would be fun to spend an evening with, but that Hoover, with his solid record of accomplishments, was the kind of man you would like your son to grow up to be. More so than in 1924, Governor Smith found Ted's vivacity to be irritating, one time saying, "If bunk was electricity, the young Colonel would be a power house." While no one ever claimed that the Republicans would have lost the election without Ted's help, he was a very effective campaigner. The Republican National Committee received more requests for Ted to speak than anyone else, except for the candidates themselves..

In 1928, the Depression was a year away, and, except for the South, the GOP was strong all over the country. In the fall, the voters liked Herbert Hoover's campaign slogan, "A chicken in every pot and a car in every garage," and elected him President by a large majority.

Ted maintained all along that he would have liked his party's '28 nomination for Governor, but he did not aggressively pursue it, as he had in 1924. Franklin Delano Roosevelt, who had spent the previous two years in Warm Springs, Georgia, battling polio, returned to New York to run for Governor as the Democratic candidate. Franklin campaigned hard and won in a close election. Had the 1928 gubernatorial contest been the Democrat FDR vs. the Republican TRJr, Ted, not having to face off against the popular Al Smith, may have won. He missed his golden opportunity because he had his mind on going hunting.[26]

On November 10, 1928, Suydam, Belle, Eleanor, Kermit, and Ted departed New York on the steamship Homeric, bound for the UK. Eleanor and Belle would accompany the men as far as Paris, then they would return home and rejoin them in Saigon the following summer. Laying over in London for three days to get all the information they could about the giant panda, Ted, Kermit, and Suydam consulted the Director of the South Kensington Museum, the Secretary of the Royal Geographical Society, the Director of the British Museum, and several British big game hunters. They promised the British Museum they would donate to it the penis and testicles of any male giant panda they killed; this would enable the museum's scientists to determine the animal's specie.[27]

From London, they crossed the English Channel to France, then took a steamer over the Red Sea and the Indian Ocean to Bombay. After riding a train to Calcutta, they traveled to Rangoon and then to Katha, Burma, where they boarded a sternwheeler up river to Bhamo. On December 26th, they traveled the final seventeen miles by truck to the village of Tengyueh, where they had horses, mules, coolies, and guides waiting. Here the hunt actually began. Mostly on horseback, but sometimes walking, they followed the centuries old Bhamo-Talifu caravan route (later to be known in history as the Burma Road) as it wound up, down, and around in a northeastwardly direction. The group would cover fifteen to twenty miles a day, stopping at night at an inn they chanced upon or pitching tents along the trailside. In the lowlands, a jungle of vines, plants, and enormous trees ran along each side of the path. Occasionally they would spot a giant termite mound in the mass of vegetation. The way the columns of termites went in and out of the holes in the mounds reminded Ted of infantry columns moving along in France a decade earlier.

A few days after starting out, the hunting caravan reached the Chinese border and they were joined by a small detail of soldiers provided to them by the Chinese government for protection against any bandits they might encounter.

Trekking along, Ted noticed that the people they encountered seldom even looked their way, and seemed to have a "live and let live" attitude. The first locals they saw were two old Chinese men on the veranda of a dilapidated grass hut. One of them was cooking an opium pill for his pipe and the other was cooking food. Both men kept to their task and never even looked up when the pack train passed by. While the binding of feet had been outlawed by authorities in recent years, women, especially older women, were often seen with horribly deformed feet as a result of the practice of this strange custom.

Even though the party had a lot of ground to cover in order to reach the giant panda territory during the best time of the year to hunt, they would halt from time to time along the trail for short periods in an attempt to find rare game. This type of hunting was not very successful, although they did manage to collect some small mammals and birds, mostly from setting overnight traps.[28]

On January 11th, they crossed the Mekong River, the same stream that would become famous forty years later when the U.S. was involved in the Vietnam War. At the place of their crossing, the river flowed through a steep gorge and it was very swift. It was not the lazy, muddy stream that the American servicemen would see many miles to the south and many years later. About fifty miles along the ancient passageway from the Mekong crossing, they reached the City of Tali, where the trail turned north, toward what was thought to be giant panda country.

Ted noticed that when they passed through a large town like Tali, the populace, especially the children, were enthralled by these strange white men passing by, and they would follow along behind them and try to touch them. This was entirely different behavior from the people they encountered in rural areas and small villages, who simply ignored them.

The hunting party stopped for four days to rest when they reached the Lamasery of Yungning. Here they were cordially received and shown the impressive temple by the Lamas. They were also allowed to exchanged their tired mules for fresh ones. Ted was now forty-one years old and not quite as spry as he used to be. For a week before reaching the Lamasery, they had been at altitudes over ten thousand feet most of the time. It was extremely cold with much ice and snow, and they had been sleeping on the ground. Climbing on the mountainside on the ice had caused Ted to fall two or three times. He was bruised up and ready for a few days rest.[29]

Departing the Lamasery on February 5th, they resumed climbing along the high mountain trail and continued following as it zigzagged down into the valleys. Soon they reached the lands of the Austro-Asiatic ethnic group known as the Lolo. These people spoke a Tibeto-Burman dialect, wore rough clothing made of homespun hemp, still practiced slavery, and were known for their hunting skills. A smallpox epidemic was raging in one Lolo village they passed through.

Stopping in one village, Ted, Kermit, and Suydam hired Lolo guides and began to hunt separately. Ted and his guide climbed up the side of a mountain to a meadow where TRJr shot a serow, a kind of antelope with horns similar to a rocky mountain goat. Hoping their luck was changing, the group decided to stay in the village overnight and hunt in the area again the next morning. When this effort drew a blank, they packed up and continued northward toward the Kingdom of Muli. The hunting caravan was in the mountains most of the time now. The snow was very deep and the wind howled, sometimes as loud as a train whistle. After some miles, they began to pass little wayside shrines, usually sheltered in a small structure about the size of an outhouse. These quaint little religious huts reminded Ted of the small shrines he saw in France during World War I. Occasionally they met a caravan headed in the opposite direction, sometimes led by Lamas dressed in red Tibetan clothing.[30]

The Kingdom of Muli is an area of vast grasslands, high plateaus, and glaciated mountains. It had been visited in 1923 by Dr. Joseph Rock, the famous botanist, who reported that the area was populated by robbers and pilgrims, but that the robbers would sometimes turn from pillage to prayer. When TRJr and the rest of the party arrived there, they found that the inhabitants were multiethnic, but mostly Tibetan, spoke many dialects, and that their principal occupations were herdsman, hunters, and collectors of medicinal herbs and mushrooms. A few of the villages were ethnically Chinese.

Continuing on to the North, they were proceeding up a river valley when Ted saw the most unusual human being he had ever laid his eyes on. The man was chopping wood. Ted said he had a, "Squat body depicting great strength, with arms that hung nearly to his knees. He was a near ape-man." Present day paleontologists would be interested in studying such a man to determine if he was some kind of throw back to the Neanderthals, who have allegedly been extinct for forty thousand years.

On up the valley they came to several small villages in which were located large stone towers. Some of the towers were shaped like six-pointed stars and some were square-shaped. They all appeared to be very old. The inhabitants said that no one knew who built them or for what purpose and that they had always been there. Ted speculated that the unusual structures had been built in ancient times for either religious or defensive purposes.[31]

They were climbing again into the mountains as they continued northward on the trail, when Ted made the first major kill of the hunt. In the bitter cold and blowing wind at an altitude of over fourteen thousand feet he brought down a sambhur (a type of deer). After the animal was skinned and the hide preserved, the carcass was divided between the men in the caravan and the local inhabitants.

Toward the latter part of February, they left the Kingdom of Muli, re-entered

Chinese territory and began to descend to lower areas as they approached the lands where they expected to find the giant panda and takin. Often along the trail they would talk with local hunters and show them pictures of the various mammals they were seeking. They soon realized that they could not rely on the information provided by the inhabitants, as they would get conflicting information from village to village, and even from hunter to hunter. Near the village of Tatsienlu, the area looked inviting and the party halted for a couple of days to hunt. Here Ted bagged two burrhel rams (a type of mountain sheep similar to the Ovis poli, except with smaller horns). The coolies and others in the caravan particularly enjoyed the tasty meat. Other hunters in the group accounted for a number of unusual squirrels and birds to add to the museum's collection.[32]

Spring was in the air by March 6th, when they reached a lower altitude and proceeded along the bank of a river. Fruit trees had sprung blooms of white and pink. Small boats with fishermen casting their nets could be seen. Before long they reached Muping, one of those strange little feudal kingdoms that fringe Tibet. This was the most northerly area on their itinerary and it was where they would begin to hunt their main prey, the giant panda and the takin. Not long after arriving, Ted and Kermit met a native hunter who showed them the hide of one of the big pandas and the horns of two takin he had recently killed. The brothers were very excited, now they had positive proof that they were getting reliable information from one of the local people. Ted promised to give the man a beautiful pearl-handled Colt pistol if he assisted them in bringing in a panda.

For several days they stayed in the Muping area, hunting in the bamboo jungles for panda and takin. While they saw lots of panda droppings and tracks, they did not see any of the elusive animals, and they failed to see any signs at all of takin. There was, however, one consolation; Ted and Kermit chanced upon a pack of golden monkeys scampering around in the trees and they managed to bring down a group of nine. The Field Museum would now be the only museum in the world to have a family group of this rare simian.[33]

By April 3rd they still had no panda or takin, and it was almost time to do a one-hundred eighty-degree turn and head back south. They had to reach the jungles of Indo-China in time to hunt before the rainy season began there. To better the chances of getting at least one panda, they decided to split up. Ted and Kermit, along with some of the coolies and guides, would go back into Lolo country but to a different location from where they had previously been. Suydam and some of the others would go into the Ningyuan area. They agreed to get back together on April 16th.

Heading south on another old caravan path and back into Lolo land, Ted and Kermit heard that a farmer in a nearby village had just the day before wounded a panda that he caught pillaging his beehive. Going straight to the village, they hunted for two days with no results. On April 12th, still having no panda, they somberly packed up in the driving rain and set out for the bamboo jungles in the vicinity of Yehli, where they would hunt for the final three days.

April 15th broke with a cold and overcast morning. A snow the night before had covered the valley floor and stuck on the spring foliage. Ted, Kermit and three Lolo guides set out to hunt this final day. They had stealthily walked in the bamboo forest for three or four miles when they turned into a ravine and suddenly came upon fresh panda tracks. With hope renewed, they tracked the animal in the snow for several hours. The trail led into an area where towering spruce trees had shaded out most of the bamboo. They found a nest of bamboo that the panda had made, but tracks were everywhere and went in every direction. Not knowing which way to go, the brothers split up with Ted and one Lolo going in one direction and Kermit and the other two Lolos going in another. If either brother found the animal he would immediately send for the other. In a short time, Kermit spied the panda slowly walking back toward the dense bamboo forest. The animal appeared to be disoriented, as if it had just woken from a sleep. Kermit immediately sent one of the Lolos to go for Ted. By the time Ted got there, the animal had recovered and was trotting into the thick bamboo. The brothers fired simultaneously, each bullet striking home, but the beast did not fall and continued into the forest. As quickly as possible, they both shot again. This time the animal fell, but it immediately recovered and made off into the jungle. About seventy-five yards into the almost impenetrable maze they found their quarry dead. It was an old male. From the day after Christmas, when the hunting began, until the downing of the panda, the expedition had covered over 1,400 miles on the ancient travel arteries.[34]

After getting the animal back to camp, they measured it, skinned it, and took proper steps to preserve the hide. Then the celebration began. The Roosevelts, all the coolies and guides, and even some of the local hunters joined in the all-night party. This had apparently been the first panda ever killed in the Yehli area. From their personal experiences hunting the giant panda, and from their readings and talks with local hunters, Ted and Kermit concluded that the elusive and extremely rare animal could be found only in the widely scattered bamboo pockets located within a fairly wide area of distribution.[35]

Since first beginning to plan for the hunt, the Roosevelts and Suydam had been warned to beware of the fierce Lolos. They were advised to take every precaution to insure the safety of themselves and the men hired to accompany them. From time to time along the route they would hear stories of Lolo attacks on villages and travelers ahead, but the Americans were cordial to the natives they met and often presented presents to the headsmen. They had no trouble with the Lolo.

After finally bagging the panda, they didn't have time to rest up for even one day. They had to get on down south to Indo-China as soon as possible. The rainy season would make the jungle there a muddy, slippery entanglement of vegetation, and they had many miles to travel to get there. After rejoining Suydam the next day, the party left for Yunnan Fu, over four hundred miles away, where there was an American Consul and a railway to Hanoi.

While Ted was busy on his hunting junket, Eleanor had been busy lobbying President-elect Hoover and other influential Republican politicians toward getting her husband an appointment in government service. The income would be nice to have, but mainly it would keep him active in the political game. She and Ted wanted Hoover to appoint him Governor General of the Philippine Islands, an American colony since the Spanish-American War. She was also busy preparing to meet Ted in Saigon in mid-July, and arranging with Signorina and the grandmothers to look after the children.

Reaching Yunnan Fu in early May, Ted, Kermit, and Suydam took great care in protecting the fruits of their hunting and in disposing of what was left of the pack train. Kermit had a distressing cable waiting for him to the effect that his shipping business was in serious financial trouble and he was needed at home as fast as he could get there. Anxious to proceed as quickly as possible, the three Americans boarded the rickety little train for Hanoi, but the old engine was slow and did not run at night. Hanoi was five hundred miles away, so the trip took several days.

Other than for Kermit's concern for his business, and Ted's and Suydam's desire to get to the jungles of south Indo-China before the rainy season set in, the leisurely journey was enjoyable. After five months in the remote backcountry of China where food compatible to American tastes was non-existent, the fare at the little hotels where the train stopped each night was good. As the train rattled along each day, the men whiled away the time enjoying the beautiful jungle scenery and thinking about their next meal. Ted thought about the tremendous cost in lives of building a railroad through the mountainous jungle terrain. Each cross tie, he said, was paid for by a human life. His thoughts were almost prophetic of the happenings in the same area less that fifteen years later when, during World War II, many thousands of Allied POWs (mostly British and Australian) lost their lives building the Thailand-Burma railroad through the jungle for their Japanese captors. While some of the survivors of the ordeal claim that the novel, *The Bridge on the River Kwai,* is not accurate as to many of the details concerning the building of the railroad, this chapter in history is best known from that book and from the award-winning movie that followed.

Hanoi was in what was then French Indo-China. When the three hunters arrived and got off the train, they felt like they were back in civilization for the first time in months. As Ted wrote, they "reveled in the flesh-pots of Egypt" by gorging themselves with delicious French food.[36]

Still making haste, the men immediately departed Hanoi for Saigon, where Kermit would board a ship for the USA, and Ted and Suydam would meet their guide and begin the last leg of the hunting expedition. On the way south, at times they skirted the South China Sea and marveled at the brilliant white sand beaches that fringed the shimmering tropical blue waters. Occasionally, they would pass a picturesque fishing village with small grass huts scattered among palm trees, or a small fleet of unpainted junks swaying at their moorings. Finally reaching Saigon in the middle of May, Kermit departed for America and Ted and Suydam met their guide, Monsieur Defosse.

Defosse was an outstanding follow. For a man of fifty, he was in remarkable physical condition. He had spent the best part of his life hunting and guiding hunters in the Indo-China area. Besides being a world-renowned professional guide and hunter, he was a highly educated scientist and had authored a number of articles for the *Atlantic Monthly* magazine. Coolies, horses, and oxcarts had been previously arranged for by the guide, so, after taking a day or two to purchase needed supplies, Ted, Suydam, Defosse, and the pack train set out into the jungle.[37]

On May 17th, President Hoover appointed Ted Governor General of Porto Rico (a.k.a. PR in this book). Both the President and Eleanor sent him cables in care of the American Consulate in Saigon notifying him of the appointment. His salary would be ten thousand dollars per year with an additional ten thousand for office and residence upkeep. Ted had been hopeful of getting the more prestigious Philippine Islands appointment and thought seriously about declining the PR job. Then, Eleanor reminded him that he had not held even an appointed political office for nearly five years, and that if he turned down this appointment there was no telling when he would have another opportunity to get back in politics. Any political job is better than no political job as far as keeping his hopes alive of some day being elected to high office. Ted knew she was right and accepted the position. He had to be in Porto Rico by early October.[38]

On the way to the primitive hunting camp Defosse had set up, they traveled for several miles through rubber plantations. Ted noticed that "strange bright-colored birds screamed harshly in the tree-tops and flashed across their path," and that swarms of butterflies seemed like showers of confetti. The natives they encountered were poor and backward, but they were not dangerous like the Lolo were reputed to be. After they unloaded their gear into the palm leaf shacks their guide had set up, they prepared to begin hunting bright and early the next morning.

The principal mammals desired by the museum from the jungles around Saigon were water buffalo, seladang and banteng. All of these animals are varieties of wild cattle or gaur. The adults stand over five feet at the shoulders and have skin as thick as two inches. Because of their large size and thick skin, and because of the heat and humidity of the jungle, extra care would have to be taken to preserve the hides. Shortly after beginning to hunt, Ted and Suydam each brought down a large water buffalo bull. With the help of the coolies, they loaded the carcasses on an oxcart, hauled them back to camp and skinned both animals. Then they scrapped off the bits of flesh still clinging to the underside of the hide, applied an arsenic compound to prevent flies and rubbed on salt as a preservative. Lastly the hides were stretched out on poles to dry.[39]

When in camp, the men did odd jobs, like dyeing their clothes with tree bark to be better camouflaged, or working on the skins, or repairing equipment. After going to bed at night, Ted was struck by the many sounds and unusual smells of the jungle. The many scents of the flowers combined with the musty aromas of unseen mammals and insects, and the putrid smell of decomposition, along with the strange calls of the fauna and the occasional crack of a falling limb, and the dampness and steaming temperature of the jungle, made sleep hard to come by. One morning when he arose, Ted discovered he had slept with two scorpions.[40]

The rains began and swarms of insects, especially mosquitoes, were everywhere. Suydam got sick and had to leave the hunt, but his place was taken by Defosse's son, Louis. Toward the end of the venture, Ted began to run a high fever interspersed with chills and he lost his appetite, but he continued to hunt. The shooters managed to bring down nice family groups of banteng, seladang, and water buffalo, along with a number of other specie, including family groups of hog deer and barking deer. Ted killed an enormous bull elephant that had only one tusk, but it was the largest tusk he had ever seen, measuring over ten-feet high from its shoulder and over five-feet around the curve.

Ted, Defosse, and young Louis had to have all their specimens to Saigon by July 15th. That was the day they were to meet Harold Coolidge and his party, who had been performing their part of the expedition in another area of Indo-China. Also that was when Ted was to meet Eleanor. The expedition had been a great success. The Roosevelts, the Defosses, Suydam, and Harold Coolidge combined in bringing in over two thousand small animals, about fifty-five hundred birds and reptiles, over forty large mammals, and, of course, the prize, the giant panda, which turned out to be in the raccoon family. The expedition in general, and especially the giant panda, received worldwide publicity. Some nineteen of the quarry turned out to be of previously unknown species. One of these, the muntjak deer, was given the scientific name, *Muntiacus rooseveltorum*. The Field Museum was the envy of the museum world. By the time the hunt was over, Harold Coolidge had a severe case of dysentery, and Ted was running a fever and felt awful.[41]

Since Kermit had to return to the States early, Belle would not be accompanying Eleanor to Saigon, as originally planned. For a girl who had been brought up sheltered, Ted's spouse had an awful lot of spunk, and the fact that she must travel halfway around the world alone to meet her husband didn't worry her a bit. From New York, she caught a train to San Francisco and there boarded a ship for Shanghai. After a few days of sightseeing in Shanghai and visiting at the home of the U.S. Consul General and his wife, she sailed to Hong Kong on a French ocean liner. At Hong Kong she had to leave the luxurious liner and board an old tramp steamer in order to get to Haiphong, where an executive with Standard Oil Co. met her and lent her a car and driver for an overnight sightseeing trip to Hanoi. From Hanoi, she sailed to Saigon and to Ted.

The American Consul General in Saigon, Mr. Henry Waterman, was waiting at the dock when Eleanor's ship moored. He took her to the U.S. Consulate where she was to meet Ted, but Ted was not there and no one knew where he was. That night, as Eleanor and the Watermans were having dinner, there was a racket at the front gate. When Eleanor looked out, she almost didn't recognize that it was Ted. He was outside shaking the gate and trying to get into the Consulate. When she got to him, she saw that he was nothing but skin and bones, was half-crazed with fever, and could not remember how to open the gate. He had lost forty-two pounds and looked worse than when she saw him in Paris, shortly after he had been gassed in the war. His fever was over 105 degrees. All he wanted in the way of nourishment was a little brandy. The doctor that was called in diagnosed Ted as having malaria and dysentery, gave him some medication, and placed him on a diet of only meat, bread, and tea.[42]

For the next couple of days, Ted stayed in bed under heavy blankets and taking aspirin and quinine. Then his fever broke, and he felt well enough to check and make sure the animal specimens were all packed and ready for shipment and also to see some of the sights of Saigon with Eleanor. Monsieur Pasquier, the French Governor General of Indo-China, gave a dinner party for the Roosevelts. Afterwards they got together with Harold Coolidge for a two-day private tour of the ruins of Angkor, conducted personally by Monsieur Henri Marchal, the curator in charge of excavations. The three Americans enjoyed very much their excursion and could easily see why Angkor was considered one of the Seven Wonders of the World.[43]

After returning to Saigon, Ted, Eleanor, and Harold boarded the Prosper, a small Norwegian freighter, and sailed for Hong Kong. Before completing the relatively short cruise to this destination two things happened. First, Ted had a severe relapse of dysentery and malaria. His temperature shot up and he looked like death itself. Then the ship got caught between two typhoons. The seas were so rough that anything not securely tied down would crash to the deck and then dangerously slide around as the ship pitched up and down with each immense wave. Ted didn't care though, he was so sick he didn't even know they were in a storm.

Just as the storm abated, the ship arrived and docked at the Port of Hong Kong. Eleanor immediately had Ted examined by a well-known British doctor. Since they were to be in port only one day, there wasn't much the doctor could do except give him some soothing medication. The next day the three Americans boarded the President Jefferson for the short journey to Shanghai. There, Ted was seen by another doctor who said he couldn't do anything for the malaria in the few days Ted was to be there, but he did give him a supply of medicine which would cure the dysentery provided it was taken as prescribed and further provided Ted stayed on his meat, bread and tea diet.

From Shanghai they sailed for Tokyo, where they had originally planned to spend a few days sightseeing. Even though Ted was feeling a little better, he looked like a ghost and weighed only 102 pounds. The brief layover in Japan was a disaster, however, for Eleanor came down with a bad case of bronchitis. Now they were both sick. When they managed to leave their hotel, intent on seeing some of the attractions, both of them were so weak they had to stop and rest after walking only a few steps. From Tokyo, they boarded the President Lincoln for San Francisco. After only one day at sea, Ted relapsed again, but this time more violently than before. Eleanor was afraid he might die. Some of the passengers were making bets on whether or not he would survive to reach the States. A couple of days later, Ted suddenly got a lot better. He then confessed to his wife that he had tired of his odious diet of meat, bread, and tea and had slipped behind her back and eaten several delicious peaches. This was the cause of his problem; Eleanor was relieved and at the same time wanted to kill him.

During the rest of the long cruise to San Francisco, most of Ted's time was occupied in learning to speak Spanish, the native tongue of Porto Rico, from a fellow passenger who was fluent in the language. He also did some study about the Island to prepare himself to perform his new job, and he began working on *Trailing the Giant Panda,* a book he co-authored with Kermit about their most recent hunting experience.

After arriving in the U.S., the Roosevelts went straight to Oyster Bay, where they checked on their children and prepared to leave again. Gracie was now seventeen; she would spend the summer visiting in France and then remain there to study at the Sorbonne. TR III and Cornelius, both in their early teens, were students at Groton. They would stay in the States under the watchful eyes of their grandmothers. Quentin, Signorina and Miss. Margaret Hensey (Ted's secretary), would accompany them to the island that TR Jr was to govern.[44]

From his general knowledge of history and geography, Ted knew that Porto Rico had been a Spanish possession for four hundred years until the Spanish-

American War when it became an American possession. The island is located in the Caribbean Sea and is nearer to South America than to the United States. Its approximately 3,500 square miles were home to 1.5 million predominantly Catholic inhabitants. Seventy-five per cent of the Porto Ricans were white descendants of Spaniards; the remaining twenty-five percent were blacks and mulattos. There were no Indians, although there was some trace of Indian blood in the people that lived in the interior mountain country.[45]

Ted's studies about the Island told him that the Jones Act of 1917 declared all Porto Ricans to be United States citizens. Since they had no elected representatives in the U.S. Congress, the principle of "no taxation without representation" applied and they were not required to pay federal income taxes. The President of the Unites States appointed the Governor General, as well as the PR Attorney-General, the Commissioner of Education, the Auditor, and the five Justices of the Supreme Court. Members of the PR House of Representatives and Senate were elected by its citizens, but the power to veto legislative acts was vested in the Governor General, with absolute veto power vested in the U.S. President should the Governor General's veto be over ridden by the legislature.

From his reading, Ted learned that the economy was mainly agricultural, with the main exports being sugar, coffee, and tobacco. From the reports filed by previous governors, he learned that since the island came under American rule, there had been a slow but steady increase in overall agricultural production as well as increases in favorable trade balances, miles of roads, telephones, and schools. He also read of how the 1928 hurricane of San Felipe had devastated the island and its agriculture.[46]

As a new appointee, Ted was determined that he would give his inaugural address in Spanish, so he spent every idle minute learning the language. By October 7th, when the ship carrying the Roosevelt party docked at San Juan, Ted had learned to speak Spanish of sorts, but still occasionally made bonehead mistakes. A large cheering crowd met them when they disembarked. The people lined the streets as the caravan of automobiles carried them to the Capitol, where a reviewing stand had been set up under a roof of palm leaves. After the Chief Justice of the Porto Rican Supreme Court administered the oath of office, Ted was introduced to the throng of onlookers by the acting governor. He then took his place at the rostrum. None of the previous Governor Generals could speak Spanish and they had all delivered their inaugural addresses in English, followed by an interpreter who would repeat the address in Spanish. When Ted began his speech with "Ladies and Gentlemen," and then read the first paragraph in English, a "here we go again" attitude settled over the crowd. Then he stopped and started over again with, "Senores y Senoras," and repeated the beginning paragraph in Spanish. The audience was electrified and began cheering. At last they had a Governor who could speak the language. The new Chief Executive had certainly gotten off on the right foot with the citizens.

Ted's inaugural speech concentrated on the economic needs of the island as he thought them to be. A parade of the National Guard, various organizations, school children, police, fire departments, bands, and the 65th U.S. Infantry Regiment marched by the reviewing stand following the address. Then the new Governor General and First Lady were driven to *La Fortaleza,* the three hundred year old palace that served as the Chief Executive's office and residence. The structure itself was impressive with ornamental pilasters and with a wide frieze of intricately sculptured mythological figures around the top. The heavy mahogany doors were decorated with hand carved designs and the tessellated floors were of gray and white marble. But the furnishings were shabby and did not match architecturally with the elegant old Spanish building. Eleanor immediately sent to New York for all their paintings, embroideries, brocades, banners, etc. She intended to transform the interior of the palace into as inspiring a place as was the exterior.

Within a few days after arriving, Ted was out into the island observing and talking to the people. He went into the slums of San Juan and the remote hill country of the interior. He rode a horse to get to isolated villages where there were no roads. He talked not with just the politicians and those of prominence, but also the laborers, the sick and the destitute. The islanders were so appreciative of their new Governor General's obvious interest in their welfare that they would often offer valuable gifts from their less-than-meager possessions, such as an egg or an orange. To his horror, Ted soon realized that the books and reports he read describing the poor economic conditions in PR were misleading, conditions on the island were worse than bad, they were deplorable. Thousands of the poor were actually starving and health conditions were no better. And this was before the stock market crash of 1929 and the onset of the Great American Depression.[47]

In the rural areas, he saw thousands of one-room shacks that were provided by the large sugar companies for their transient laborers. Almost all of them had dirt floors, and the cooking done outside by building a fire between two rocks. In the cities, he observed hovels constructed of cardboard and tin cans, jammed together in a maze of paths. Also in the cities, he saw the "wolf gangs" of filthy street children who robbed and stole, and protected parked cars to survive. Often these waifs would steal or destroy property in plain view of the police so they would be arrested and get free board and lodging for awhile, even if it was in a jail cell.[48]

Health conditions on Porto Rico were horrible. Malaria, tuberculosis, and gastrointestinal diseases took a staggering toll of the weak and, underfed people. Over three-fourths of the small children were suffering from chronic intestinal troubles. Thousands of children had never had a glass of milk and seventy percent of the young were both underweight and under-sized. Most of the children had decaying teeth. Many thousands of the islanders were infected with TB, and there were only seven hundred hospital beds allocated for those afflicted. It was estimated that over forty percent of the population were hosts to hookworms. Hookworms and insufficient nourishment were the primary reasons that Porto Ricans were said to be lazy and apathetic.[49]

The average annual income for rural workers was $150, and that of workers in the towns and cities was only slightly higher. Prices for necessities were not responsive to wages because beans, rice, and salted cod fish, the main foods consumed by the citizens, were imported, rather than being raised and harvested on the island. The principal farming activity was the growing of sugar cane on the approximately 250,000 acres of land on the fertile coastal plain. This excellent farmland was almost entirely owned or controlled by four absentee American sugar companies. The remaining arable land, about 230,000 acres, was less productive and was devoted mostly to raising coffee and tobacco. Very little land was planted in vegetables or other crops for local consumption. Practically all of the agricultural production was exported, with 90% of it being shipped to the U.S. This meant that the prices received for Porto Rican products were directly dependent on the demand for them in North America. The sugar plantations yielded good profits for their absentee owners. While agriculture was far and above the main income producing activity, it was seasonal in nature and, due to the abundance of labor, the wages paid the workers were extremely low. Even in rush season, a laborer earned only $1.25 per day. Over sixty percent of the adult male population was out of work at least part of the year, and thirty-six percent was unemployed the year-round.[50]

Although forty percent of all the government revenues were devoted to education, Ted found that half of the children received no schooling at all, and that of those that did, eighty-four out of every one hundred never reached the fourth grade. The fifth grade classes and above were taught in English, even though the native tongue of Porto Rico was Spanish. All this aside, Ted well knew that a hungry and undernourished child couldn't learn much.

Instead of the Porto Ricans themselves, the Americans had control of the island's banking industry. Sixty percent of the capital of local banks and almost all of the capital of foreign banks was owned by outside interests.[51],

Ted knew the old saying that when the hole in the dam is the size of a cow and all you have to plug it with is a finger, you desperately need outside help. In this case, the two sources to go to for the kind of help Porto Rico needed was the U.S. Government and the American people. He thus began an extensive campaign to inform the federal government and the American public of the horrendous conditions in their island colony. On December 8, 1929, the *New York Herald Tribune* printed an article written by Governor General Roosevelt describing some of the sights that greeted him during his initial inspection of the island:

I write not of what I have heard or read, but what I have seen with my own eyes. I have seen mothers carrying babies who were little skeletons. I have watched in a classroom, thin, pallid boys and girls trying to spur their brain to action when their bodies were underfed. I have seen them trying to study on only one scanty meal a day, of a few beans and some rice. On the roads time and again I have passed pathetic little groups carrying tiny homemade coffins. I have looked into the kitchens of houses where a handful of beans and a few plantains were the fare for the whole family. Riding through the hills, I have stopped at farm after farm where lean, underfed women and sickly men repeated time and time again the same story—little food and no opportunity to get more. From these hills the people have streamed into the coastal towns, increasing the already severe unemployment situation there. Housing facilities, of course, are woefully inadequate, besides, the lack of funds and the increased work have rendered it impossible for our Health Department to cope satisfactorily with our increasing problem. Sixty percent of the children of the entire island are undernourished; many are literally slowly starving. Of the 710 boys and girls in one public school in San Juan, 223 come to school each day without breakfast—278 have no lunch.[52]

This was only the first of many articles Ted wrote describing the distressing conditions in PR that appeared in newspapers and magazines in the U.S. He also testified before U.S. congressional committees, lobbied congressmen, and spoke before and corresponded with many private charitable organizations. At that time, the island was under the supervision of the U.S. Bureau of Insular Affairs of the War Department, and when Ted began his publicity campaign, it reflected badly on the bureau for allowing such terrible conditions to exist in an American possession. The bureau notified Ted to stop what he was doing, but he politely replied that the statistics and facts he had been reciting were correct and he continued his efforts.

In '29, the year following the San Felipe hurricane, Congress appropriated two million dollars for relief of the island. Ted's publicity efforts attracted President Hoover's interest, leading the President to request a study of conditions in PR by the American Child Health Association. This study substantiated the Governor General's claims and spurred Congress to appropriate another two million dollars the following year. In view of the fact that Black Thursday and the onset of the Great Depression pre-dated this second appropriation, it is certain that this last money was made available only because of Ted's activities.[53]

A number of private charities came to the aid of Porto Rico after the island's plight was brought to their attention. The Golden Rule Foundation donated $50,000 for milk stations for babies and school lunches for students. The American Relief Association Children's Fund gave $100,000. A group of big charitable organizations got together and formed the Porto Rico Child Health Committee and formulated a plan to raise $7,300,000 over a five-year period to aid in the dreadful health and food problems.[54]

Besides the humanitarian relief provided by the federal government and private philanthropic organizations, Governor General Roosevelt initiated a number of programs designed to aid the inhabitants in other ways. The first thing he did was to surround himself with extremely capable, mostly Porto Rican men on his Cabinet and on the Executive Council. In making these appointments he ignored the political party affiliation of the appointee and chose the man best qualified to do the job. Based on Ted's recommendations, President Hoover appointed American educated Jos'e Padin the head of the Department of Education, and the respected Socialist Prudencio Rivera Martinez to lead the Department of Labor.[55]

Ted prevailed upon the sugar companies to allow their workers small plots of land to plant vegetable gardens on. He knew, however, that the uneducated laborers would simply plant their parcels in sugar cane and then sell their production back to the sugar companies at a disadvantaged price unless some form of education was included to teach them how to raise truck gardens and to look after a cow or a few goats.

One of the first things Ted and his Commissioner of Education did was to order classroom instruction to be given in Spanish rather than English, with English made a required subject. Then they reshaped the educational system to conform to the island's needs by locating rural schools on small farms ranging from five to fifteen acres each. The children were taught reading, writing, arithmetic, and English. They also received vocational training in elementary agricultural methods, health, hygiene, and practical crafts like carpentry and cobbling for the boys and home economics and embroidery for the girls. The boys made tables, chairs, beds, washboards, and other things of a practical value that could be sold or used in the home, while the girls learned to cook on a charcoal stove, like the ones used in the homes, and were taught to sew and make their own clothes. The embroidery and cobbling were particularly important; nothing is more effective in preventing hookworms than a good pair of shoes, and the girls could pick up some extra money with their embroidery. The acreage surrounding the schools was utilized by the agricultural teachers to teach the boys the basics of raising vegetables and other produce for family consumption. Instruction in the tending of domesticated farm animals was also given. Some of the farm production would be cooked and eaten by the students in the lunchroom, and some would be sold. The proceeds from the sales would be divided, two-thirds back to school funds and one-third to the boys themselves. Seeds would be furnished by the school for the students to plant in small, at-home gardens. The best gardens were awarded inexpensive prizes, such as a rabbit or a chicken. During Ted's term as Governor General, there was nearly a threefold increase in the number of rural high schools on PR.[56]

At night the schoolhouses were made into community centers where the adults would meet and learn up-to-date agricultural methods for the raising of vegetables and other food for home consumption, as well as proper health and hygiene habits. Social workers, health professionals, and men with agricultural training and/or experience would be scheduled to attend and give instruction in their fields. Mothers clubs and parent-teacher associations were formed, fairs were held to display the student's handiwork, and dances were sometimes scheduled to strengthen the community aspect of this new school concept.[57]

The Porto Rican Homestead Commission had been established pursuant to legislation passed in 1915. Under this law, the Commission was given the authority to acquire land and in turn to convey parcels thereof to poor PR citizens for homestead purposes. Property could be acquired by the Commission by purchase from willing landowners or taken from unwilling owners by paying the fair appraised value through condemnation proceedings. A type of lease-sale arrangement was used when conveying a plot to a homesteader, where if the person failed to occupy the tract for the required number of years or failed to pay for it as agreed, the land would revert to the Commission. By the time Ted became Governor General, almost all of the public land available had already been homesteaded by citizens and there were no funds in the island's treasury to use to acquire additional property. At Ted's urging, the PR government issued $500,000 worth of bonds so funds would be available for the Homestead Commission to purchase additional land and also to have money to pay for any land taken by condemnation. After obtaining property, the Commission would subdivide the tracts into plots of from 2 to 10 acres each, then sell the plots to deserving homesteaders and withhold delivery of the title until the person had completed payment.[58]

Two federal statutes provided money for use in agricultural extension programs. To take full advantage of this money, Ted had the Homestead Commission retain ownership of specific parcels in the middle of the subdivided plots sold to citizens. These retained parcels were used as demonstration farms. There professional agricultural agents would teach the homesteaders practical farming and harvesting methods, and, considering the lay of the land and the fertility of the soil, give advice on what crops could be successfully grown on any individual plot. Seeds were furnished at no charge to the homesteaders.[59]

Under Ted's leadership, the Bureau of Commerce and Industry was established. Because there were no funds available to pay the personnel working in this new bureau, Ted appointed his military aide, Major Gary Crockett, Commissioner of Commerce and Industry. The other employees were borrowed from other government agencies. This new bureau was given a number of different responsibilities, including: assisting local manufacturers, publicizing the industrial potential of the island, developing markets for PR products, aiding in the development of local fisheries, and reporting to the Governor General any unnecessary government restrictions on business that it discovered. Through hard work, Major Crockett and his borrowed assistants were responsible for bringing in a number of new industries to PR and for the reduction in the local cost of fish, meat, dairy products, and bread.[60]

Another idea Ted followed through on that was aimed at increasing the revenue available to the local government was in having the PR tax laws strictly enforced against wealthy citizens and absentee corporations. He also worked to increase the tourist industry. Like all of the Caribbean Islands, Porto Rico possessed beautiful waters and beaches, and a warm and sunny climate. Ted was quick to see that they needed something extra to attract tourists, particularly the cruise ship trade. Besides having the Bureau of Commerce and Industry advertise the Island as a good vacation spot, Ted would take time from his busy schedule to personally greet the passengers when a cruise ship docked and invite them to a reception at *La Fortaleza*. There Eleanor and Signorina would give them a tour of the palace and its beautiful gardens. Thirteen cruise ships visited PR in 1929; over thirty moored there in 1930, and that was after the onset of the Depression.[61]

Besides helping with tourists, Eleanor tended to her own family, oversaw the operation of the residence, and was a gracious First Lady at the many luncheons, dinner parties, and balls hosted by the Governor General at *La Fortaleza*. Some of the balls would be attended by over a thousand people, and orchestras would be on the main floor and on the dancing pavilion beside the sea wall. From an appeal to her New York friends for help, Mrs. Ted raised over eight thousand dollars that she used to buy ten cows and eighty goats, which were promptly given to some of the dirt poor islanders.

The most significant contribution Ted's spouse made to the island's welfare was her work in promoting the stitching and sale of fine Porto Rican embroidery. Eleanor learned that in previous years needlework had been second only to sugar as a PR export product, but recently it had fallen to almost nothing in both quality and quantity. What little of it that was still sold in the U.S., was simply labeled "imported" by the retailer and marked with a low price. Visualizing an opportunity to teach the women of the island a craft that would benefit them financially, she prevailed on her husband to allow her to use an old, abandoned insane asylum building. Then she hired twenty women who would work for one dollar a day to embroider fine linen, organdy, and Crepe de Chine fabrics to sell to tourists and to her friends in New York. As sales increased, Eleanor began, at her own expense, carrying samples to New York and making sales calls on the finest New York stores, such as Saks Fifth Avenue. Soon there were over one hundred poor women stitching, and the retailers were advertising that they had "Exquisite Porto Rican Embroidery" for sale. The business began with a $5,000 personal loan from Eleanor. When she and Ted moved from the island, there was a remaining balance on the loan of $1,500, which she never tried to collect.[62]

While Ted saw himself as a staunch Republican in the U.S., he pictured himself in Porto Rico as simply Governor General, not as Republican Governor General, and he tried to keep neutral with respect to the island's party politics. There were three occasions, however, when he felt compelled to get involved in the local political game. The City of San Juan was on the verge of bankruptcy under the inefficient leadership of its long-time Mayor, and its financial deficit was increasing daily. San Juan bonds had no buyers on the open market, and the Mayor refused to step down. At Ted's urging, the legislature passed a bill abolishing the position of Mayor of San Juan and converted the city's municipal government to the commission form. In a similar bill Ted pushed through the legislature, the Governor General was granted the authority to appoint municipal auditors and to remove any municipal official from any of the Porto Rican municipalities if there was just cause to do so. The third time he crossed horns with the local political parties was when he vetoed a new election law because it left the Election Supervisory Committees in each ward in the hands of the old established political parties without making a place on the Committee for any newly formed party. Ted felt that if this new law was allowed to remain, it would encourage vote fixing on the part of the established political parties. Shortly before Ted left the island, he called the legislature into special session in an attempt to get an election law passed that would properly protect any newly formed political party. His attempt was unsuccessful, however, and no such new legislation passed until six months after the Roosevelts departed.[63]

There were a number of other accomplishments made during Ted's administration for which he could be justly proud. One of these was converting the material used for the construction and repair of the island's roads from macadam to asphalt. This alone resulted in annual governmental savings of $350,000. Sixteen new medical centers were constructed. These provided health care to thousands of citizens who had previously been without. Probably though, the thing which gave Ted the most personal satisfaction was the fact that, with his intelligent use of the line item veto to eliminate unnecessary government spending, Porto Rico had a balanced budget for the first time in seventeen years.

When the Roosevelts went down to Porto Rico, three of their children remained in the States. Gracie, who returned from France and enrolled in a business course in New York, resided with Eleanor's mother. Occasionally she would come down to see her parents, sometimes bringing friends. TR III and Cornelius were students at Groton, but they spent their summers with their parents in PR, where they swam, fished, and enjoyed hiking around and observing the plants and animals native to the area.

Quentin, the baby of the family, had a wonderful time living on the beautiful tropical island with his parents near at hand. When they first arrived, Quentin was enrolled in an American school in San Juan and lived in the residence with his parents. But when he made friends with the convicts that worked at *La Fortaleza*, Ted and Eleanor decided that he needed to learn more about the Spanish culture and sent him to a boarding school in a nearby town. Most of the students in Quentin's new school were Porto Rican, but the teachers were American and he could come home every weekend. At this stage in his life, Quentin was developing a keen interest in nature. When at *La Fortaleza*, he would often go out in the gardens and catch butterflies and other insects for his collection.[64]

To the surprise of Ted and Eleanor, Edith came down to visit them on three occasions during the two plus years they were on PR. Her first trip was in January 1930, for two weeks, and again the following September for nearly a month. Ted was flattered to have his mother as a houseguest because he felt he had slipped from her graces somewhat in recent years. The former American First Lady was spry for her age and enjoyed a daily swim in the ocean and basking in the palace gardens. On one of her visits she and Eleanor made an enjoyable side trip to neighboring Haiti.[65]

The Republican Party sustained devastating losses in the 1930 off-year elections, including the landslide reelection of Franklin Delano Roosevelt as Governor of New York. It was obvious to Ted that most Americans blamed the Republicans for the Depression, and that whatever slim chance he had had to resurrect his political future was gone. Right after the election, he prophetically wrote his mother:

Well, as far as I can see, the ship went down with all on board. Your cousin Franklin now, I suppose, will run for the Presidency, and I am already beginning to think of nasty things to say concerning him.[66]

Edith's third trip to Porto Rico came in December, shortly after receiving her eldest son's letter. By nature, Ted was an optimist, but it was apparent from his letters that he was despondent. She went as a gesture to Ted that he had carried his father's standard admirably and to the best of his ability. No doubt Ted appreciated his mother's intimation, but the namesake was his father's political heir, and he still felt unworthy. But for the deaths of Alice's husband, Nick Longworth, and TR's sister, Bamie Roosevelt Crowles, Edith might have come back again in 1931. Teddy's last surviving sibling, Corinne Roosevelt Robinson, passed away in early 1933.[67]

The Porto Ricans took the three-day visit made by President Herbert Hoover in early spring 1931 as a hopeful signal that the neglect of Porto Rico by the United States was at an end. Hoover was the first President to come to the island since Ted's father, twenty-five years before. The Chief Executive and his entourage arrived at San Juan harbor aboard the later-to-be enshrined U.S.S. Arizona, and were loudly cheered by the enthusiastic crowd as the motorcade took them to their quarters at *La Fortaleza*. Ted had arranged for two receptions, one private and one public, so that the President could meet influential citizens as well as some of the common folk. Hoover seemed to enjoy his visit and, after he returned to Washington, rumors began to circulate that Ted would be Hoover's running mate in the upcoming '32 elections.[68]

The previous American Governor Generals had tried to Americanize the Porto Rican people by doing such things as having school instruction taught in English and influencing them to accept Santa Claus on December 25th, in lieu of their traditional Three Kings Day on January 6th. Ted was just the opposite. He looked on the island as a gateway from the U.S. to the predominately Spanish speaking countries in South America and considered PR to be "a show window looking south." He encouraged the people to be proud of their Spanish heritage. Munoz Marin, a bright young Porto Rican Socialist and journalist that became a close friend to Ted and Eleanor and was eventually elected Governor of the island, described how TRJr told some of the students to use their pennies to buy breakfast rather than to purchase small American flags, as they had been instructed to do by the school superintendent. Marin also wrote about the time Roosevelt nixed an attempt to substitute the visit of the Three Kings with Santa Claus.

The United States Army's 65th Infantry Regiment was based in PR and was composed of American officers and Porto Rican enlisted men. In selecting any particular officer to be sent there, the Army gave little consideration to his character and whether or not he could speak Spanish. Desiring for the native enlisted men to take pride in their Spanish ancestry, in 1931 Ted wrote the newly appointed United States Army Chief of Staff, General Douglas MacArthur, a letter requesting that henceforth the Army take extra care to send to the island only top quality officers who were reasonably fluent in Spanish.[69]

After the island came under American rule in the late 1800s, one of the first things the U.S. did was change the official name of its new possession from Puerto Rico to Porto Rico. The islanders were very resentful of this for they felt that in its attempt to Americanize them, the parent country had even robbed them of the correct spelling of the name. Ted made himself a permanent place in the hearts of the Puerto Ricans when he became the driving force in doing the one thing, among all others, that would help them to re-establish their rich Spanish heritage. The spelling was again amended, and Porto Rico again became Puerto Rico.[70]

Besides performing his duties as Governor General during the years 1931–1932, TRJr. completed his work on a book he co-authored with Harold J. Coolidge entitled *Three Kingdoms of Indo-China* about their experiences in Southeast Asia while on the last Field Museum hunt. At his own expense, Ted made four trips to the States during this same time period. On one of these trips, he was in Washington meeting with President Hoover to discuss his future with the national administration when he received a message that a run was being made on the Puerto Rican banks. One bank had closed and others were in distress. Massive bank closures would mean financial chaos for the island. As soon as he could get back, Ted gave his personal note for one hundred thousand dollars ($^{1}/_{4}$ of his net worth) to the Insular Treasurer with instructions to deposit that sum in the threatened bank. He then went on the radio and assured the people that the Puerto Rican banks were solvent and urged them to have confidence in their financial system. The bank crisis was averted.[71]

From the beginning, Ted had no illusions about being able to make any dramatic change for the better in Puerto Rico. While he could take pride in the positive things he had accomplished, and they did help to a certain extent, the basic problems (poverty, disease, poor health care, overpopulation, ignorance, and passive acceptance of deplorable conditions by the populace) took decades, even centuries, to develop and would take a lot of then unavailable money and many years to solve. Most of the Puerto Rican people felt that their present Governor General was sincere in his sympathy for them, and they appreciated the hard work he had given to their cause. As always, however, there were detractors who said he was not genuine in his concern. They credited the fact that he spent most of his personal salary on the islander's welfare and once personally guaranteed a bank note for $200,000 so the PR government would have sufficient funds to pay its employees their salaries as merely being a bad case of "the white man's burden."[72]

The fact that Puerto Rico was heavily overpopulated created a special dilemma for Ted. He was well aware that PR's population had increased over 50% during the thirty years of U.S. control and that presently, the birth rate was increasing while the death rate was declining. He also knew that the Catholic Church and the predominantly Catholic population would not accept an effective birth control program. The people would most certainly be antagonized by any attempt, and he might lose their cooperation and confidence in other programs that had a better chance of being successful. He let discretion prevail, and did not tackle the problem.[73]

In the fall of 1931 Ted was informed that Dwight Davis, the current Governor General of the Philippine Islands, was going to resign to accept an ambassadorship and that he would be appointed Davis's successor. Mr. Davis got upset because his impending resignation was leaked to the press, and he balked at resigning for a number of weeks. Ted and Eleanor began to wonder about the sincerity of the promised promotion. In early November, Eleanor, who was in Washington at the time, sought the advice of Secretary of War Pat Hurley, and General Douglas MacArthur, who was stationed in Washington but had recently completed a tour of duty as Army Commander in the Philippines. They both essentially told her that Ted should just sit tight and do nothing drastic, and that his promotion would come as soon as something could be worked out with Mr. Davis.

Davis was still holding out when Ted made a trip to the States during the Christmas season. By now Ted was beginning to suspect that the current administration was kicking him around by making only promises, instead of giving him the well-deserved, more prestigious job for the final year the Republicans would be in power. He let it be known that he was giving serious consideration to resigning his governor generalship. Hoover, who by all accounts was a good man, still had hopes, some would say irrational hopes, that somehow the Republicans could turn things around and salvage victory in the 1932 elections. Others in his administration, seeing the handwriting on the wall, were beginning to jump ship. Defections are bad publicity in an upcoming election. Hoover, who knew that TRJr would be an important asset in the fall elections, particularly since the Democratic nominee was expected to be New York Governor Franklin Delano Roosevelt, bowed to the pressure Ted put on him by threatening to resign and instructed Davis to immediately submit his resignation. Ted then arranged a meeting between Douglas MacArthur, Manuel Quezon, and himself. Quezon, who was the President of the Philippine Senate, made his apartment in Washington available for the meeting. The Philippine leader was impressed with what he saw and gave Ted his enthusiastic support. In early January 1932, Ted was finally given his long sought after appointment as Governor General of the Philippine Islands. He would be the youngest man to ever hold the most important United States' administrative office outside of Washington, D.C.[74]

The Puerto Rican people were sorely disappointed to lose the one governor general they had come to love and respect, and they were particularly disappointed that he didn't return to the island to say goodbye and allow them to personally thank him for his earnest efforts. They generally considered Ted to be the most philanthropic, most dynamic, and best loved of all the mainlanders sent to them by the U.S. American newspapers called him the best colonial governor in American history.[75]

Perhaps the most flattering article concerning TRJr's performance in Puerto Rico was written by Daniel Rochford as a result of an independent study he made of conditions on the island. He wrote:

> Roosevelt does not claim to have started all these things. He claims nothing. But until he arrived the plans which are now raising the the whole standard of life in Porto Rico were not in operation. It took his fire and enthusiasm and his leadership to get the forces in motion.[76]

At the time of his appointment, the Philippine Islands (a.k.a. PI) were in considerably better condition with respect to diet, nutrition, employment, and the general health of the population than had been the case two years before in Puerto Rico. Most of the 14,000,000 inhabitants were from poor, uneducated small-farm families, but neither starvation nor unemployment was a major problem. The standard of living was at an acceptable level and most of the towns had a medical facility, high school, movie theater, playgrounds, and automobiles. Like Puerto Rico, the islands had been under U.S. rule since the Spanish-American War. The government, which was running an enormous deficit, was made up of a Senate and a House of Representatives, both elected by the people, and a Supreme Court and Governor General appointed by the American President. Catholicism was the dominant religion, but there was a strong Moslem element on some of the most populated islands. In all, the complex consisted of over seven thousand islands, some of which were uninhabited.[77]

TR III, who was now a freshman at Harvard, and Cornelius and Quentin, who were students at Groton, were left behind, but Ted, Eleanor, Gracie, Signorina, Miss Hensey, and Colonel Crockett (formerly Major Crockett from Puerto Rico) departed New York shortly after Ted's appointment and boarded a train bound for Seattle. From there, they sailed west into the Pacific Ocean aboard the S.S. President Taft. The ship's itinerary called for stops of one or two days each at Yokohama, Kobe, Shanghai, and Hong Kong, before finally docking at Manila, where the Roosevelt party would disembark. There had been a lot of publicity given to Ted's appointment and to their departure from New York, and at several stations across the country, a crowd was waiting when their train pulled in. Being the accommodating person that he was, Ted was happy to greet his fans and speak a few words.

Except for some rough weather, the long trip across the Pacific was uneventful. Ted had decided to be sworn in after he reached Manila. In dong so, he would be the first American Governor General to be sworn in on Philippine soil. The leisurely days at sea gave Ted ample time to prepare his acceptance speech. Many of the older Philippine citizens spoke Spanish, but English had been the official language for thirty years and most of the young people were fluent in it. There were some seventeen different native dialects and tongues, so there was no universal language which all the citizens would understand. With this in mind, and the fact that he spoke less than perfect Spanish, TR Jr decided to make his remarks in English and have an interpreter standing beside him to repeat his words in Spanish.

After the ship docked at Yokohama, Gracie, Eleanor, and Ted journeyed the short distance to Tokyo, where they had an audience with the Emperor and Empress, and where they renewed acquaintances with Japanese friends from their Washington Arms Limitation Conference days.

Later in the trip, as they approached Shanghai, the Captain of the President Taft announced to the passengers that there had been active fighting in the city between Chinese and Japanese military forces, and that he was awaiting orders from his company as to whether to dock there or not. Permission to moor was received after only a few hours wait and as the President Taft entered port, it passed warships of Great Britain, France, Japan, Portugal, and the United States anchored in the harbor. As their ship approached its assigned pier, it could be plainly seen that part of the city was on fire. An occasional explosion could be heard in the distance. The fighting in what would eventually escalate into the bloodiest conflict in the history of mankind had begun. There had never been a more paradoxical situation than the Roosevelt party encountered in Shanghai. While part of the city was being devastated by a war going on, the other part was normal with business as usual. The ladies in the party attended a tea given by the mayor and went shopping, and Ted addressed the Boy Scouts. That night, after attending a large dinner party, Ted, Colonel Crockett, and two other military officers excused themselves to go visit the war front.[78]

On February 29th, (leap year day) when the President Taft entered Manila Bay and sailed past the Island of Corregidor, squadrons of American war planes flew overhead and a flotilla of decorated motor launches crammed with well-wishers accompanied the big liner to its mooring pier. After Ted inspected the honor guard, a company of Philippine Scouts led the motorcade to the Luneta, a public square in Manila, where a large grandstand had been erected. Ted was sworn in before the crowd of approximately forty thousand islanders. In his inaugural address he promised to work toward improving the education and health care of the Filipinos and to create a better business atmosphere for the small farmer. He asked the people to judge him by his subsequent acts.[79]

After the swearing in ceremony, the Roosevelts were escorted to *Malacanan,* the beautiful Spanish-style white stucco Governor's palace overlooking the Pasig

River. The residence was surrounded by immaculately manicured lawns with exotic tropical trees and flowers. There was a swimming pool, tennis court, patio, and fountain. Ted's office was in a nearby building connected to the residence by a covered passageway. All in all, the Governor General's quarters were much more livable than had been *La Fortaleza* in Puerto Rico.[80]

As in Puerto Rico, Ted's plan called for first making get-acquainted trips to as many of the forty-nine island provinces as possible. He wanted to talk face to face with as many of the small farmers and common folk as he could to find out what the problems were from their point of view. He also wanted to explain to them why taxes were necessary and what their tax money was spent for. The Governor General's staff would advertise his itinerary in any province he intended to visit a couple of weeks in advance, so the people that wanted to see, hear, or talk with him would have sufficient notice of when and where he would be in their community.

Ted set up his appearance in any particular community something like an old fashioned American political rally. Eleanor would often go, and all the local politicos would be there. Some type of entertainment, like a band, singers, or dancers, and an assortment of experts in agriculture, health, or whatever that was relevant to the particular area were included in the entourage. Ted would speak and then mingle and talk with the citizens (and most likely kiss the babies). He would ask the people about their particular problems, and request their suggestions and support for his efforts to improve the islands. The experts would lecture and instruct in their fields, such as practical and efficient farming practices, sanitation, and vegetable gardening. The audience would enjoy the entertainment. Sometimes, on the way from one community to another, he would stop and talk to some man or woman who didn't even know what a Governor General was. He traveled variously by boat, train, auto, horseback, airplane, and on foot, sometimes making as many as twenty speeches a day. These meetings were so successful and so well-attended (nearly ten thousand people attended the very first one) that they became known as community assemblies. Over the next year, Ted attended one or more assembly in forty-eight of the forty-nine Philippine provinces. Through these community gatherings, he learned of the people's most pressing troubles, and in doing so he gained their friendship and support as no other foreigner ever had.[81] Manuel Quezon, who would one day be elected the first President of the Commonwealth of the Philippines, said of Ted:

No Governor General has had, in all the years of American occupation, more direct and intimate contact with the Filipinos in Manila and in the provinces, and more friends both among officials and private citizens.[82]

From the standpoint of Ted and Eleanor, the most touching assembly was held at the leper colony funded by the Catholic Church on the island of Culion. Waiting at the dock for their boat to land were most of the six thousand lepers, along with the nuns, priests, and public health doctors and nurses. An archway had been erected over the colony entrance with a big sign reading, "Mabuhay Governor General and Mrs. Roosevelt." Ted spoke to the crowd, and then mingled and met a large number of them. He next went into the hospital, to see and talk with those too sick to be outside with the others. As he walked down the aisles between the lepers' beds, many of them would hold out their hands to him. He shook every hand offered. Eleanor couldn't forget the colony's troop of Boy Scouts; they were all lepers. Later in her life, she wrote that that group of young boys was the saddest thing she ever saw.[83]

Recognizing that the community assemblies were a way to raise the level of citizenship and a means of providing the people with information concerning public affairs and other matters of a practical nature, the PI legislature passed Act No. 4046 in 1932. This law made sponsorship of community assemblies an official act of the government. Private organizations, such as women's clubs, got involved and broadened the purpose of the assemblies by providing reading lessons to adult illiterates, even in the remote villages.[84]

From his studies and his many discussions with officials and ordinary citizens, Ted came to the conclusion that the most pressing needs of the Philippine Islands were to get help for the small farmers and to restructure the government to live within its income. Other, though perhaps not as immediate, problems included deficiencies in health care and education.

To make any substantial headway in alleviating the PI's troubles, the legislature would have to be cooperative with Ted and pass the ameliorating legislation he requested. The raging side issue in the Philippines at the time was the question of independence. Most of the citizens desired the islands to be free of any other government, be it American, Spanish, Japanese, or any other. There were some, however, including Ted, and even Mamuel Quezon, who thought the Philippines were not yet ready for independence. They felt that to suddenly set islands on their own would result in economic chaos. Ted was politically astute enough to realize that he couldn't personally get involved in the independence issue or have his reform programs tied to it in any way. By publicly remaining mute with respect to independence, Ted placed the legislators in the position of having to commit to being for or against a particular program. Otherwise, some of the lawmakers might avoid supporting a piece of reform legislation by claiming it was somehow tied to Ted's stand on the independence issue. Another advantage Ted had was the fact that the majority of the voters were behind him with respect to governmental reform.[85]

On one occasion when he was speaking before the islands' legislature in support of his programs for land reform and aid to small farmers, Ted congratulated the Senate and House members for having the foresight to pass an enforceable law preventing any corporation from owning over 2,500 acres of land. Puerto Rico had a somewhat similar law restricting ownership to 500 acres, but it had many loopholes and failed to accomplish its intended purpose. The Philippines didn't have the problem PR had where a few large companies owned or controlled most of the good farmland. He went on to say:

> As part of this program for the small farmer large areas of public lands are available for homesteaders, as in Mindanao. This is still a pioneering country, it must be remembered. Mindanao contains at present 1,300,000 inhabitants, and can easily support 15,000,000, more than the entire population of the islands at present.
>
> Plans now under way, which we are working out with the aid of various bureaus, provide for the gradual opening of some of this virgin territory for settlers who will clear the land and operate small farms. The government is giving them all possible assistance, and the Filipino leaders are cooperating to the fullest extent.[86]

Another part of Ted's plan for help to the small farmer that was approved by the legislature was the reassessment of land values for tax purposes. This set real estate values for tax purposes at a lower, more realistic level. Tax penalties were reduced and extensions for the payment of taxes could be granted. His philosophy was that it didn't profit the Philippines to confiscate the property of a small farmer because he couldn't pay tax penalties. Credit was made more available to farmers by the establishment of banks and credit associations in the rural areas, and the usury laws were tightened and enforced. The Rice Share Tenancy Act was passed for the purpose of protecting the rice-producing share tenant against abuses by the landlord, but the local political bosses later got this law amended to make it largely ineffective.[87]

A major improvement in the efficiency of the Philippine government was made during Ted's administration. In prior years, due mainly to nepotism, there were entirely too many government employees working in the myriad bureaus, and there was an overlap in their duties and the services they offered. The legislature, at Ted's insistence, terminated many of the unnecessary bureaucrats and reduced the salaries of those retained of from 5 to 10 percent. Some bureaus were eliminated entirely, and others were reduced in size or consolidated. The purpose of some of the government agencies was re-defined so that there would be no duplication in their duties and services. Any employee discharged under

Ted's reform program was given a termination bonus of one months pay for each year of service or a farm of their own on government land (most chose the farm). The legislators voluntarily reduced their own salaries commensurate with the reduction forced on the employees.[88] Speaking on the subject of government reform, Ted said:

> There was immediate need of reduction when I arrived, and appropriations were at once cut ten percent, including the salaries of insular officials, my own among them. I am gratified to be able to say that every Filipino in the Cabinet gave the measure his support. All felt economies necessary and were perfectly willing to accept them. The provinces and municipalities have been cutting salaries also. No government can exist without balancing its budget.[89]

Except in Manila and the other large metropolitan communities, white-collar jobs were few and far between in the Philippine Islands. Wanting to get the most out of every dollar spent for education, Ted expressed his ideas on how the islands' educational system could best serve the people when he said:

> That is why, in the Philippines, education by government should at present be confined to primary, grade and vocational schools. Every man should know how to read, write, subtract and multiply, the famous three Rs, but what use to the man who must win prosperity by honest toil in his fields are algebra, geometry or Latin? None at all except to supply the cultural needs which he does not have. He needs also a primary business education that he may fulfill the duties of a good citizen. So I believe the government funds should be used for primary schools, and that high schools and colleges should be self-supporting.[90]

Under Ted's plan, high schools and colleges would eventually become self-supporting and scholarships would be made available to cover any exceptionally gifted rural student.

An education in the public supported Manila High School had previously been available only to children of Anglo-Saxon descent. A belief in racial equality was one of the things that was ingrained into the soul of TRJr, as it had been in that of his father. The new Governor General immediately put an end to racial segregation in Manila High, to the displeasure of most of the Americans residing in that city. They began to refer to him as a Manila American.[91]

The administration of the health and welfare agencies of the Philippine government had been in a shamble before Roosevelt arrived on the scene. These services were scattered among several different departments and bureaus. Some had even been operating directly under the supervision of the Governor General. At Ted's urging, the legislature passed the Reorganization Act of 1932. This act consolidated all the government agencies relating to health, sanitation, social welfare, hospitals, and the examining boards of the health professions and put them under the direction and control of a newly created Commissioner of Health and Welfare. Besides increasing the efficiency of the government administration of the PI health care programs, the streamlining of these services made them more responsive to the needs of the people, which improved the general health of the populous. Strides were made in the control and treatment of leprosy and TB, which would not have been made had the public health system not been revamped.[92]

Besides his official duties, the office of governor general carried certain unofficial, but obligatory, duties of a social nature. There were many dinner parties for officials and influential Filipinos as well as a number of formal dances and balls. One ball required the ladies to wear traditional Filipino dress, and another was in honor of the legislature. Prior to Ted's appointment, the Manila Hotel had catered the balls and the guests were served elaborate suppers. When Eleanor became First Lady, she took over the management of these events and reduced the meals to salads and other food of a less expensive nature, in line with Ted's policy of government economy. At the final ball given by the Roosevelts before they left the islands, over three thousand guests attended.[93]

The Philippine Islands were so distant from the U.S. and Europe that there were few visitors from the western world. Some notables that did call were King Leopold III and Queen Astrid of Belgium, Henry Cabot Lodge, Jr. (the son of Teddy's old friend), and Mr. and Mrs. George Bernard Shaw.[94]

General Douglas MacArthur came back to visit the Philippines in his official capacity as Chief of Staff of the United States Army. While he was there, he gave a formal dinner at No. 1 Military Plaza, Manila in honor of Governor General and Mrs. Roosevelt. Mrs. Joshena Ingersoll was one of the invited guests and she later described the event as being the most elegant affair she had ever attended. When dinner was announced, the General, with Eleanor Roosevelt on his arm, led the guests into the impressive dinning room. To Mrs. Ingersoll, Eleanor appeared to "float across the floor like a fairy princes," rather than just walk like an ordinary women. Throughout the elaborate meal, a military orchestra entertained the guests with appropriate music.[95]

TR III came from Harvard, and Cornelius and Quentin came from Groton for a three-week stay in the summer. Colonel Crockett's daughter, Lucy, was a teenager and the four of them had a great time shooting whitewater rapids in canoes, swimming, fishing, playing tennis, badminton, and horseback riding. Most of all, they enjoyed driving around in the bright yellow roadster furnished for their pleasure by General Motors.

It wasn't all work and social duties for Ted during the time he was in the Philippines. He and Grantland Rice managed to complete an anthology they had been compiling entitled, *Taps: Selected Poems of the Great War.* Some of the poems chosen for inclusion in the book had unknown writers. There was some speculation that Ted actually wrote the poem entitled, "To An Aviator Killed In Action," rather than some unknown poet, as stated in the book.

On two occasions, he was able to get away for a few days hunting. One of the newspapers had run stories about Ted's hunting exploits and the islanders looked on him as a great white hunter. When he was invited to spend a couple of days hunting for wild carabao, there was wide interest and much publicity given by the Philippine press. Ted knew that technically the carabao on the islands were not wild, but were simply animals whose domesticated ancestors had wandered into the jungle. He didn't really want to go. But to decline would be like saying that the Philippine carabao was not the vicious animal the people thought it to be and that it was not worthy of being hunted. Much fanfare was given, and reporters and citizens gathered to observe the mighty hunter in action. During the hunt, Ted was able to spot only one of the animals. It was about a hundred yards away and running fast toward the jungle. With a quick shot, he brought it down. When he got to the dead animal, he breathed a sigh of relief to find that it was not branded. The other time he got away to hunt was toward the end of his service as Governor General when he flew to the island of Mindoro and killed two scientifically wild timarau, a species of small ox.[96]

Early during his trips to the various provinces, Ted had gone to the island of Jolo Many of the citizens there were Moros, a truculent Islamic people generally more primitive than most of the Filipinos. While his initial visit was without incident, during the summer a group of the local police were ambushed by the Moros and thirteen law officers were killed, including a police lieutenant. The constabulary retaliated in kind, and conditions on Jolo deteriorated to the point that civil law and order were threatened. Ted and his military aide, Major Matthew B. Ridgway, immediately went to Jolo, where they conferred with officials, talked to witnesses, and walked on foot to view the scene where the massacre took place. With his experiences in facing danger during the Great War, going to Jolo with only one other man was nothing to Ted, but it must have impressed the outlaws, for there was no more trouble.[97]

In 1932, as expected, incumbent President Herbert Hoover was nominated by the Republican Party for a second term. As Ted predicted, Franklin Delano Roosevelt received the Democratic nod for President, even though Al Smith had turned on FDR and supported another candidate. Ted might well have gotten the Republican V-P nomination had he sought it, but he, like almost everyone else except Hoover, realized the inevitability of a Democrat victory and was not interested. In September, TRJr wrote letters to his mother speculating that his Governor Generalship in the Philippines would mark the end of his active political career. He said in one letter that he felt he had done his best and did not "have anything to be ashamed of." And in another he wrote that his efforts in the past few years "have given me enough in the way of accomplishments to make me feel

I have left sufficient to the children in that way." By inference, Ted was saying that he knew he had not matched his father's achievements, nor lived up to his own expectations, or those of his family, but that he had done his best and felt O.K. about himself.[98]

With the approach of fall, some members of the President's Staff and Republican Party political strategists began to put pressure on Ted to return to the U.S. to campaign for Hoover, as he had in 1928. They said he could refute any claim by FDR of connections with Teddy Roosevelt. By now, however, it had been over twenty years since Teddy had been President, and he had been dead for nearly thirteen years. TRJr, knowing that the political memory of voters is short, reasoned that any claim by FDR to links with Teddy would not be effectual, even without his help. Also, Ted knew that his work in the Philippines was important and that if he had to return home for three months to campaign, many of his programs for the betterment of the islands would be put in jeopardy. Ted replied by letter that he would come only if President Hoover indicated that it was vital that he do so. When further insistence by members of Hoover's campaign staff were sent by open cable, rather than encoded, the American press picked up on the story and wrote that the Philippine Governor General was being drafted to come home and work for the President's reelection. Then the Philippine press took up the story and the Philippine people realized that Ted might be called home. There arose such an outcry of protest from the municipalities, the provinces, the newspapers, the Philippine Legislature, and the islanders in general, that an announcement was made by one of Hoover's top campaign officials that Ted was not being made to come home, but was doing so voluntarily. This, of course, was an outright lie. The New York Times easily saw through that, and immediately printed a story pointing out how ludicrous it was for the campaign committee to claim that Ted was coming home of his own accord, against the wishes of almost every Filipino. The Times went on to say that it was a shame to see a man with the grave responsibilities of the Governor General of the Philippines become "a traveling lecturer managed by the Republican National Committee."[99]

After the Times wrote its story, protests arose in the States. The Republican campaign officials finally backed down and cabled Ted that in view of all the circumstances, it was his duty to remain at his post. It was, however, arranged for Ted to do a radio address from Manila on behalf of President Hoover. This was an historic event because it was the first live broadcast across the Pacific Ocean. Ted began speaking into the microphone at 7:00 a.m. Manila time; half way around the world in New York it was 6:00 p.m. The date was October 27, 1932.[100]

Before the fall general election, Edith had briefly departed from her private, somewhat secluded life style and campaigned in public for Herbert Hoover both in Washington and New York. In January, she made the over ten thousand mile trip from Sagamore Hill to spend a few weeks with her eldest son and his wife in Manila. Even though she was now in her seventies, the long journey didn't overly tire her and she seemed to enjoy herself immensely. Perhaps the real reason for her visit was so she, Ted, and Eleanor could console each other over Franklin Delano Roosevelt, the bane of the Oyster Bay Roosevelts, being elected President of the United States by a landslide.[101]

Kermit and his wife Belle were not by their nature as politically oriented as was the rest of the immediate family. They never had the animosity toward Franklin Roosevelt that so consumed the others of the Oyster Bay clan. While Edith was still in the Philippines, the newspapers picked up a story that Kermit and Belle were vacationing with FDR aboard Vincent Astor's yacht. Ted felt that his brother had let him down and was annoyed that it might appear Kermit was attempting to propitiate the incoming President to allow Ted to keep his job. To think that her own flesh and blood was playing with the enemy infuriated Edith, however. At a news conference a reporter asked Ted why his brother was out yachting with FDR. Before he could answer, Edith broke in and snapped: "Because his mother was not there."[102]

With the Depression raging and many banks failing in the States, one of FDRs first acts after his inauguration was to declare a "Bank Holiday." This meant that all the banks in the U.S. and its insular possessions would close for as much as four days to allow the public concern over economic conditions to have a cooling off period, and also to give Congress the opportunity to pass some emergency banking legislation, and to allow the U.S. Treasury Department to print and distribute more currency. This would discourage runs on the banks by depositors, and thereby prevent mass bank failures. Ted did not believe such action was necessary in the PIs, and immediately called a meeting of the islands' bankers, prominent businessmen, and government officials. He suggested they should pool their resources and agree to abide by whatever strict regulations the U.S. banking authorities might require, provided the President rescinded his bank holiday order with respect to the Philippines. The local group agreed with their Governor General without dissent. After the U.S. Government and FDR agreed that the Bank Holiday would not apply to the Philippines, Ted went on the radio and told the people that the islands' banks were strong and that they should have confidence in the local economy. No runs were made on the Philippine banks; they were the only banks under the American flag to remain open and carry on normal business during the National Banking Holiday of March, 1933.[103]

For many years the appointments of governors general for United States' island possessions had been kept out of politics. The only concern of the sitting President had been to select a man of integrity with experience in colonial government. With, however, the presidency of Woodrow Wilson came the custom of the appointments being a plum given to a man with influence in the President's political party. After the election of Franklin D. Roosevelt, a campaign was begun by organizations and governmental authorities in the Philippines, and then taken up by the Scripps Howard newspapers in the States, to persuade President-Elect

Roosevelt and the Democrats to refuse to accept the courtesy resignation Ted submitted and leave him at his post. The Philippine legislature passed a resolution expressing "admiration for the ability, earnestness, and loftiness of purpose which have characterized the administration of Governor General Roosevelt." Many municipalities and most of the provinces passed resolutions urging the President-elect to leave Ted at his job. Ted, though, well understood the American political concept that you help your friends and to hell with your enemies. He knew he was gone and answered an inquiry as to how he was related to FDR by saying he, "was a fifth cousin about to be removed."

As expected, Ted's resignation was routinely accepted and he and Eleanor prepared to leave the islands.

From the influential to the ordinary citizen, the Filipinos were upset at FDR for continuing to treat their governor generalship as a reward for a political crony, but at the same time they realized there was not a thing they could do about it. They, therefore, focused their attention on making the Ted Roosevelts' last few days in the Philippine Islands memorable ones and letting them know how much they appreciated the good things they had accomplished. A three-day round of dinners, receptions, and parties began. Many of the Roosevelts' native friends presented them with gifts, such as Mrs. Emilio Aguinaldo who, with tears streaming down her face, presented Eleanor with a beautiful gold and pearl pendant that had been passed down from her great-grandmother. Mrs. Elpidio Quirino, later to be executed along with her two children by the Japanese during World War II, gave her an exquisite gold bracelet.[104]

Accolades attesting to Ted's superior job performance came pouring in. *The Tribune,* a Filipino daily newspaper, said that his first spoken words to the citizens was a plea that he be judged by his subsequent acts, and that:

Mr. Roosevelt's career in these Islands will be written large across the book of his life. It has been a career of splendid initiative, keen foresight, and unfailing tact.

As the first citizen of the land he has proved to be a big heart, a true and loyal friend.

No narrow prejudices ever tinged his policies. He brushed aside odious traditions of colonial rule and approached his task in the spirit of a plain citizen without pretense and sham.

Mr. Roosevelt stood out to inspire the public with confidence in the eventual stabilization of the public business.[105]

A Scripps-Howard report said the Filipinos considered Ted to be the best Governor General in U.S. history, and that:

He worked like an ox. Speaking Spanish when he arrived, he quickly learned enough of some of the native dialects to understand and make himself understood as he moved about the country.

And move about he did. He went everywhere observing how people lived, what their problems were, child health conditions, education, sanitation, recreation—everything.[106]

Colonel George C. Marshall read Ted's final report as Governor General and wrote that his work in the Philippines was "one of the most remarkable examples of Colonial government in American history, where harmony, efficiency and patriotism prevail throughout.[107]

Carlos Romulo, famous Philippine patriot, author, and educator, who was President of the United Nations General Assembly in 1949, and was President of the United Nations Security Council in 1957, said:

Theodore Roosevelt, Jr. has established the first 'Era of Good Feeling' our government has ever known.[108]

The *New York Times* reported that Ted "likes the Filipinos genuinely, and they like him," and that he was called "the poor man's Governor." The *Philippine Herald* described Ted as being "fair and friendly, wise and human, and far seeing and sincere." He received many other public and private compliments for his good work.[109]

When the March departure date came, the members of the cabinet and their wives met Ted and Eleanor at the Governor General's residence to go with them to their ship. The Roosevelts said their good-byes to the *Malacanan* household staff. As they went out of the front door, the Constabulary band waiting outside struck up "Hail to the Chief." Ted knew that he would never hear that tune again when it was honoring him personally. As they drove away, the band began to play, "Auld Lang Syne."

Thousands of Filipinos were at the pier to wish them well along their way; many more were there than had been awaiting them when they first arrived a little over a year before. The Roosevelts were mobbed with people trying to shake their hands and pat them on the back. So many flowers were handed to Eleanor that she couldn't see over the top. As they boarded their ship, the cabinet and many in the crowd were openly crying, so was Eleanor. As the ship left its mooring and slowly made its way into Manila Bay, an escort of four American destroyers took positions on each quarter. Ted received a seventeen-gun salute as the flotilla passed Fort Santiago and again when they went by the U.S.S. Canopus. As they reached the mouth of the bay, the destroyers broke away and Ted received a final salute from the guns of Corregidor Island as his ship, the Arayat, sailed by and out into the open sea. Had he known the significance Corregidor would have to American history within the next decade, Ted no doubt would have saluted first.

After some inside maneuvering by American and Filipino politicians, in 1934, the Tydings-McDuffee Act was passed by the United States Congress, signed by President FDR, and ratified by the vote of the Filipino people. This law called for full Philippine independence after a ten-year period of adjustment as a United States Commonwealth. World War II delayed the granting of independence, but on July 4th, 1946, the United States fulfilled its agreement and granted the Philippine Islands its rightful status as an independent and free nation.

Gracie and Signorina had previously left the Philippines and were now at home. Military Aide Major Matthew Ridgway accompanied the Roosevelts when they left. He would return to Manila on the Arayat after Ted and Eleanor disembarked at Udjung Pandang in Indonesia, where they would transfer to a larger vessel. Ted had decided to give his wife the trip of her lifetime by taking a much longer western route to get home, rather than going east to Seattle or one of the California ports. They would apply the funds the United States owed them for moving expenses back to New York toward the additional cost of going the long way.

While the Arayat was still among the Philippine Islands, it ran aground on a submerged reef and had to jettison much of its fuel and water supply in order to free itself. The captain then ordered the ship to the nearby port of Zamboanga, P.I., to replenish its fuel and water before continuing on to Udjung Pandang, Ted and Matt, (The same Matthew Ridgway who gained fame as a World War II General and later as Chief of Staff of the United States Army) decided to take the ship's launch and do some fishing in the area until the ship returned. Because of unexpected delays in Zamboanga, the Arayat did not get back to Ted and Matt until after midnight. The seas were rough and it was raining hard when they got back aboard. During the wait, both men received numerous mosquito bites and Ridgway had a severe attack of indigestion. For a while, Ted thought his aide might be having a heart attack, but he had completely recovered by morning.

In her book, *Day Before Yesterday,* Eleanor writes in detail about their long trip back to Oyster Bay. It was indeed the trip of her lifetime. Along the way, she and Ted saw many ancient ruins, temples, tombs, palaces, some of the wonders of the world, and other sights which they would never forget. They even managed to get in some fishing, tennis, and squash. As famous children of a famous American President, they met many interesting people and were wined, dined, and accommodated by royalty and government officials all along the way.

One of the most entertaining experiences they had was at the stop they made at Surabaja in Java, where the Dutch Governor invited them to attend a rice festival at the Court of His Highness the Soesoehunan of Solo, who was the titular ruler. As the festival started, a parade began. First came the Soesoehunan's female bodyguards dressed in green and gold sarongs and each carrying one of his possessions, such as a bird, chest, or golden idol. Next came two dwarfs leading his concubines and a troupe of dancing girls dressed like the bodyguards. A line of blind men, who went out into the city each day to hear the news and relay it to the Soesoehunan, who was unable to read or write, came behind the dancers. They were followed by a detachment of solders, including a squad of archers, in scarlet, green, yellow, and white uniforms. Last came the servants in green uniforms with a plume of orange feathers attached to their hats. His Highness then entered and took his place on the throne. The Soesoehunan's four wives and seventy-nine children were nowhere to be seen. The several hours of music, toasts, speeches, and colorful ceremony were similar to the British investiture dinner Ted and Eleanor had attended several years before in India.

Their last stop in the Dutch East Indies area was at the city of Pinang, where they met William McMillan of Baltimore and Alan Stuyvesant of New Jersey, who were on their way home after having been tiger and elephant hunting in Indo-China. An immediate friendship began between the two young Americans and the Roosevelts, and they decided to continue on the journey together. It wasn't long before Eleanor was thinking that Bill McMillan might be just right for Gracie.

In 1925, when Ted and Eleanor had been in India, they went through the Khyber Pass intent on entering Afghanistan, only to find the border closed. Eleanor had always wanted to go back someday and spend some time in that mysterious land. This was her chance. Ted got permission from the British Government for their party to travel across India and go through the Khyber Pass, and he also received permission from the Afghani Government to enter that country. From Pinang, Ted, Eleanor, Bill, and Alan sailed across the Indian Ocean to Bombay, then they took a train to Agra, so the Roosevelts could again view the magnificent Taj Mahal, and finally they traveled to Peshawar and into the famous pass.

Reaching the Afghan border and presenting the armed guards with their passports and other credentials, they were surprised when an honor guard turned out and they were told they would be in the country as special guests. They had even been assigned an assistant to the Prime Minister as their personal guide. In this desolate country, they crossed deserts, and spent time in Jalalabad, Nimlah, Bamian, and Kabul. They met Afghan royalty and government officials, and a number of European diplomats. Ted even had an audience with the King, who was assassinated a few months later.

From Afghanistan the party next went to Quetta in what is now Pakistan, where, after a brief stay, they left by car for Teheran, in what was then Persia and is now Iran. The trip took four days, all of it across the desert. At one stop on the way, an old Persian man accidentally spilled a jug of scalding hot water on Ted's leg, causing a deep and painful third-degree burn. Eleanor rubbed Unguentine, which was the only medication they had with them, all over the burned area and they headed to the nearest doctor, in Meshed, two days away. The doctor there was very complimentary of how well Eleanor had cared for her husband's burn, and he had Ted back up and around in no time.

In Teheran, Ted had an audience with the Reza Shah Pahlavi (head of government). When he went to the Shah's palace to keep the appointment, TRJr was accompanied by George Wadsworth of the American Legation to Persia. Most audiences with the Shah lasted for only a few minutes, but Ted stayed in with His Highness for well over an hour. When an aide went in to check on them, he found both men sitting on the floor together dismantling a machine gun while Ted explained the capabilities and deficiencies of that particular type of weapon. After getting back to the States, TRJr wrote Army Chief of Staff Douglas MacArthur that he had visited the Shah and promised to send him a modern U.S. machine gun. General MacArthur promptly replied and told him how to go about getting the gun shipped to the Shah.

On one occasion during their trip, Ted became concerned for Eleanor's safety and got angry with her at the same time. It was similar to the time in France in 1918, when he thought the Germans were about to break through and capture both Paris and his wife. This time, they were in the Islamic Holy City of Qum. Eleanor wanted to go into the local mosque and see the great gold dome and the tall slender minarets. The Police Chief said he thought it would be all right, but Ted knew that the town was packed with religious pilgrims and he was reluctant. Eleanor had her mind made up, however, and, in the company of the Police Chief, they stepped into the courtyard of the mosque. There instantly arose a low sound of protest from the worshipers that quickly swelled into a roaring grumble. Realizing the danger in aggravating religious zealots in the place of their worship, Ted whispered in a stern tone that meant he didn't want any argument, "Turn around slowly and walk out. Keep your head up; don't look back; I am right behind you." As soon as they were outside, he berated his wife and questioned her intelligence, telling her he expected the upset Muslims to start throwing stones at any moment, and that one day she was going to get into real trouble.

Some of the other places where they stopped included Baghdad, Jerusalem, Bethlehem, Damascus, Beirut, Istanbul, Venice, Florence, Rome, the French Riviera, and Monte Carlo. When they got to Nice, they met up with Cornelius, who had spent the summer in Europe. Their last stop before sailing for home was London, where they took a few days to visit with their old friend, Rudyard Kipling, and to pick up Gracie, who spent part of the summer there as the guest of Belle's sister, Elizabeth Herbert.[110]

The Years Abroad Source Notes

1. Collier p 305; Roosevelt, Mrs. T Jr. p 167–168; Roosevelt, T Jr., *East of the Sun* p 1–8; Lowell Thomas Broadcast of 7/14/44, LOC c-56; Diary entry page 605, LOC c-2.

2. Roosevelt, Mrs. T Jr. p 168–169; Roosevelt, T Jr., *East of the Sun* p 11; Miller, Nathan p 329.

3. Roosevelt, Mrs. T Jr. p 168, 186; Roosevelt, T Jr., *East of the Sun* p 13–15

4. Roosevelt, Mrs. T Jr. p 169.

5. Roosevelt, T Jr., *East of the Sun* p 277; Roosevelt, T Jr., *All in the Family* p 22; Gerald Darr statement, Sagamore Hill Archives.

6. Roosevelt, T Jr., *East of the Sun* p 226, 235.

7. Ibid p 241–261.

8. Roosevelt, Mrs. T Jr. p 169–198.

9. Roosevelt, Mrs. T Jr. p 168; Lowell Thomas broadcast of 7/14/44, LOC c-56

10. Roosevelt, Mrs. T Jr. p 199–201.

11. Ibid p 204–205.

12. Roosevelt, Mrs. T Jr. p 206–207; T. Roosevelt Jr. papers Sagamore Hill Archives.

13. Roosevelt, T Jr., Foreword to *Rank and File*

14. Hemingway, *The Best War Stories.*

15. Chicago Natural History Museum bulletin of Sept.—Oct. 1944, LOC c-56.

16. Roosevelt, T Jr., *All in the Family.*

17. TR Jr. letter to Ethel Derby of 8/23/28, TR Collection, Harvard U. 87M-100

18. Collier p 308; Madaras p 245; NY Times 4/1/26; NY Times 4/5/26.

19. Pringle p 253; NY Times 10/1/27

20. Nations p 67–69

21. Pringle p 254.

22. Collier p 323.

23. Roosevelt, Mrs. T Jr. p 208.

24. Roosevelt, T Jr., Trailing the Giant Panda p 6; Roosevelt, T Jr., Three Kingoms of Indo China, p 11–12.

25. Roosevelt, Mrs. T Jr. p 209; Roosevelt, T Jr., Trailing the Giant Panda p 15, 88

26. Madaras p 249; Roosevelt, Mrs. T Jr. p 209; Pringle p 241.

27. Collier p 324; Roosevelt, T Jr., Trailing the Giant Panda p 18.

28. Roosevelt, T Jr., Trailing the Giant Panda p 28–32.

29. Ibid p 88

30. Ibid p 93, 204–205.

31. Roosevelt, T Jr., Trailing the Giant Panda p 12; Jan. 1931 National Geographic.

32. Roosevelt, T Jr., Trailing the Giant Panda p 124, 143

33. Ibid p 157–166, 195.

34. Ibid p 221–229.

35. Ibid p 229–261.

36. Roosevelt, T Jr., Three Kingdoms p 235–236; Boulle, Pierre, Bridge of the River Kwai

37. Roosevelt, T Jr. Three Kingdoms p 336–338.

38. Collier p 325; Madaras p 253; Roosevelt, Mrs. T Jr. p 209.

39. Roosevelt, T Jr., Three Kingdoms p 240–242

40. Ibid 169

41. Roosevelt, Mrs. T Jr. p 216–217; Roosevelt, T Jr., Three Kingdoms p 220.

42. Roosevelt, Mrs. T Jr. p 210-217.

43. Roosevelt, Mrs. T Jr., p 220–223; Roosevelt, T Jr., Three Kingdoms p 222.

44. Roosevelt, Mrs. T Jr. p 209–210, 223–225; LOC c-62.

45. Clark p xxiv—1; Lynskey/Catholic Assn. p 5; Roosevelt, T. Jr. Geo. Review p 182.

46. Hanson p 76; Johnson p 18; Lynskey p 38; Mathews p 1–19.

47. Diffie p 40–44; Roosevelt, Mrs. T Jr., p 226–230; Article in the NY Herald Tribune of 2/10/30 and NY Times article of 10/14/29, LOC c-63& c-47.

48. Clark p 18, 43, 69; Hanson p 77; Lynskey p 26–27; Article by Theodore Schroeder, LOC c-63.

49. Diffie p 4–6; Hanson p 77; Lynskey p 29; Madaras p 255; NY Times article of 2/5/30, LOC c-63

50. Carrion p 216; Clark p xix and 15–20; Johnson p 18; Lynskey p 6–8; Madaras p 258–260; Report of the Governor General for 1930, LOC c-47.

51. Diffie p 162–183; Lynskey p 19, 28.

52. Hanson p 77; Johnson, R.A., p 18; LOC c-47.

53. Roosevelt, T. Jr. Geo. Review p 191; Roosevelt, Mrs. T Jr., p 232.

54. Roosevelt, Mrs. T Jr., p 233; Lynskey p 31.

55. Carrion p 213–216; Hanson p 250; Mathews p 110.

56. Roosevelt, Mrs. T Jr., p 234; Hanson p 250; Madaras p 266–267.

57. Hanson p 251; Madaras p 267–268.

58. Madaras p 262–264; Roosevelt, T. Jr. Geo. Review p 187–189; Roosevelt, Mrs. T Jr., p 233.

59. TRJr's speeches of 9/1/30 and 2/9/31, LOC c-47.

60. Roosevelt, Mrs. T Jr., p 237; TRJr letter to Bailey Diffie of 11/30/31, LOC c-16.

61. Collier p 331; Roosevelt, Mrs. T Jr. p 237.

62. Collier p 331; Roosevelt, Mrs. T Jr. p 235–240; Article in Cincinnati Times, LOC c-63.

63. Madaras p 271–273; Roosevelt, Mrs. T Jr. p 241; San Francisco Chronicle 6/30/31, LOC c-63.

64. Roosevelt, Mrs. T Jr., p 232, 245–246, 250.

65. Collier p 329–331; S. Morris p 474.

66. Collier p 330–331.

67. Ibid

68. Roosevelt, Mrs. T Jr., p 246–247; Article in the Macon Telegraph of 3/29/31, LOC c-63.

69. Hanson p 60–61; Lewis p 225; Office of Puerto Rican Commonwealth p 14; LOC c-29; LOC c-63.

70. Hanson p 61n.

71. Collier p 331; Roosevelt, Mrs. T Jr., p 242, 250.

72. Carrion p 213.

73. Madaras p 259.

74. Collier p 331; Roosevelt, Mrs. T Jr., p 252, 261; Quezon p 143; Eleanor's letter to Ted, 11/13/31, LOC c-6.

75. Mathews p 64, 67, and 208; Roosevelt, Mrs. T Jr., p 249; Lewis p 220; Office of Commonwealth of Puerto Rico Pamphlet p 15; NY Times 1/24/32; Boston Herald of 9/14/31, Boston Evening Transcript of 9/2/31, NY Times of 9/12/31 & 1/10/32, all in LOC c-63.

76. Roosevelt, Mrs. T Jr., p 234; Governor General's Official Reports of 1930 and 1931, LOC c-47 & c-63.

77. Madaras p 278; Roosevelt, T. Jr. Geo. Review p 192; Roosevelt, Mrs. T Jr., p 266; Keesing p 15–19.

78. Roosevelt, Mrs. T Jr., p 252–258.

79. Roosevelt, Mrs. T Jr., p 260–261; The Tribune, March 1933 and Atlanta Constitution, 5/15/32, LOC c-63; Copy of Inaugural Address in LOC c-47

80. Roosevelt, Mrs. T Jr., p 262; TRJr Diary entry of 2/29/32, LOC c-2.

81. Madaras p 279; Roosevelt, T. Jr., Geo. Review p 203; Roosevelt, Mrs. T. Jr. p 292–293.

82. Rizal Program, LOC c-56; Hearst Newspaper articles, LOC c-63; TRJr's Diary entry of 3/22/32 and various other entries in March and April 1932, LOC c-2.

83. Roosevelt, Mrs. T Jr., p 282–283.

84. Hayden p 531–532.

85. Roosevelt, Mrs. T Jr., p 295; Chicago American of 4/20/32, LOC c-63.

86. NY Times 6/13/32, LOC c-55.

87. Madaras p 280, Taylor p 84–85; NY Times 6/13/32, LOC c-55.

88. Roosevelt, Mrs. T Jr., p 294–296; Official Order Reducing Salaries, LOC c-47.

89. Ibid

90. NY Times 6/13/32, LOC c-55

91. Grunder p 189; NY Times 6/13/32, LOC c-55

92. Hayden p 647; Madaras p 280; Official Report of the Governor General 1932, LOC c-47, various letters TRJr. wrote describing his programs, LOC c-42.

93. Roosevelt, Mrs. T Jr., p 269–271.

94. Ibid p 266, 273, 291.

95. Ingersoll p 193.

96. Roosevelt, Mrs. T Jr., p 277–278; Rice & Roosevelt, TAPS p 207

97. Roosevelt, Mrs. T Jr., p 284–285; Manila Tribune article, LOC c-63.

98. Collier p 334–335.

99. Roosevelt, Mrs. T Jr. p 298–300; LOC c-56

100. Roosevelt, Mrs. T Jr., p 300; A copy of the address is in the LOC c-47.

101. Collier p 334.

102. Morris, S., p 479–480.

103. Roosevelt, Mrs. T Jr., p 302; Rizal Program, LOC c-56.

104. Roosevelt, Mrs. T Jr., p 304–305, LOC c-56; Scripps Howard Newspapers of 2/27/33, LOC c-63.

105. LOC c-63

106. LOC c-63

107. LOC c-29.

108. Roosevelt, Mrs. T Jr., p 296.

109. NY Times 6/13/32, LOC c-55; Minkota Free Press and NY World Telegram of 3/27/33, and The Philippine Herald of 4/28/33, all in LOC c-63 Philippine Herald 3/16/33, LOC c-76 (Misc. Folder)

110. Roosevelt, Mrs. T Jr., p 305–366.

THE NORMAL YEARS

When Ted and Eleanor landed in New York in the fall of 1933, for the first time in years they didn't have anything to do except to find a home and begin living a normal life for a change. After first finding an acceptable home to rent near Sagamore Hill, Ted went out job hunting. Keeping three boys in Groton and Harvard, along with the Depression, had depleted the Roosevelt's finances somewhat. While they were certainly not broke, Ted needed a job if they were going to maintain their accustomed lifestyle without dipping into their savings.

Even though the Philippine Islands had been promised total independence by the United States, a bill must first be approved by the U.S. House and Senate setting a specific date for sovereignty to be granted. For political reasons, Manuel Quezon and some of the other influential Filipinos wanted Congress to delay for a short time passing such a bill. Knowing that Ted had just spent the past year as Governor General and would be well versed in Philippine politics, President Franklin Roosevelt invited him to have lunch at the White House. After talking privately with FDR about the islands' politics and independence for nearly an hour, they were joined by Gerald Swope and J. H. Perkins for a nice lunch. Over the next few months, Ted and FDR exchanged several letters about the Philippine situation and they got together for another White House lunch.[1]

After returning from his visit with the President in the nation's capital, Ted began to worry about getting his Reserve Army Officer's Commission renewed. It was about to expire and he knew he didn't have the required active duty time to get it extended. With his fingers crossed for luck, he wrote Army Chief of Staff Douglas MacArthur a letter pointing out that while he technically did not qualify for renewal, he had been in contact with troops on an almost daily basis during the three years he had been Governor General of Puerto Rico and of the Philippines, and he greatly desired to maintain his reserve officer's status. MacArthur promptly responded that his commission would be extended for a five-year period if he could pass the army physical examination. Other than smoking cigarettes and moderate to heavy social drinking, Ted always maintained proper health habits. He ate nourishing foods, got plenty of exercise by playing squash and tennis often, and always kept himself in top condition. He had no trouble passing the physical.[2]

Due to a change in the way the company's business was being conducted, several members of the Board of Directors of the American Express Company had resigned. Ted and Eleanor owned stock in the company, and, with the help of a relative of Eleanor's, in January '34, Ted was elected to fill one of the vacancies on the Board. While being a director took but little of his time and paid only a modest compensation, Ted was glad to have the job; every little bit helped.[3]

All fall Gracie had been dating Bill McMillan, the young architect Ted and Eleanor had met on their return trip from the Philippines. Both of her parents had said all along that Bill was a perfect young man for Gracie, so naturally they were pleased when the couple announced their engagement. The wedding took place in March at Christ Church in Oyster Bay. To give the bride away, Ted dressed in the same formal attire he wore at his own wedding, twenty-four years before, and Gracie wore her mother's wedding dress. TR III and Cornelius were ushers, and Quentin, who had developed into quite a musician, played the piano at the reception. Despite some bad weather, it was a beautiful wedding. The newly-weds would live near Baltimore. The following January, when Gracie and Bill had their first child, Ted and Eleanor flew to Baltimore for the birth. They couldn't wait to get a peek at their first grandchild, a beautiful little girl. Some in the news media got confused and reported that it was Ted and Eleanor who had had a baby. Tickled to death at the accusation, Ted didn't deny it. When the Associated Press called about the report, he led them to believe he was the father by telling them he was certainly not going to plow the new little Roosevelt under.[4]

Because Ted had been out of the country so much of the past eight years, his chances of receiving the Republican nomination for any political office were remote, but he couldn't resist getting his hands back in American politics in some way. Due to being blamed for causing the Depression, the Grand Old Party was at its lowest point in history. Ted knew that the Party had absolutely nothing to do with bringing on the hard times, but this did not hold true with respect to many of the voters. When the opportunity arose for him to seek the Presidency of the National Republican Club with an almost 100% chance of being elected, he jumped at it. Like the Party, the Club was in extremely bad shape. Many of its members had dropped out and it was operating with an ever-increasing financial deficit.

Two totally unrelated meetings were held on April 12, 1934. At one of the meetings Ted was elected President of the National Republican Club, and at the other he was elected Chairman of the Board of Directors of American Express Co.

Both these jobs would help the Roosevelts' perceived money problems, especially the American Express job; it paid a salary of $15,000 per year.[5]

Over the next year, Ted and Eleanor lived the quiet life. Unless he was gone on one of his occasional political speaking engagements or off hunting, Ted was at home every night. In mid-1935 he took advantage of the opportunity to go on a hunting expedition to Brazil for the American Museum of Natural History. On his way down to South America, he made a stopover in Puerto Rico. It was the first time he had been back since he left three years before, and the Puerto Ricans gave him a warm welcome. Ted enjoyed immensely seeing his many good friends there. To add to the fun and success of his trip, he managed to down a magnificent jaguar to put in the museum's collection. In addition to specimen for the American Museum, he brought back two Sakiwinki monkeys for pets. In winter, these delicate, slender creatures lived in the basement of Balocca's bungalow, but in warm weather they had the run of the yard surrounding Ted and Eleanor's residence. They were curious little animals and gave many a guest on the veranda a chuckle as they scampered about and tried to examine the visitors' eyeglasses, cups, spoons, etc.[6]

Nelson Doubleday, the CEO of Doubleday Doran Publishing Co., had been a personal friend of the Ted Roosevelts for years, and his father and TR were close. When the company lost the services of Walter Page, a partner and former Ambassador to the Court of St. James, Mr. Doubleday decided that Ted, with his vast knowledge of government and extensive writing experience, would be an excellent replacement for his departed employee, and offered him a job with the company as an editor. Delighted at the offer, Ted immediately accepted. With the duties of his new job, Ted would not have time to continue as Chairman of the Board at American Express, although he would be able to remain as a board member and could also retain his presidency of the National Republican Club. When news of his career change broke, a reporter asked him if he was ready to settle down to a sedate existence after having lived such an exciting life for the past thirty years. Ted responded, "Oh yes, you forget that I'm a grandfather now and it is time I settled down."[7]

The work at Doubleday was enjoyable and interesting. Part of the job entailed Ted trying to think of a good plot and then hunt for the right writer to put it into the form of a marketable book. Another thing he did was contact his influential friends and encourage them to begin to work on their autobiographies for Doubleday to publish. He wrote Douglas MacArthur with the suggestion that he write his memoirs. In a rare bit of humor, the General promptly wrote back that the thought of writing his memoirs made him laugh, for if he told half of what he knew, many reputations would be ruined and he would be an outcast. Ted responded that if he did not feel the time was right, he should go ahead and start making notes but hold off publication until the proper time. Years later, during World War II, Ted made a similar suggestion to General Omar Bradley. After the war, when Bradley wrote *A Soldier's Story,* he gave Ted credit for having planted the seed in his mind to write the book.[8]

It had been assumed for years that Ted and Eleanor would eventually acquire Sagamore Hill from Edith and make it their home. They had been married since 1910, and had never owned a home of their own. Archie, Kermit, Alice, and Ethel all had their own homes, but Ted and Eleanor had always lived in a rented house or a house furnished to them by the government. Over the years, Edith had mentioned to Ted several times that she would move out of Sagamore Hill and turn it over to Eleanor and him, but somehow it just never came about. Among themselves, he and Eleanor decided it was now or never and put some pressure on Edith to go ahead and vacate the old family home. Edith, who by now spoke mostly of the past and showed other signs of aging, resisted. When Archie took his mother's side in the issue, there developed some hurt feelings in what had at one time been an exceptionally close-knit family. Ted wrote Ethel of his mother, "The 'old hero beyant' is well. Like Bugaboo Bill, she is 'sitting on top of the hill, entertaining occasional grandchildren.'" He wrote Archie, saying that while he and Eleanor had "received far less from the family than any of the other children," they were now the only ones with the financial means to take over the old home place, and that otherwise Sagamore would have to be sold on Edith's death. Actually, Edith lived in Sagamore Hill until her death in 1948. Afterwards, the unusual old residence was deeded to the United States Government and then made into the Sagamore Hill National Historic Site, as it remains today.[9]

Finally giving up on ever acquiring Sagamore Hill, Ted and Eleanor bought a tract adjacent to Sagamore, which at one time had been planted in fruit trees, and then they got their architect son-in-law Bill McMillan to design a home for them to build on their new property. The new home was named "Old Orchard."

Nineteen thirty-seven was an extremely busy year for the TRJrs First, they spent several weeks in the United Kingdom, where Ted earned some extra money by delivering the Watson Chair Lectures at the University College London, and he and Eleanor shopped for things for their new home. They even had lunch with Winston Churchill.

The Watson Chair had been founded shortly after the First World War for the purpose of offering annual lectures by a highly qualified person in the fields of American history, literature or institutions. Just being asked to give the lectures was an honor within itself. Ted chose as his subject Imperialism and the United States. Based primarily on his research and lecture notes, he later wrote *Colonial Policies of the United States,* which was by far his most serious, and last book length composition. In his lectures, and also in the book, Ted rejected the imperialistic policies of his father and also those of the UK, stating that colonialism is alien to democratic traditions and that the primary reason for a ruling nation to have a colony is to benefit the ruling nation. He did, however, admit that with respect to Puerto Rico, the cost of maintaining the colony had been greater than the benefit received. Teddy Roosevelt had been a staunch advocate of colonialism and the U.S. acquired several colonies because of his efforts. By repudiating one of his famous father's most noted accomplishments, Ted, at age fifty, was in a sense cutting the strings and proclaiming his emotional independence from TR. He had first publicly asserted his freedom when he spoke earlier in the year at the Lincoln Day dinner held by the National Republican Club. In this speech, he, by inference, disavowed TR's progressivism. He was still proud to be who he was, but he had at last overcome his feelings that he had to live up to what he perceived to be his father's expectations, unattainable expectations. Ted had finally exorcised himself of what to him was an emotional demon, the demon of feeling he was unworthy of being the son and namesake of President Theodore Roosevelt.[10]

In April, after serving for three years, Ted resigned his leadership roll in the National Republican Club. During his tenure, he had greatly increased the club's membership with primarily young members, and had gotten the organization to a sound financial footing.

During the decade of the 30s, TRJr wrote articles for numerous magazines, including pieces on hunting for *Country Gentlemen* and *Cosmopolitan,* one on the development of modern medicine for the *Journal of the Philippine Islands Medical Association,* and articles on various other subjects for *Foreign Affairs Magazine, The Geographical Review, Readers Digest,* and *Look,* to name a few. In the latter part of 1937, he and Eleanor were chosen as the co-travel editors for *House and Garden Magazine* Since this was only a part-time job, Ted was able to continue working at his position with Doubleday Doran. Together, the TRJrs wrote a regular travel column for their new employer.[11]

In early spring of '38, just about the time Ted was promoted to Vice President of Doubleday Doran, the Roosevelts moved into their brand new, ninety thousand dollar, two story, Georgian style home, Old Orchard. The structure was large, made of old brick, with high ceilings and a hall running down the center from the front door to the back door. The interior was designed with a living room, dining room, formal drawing room, and six individually named bedrooms. Ted's and Eleanor's was the "Vermont," Signorina chose hers to be "Cuneo," after her home town in Italy; the others were "Manila," "Chengtu," "Puerto Rico," and "France." Quentin hand painted the names on all the bedroom doors. Bookshelves were everywhere, both upstairs and down. Over the years, Ted and Eleanor had acquired hundreds of unusual furnishings and items for the home they hoped to have one day, and they finally had a place to put them. For instance, they had scrolls and paintings from Tibet, tiles from China, an ornate bronze chime clock from Turkey, primitive carvings from the Philippines, carved figures from Java, and embroideries from Szechwan to go along with some of the beautiful things Eleanor had sewn herself. Other furnishings in Old Orchard included a large table with its top made from a single piece of Philippine mahogany, Ming lamps, a Chinese palace carpet, an antique white marble mantelpiece with intricately carved baskets of flowers, and two antique chandeliers. The antique front door came from an old house in Dublin. They had the antique, bronze, muzzle-loading swivel canon that had been given to Ted by a Moro Chief, mounted in the yard. Each afternoon when Ted came home from work he would begin his second job, improving the grounds around Old Orchard. Balocca handled the general yard upkeep, but Ted did the heavier work, like clearing away unwanted trees and brush. During World War II, the TRJrs started working on what they called the "War Corner," where memorabilia from Ted's war service would be displayed.

Some of their friends laughingly said that the place was so full of unusual things that it reminded them of a museum, but others said that Old Orchard was Ted and Eleanor to a tee. One wrote them that it was "as indisputably yours as your toothbrush." Whatever it was to others, Ted and Eleanor loved it; it was their long awaited home of their own. One of the first things they did was place a guest book in the hall. The first names in it appeared on April 21, 1938. Even though fighting was going on between Japan and China, and Hitler was in power in Germany, the shooting war in Europe had not yet started The TRJrs had no inkling that they would do anything other than live out the rest of their lives quietly at Old Orchard in Oyster Bay.[12]

All of the Roosevelt children grew up and left home during the 1930s except the youngest, Quentin, who by 1939 was a junior at Harvard. Gracie was a young mother and living near Baltimore. TR III graduated from Harvard in 1936 and got a job with E.I. du Pont de Nemours in Philadelphia. Within the next two years, he was transferred twice by du Pont, and ended up in Louisville, Kentucky. While there, he met and fell in love with a local girl named Anne Babcock. When he brought her home to meet his parents, Eleanor and Ted immediately liked her, and by the time the weekend was over, they knew she was the right girl for their middle son. TRIII and Anne were married in 1939. Eleanor called Anne "the daughter-in-law of my dreams." Cornelius attended Harvard for two years, and then transferred to MIT. There he studied mining engineering and graduated with honors in 1938. He then went to work in Mexico for American Smelting and Refining Co. The President of that company had intended to employ Cornelius' Uncle Quentin after World War I was over, and he had kept a job open all those years for the first member of the Roosevelt family who graduated with an engineering degree.[13]

Even though he had a job that he was successful in and liked very much, and was busy with their brand new home, and did volunteer work in several worthy causes, Ted was not content unless he was actively participating in politics in some way. Especially during the election years of 1936 and 1940, he made numerous speeches blasting the liberal spending policies of the Democrats in general, and the New Deal of FDR in particular. Ted was still the most sought after speaker in the Republican ranks, except for the actual candidates that were running. While many, if not most, politicians are able to adjust their personal philosophies on matters to fit the view that will win them the most votes, Ted Roosevelt was too honest to fit into that category. He was an uncompromising, true believer. In his mind, the welfare state of the New Dealers would lead to the ruination of the country. At times he was so forceful in denouncing the Democrats that some of the more liberal members of his own party were embarrassed. Still, trying as hard as he did, he made no appreciable difference in the results of any of the races. The Republicans were out and the Democrats were in. During the latter years of the '30s, Ted was mentioned as a possible candidate for Governor and Vice President, but he never actively sought either office and would most likely have refused to run had the opportunity presented itself.[14]

All his adult life, Ted had been a worker in a number of causes and civic organizations which he considered to be worthwhile. At one time or another, he had actively worked on behalf of the American Poets' Academy, Howard University, Tuskegee Institute, the National Council for Civilian Relief of China, the Royal Geographical Society, the Elks, the Masons, the American Legion, the Salvation Army, the Harvard Club, the Sons of the American Revolution, the Knickerbocker Club, the Izach Walton League, the Boone and Crocket Club, the First Division Society, the Traveling Salesmen's Association, the YMCA, the American Museum of Natural History, and the Field Museum of Natural History in Chicago, to name a few. For several years, he was Sunday School Superintendent at Christ Church in Oyster Bay.[15]

Having absolutely no tolerance for intolerance and racial prejudice, TRJr denounced these unreasoned views in speeches and letters over the years. Saying in a letter he wrote shortly after the beginning of World War II,

Last war I felt that our people would be greatly helped specifically by the war—
I thought intolerance, snobbery, greed would be driven into the background.
They were not, If anything they seemed to be fostered.[16]

He was an active worker in both the National Association for the Advancement of Colored People and the National Conference of Christians and Jews, and served on the Board of Directors of both of these organizations. Probably, however, the organization that he devoted more time to than any of the others was the Boy Scouts. For many years, Ted was on its National Executive Committee, and he received the organization's Silver Buffalo Award. When Irving Berlin signed over the rights to his song "God Bless America" to a trust for the Boy Scouts, he requested that the trust be administered by three trustees, made up of a Catholic, a Jew, and a Protestant. The initial trustees chosen were Herbert Swope, Gene Tunney, and Theodore Roosevelt, Jr. Ted's sarcastic wit displayed itself in an incident that arose out of a remark he made in a speech for the Boy Scouts. He mentioned that the Scouts maintained a secret "red flag" list of persons alleged to be unfit to lead or influence boys. A particular newspaper reporter in the audience took exception to the fact that there was such a list and, in his column the next day, demanded that the list be made public and further demanded to know if his (the reporter's) name was on the list. Ted promptly wrote him that the red flag list had nothing to do with communism or any other political doctrine, but that the list was composed of the names of men whose moral character rendered them unfit to be associated with the training of boys. As to whether the reporter's name was on the list, Ted said that he had not studied the list and, "therefore, I cannot tell you positively whether your name is on it or not. Have you any reason to suppose that it is?"[17]

You would think that being the "man's man" that he was, Ted's best friend would have been some sportsman, or famous athlete, or maybe a politician, as was true with respect to his father, but this was not the case for Ted. Over the last decade of his life, his best friend was Alexander Woollcott, a literary critic, broadcaster, and prominent member of the Algonquin Round Table. Woollcott and Roosevelt had known each other for years, and, shortly after Armistice Day, they had worked together on the formation of the American Legion. The initial friendship continued and broadened and as the years passed TRJr and Eleanor settled into a warm friendship with the noted literatus. They spent many weekends visiting in each other's homes and carried on an extensive correspondence by letter. One of Ted's favorite subjects in letters to his pal was Eleanor. He often referred to her as "Mickey Herself McQuire," apparently after a character named Mickey McQuire played by child actor Mickey Rooney on a radio show. Mickey McGuire was always getting into trouble by doing things his peculiar way, and Ted loved to describe Mickey Herself McGuire's undertakings in his letters. Once he wrote Alex (or Aleck, they referred to him both ways) that "Herself" was mad at him because his shoes had holes in the soles, and he refused to concede to her demands and buy a new pair. He went on to write that she retaliated by calling him "a goddamn ape." Naturally, Alex was one of the Roosevelts' first overnight guests after Old Orchard was completed. Woollcott was funny about signing guest books, at least funny about signing the Old Orchard guest book; he wouldn't sign it. Finally, after being berated by Ted and Eleanor to please sign, Alex decided that he would teach them a lesson and at the same time show them what good friends were for. On 11/3/1940 he went ahead and signed the guest book. The only thing was he used an alias; he signed "Franklin D. Roosevelt."[18]

In 1935, Alex suggested to Ted and his half-sister, Alice Longworth, that people must have thousands of wonderful poems hidden away in nooks and crannies around the house which would never be seen by the general public unless someone sought them out and presented them for publication. Woollcott had a popular radio program at the time and he volunteered to request on the air that his listeners search their hiding places for unpublished poems, and send in any found to Ted and Alice for possible inclusion in a book. Ted and his sister were charged with going through the lyrics submitted and selecting the best ones for publication. Of course, they would also have to handle the matter of obtaining the poets' permission to publish and negotiating with Doubleday, the expected publisher. When all was agreed, Alex's request to his listeners was answered with some thirty thousand poems sent in, so Ted and Alice had quite a job. Thusly, the delightful book of several hundred poems entitled *Desk Drawer Anthology*, came into being. It sold well in the U.S., but it was especially popular in England and stayed in print for years. One of the poems included is entitled, "God in His Goodness Sent the Grapes." The poet is unknown. It reads in part:

> God in His goodness sent the grapes
> To cheer both great and small
> Little fools will drink too much,
> And great fools not at all!

Unless disguised by a pseudonym, none of Ted's poems appear in the book.[19]

Ted had a kind of love/hate relationship with H. L. Mencken. They addressed each other as "Ted" and "Henry," shared similar political philosophies, and carried on an intense correspondence mostly about politics. Privately though, Ted didn't think much of his friend as a writer. In one letter Ted wrote to a young relative, he said that Mencken and some of the other modern writers, "Tend to make half-truths appear as whole truths. They take for their theme indecency and label it realism. Some of them are bright. They shine with a phosphorescence that gathers on rotten flesh."[20]

Other close friends of the TRJrs included Helen Hayes, Charlie MacArthur, the Lunts, Thornton Wilder, Gertrude Lawrence, Susan and Harpo Marx, Henry and Elizabeth Beston, and the DuPonts. These were what might be called their high-class friends, and they would get together with them on occasional weekends for croquet, badminton, and parlor games. Ted's sister, Ethel Derby, was critical of this particular group of their companions, one time writing her mother, "How can they love the DuPonts?"[21]

Gene Tunney, Grantland Rice, Quintin Reynolds, and Suydam Cutting were some of Ted's more macho chums, and he also remained in touch with many of his World War I friends. After returning home from the Philippine Islands, Ted entertained his old comrades from the 26th Infantry Regiment with an annual luncheon at his home in Oyster Bay. Many of the old veterans traveled for miles to attend. One year, General George C. Marshall was the guest of honor.[22]

In the late '30s there were a number of celebrity softball games played to raise money for the Theodore Roosevelt Park in Oyster Bay. One of the teams was named the "Nine Old Men" and was captained by Lowell Thomas. The opposing team, named the "Oyster Bay Oysters," was led by Ted. The games were played on different fields in the area, once even at Madison Square Garden. Some of the players were Eddie Rickenbacker, Rube Goldberg, Grantland Rice, Gene Tunney, Hamilton Fish, Jimmy Dolittle, Gene Sarazen, Quintin Reynolds, Babe Ruth, and Nelson Doubleday. There was always a party before, during, and after the games for the participants, their wives, and friends. Everyone always had a wonderful time. Another thing of a local nature that Ted got a lot of personal pleasure from was the Dutch Treat Club. Its membership was made up primarily of broadcasters, publishers, and writers, but there were a few others. Some of the members of this informal group were Lowell Thomas, H. V. Kaltenborn (a Harvard classmate of Ted's), Roy Howard, and John T. Flynn The club met for a weekly luncheon and always had a prominent person as speaker. The only rule was that nothing said ever went beyond the club.[23]

As FDR's second term was winding down and the war clouds were gathering in Europe, there was an element in the United States, including Ted Roosevelt, that believed the national administration was intentionally guiding the country into a war that was about to start. In 1937, the First Lady (FDR's Eleanor) sent her first cousin, Ted Roosevelt, a book about war as a Christmas present. In his letter thanking her for the present, Ted wrote:

> I myself am a convinced pacifist, but when I use the term pacifist I use it in what I believe to be the true significance,—i.e., I do not believe that my country should get into any war that can possibly be avoided. I do not believe in wars of conquest.
>
> My feelings on the matter are so deep that this year I tried to get Philip Gibbs to write for us a book which was to be called NOBODY WINS A WAR. As I see it, the matter can be summed up in this fashion. A country always loses by a war. At times it loses less by having a war than by refusing to fight. So far I am sure we are both entirely in agreement.
>
> Next, I believe most emphatically that the real losses from war are not what occur during the war, but the after effects of it.

The letter goes on to say that he does not believe the League of Nations is a practical instrument for peace other than being a forum where nations may air grievances, and that he would not trust other nations to make the decision on whether the United States should go to war or not. The President's wife promptly wrote back, thanking Ted for his letter, and then she went on to write,

> This is a terribly complicated question, however, and I do not know that anybody wants peace! I have moments when I think we all believe that complete peace is so complicated we might better go to war![24]

This is a very peculiar and revealing off-the-cuff comment by the wife of the President of the United States. It could easily be construed to confirm what Ted suspected. FDR was trying to get the country into a war.

While there was never a split within the TR family to the extent that they refused to speak to one another, by the mid-1930s, Teddy had been dead for fifteen years, and Edith was showing signs of old age. The glue that held the family together was beginning to dissolve. The row over Sagamore Hill caused some of the problems, and it didn't help any when Ted's Eleanor sent her mother-in-law a bill for $140 for trees she and Ted had planted on the property line between Old Orchard and Sagamore Hill. Ethel didn't approve of some of Ted's and Eleanor's friends, and she may have been jealous of how well off financially her oldest brother was. When Aunt Emily Carow died and left most of her small estate to Ted, who really didn't need it, the ill feelings over money escalated. Kermit's drinking and promiscuity could not be tolerated by the family, especially not by Ted. Alice, who was only a half-sibling, was the only one not caught up in the family bickering. While Alice certainly had her wild side and did her own thing, the family seems to have accepted it as just Alice, the free spirit, living her own life.[25]

After Germany invaded Poland in 1939 and World War II began in Europe, there developed in the U.S. two totally different views with respect to the proper political roll for the United States to take. The interventionists, which included FDR and his administration, thought the country should enter the war as a combatant, or at least give all the aid possible to the British and French. The non-interventionists, of which Ted Roosevelt was one, believed no one won in a war and that the U.S. should do everything possible to stay completely neutral. In 1940, Alice Roosevelt Longworth and a number of other influential non-interventionists, including Hanford MacNider, a former national commander of the American Legion, formed the America First Committee and issued the following statement of principles:

1. The U.S. must build an impregnable national defense.

2. No foreign power, nor group of powers, can successfully attack a prepared America.

3. American democracy can be preserved only by keeping out of the European war.

4. "Aid short of war" weakens national defense at home and threatens to involve America in war abroad.[26]

With their strong anti-war sentiments and wanting the organization to become a thorn in the side of the FDR administration, Ted and Charles Lindberg, the famous flyer, were among the first to join. The organization set about attempting to influence public and political opinion toward keeping the country out of the war and, at the same time, encouraging the building of a strong national defense. Being the hawk that he was, if Teddy Roosevelt had still been alive he most certainly would have been a strong interventionist. In a sense, Ted's pacifist beliefs and his action in joining America First were other examples of his asserting independence from his famous father.

When it became publicly known that Ted was an "America Firster," he began to receive hate mail and ridicule, some saying he was a Nazi, a Communist, a traitor, a white-livered coward, and that he was certainly not the son of his father. These detractors had obviously forgotten Ted's exemplary record in the Great War. When France fell and Germany invaded Russia, Ted realized that the U.S. could be drawn into the war at any time. In late 1940, he was at an America First meeting when some of the members present stated that they would refuse to fight, even if America was in the war. This really went against Ted's principles. While he was a pacifist, he still strongly believed in his father's "blood tax." If the United States was at war, every able-bodied man had the obligation to fight for his country. Ted immediately resigned his membership in America First.[27]

With the onset of 1941, the years of being a civilian working man, of children growing up, of a home of their own, of politicking, of good causes and of good times with good friends were over. The normal years for the Ted Roosevelt family were at an end. Ted was fifty-three years old. The family had lived in Old Orchard for three years. A visitor's name was entered in the Old Orchard guest book on May 10, 1941. It wasn't signed again until 1945.[28]

The Normal Years Source Notes

1. Franklin D Roosevelt, Day by Day, 9/8/33, FDR Library, Hyde Park; LOC c-29; NY Times 2/10/34; T letter to FDR of 2/12/34, LOC c-30.

2. LOC c-29 & c-30.

3. Ted's letter to Ethel and Dick Derby of 10/30/32, TR Collection, Harvard U., 87M-100.

4. Roosevelt, Mrs. T. Jr., p 377–378; Ted's letter to Edith of 1/31/35, TR Col. HU, 87M-101; Ted's letter to James Beverly of 1/9/33, LOC c-27.

5. Roosevelt, Mrs. T. Jr., p 368; Board minutes of American Express of 4/12/34 & 8/1/44; Ted's letter to Ethel Derby, TR Col. 87M-100.

6. NY Times, 6/8/35 & 7/25/35; Roosevelt, Mrs. T. Jr., p 370.

7. Roosevelt, Mrs. T. Jr., p 371 & 380; NY Times, 9/16/35

8. LOC c-29; Acknowledgements in A SOLDIERS STORY by Omar Bradley

9. Ted letter to Ethel Derby of 8/23/28, TR Col., 87M-100; Collier p 391; Sylvia Morris p 490.

10. Roosevelt, Mrs. T Jr., p 398; Roosevelt, T Jr., Colonial Policies of US; Ted letters to Ethel Derby of 2/1/37 & 2/13/37, TR Col. 87M-100, 33–41.

11. Miller, N. The Roosevelt Chronicles p 329; NY Times, 11/13/37; LOC c-51.

12. Roosevelt, Mrs. T Jr., p 404–409; Ted letters to Eleanor, LOC c-61; Time Magazine 7/24/44; The Guest Book is now in the LOC c-60.

13. Roosevelt, Mrs. T. Jr., p 382 & 385.

14. Roosevelt, Mrs. T. Jr., p 374; NY Times, 6/1/35.

15. LOC c-37 & c-59; NY Times 5/23/39; NY Herald Tribune 7/14/44; Madaras p 218; Roosevelt, Mrs. T. Jr., p 369.

16. Ted letter to Woollcott of 5/2/42, TR Col., HU.

17. Collier p 389; Roosevelt, Mrs. T Jr., p 368–369; The Article and Ted's letter are in LOC c-41.

18. Ted letter to Woollcott of 10/11/38, TR Col. bMS Am 1449[1442] 33–41; Guest Book in LOC c-60.

19. Roosevelt, Mrs. T. Jr., p 373.

20. LOC c-56 & c-29; Ted letter to Joseph Alsop, Jr., TR Col. 87M-102.

21. Caroli p 362; Roosevelt, Mrs. T. Jr., p 372; LOC c-46.

22. LOC c-29.

23. LOC c-29 & c-36; Ted's diary entry of 11/23/21, LOC c-1.

24. Ted letter to Mrs. FDR of 1/14/38 & her response of 1/20/38, LOC c-30.

25. Morris, S. p 139 & 496–498.

26. Cole p 9–15.

27. Downs; Roosevelt, Mrs. T. Jr., p 418.

28. The Guest Book is in the LOC c-60.

THE TERRY AND TEDDY SHOW

With the deteriorating world political situation in general, and particularly with respect to the United States' relations with Germany and Japan, by the end of 1940 Ted was convinced that the country would soon be drawn into the war raging both in Europe and the Far East. While he still believed nobody won in a war, he also believed in a strong national defense. If there was to be a war, he could help the country more by being at the battlefront than in any other way. Still holding his reserve officer's rank of Colonel, (commonly called "Full" Colonel, "Bird" Colonel or "Chicken" Colonel) in early 1941 Ted applied for active duty in the Army. On April 15th his request was granted; for the first time in over twenty years he was back in military service. When his first duty assignment was to command his old World War I outfit, the 26th Infantry Regiment, then stationed at Fort Devens, Massachusetts, he was more than happy, he was elated. As had been the case during his 1917–1918 wartime service, the 26th Infantry was a component of the First Infantry Division. Now though, due to a change in Army philosophy with respect to the optimum size of various units, the authorized strength of infantry divisions had been reduced from approximately 28,000 to 15,000 officers and men. The Big Red One was now made up of the 16th, 18th, and 26th Infantry Regiments, together with four battalions of artillery, an engineer battalion, a medical battalion, a quartermaster battalion, a reconnaissance company, a signal company, and a detachment of military police.[1]

Almost immediately after Ted's re-entry into the service, his family and friends began to notice that he somehow looked younger, and was always in the best of spirits. He was back in the one element in which he knew he was as good, or better, than his father. In fact, being constantly compared to his father didn't bother him so much any more. Throughout their married life, Eleanor had always been her husband's biggest fan, and she wrote her mother that Ted was in, "splendid shape and looked dashing in his uniform with all his ribbons and decorations."[2]

No doubt Eleanor and Ted both had some thoughts that with war likely to break out at any time and Ted going back into the Army, their remaining life together might be limited. Though he was unlucky in politics, he was lucky in marriage. What a wonderful wife Eleanor had been for Ted, and what a marvelous marriage they had had. One friend called them a "dramatic cultured, articulate, witty, completely charming and devoted couple." Ted liked nothing better than to kid his spouse and tell friends of the many funny things she had done. One time he wrote, "My wife is usually of a sweet disposition. Just before a delayed meal she sometimes becomes actually ferocious. Often I have wished to paraphrase the words of the native servants in 'Kim,' and shout, 'Bring her her food and stop her mouth of illomen!'" Eleanor was determined to make the most out of whatever time they had left together, so she rented a suite at the Groton Inn near Fort Devens to be near Ted during his training and to see him when he could get away.[3]

The Division CO, Major General Donald C. Cubbison, had the Big Red One on a vigorous training schedule. Besides the normal training activities infantry divisions would be expected to engaged in, such as close order drill, bayonet practice, weapon's ranges, first aid, signal training, etc., they often practiced loading on boats and landing on the beach near Buzzards Bay, Massachusetts. Ted and the few other World War I veterans in the division were like celebrities to the younger men; they were treated with great respect. One soldier wrote that the old World War I heroes were, "an inspiring force" to have around.[4]

The West Indies Island of Martinique was a possession of France, and it was the location of a French military station with several thousand troops and a strong air contingent. France was, at the time, a defeated nation and was occupied by the German Army. Martinique was therefore a likely hostile base in the event the U.S. went to war with Germany. By May, there were rumors circulating in Devens that the Big Red One was going to be the spearhead of an amphibious assault on the island to keep it from falling into German hands. This rumor did not materialize, but the Division did temporarily transfer to North Carolina for more amphibious training. After returning to Devens in late summer, they continued an intensive training schedule with special emphasis on amphibious operations.[5]

Ted and Eleanor were both delighted when Quentin, who had recently graduated cum laude from Harvard, was assigned to the 33rd Field Artillery Battalion, a component of the 1st Division Artillery (Divarty), and was also stationed at Devens. Now Eleanor could have them both, almost every Sunday. One of their favorite things to do on weekends was leisurely drive around the old New England countryside and just take in the scenery and talk. Sometimes they would stop and read inscriptions on the large, ornate tombstones in some old graveyard they had noticed, or they might window shop the beautiful old New England homes. One time on an afternoon outing, the three of them spied an unusual-looking old house with the front yard all grown up in weeds. They stopped, and Eleanor got out to take a photo of the place, while Ted and Quentin, engrossed in conversation, stayed in the car. Seeing a new playmate, an enormous dog bounded out from a neighbor's yard and jumped up on Eleanor, knocking her to the ground. When Ted and Quentin heard her screams and came running to her rescue, the dog abandoned Eleanor and exuberantly headed for the retreating Ted, who, in an increasingly impassioned voice was yelling, "Good dog! Nice fellow, good dog! Down! Down you bastard!" Quentin was standing there taking it all in and laughing his head off. They liked just being together, killing time on lazy Sunday afternoons, like ordinary folks.[6]

In early September, the 1st Division was notified that in mid-October it would again be temporarily transferred to North Carolina for seven weeks of special training. Before they left, Ted held a Regimental Organization Day where the twenty-two noncoms and five officers that were veterans of World War I were honored with a Regimental Parade.

When the Division left for North Carolina, Eleanor gave up her small apartment and went back to Old Orchard for a short while. When Ted and Quentin could get weekend passes they would join her there. These occasions would not be a lively and jovial two days, as would have been expected, but were sentimental and pensive times. They usually would walk over to Sagamore Hill and visit Edith, and then mosey down to the old barn. They did a lot of talking about bygone days. The feelings they had were like the ones they had back in 1917 when Archie and Grace Lockwood got married, right after war had been declared against Germany.[7]

For the next month and a half, the Big Red One was headquartered near Samarcand, North Carolina, and engaged in extensive maneuvers and practice landing operations at Onslo Beach. Like most Army maneuvers, the forces were divided up to engage in mock battles against each other. The opposing force hatched up a plan to slip up on the 26th Infantry Headquarters and capture Ted, but the plan failed because Ted spent most of his time out in the field with his battalions and companies. He was in his headquarters very little. The opposing force was not completely foiled, however, for they did manage to capture General Karl Truesdell, the former CO of the Division.[8]

After a few weeks at Old Orchard, Eleanor packed her clothes, drove to North Carolina, and rented a room in Pinehurst, so she would be close to Ted's headquarters. Her husband and son were so busy that she didn't get to see much of them, but she would drive around in the general area where they were and occasionally catch a glimpse of one of them or even get to share a few words. The men in Ted's Regiment would see her pass by, and if they were off duty, she would give a ride to as many of them as could cram into her car. While in North Carolina, Eleanor was impressed by the hospitality the Southerners showed to those strange soldiers suddenly cast in their midst. Every Sunday, the neighborly locals would invite many of the troops (they called them boys) for dinner and a relaxing afternoon.[9]

By the fall of 1941, the Selective Service Act had been in effect long enough that, through the induction of draftees, the manpower of all the military services had ballooned. For this reason, after having been practically frozen for years, promotions within the officer corps were being handed out at an accelerated rate and with little consideration as to date of rank. For instance, Dwight Eisenhower had been a Lieutenant Colonel in 1939 and was now a Brigadier General. Ted always knew that there were some within the Army high echelon who thought of him as a show-off who had not actually paid his dues. Those of the top brass that felt that way were, for the most part, the ones that had had no personal experience with him. Knowing that with his extensive combat experience from World War I and his date of rank as a full Colonel being from August 1919, he should have already been made a Brigadier General, Ted inquired of his promotion status to the War Department. When the answer he received was not responsive, it was obvious to Ted that he was being discriminated against and was getting the run-a-round. He compared his situation to a well-known Albert Lasker story. It was a yarn about an old man who refused to contribute to a particular charity and as a reason for his refusal, said that it was because he didn't like apple pie. When Mr. Lasker asked him what that had to do with it, the man answered that if you didn't intend to do something, one reason was as good as another.[10]

When training was completed in North Carolina, the Division, with Eleanor following, moved back to Massachusetts. A little over a month later when the Japanese attacked Pearl Harbor, all leaves were cancelled and the rumor mill began to grind. The Big Red One was one of the few combat-ready divisions in the Army, so everyone knew it wouldn't be long before they would be sent somewhere to fight. One report had it that Ted would be transferred to the Philippines, and this made a lot of sense because of his having previously been Governor General of the islands and was so well-liked by the Filipinos. Whether there was any substance to this report is mystery, but nothing came of it.[11]

On December 17th, Ted received his long overdue promotion to Brigadier General, and at the same time he was elevated to Assistant Commander of the First Infantry Division. He and General Julius Adler, the former General Manager of the New York Times, were the only combat experienced generals in the Army who did not have regular army commissions. However, Ted was the only general with a reserve commission who was permanently entitled to wear the Fouragere. The Fouragere had been awarded to the Big Red One by the French Government for its distinguished service in World War I. The decoration consists of a small rope with a hangman's knot and a metal spike on the end. It is worn over the shoulder. All soldiers presently serving in the Division were entitled to wear it, but only those actually serving in the 1st Division during World War I when the award was made were entitled to wear it, no matter what division they were presently serving in.[12]

Toward the latter part of December, the leave cancellation policy was relaxed so that as many troops as possible would have a few days off at Christmas time. All the men were to report back shortly after New Year's Day. During the holidays, the barracks were cleaned out and all the Division's property and equipment was crated up. On January 9th, the entire Division, with full field packs, climbed on Army trucks with the ID numbers painted out, and was transported to a nearby train station. There, the troops boarded a train with the coach windows painted black and were hauled away. When the train came to a halt, they were at New York harbor. They were then combat loaded on troop ships and immediately sailed out to an unknown destination. Even though there was a strict Navy regulation against booze being carried on the ships, Ted had slipped a bottle on board. He was nipping and was in a jovial mood. He was celebrating being back with comrades, where he felt he was meant to be during times of crisis.

When morning came and the men were allowed on deck, they could see that they were part of a large convoy of ships, including warships, with flying boats and Navy blimps overhead for submarine protection. Ted and the Division staff were studying maps and feverishly working on plans for an amphibious assault of Martinique. The word was that the 1st Division, with the support of the 70th Tank Battalion and the 1st Marine Raider Battalion, was actually going to invade that Vichy French-controlled island. After being at sea for a few days, the entire force turned around and sailed back to the mainland. Upon arrival, they conducted a practice landing at Virginia Beach, Virginia. At the conclusion of that tactical problem, the Big Red One returned to New York Harbor and then, again by secured transportation, back to Fort Devens. Regular training was resumed. After the war, it was revealed that the original destination of the force had been Martinique, but before reaching the island diplomatic negotiations had neutralized it with respect to it being a threat to the United States. The invasion force was then diverted to its secondary mission at Virginia Beach.[13]

With a star now on his shoulders, Ted was entitled to a furnished general's house on post. He was delighted to have a home away from home. Eleanor promptly moved in, bought some pots and pans, and, for the first time in her life, began to cook family meals for Ted, and Quentin too when he could come. Occasionally they would entertain guests. Ted and Eleanor both savored the home life and both of them were proud of Eleanor.[14]

In the middle of February, the Division began moving to Camp Blanding, Florida, for three months of advanced infantry training. The emphasis would be on battle tactics. As always, Eleanor pulled up stakes and went too. She rented a two-story, three-bedroom house, which she called a cottage, overlooking the beach at Ponte Verda, Florida. Now Ted and Quentin had a place to come on the weekends. By this time TRIII, who was a naval officer, was receiving flight training at the Naval Air Station in Jacksonville, Florida. Anne was there with him. Most of the time, they were able to get away and come to Ponte Verda too, so on those occasions all the boys were there except Cornelius. Signorina came down from Oyster Bay to join the family. Eleanor made sure everyone could relax and enjoy this last vestige of home life before her warriors were sent in harms way. Everybody tried to stay upbeat. Eleanor and Signorina would start preparing for the men and Anne on Thursdays by cooking up a big pot of clams, oysters, shrimp, scallops, crabmeat, and lobster. They would then pour a rich cheese sauce over the seafood, it was everybody's favorite. They would also fix some real Southern dishes, like grits, cornbread, and collard greens cooked in salt pork.

Sometimes they would walk on the beach and pick up shells. Ted bought a book on mollusks and they would try to identify what animal lived in the different types of shells. Once they went to Marineland, and a couple of times they drove over to historic old St. Augustine. One night, the war was brought close to home when a German U-Boat torpedoed and sank a big oil tanker a few miles off shore. The flames lit up the sky. Planes flew overhead dropping flares in an effort to find the enemy sub. Hundreds of sea birds and fish were killed from the huge oil slick.[15]

Many of the civilians living around Camp Blanding got to know Ted and made friends with him, which was not hard to do. He was all over the place in his jeep, supervising training and encouraging the men. When the troops had some free time and got out into the community, the locals found them to be a tobacco chewing, tough division that brooked no back talk from the men in other units. Some said the Big Red One was the "cockiest bunch you ever saw."[16]

Like his father and grandfather before him, Cornelius had less than perfect eyesight, but, with his engineering education and experience, the Navy was glad to have him and immediately put him to work on a classified research project. When he first started his secret work, Cornelius asked his superior officer how much he could tell his family about what he was doing. Being an acquaintance of the Roosevelts, his boss answered that he could tell his parents anything he wanted to, but that he could not tell his brothers anything at all because they would understand what he was talking about. Ted had a big laugh when he heard what Cornelius' boss told him and loved to repeat the story to friends.[17]

During training, one thing Ted always looked forward to doing was observing Company G of the 16th Infantry. He knew they were a top-flight outfit for one thing, but mainly he got a kick out of petting their friendly little mascot, a dog named "Whitey."[18]

On May 1st, Chief of Staff of the Army General George C. Marshall, along with British Field Marshall Sir John Dill and various other high-ranking staff officers came down to Blanding and paid a surprise visit on the Big Red One. They must have liked what they saw, for three weeks later the Division was sent to Fort Benning, Georgia, for some final air-ground training and demonstrations. At Benning, Private Henry Bowles of the 26th Infantry Regiment remembers an occasion when General Roosevelt came upon two of the soldiers in a violent argument and threatening to fight. Ted had both men take their shirts off and then let them go at it. When the fight was over, he had them shake hands and put their shirts back on. Training then resumed.

In late May, the Division was moved to Indiantown Gap, Pennsylvania, for final overseas staging. There, General Donald Cubbison was relieved of command, and Ted was made temporary Division Commander, pending the appointment of a permanent replacement for Cubbison. On May 28th, Brigadier General Terry de la Mesa Allen was placed in command of the Division. For the men who would serve in the Big Red One for the next 15 months, this was a historic event, for it was the beginning of the famous "Terry and Teddy Show."[19]

Terry de la Mesa Allen was a tough, hard drinking, flamboyant, confident, and outstanding career Army officer. He was the son of a West Point graduate and had himself entered the Academy scheduled for graduation in the class of 1911. Failing math, he was put back to the class of 1912, but, after failing a course during his senior year, he was discharged from the school. Transferring to the Catholic University of America in Washington D.C., he graduated in 1912, was granted an Army commission, and placed on active duty. He served as a battalion commander during World War I, and by 1942 had thirty years of active military service behind him. Even though he had flunked out of the Military Academy, when he was promoted to Brigadier General in 1940, he became a general officer before any of the West Pointers graduating in the class of 1912. Three weeks after being placed in command of the 1st Division, Allen was promoted to Mayor General. Like Ted's old friend Leslie McNair, General Allen would later lose a son in the service of his country, when, in 1963, Lieutenant Colonel Terry de la Mesa Allen, Jr. was killed in action in Vietnam.

On July 1st, Ted, along with an advanced Division Headquarters detachment and the 2nd Battalion of the 16th Infantry Regiment, boarded the Duchess of Bedford at Brooklyn, New York Harbor, and sailed for England. Strict Army and naval regulations prohibited any contraband and animals from being taken aboard ship, and any violation was a court martial offense. Disregarding the rules, someone had smuggled Whitey, the G Company mongrel mascot, onto the ship.[20]

With her husband headed overseas, Eleanor and Signorina drove back to Oyster Bay and, except for a service wing they kept open to live in, closed up Old Orchard for the duration. Balocca and one general maid-cook-seamstress were retained, but the other household staff were let go. Eleanor applied to the American Red Cross for volunteer work overseas. She was confident that with her experience in YMCA work during World War I she would get an assignment somewhere. She knew that no matter what happened in this war, things would never be the same for Ted and her and their family. As she was packing her clothes and getting things at Old Orchard ready for her to depart, she succinctly expressed her resignation by writing, " A chapter of our lives has ended."[21]

Ted and the military contingent that was with him on the Duchess of Bedford crossed the Atlantic without incident. On the way over, to occupy time if for nothing else, Ted lectured the men on the outstanding qualities of the English people and how they were much to be admired. He told the troops that most of the local citizens they came in contact with had never been around Americans before, so they should be on their best behavior when they were with the British civilians. After all, he said, we certainly want our ally to think well of us, since we are their former colonists.[22]

After being at sea for a little over a week, the Duchess of Bedford arrived in the United Kingdom and the men disembarked. They had been ordered to Tidworth Military Barracks, near Salisbury, Wiltshire. The rest of the Division was scheduled to cross the Atlantic on the Queen Mary and would join them a few weeks later. As the troops were marching from the ship to the train station to board the troop train to Tidworth Barracks, Whitey escaped from his benefactor and was running around and barking at all the excitement outside the station. As some of the men were calling to the dog and trying to catch him, Ted came along. He pointed to the mutt and said, "Look at that English dog." Without thinking, one of the soldiers piped up and told Ted that it was not English, but was Whitey, the G Company mascot. Ted replied, "Nonsense, soldier, he has to be an English dog. He barks like an English dog. Somebody pick him up. We'll take him with us." Nobody got in trouble for sneaking the little canine onto the troop ship and into the UK. That story got around among the men and the privates and the pfcs in the Big Red One knew that they had a friend in Ted Roosevelt. He was truly one of their own.[23]

Before the Queen Mary arrived with the rest of the troops and the Division's supplies and equipment, including all the Class A uniforms, a group of the advanced element had some time off and took a bus into Salisbury. It wasn't long before the MP's arrested the men, charged them with being out of uniform for not having on their class A's, and brought them back to the post. When Ted found out what was happening, he immediately accosted the military police, ordered them to release the men, and instructed them that henceforth they were not to bother with any of the 1st Division soldiers for anything unless they were being disorderly.[24]

By pulling some strings, Eleanor got the American Red Cross to waive its rule that overseas volunteers must be no older than twenty-eight. She also got herself approved for assignment to England. After spending a month in Washington, taking a Red Cross orientation course, she flew to London, arriving there on the same day the Queen Mary docked and General Allen and the rest of the Division disembarked. With blackouts, rationing, and the blitz, during which whole blocks of London and other British cities were devastated, it didn't take long for all of the newly arrived Americans to realize that they were now in a war zone.

The Red Cross had assigned Eleanor the job of establishing centers where the enlisted men in the U.S. Army could relax and have a good time when they were off duty. This was practically the same thing she had done twenty-four years before in France, so she knew how to perform her duties.

The buildup of U.S. forces in England had just begun, and the majority of the American servicemen there were stationed at Tidworth Barracks. A major problem for the troops at Tidworth was that there were no after hours facilities for their use. When off-duty, all they had to do was lay around the barracks, or take a bus to Salisbury or to some other nearby town and further crowd the already overcrowded pubs and movie theaters. Within hours after landing, Eleanor placed a call to Ted and managed to get him on the phone. He told her that the only place in the area he was aware of that might suffice as a service club was the old Tidworth House.

Eleanor reported in to the head of the Red Cross in London, made a courtesy call on General Eisenhower, and then took a train to Salisbury to see Ted and to look over the Tidworth House. She found the two hundred year old mansion to have over a hundred rooms, beautiful grounds, several outbuildings, and a glass enclosed tennis court. With some cleaning, painting, and modernizing it would be perfect. Using all of her considerable charm and influence, Eleanor cut through the red tape and quickly got the approval of the British Government to convert the historic old structure into a club for the soldiers. With the help of several Red Cross volunteers and the nine Voluntary Aid Detachment girls allotted to her by the British War Office, she proceeded to get the facility ready to open.

Unless Ted was away on some training problem, Eleanor went to his snug and warm quarters at Tidworth Barracks every night. Quentin would come over often and the three of them, and sometimes one of Ted's aides, would play cards, or Monopoly, or just listen to the radio and talk.[25]

Out in the training area, Ted was all over the place. He observed, advised and encouraged the men. By now he knew many of the men by name, including practically all the sergeants and officers. He liked nothing better than to jaw with them, e.g. joking, telling stories, and reciting poetry. The men were comfortable around Ted, contrary to their feelings about most other officers, especially high-ranking officers. Typical of his behavior with the men, was the time he spotted a first sergeant he knew. Grinning, Ted bellowed, "Goddammit, Merrill, but you're ugly and getting uglier every day." Pleased at being singled out, the tough old enlisted man snapped to attention and replied, "The General isn't a handsome man himself." Ted let out a hearty laugh, slapped his leg, and drove away in his jeep.[26]

After Eleanor got the club opened, the men had a place where they could relax; play cards, pool, and ping pong; and get a hamburger, a cup of coffee, or a haircut. Some just wanted to sit in an easy chair and talk. Usually there was a pretty girl around to listen. They had a jukebox and weekly dances were held. Eleanor had the glass covered tennis court fixed up into a nice auditorium where over a thousand men at a time could enjoy USO shows and movies. Some of the top show business personalities performed there. The men would never forget those shows. Sgt. Joe Morell, a 1st Division veteran, still remembers seeing Al Jolson and his troupe when they entertained the troops there. He said it seemed like yesterday.[27]

As September approached, the Big Red One continued amphibious training and took its first battle casualties when a Luftwaffe fighter-bomber came over in daylight and strafed one of the units. In early September, a high level conference was held in London. There, Ted, Terry, and the other Division top brass learned that they would soon be heading out to invade Algeria, in North Africa. A month later, the Division, traveling under strict security as always, departed Tidworth Barracks by troop train for Glasgow, the port of embarkation. There the troops combat loaded on ships and made another practice landings, this time near Inverarry.[28]

While driving his jeep around inspecting the troops during their training activities, Ted developed a practice of never putting up the canvas jeep top. His idea was that if the men were out training in every type of weather, it was only fair that he be exposed to the same weather in his jeep. Major Kenneth Downs, who had recently been transferred from the OSS to the First Infantry Division's staff, met Ted and was invited to accompany him on a drive around to observe the training in progress. On that particular day, Eleanor had come up from Salisbury to visit with her husband and was sitting in the jeep beside him when Major Downs got in. In describing this first meeting some years later, Downs said that the three of them conducted their tour in the "heaviest downpour of rain I have ever seen," with the jeep top down.[29]

Shortly before the embarkation date, the Division had one final practice amphibious assault. After Ted had come ashore and was walking inland from the beach, he chanced upon General Eisenhower and his aide, Harry Butcher. Ike inquired how the landing had gone. Ted told him that the troops looked good and the landing had gone off like clockwork, but the Supreme Commander had observed the mock invasion himself and thought he saw some serious problems, especially with respect to the leadership abilities of the junior officers.[30]

The night before her spouse had to be aboard his troopship to embark for the invasion of North Africa, Eleanor managed to sneak away from the Tidworth House and joined him at the Central Hotel in Glasgow. At 1:00 a.m. the lady at the hotel desk gave a requested wake-up call to Ted's room. When Eleanor answered the phone, the desk clerk assumed that Ted had a girl friend in for the night and spread the rumor to everyone who would listen that "General Roosevelt need not pretend he's so pure. I called up his room and a woman answered the phone." Weeks later, word of the story the woman spread got back to Ted and Eleanor, and they, by letters, had a nice laugh about it. Ted wrote his wife, "How could you! And after I've been so careful. Never doing the least thing to cause a lifted eyebrow, year after dreary year, and now all for nothing. My reputation gone in the twinkling of an eye."

Throughout their life together, Ted had developed a habit of making complimentary remarks about Eleanor. There are numerous entries in the diary he kept during the 1920s as to how nice she looked on some particular occasion, and how much he missed her during the times she was away. Typical of his observations was in the summer of 1922 when he wrote that Eleanor looked "perfectly gorgeous in her new scarlet bathing suit." What an exciting joy their marriage had been. Unlike her mother-in-law, Eleanor had been no stay-at-home wife and mother. Ted had been everywhere and done everything, most of the time with Eleanor by his side. When the time came for Ted to leave the hotel and join his Division, his one and only love, his "Bunny," his "Mickey Herself McGuire," with a sense of concern, perhaps even a sense of foreboding, returned to her job with the Red Cross. They would never see each other again.[31]

On October 26th, the invasion convoy sailed from the Firth of Clyde, Scotland, for the North African coast. Operation Torch, the first major Allied offensive action in the European Theater of Operations (as that term is broadly defined) had begun. After returning to the Tidworth House, Eleanor applied to the Red Cross for a transfer to North Africa. However, her application was denied because of a rule that no wife could be transferred to the same combat zone in which her husband was stationed.[32]

There were several reasons why the United States and Great Britain felt compelled to undertake a major offensive operation against the Germans in 1942. For one thing, they had to take some pressure off of the Russians. Except for actions by the British Eighth Army against Rommel's Africa Corps, the Russians were fighting the Germans single handedly. FDR and Winston Churchill were scared to death that Joseph Stalin would make a separate peace with Hitler. This had to be prevented if at all possible, for if Russia dropped out the Germans could concentrate all their forces against Britain, the US, and Canada. There was also a case of sagging morale being experienced by all of the Western Allies. It appeared to the general public that the Americans were doing nothing toward the defeat of Germany and Italy. In early '42, when the Allied decision makers first began discussing some appropriate offensive action, there had been disagreement between the U.S. planners and those of Great Britain over just what, where, and when the initial offense against the Axis should take place. General Marshall and the U.S. War Plans Division initially recommended an invasion across the English Channel into France, but the British argued, successfully, that sufficient forces were not yet trained or available to undertake an offense of this magnitude. A more appropriate operation in North Africa was finally agreed upon.

The general plan called for simultaneous landings to be made at three locations on the North African coast by three independent Allied forces. The Western Task Force, with General George Patton and the U.S. 3rd Infantry Division, would embark from United States ports, sail across the Atlantic, and assault the Atlantic coast of Morocco both north and south of the City of Casablanca. Ships making up the Center Task Force, with the Big Red One and attached units, and the vessels of the Eastern Task Force, with British units aboard, would embark from the UK, enter the Mediterranean Sea through the Strait of Gibraltar, and land troops on the Algerian coast. The initial mission of the First Infantry Division was the seizure of Oran. This objective was to be taken by an amphibious assault made on the coast in the general vicinity of that city. The convoy with the British troops aboard would continue eastward well off the Algerian shore and land its forces at Algiers.

Oran, a city of approximately 350,000 inhabitants, was controlled by the Vichy French Government and was protected by a strong element of French troops. It was a major port on the Mediterranean coast and was considered vital as both a supply base and air base for the Allied forces. How the French military in and around the city would react to an American invasion of French territory was an unknown factor. It was hoped that they would welcome the Allies and even join them in fighting the German and Italian forces located further to the east, but the Americans and Brits had to be prepared in case the French offered stiff resistance.

The final plan for the capture of Oran, as drawn up by General Allen, Ted, and the division operations staff, called for the 1st Division to be broken up into two combat teams and employ the double envelopment scheme of maneuver. The "Y" force would be under Ted's command and included the 26th Infantry Regiment, the 33rd Field Artillery Battalion (Quentin's outfit), and other attached units. It would land at the village of Les Andelouses, fourteen miles west of Oran, and drive on the city from the west. The "Z" force, under General Terry Allen, was composed of the rest of the Division with the 1st Ranger Battalion attached. It would come ashore twenty-five miles east of Oran and drive directly on the city from the east.[33]

The armada transporting the "Y" force arrived off the invasion beach in the late hours of November 7th, and dropped anchor. The leading assault wave, composed of troops of the 3rd Battalion, 26th Infantry Regiment, climbed down the big rope nets strung from the sides of the troopship and jumped into the assigned landing craft. Ted climbed down too, and got in one of the first wave boats. After circling around while the warships were firing a shore bombardment, the little assault boats formed into ranks according to the specified waves and headed toward the North African coast. When they reached the beach and ground to a halt, the men scrambled out and ran inland toward their first objective, the guns atop Djebel Murdjadjo, a coastal mountain overlooking the port and the City. It was 0100 hours; they were right on time. Ted's optimism of a couple of weeks earlier, when he ran into General Eisenhower after the final practice landing, was vindicated. Instantly realizing the landing was unopposed, the "Y" Force Commander remained on the beach for a short time to make sure the beachhead was properly secured and to supervise the landing of the rest of the 3rd Battalion. He then got in his jeep, which had been unloaded from one of the subsequent waves, and drove off toward the advancing companies. The men were already climbing up the heights of Djebel Murdjadjo.

At dawn, as the men of the lead company were continuing to climb and getting close to the crest of Djebel Murdjadjo, hostile anti-aircraft fire began to explode hundreds of feet above their heads. The green troops, experiencing their first enemy fire, stopped advancing and begun to dig in. Just then a jeep with "Rough Rider" painted on its bumper and with a large American flag flying from its hood, raced up and abruptly stopped. Ted, carrying only his walking stick and a pistol in his shoulder holster, jumped out, strode up and down among the troops, and bellowed in his moose call voice, "Alright men, let's go, no one is shooting at you; let's get to those guns, get up now, come on! I'm going in men, let's go!" This was the first time Private Thomas Bowles had been under enemy fire. While everyone else was digging in the dirt, he saw General Roosevelt walking around encouraging the men as if he was out for a Sunday afternoon walk down Main Street. Returning to his jeep, Ted and the three men with him drove on forward, past the assault company's most advanced elements, to reconnoiter the terrain ahead. Suddenly, Ted and his small group were attacked by a ten-man patrol of French cavalry. Although exposed to enemy fire, Ted picked up a rifle and engaged the enemy in a firefight. Soon, the French unit withdrew. Inspired by the audacity of this fifty-five year old grandfather, who had lived and trained among them for the past eighteen months, the now not-quite-so green troops began to get up and move forward. The NCOs and junior officers took up Ted's lead, and the attack got

254 / Robert W. Walker

underway again. It had been nearly a quarter of a century, but he had not lost his touch. For his actions on November 8th, Ted was awarded the Bronze Star with "V" device.[34]

Both Major R. H. Critz, the Assistant Division Chief of Staff, and General Terry Allen recommended Ted for the Distinguished Service Medal for his planning, directing, and leading the landing at Les Andalouses. But, according to official Army records, the award was never made, nor denied; no reason is given. With typical Army efficiency, it was probably simply overlooked. Had the decoration been issued, it would have been Ted's second DSM, as he had received one for his service during the Great War.[35]

The 3rd Battalion continued to advance for several thousand yards, until the troops got near the major French coast defense batteries at Ferme Combier and Ferme Ste Marie, atop Djebel Murdjadjo. There the men were again halted, this time by heavy rifle and machine gun fire directed at them. They began to take casualties. Soon French mortars found the range and sporadic artillery fire came in. The men dug in.

Meanwhile, the 1st Battalion had captured the town of El Anco, thus giving the "Y" Force protection on its right flank. Meanwhile, the 2nd Battalion had occupied Ain et Turk and soon overran the heavy coastal battery at Mers el Kebir.

By November 10th, the 1st Division's artillery fire had reduced the Vichy French opposition on the Djebel Murdjadjo heights to scattered small arms fire. Then, the GIs of the Big Red One, who by now had earned the honored title of "dog face," or "combat infantrymen," got up out of their foxholes, formed a line of skirmishers, and moved forward to capture the guns at Ferma Combier and Ferme Ste Marie.

The Division now controlled the high ground and looked down upon the City of Oran, and its port, but there still remained a strong French military contingent to contend with. The Division brass began to think about their option of just pounding the city into submission with artillery, but no one on the Staff really liked that idea, particularly against a potential ally. There were sure to be many innocent civilian deaths and injuries from the indiscriminate firing of artillery concentrations into the city. Ted suggested that they hold up resorting to this drastic measure until he made an attempt at getting their Vichy French opponents to surrender. The little General told his artillery commander, "If I'm not back in two hours, give it all you've got." With that, he and Lieutenant Bill Gordon mounted a half track, borrowed a dirty white undershirt from Major Clancey Beck, tied it on the antenna, and drove down into Oran. It didn't take long. Shortly after he entered the city, the French forces surrendered without further bloodshed. When the men of the Big Red One marched into Oran, pandemonium broke loose. It was just like the Paris Armistice Day celebration in 1918, but on a smaller scale. The entire 350,000 population went wild with joy. The French really didn't have their hearts into resisting the Americans, but had fought long enough and hard enough to preserve the honor of their homeland. All in all, 416 First Infantry Division soldiers were killed, wounded or missing in action during the Oran campaign. Sadly, Texas-born Lieutenant Robert Emery was one of those killed in action; he had been assigned as an aide to the Assistant Division Commander.[36]

Shortly after the North African invasion, the Allies prevailed upon Admiral Jean Francois Darlan, the overall commander of all French forces, to terminate all military opposition directed against them, and join them in fighting the Axis. At this time in history, the French sincerely hated the British; the only thing was they hated the Germans more. Admiral Darlan reconsidered the situation and did in fact order the French forces to cease resistance. They soon became a valuable ally in the battle against Hitler's and Mussolini's tyranny.

With Oran, the 1st Division's primary objective in hand, and the North African landings a great success, the Allies attacked to the East, in a race to seize Tunisia and cut off the Germans and Italians from their supplies. The Axis forces won the race, however, and the campaign was prolonged. At this point, Dwight Eisenhower agreed to a decision made by General Lloyd Fredendall, the American Corps Commander, to break down the Big Red One into regimental and battalion size combat units. These regiments and battalions were then individually attached to British and French divisions at the front. It was claimed that this was a way to reinforce the Allied Eastern front. General Eisenhower said that there simply was not enough transportation available to utilize the First Infantry Division in any way other than by a piecemeal process. This was a very bizarre and controversial decision, particularly in view of the fact that the Big Red One was the best trained U.S. division and was made up primarily of regular Army officers and enlisted men. Breaking up American divisions and having the various battalions and regiments attached to British and French forces was the very thing General John Pershing had refused to do during World War I.[37]

Besides the decision to bust up the best U.S. division with the best combat leadership, another strange thing involving the Oran Campaign was the numerous news reports that described Ted's actions during the initial landing and subsequent three-day fight, but did not specifically name him. One of the articles referred to a Brigadier General who recited poetry, and another story gave only the name of his aide. Eleanor and the rest of the family knew these various news reports were about Ted, but they couldn't understand why his name was not mentioned.[38]

Ted wanted to get another Texan to replace Lieutenant Emery, his aide that had been killed-in-action. Knowing that Lt. Marcus O. Stevenson, a platoon leader in the 3rd Battalion, was from Texas, Ted sent for him and, after talking with him a while, offered him the job. Stevenson told Ted that he would do it, but that he was "no spit and polish soldier," and that "maybe you should get somebody else." In describing the General's reaction, Stevenson said he laughed and replied, "I can promise you that we won't be doing any social work." During the nearly two years the little General and Stevenson were together, they became almost like father and son. There was hardly an hour that they were not within eyesight of each other. Ted called him "Stevie," and "the ole Texas longhorn." Of course the new aide said "Sir" and called his boss "General Roosevelt." Stevie always intended to write a book about his wartime experiences, but somehow just never got around to it. [39]

As soon as the Division was split up and its various units assigned to the British at the battlefront, Ted, Stevie, and their driver, Kurt Show, would pile into the jeep each morning and go to the front to visit one of the 1st Division's units. Hopefully, they would be of assistance and cheer to the men. Ted was aware of the miseries of front line combat from his 1st World War experiences. He knew the men would be sleeping on the ground in the wet and cold, that they would never take off their clothes, and their boots only at night. They would never have time off to go to town, and would lose track of what day it was. They would get little sleep, and what sleep they did get wasn't sound. Often they would be roused out for a night move, and would never get enough hot food. If Ted sensed that one of the units was about to be in a fight, that was where they went that day. It wasn't long before a piece of shrapnel hit his jeep's (the Rough Rider) windshield causing a starburst hole. Within the next couple of months probably every man in the Big Red One got several good chuckles out of seeing the craggy faced, fifty-five year old, little general, always with a wide mouth smile, drive up in a jeep with Rough Rider painted on the front bumper, and combat damage on the windshield. He would come to a screeching halt, jump out and immediately start talking to privates and colonels alike. He usually went to the front in the mornings, and was just as likely to crawl into the most forward outpost as visit a battalion headquarters. He always asked the men if they were getting enough food and how it was, and where they were from. From his travels, Ted had at one time or another been almost everywhere in the States, so no matter where a man said he called home, Ted could make some comment like, "O yea, I know that place well, you have the prettiest girls in the world there," or "I had a great time there hunting one time." If there was a field mess nearby, he always went there and had a few words with the mess sergeant, and usually a quick cup of black coffee. He never failed to ask the CO, no matter the level of command, if there was anything he could do for him.

It is very cold and very wet on the Mediterranean coast of North Africa in the winter, especially down in a foxhole. Stevie remembered one of Ted's favorite ways to get a smile out of a group of GIs on the front was to say, "Fine weather men, remember the Army pamphlets we read on African weather, always wear a sun helmet, and be sure the house has a good roof to keep the sun off, and to avoid sunstroke. Damn! I wish it would warm up and stop raining." He knew by heart thousands of poems, and was always reciting poetry to the men. It might be a masterpiece by Kipling or Keats, or a ribald rhyme composed by some unknown GI. One of the poems he would often repeat to emphasize that the men should avoid something that might be booby-trapped, was, "Keep your rifle clean, and use your eyes and ears. Don't go wandering off the scene, alooking for souvenirs."[40]

Private Kenneth Anderson of Interlachen, Florida was one of the 1st Division GIs at the time, and remembers one occasion when, just as his artillery battery was lining up for noon chow, the Rough Rider roared up, General Roosevelt got out and proceeded to the rear of the chow line. Anderson described what happened:

Whereupon one of the dogrobbers (cooks) rushed over to the General to tell him that a place had been set up for him at the table under the shelter with the officers. The General brushed him off and said he wanted to eat with the boys. Filling his messkit, he walked over to where we were randomly sprawled and started talking to us as though we were of common bondage.

One soldier in the group said, "That's our dollar-a-year man." Anderson caught a glimpse of Ted a number of other times in North Africa and said, "If he was driving by in his jeep, he always stood up and waved to the men."[41]

Afternoons were usually spent at one of the regimental or battalion headquarters. One thing Ted noticed in the rear areas was that there seemed to be many more support troops, as compared to combat soldiers, than there had been during the 1st World War. At night, his little party would head back to their quarters near Oran. The next day the routine started anew.[42]

Ted knew practically all the officers and most of the sergeants in the Division, and it was said that he knew over a thousand of the men by name. Almost every man knew him by sight and also by the unique sound of his foghorn voice. One pitch-black night, Ted was accompanying Ernie Pyle on a visit near the front. He had boasted to the famous war correspondent that he had been around his men so much that they would recognize him when they heard him speak. As the journalist and the one star general approached a group of GIs in the dark, Ted asked what company they were from. The answer come back, "Company K, General Roosevelt." General Omar Bradley (a.k.a. Brad) had a similar experience when 1st Division men in a blacked out truck recognized Ted by his voice.[43]

Late in '42, Ted was placed in command of a special unit made up of three battalions of the 26th Infantry Regiment, 6000 Goums (Arab irregulars) with French officers, a battalion of British artillery, and a company of American light tanks. The hodge-podge outfit was given the name, "Groupment Roosevelt" and was ordered to defend at all costs the Ousseltia Valley against being overrun by the Germans and Italians. While this special command was in existence only a short time, Ted and it successfully completed the mission. The important valley was not captured by the Krauts. In handling this assignment, Ted demonstrated his ability to lead soldiers of different nationalities and he made friends with many of the French officers that he would serve with in the future. The experiences he had during WW I in France, his Field Museum hunts to the Far East together with his work with the Puerto Ricans and the Filipinos were of enormous benefit in aiding Ted to successfully command the multi national Groupment Roosevelt.[44]

In a letter to General Eisenhower about Ted's performance in heading up Groupment Roosevelt, Terry Allen wrote:

When this sector was first taken over, because of the deficiencies in French equipment and the recent losses suffered, the morale of of the units was not high and the sector was not capable of vigorous defense.

General Roosevelt has displayed extraordinary executive ability, exceptional initiative and a practical knowledge of combat needs, in taking over his sector. As a result of his efforts, the morale of all units and the defensive organization of the sector is greatly improved.

I attribute the results accomplished to the energy, initiative and leadership of General Roosevelt. His knowledge of the French language and his previous battlefield acquaintance (during the last war) with many of the French officers contacted, assisted him materially. I know few officers who could have done as well on this mission.

This information is submitted because General Roosevelt's value to this Division has been discussed from various aspects, I believe that his recent accomplishments demonstrate his outstanding value to this Division, particularly under combat conditions.[45]

Just before the end of the year, Eleanor found out why so many news stories out of North Africa described Ted's exploits without naming him. A public relations officer she knew gave her a copy of a "Stop Order" issued by the British Ministry of Information. The effect of this document was to prohibit all news correspondent naming Ted, or his son Quentin, or Henry Wallace, Jr., the son of the U.S. Vice President, in a news story. A reporter was permitted to describe their exploits and identify the people around them, he just couldn't put their names in the story. Eleanor immediately wrote Ted about the matter, but he didn't know the purpose of the order or who was responsible for it being issued. Occasionally, some news of Ted's activities would be picked up in the States from some soldier sent home to recover from a wound, or from a War Department bulletin issued from Washington, but his name would be automatically censored from any news reports emanating from North Africa or England. The extensive publicity Ted's heroics garnered in World War I was sorely lacking in World War II.[46]

The Germans had air superiority during the first months of the North African Campaign, and Ted, Stevie, and Show often saw Luftwaffe planes in the air as they were driving to or from one of the Division's units. Ted's policy was that they would simply keep an eye on the enemy planes and continue on to where they were going. He knew the planes would probably not bother with a single jeep, and he told Stevie and Show, "If they make you stop and leave your vehicle, they've accomplished part of their mission, so just keep on going until they attack us." One day as they were driving along, Ted was reciting one of his many poems when a flight of Messerschmitts loomed on them in a strafing attack. Show immediately stopped the jeep and the three men jumped into the roadside ditch. As soon as the planes were gone, they got back in the jeep and started on down the road. Ted instantly picked back up on his recitation of the poem right where he had left off when the attack began. In describing this incident several years later, Stevie couldn't remember the name of the rhyme, but he did remember that it was a Grantland Rice lyric from the 1917–1918 Great War, and it went:[47]

All wars are planned by older men
In council rooms apart,
Who call for greater armament
And map the battle chart.

But out along the shattered field
Where golden dreams turn gray,
How very young the faces were
Where all the dead men lay.

Ted and Eleanor wrote each other almost every day, although the war usually caused a delay in delivery of their letters of several weeks. He wrote her about everything. He wrote about what he was doing and who he had seen. They wrote back and forth about Old Orchard and its grounds, and the "war corner" he was saving souvenirs for. In one letter, he said he liked the fact that the foreign women went barelegged, but wished their legs were not always dirty. In another letter, he said that he was sick of the war and the misery it brought, and longed to just get it over with and get back home. In early February, he wrote her of his visualization of his first day home after the war was over. In his daydream, all the adults in the family would meet at Eleanor's club for cocktails. Ted and his three sons and son-in-law would all be dressed spick and span in their military uniforms, three Navy and two Army, with all their campaign ribbons on their chests. Eleanor would be radiant in her best clothes, or her Red Cross uniform, and Gracie and Ann would be pictures of loveliness in their finery. Then, they would all go to some fine restaurant for a gourmet dinner, and afterwards take in a good play at one of the Broadway theaters. The night would be completed with drinks at Club 21 or the Stork Club. Throughout all the gay activities, friends and even strangers would be ooing and aahing over them, and coming over to their table to say hello. The Roosevelts would be very gracious to all. Then, Ted wrote, they would all drive back to Oyster Bay and, "revert to type."[48]

In mid-February, while the Big Red One was still split up, came the American defeats at Sidi-bou-Zid and Kasserine Pass. Personnel casualties, mostly infantry and armor, ran into the thousands and equipment losses included over 200 tanks and half-tracks, and about that many trucks. The 33rd Field Artillery Battalion was in the thick of the battle when Quentin was shot in the torso by a strafing Messerschmitt. His lung was pierced and the bullet lodged in his liver; his life hung in the balance. Scared to death for the life of his son, as soon as he could get away Ted sped to the field hospital where Quentin had been taken. However, by the time he got there Quentin had taken a turn for the better and he was no longer in mortal danger. Before young Captain Quentin Roosevelt was furloughed home to recuperate, he was awarded the Silver Star and the French Croix de Guerre for his actions in North Africa.[49]

Neither Ted nor General Terry Allen were impressed with the American II Corps Commander, Major General Lloyd Fredendall, and when the 1st Division was broken up and piecemeal sent to fight with other divisions, they had even less respect for his judgment. After the Kasserine clobbering, General Eisenhower relieved Fredendall and picked General George Patton to Command the II Corps. Immediately changes were made. For one thing, the 1st Division was brought back together as a fighting unit, and allowed a few days to get itself reorganized before being sent to the front. For another, Patton adopted a policy, most of the GIs would call it a "chickenshit policy," requiring the men to be in uniform with neckties and helmets on. By now these men were tough combat veterans and they just didn't see how a dress code would improve their fighting efficiency.

With the return of the various 1st Division units to American command, Ted's work with the French and British was temporarily completed. Both governments deeply appreciated his efforts in their behalf. The French awarded him another palm to his Croix de Guerre.[50]

The re-assembly process for the Big Red One began on March 1st in the mountainous area near Morsott, about twenty miles north of Tebessa. After a few days to rest, reorganize, and give a short combat training course to the new replacements, the Division was ordered to assault and occupy Gafsa, a former French garrison town that had been seized by the Germans during their recent offensive. Retaking this objective was vital to the Allies for it was needed as a supply base for General Montgomery's Eighth Army, then attacking the Germans from another direction. Gafsa was defended by both German and Italian units. The attack was set to begin on March 17th. Plans for the operation called for the Big Red One to cross some fifty miles of desert by a well-organized motor movement on the night of March 16th. The attack was to begin at 0600 the next morning.[51]

One time Ted had said to Stevie, "You can't tell much about the terrain from the map, a map maneuver is definitely bad and I would like to have my hand on the guy who invented the 'goose egg,' a blob on the map you are supposed to take." TRJr knew that the ground the Division must cross to get to the line of departure for the attack contained numerous rocky hills and dry river beds, and that it was crucial that an expedient route be selected. He, therefore, took it upon himself to accompany the detachment of combat engineers that had been ordered to make a reconnaissance and pick the best route for the Division to take. On March 14th, while they were doing their work, Ted and his small engineering party were joined by none other than the Corps Commander, General George Patton. In writing in his diary about the occasion, Patton said:

Yesterday Gen. T.R. (Teddy Roosevelt) and I got a little lost and were about six miles outside our front line. I felt scared till I came on some air listening post men who were putting up a station. I said do you know where you are, and they said no. So I told them to move on to a healthier place. They had put out no sentinels—soldiers are funny.[52]

Patton did not know that in reconnoitering the approach route to the line of departure, Ted, Stevie, and their little engineering party had at times been as much as twenty-five miles ahead of the front lines.[53]

On the 17th, after a supporting aerial bombardment, elements of the 18th Infantry Regiment formed in a line of skirmishers and led the assault across the LD. The front assault units were ready for a fight, but met no enemy opposition. The twelve hundred Italian troops, along with the 580th German Reconnaissance Battalion that had been defending the town were gone; they had pulled out. Entering Gafsa, Ted set up the Division CP and then he and Colonel Greer, the CO of the 18th Infantry, drove on out of town to the south. Soon they encountered six enemy armored scout cars speeding away in the direction of El Guettar. The General and the Colonel, acting as forward observers, called in an artillery fire mission to the 18th Infantry Cannon Company. The barrage succeeded in hitting and destroying two of the escaping vehicles.[54]

It was raining hard the day of the attack. Tom Lancer, an engineer in the Division, was out with his men working on a section of road that had been destroyed when Ted drove up in the Rough Rider. The top was down, as usual. Tom saluted. Ted, pleased that the enemy had pulled out, and knowing of Lancer's heritage, smiled and bellowed, "Tom, it's a great day for the Irish."[55]

As soon as orders were received from higher headquarters, the Big Red One continued it's offensive operation along the main highway toward the town of El Guettar, twelve miles to the east. Jumping off at 0200 hours on March 21st, the leading elements, including Ted, met only light opposition from the defending Italian Centauro Division. The "Eyeties" had lost their will to fight and seemed to be interested only in surviving and getting back home. Many prisoners were taken. Several battalions of Italian troops surrendered en masse. While little opposition was received from the Italians, it was a different story with respect to the Krauts. The Germans had concrete runways at their airfields in Sardinia and Sicily and didn't have to worry about their planes taking off in the mud, as the Allies did. The Luftwaffe was intensely active during the entire El Guettar operation. Enemy planes savagely bombed and strafed the 1st Division infantry and artillery units many times. These air attacks did not, however, prevent the Division from seizing it's objective, the town of El Guettar.[56]

With the 1st Division now in control of the town, the German Africa Corps wasted no time in counterattacking with its premier combat unit, the 10th Panzer Division. Ted was asleep when he first became aware that something was amiss. At 0200 on March 23rd, he heard, "German automatic fire in my sleep." He immediately got up and went to the point where the Germans were concentrating their attack. After checking the line, he went to the 18th Infantry Regiment's forward observation post and remained there, under almost continuous enemy artillery and small arms fire, for the next three days. Once when the other men in the OP threatened to withdraw, Ted told them, "I'm staying in this position. You leave it and you leave me behind." The men stayed.[57]

Captain Joe Dawson of the 1st Division, who would later gain fame as one of the heroes of Omaha Beach on D-Day, made a statement describing Ted's actions on March 23rd, saying:

*** two direct assaults were made during the day along with constant and heavy harassing fire falling on our positions from early morning till late in the evening when the second attack had been successfully repulsed. During the period the enemy employed fifty tanks, infantry, artillery and dive bombers in an effort to destroy our defense but was unable to do so. Throughout the entire day and the following night General Roosevelt remained on the front lines situated on the Djubel el Kaddab which was occupied by the 18th Infantry. From this position he personally supervised the forward elements of the division and his personal observation assisted in the coordination of the defense of the entire Divisional sector. The position from which he operated was situated on the highest point of the ridge occupied by our forces and subjected to heavy enemy fire of all types. The only natural protection afforded in this position was a slit trench from which he supervised our forces. His timely decisions in calling for artillery fire on advancing enemy infantry resulted in virtual annihilation of these advancing troops. Throughout the entire battle he constantly exposed himself while under intensive enemy fire. Shouting words of encouragement to our men and officers and displayed great fortitude and courage in remaining at his post where he could personally direct the actions of our elements . . .[58]

Unbeknown to Ted, General Patton was at another vantage point where he could observe first hand the slaughter of the German infantry by the artillery Ted called in, and by the fire from the defending 1st Division infantry. Shaking his head in disbelief and in sympathy with the German soldiers that were being slaughtered, Patton said, "They're murdering good infantry! What a helluva way to waste good infantry troops." When the final German counterattack had been repulsed, at least fifty Kraut tanks had been destroyed and an untold number of enemy ground troops had been made battle casualties. After the battle, George Patton wrote a letter of commendation to Terry Allen, stating:

Now that the battle of El Guettar has been won, please accept for yourself and for the officers and men of your magnificent division my sincere congratulations and heartfelt thanks for your truly great performance.

For twenty-two days of relentless battle, you have never faltered. Over country whose rugged difficulty beggars description and against a veteran enemy cunningly disposed, you have pressed on. Undeterred by cold, by lack of sleep, and by continued losses, you have conquered. Your valorous exploits have brought undying fame to the soldiers of the United States.[59]

Terry Allen recommended that Ted be awarded the Distinguished Service Cross for his actions on March 23rd. Had General Allen's recommendation been approved, it would have been the second time Ted had earned his nation's second highest combat decoration. He had previously received the DSC for his heroism during World War I. For some unknown reason, the award was reduced to the Silver Star; Ted's third in two wars.[60]

Now an outlandish event occurred, especially since it involved the top echelon of American World War II commanders. In the early morning, after the final German counterattack had been repulsed, Ted had just returned to the Division command post after having spent seventy-two straight hours at the front and gone to bed. Terry Allen was also asleep. Unexpectedly, Generals George Patton and Omar Bradley made a visit to the Division CP and asked for Ted and Terry. Aides roused them; Ted appeared in his bathrobe. Patton was highly agitated, apparently because Terry and Ted had been asleep. As he looked around, Patton spied a number of slit trenches in the area. Pointing to them, he asked General Allen what they were for. Allen responded that they were for cover in the event of an air attack, Patton then asked, "Which one is yours?" Being shown, he went over to Allen's trench, unzipped his fly, sprayed the hole with urine, and then said, "There, now try to use it." The silence that followed was broken only by the click of the safeties being taken off their Thompson submachine guns by Allen's and Roosevelt's bodyguards. Knowing not to push the incident further, Patton and Bradley immediately got in their staff car and departed. Omar Bradley later wrote of this incident in his book, *A General's Life.*[61]

A scary incident took place shortly after the defeat of the German counterattacks at El Guettar. Just after Ted, Stevie and Show pulled into a temporary command post located in a little valley, a flight of sixteen Luftwaffe Stukas suddenly came in on a dive-bombing and strafing attack. Everyone jumped into whatever cover he could find. Stevie, writing about what happened, said, "The earth shook so that each explosion knocked the breath out of you like a blow to the stomach." After the initial bombing, "the planes came back with their machine guns going." Stevie's head was aching and his mouth was full of dirt. "As soon as the planes had gone, General Roosevelt emerged out from the smoke and dust. He calmly took charge, getting medical help for the wounded and reassuring the survivors." One hundred and twenty-five soldiers had been killed or wounded during this single attack. After the excitement had subsided, Ted told Stevie that one of the bomb blasts had knocked his helmet off and that if his chinstrap had been buckled it would have broken his neck. He asked Stevie to remind him, "to tell the troops to keep their helmet straps loose."[62]

While the Big Red One continued its offensive, now directed toward Maknassy, the major battle at El Guettar was over. On April 8th, the Division was reassembled and moved back to the Morsott area, near Tebessa, for a brief period of rest and refitting. On the 15th, the battle-hardened troops began loading on trucks for the 150-mile trip to the north flank of the British First Army in northern Tunisia, for what would develop into the battle of Mateur. As usual, Ted was in the advanced detachment to select the best route, gather information, find assembly areas, and reconnoiter the front where the Division would be inserted. By this time in the war, the German and Italian forces had been pushed back into a relatively small area around Bizerte, Mateur, Tunis, and the Cap Bon Peninsula.

The Allies could smell victory in North Africa. At this time General Patton was transferred to a new command, and General Bradley was made CO of II Corps.

After arriving near Mateur and replacing a British unit in the front line, just before dawn on April 23rd, the Division jumped off in an attack on a six-mile front. The tactic employed had the three infantry regiments abreast. Each regiment had been assigned a different hill as its objective. The approaches to the lines of departure for all three of the regiments were through low-lying hills and offered little in the way of concealment. The enemy positions were well camouflaged, afforded excellent protection against American artillery, were at higher elevations, and had good fields of fire. Defending for the Germans and Italians were elements of several units, including the 1st Division's old nemesis, the 10th Panzer Division.[63]

The day before the assault was set to begin, Ted picked out a spot for his observation post that would give him a good view of the attack as it progressed. The only trouble was as he scampered into the position he would be in plain view of the Huns, so to avoid detection, he slipped into his OP the night before. The attack got under way early the next morning as scheduled, and the infantry began to advance. Shortly, the advancing foot soldiers began receiving enemy artillery, mortar, and small arms fire. Just then the field telephone rang, and Ted was informed that his old buddy from the early days of World War I, Leslie "Whitey" McNair, now a Lieutenant General and Chief of Infantry of the United States Army, was on his way to the OP to observe the attack. It was now broad open daylight and Ted knew the Germans would see McNair enter the site and probably fire an artillery barrage at them. He was a little perturbed, but he went and got his friend and led him into the post. How glad to see each other those old doughboys of twenty-five years before must have been. After he greeted the three star general, their conversation, according to Stevie, went as follows:

Ted—What are you doing here, Leslie?

McNair—Come to see the war, Ted, you can't see it from Washington.

Shellfire started coming in and hitting close-by.

Ted—The Germans know we are here, we are in full observation, and I suggest you take a quick look and get off this hill. Now last war when you were a Major, it would have been a different matter, but Lieutenant Generals aren't expendable.

McNair—Oh, that's O.K., I was a better man then than I am now anyway, Ted.

Ted's friend, after watching the progress of the attack for a little while, made it back down the hill safely. Later that same day, McNair was wounded by shrapnel while observing another of the 1st Division's regiments.[64]

After two days of constant day and night attacks, supported by concentrated Corps and Division Artillery barrages, the regiments succeeded in taking their initial objectives. One incident during the battle reminded Ted of a lesson he learned in World War I, that experienced combat troops have a much better chance of survival than do inexperienced rookies. One of the companies was dug in on a rocky hill when they were counterattacked by the Boche. The new replacements in the unit broke and ran, but the veterans stayed in their foxholes and returned fire. Both the Krauts and the panicking recruits suffered heavy losses while the veteran soldiers held the hill.

The Big Red One continued its attacks on the strong enemy positions through May 7th. The fighting was fierce and included a bayonet attack. The last Axis forces holding out surrendered on May 9th, and all combat operations ceased. During the last seventeen days of the campaign in Tunisia, the First Infantry Division suffered over 2000 battle casualties. That casualty rate was consistent with the casualty rate sustained by the Division in its previous North African battles.[65]

Of the campaign in North Africa, Ernie Pyle wrote, "It was a battle without letup. It was a war of drenching artillery and hidden mines and walls of machinegun fire and even the barbaric bayonet. It was an exhausting, cruel, last ditch kind of war *****."[66]

The GIs of the Big Red One had been in combat almost continually for six months, living in holes in the ground in the rain and cold, with little sleep and sporadic meals, many of which were cold. Every man in the Division was exhausted by the time the last shot was fired. They were happy when they climbed into trucks to be transported back to Oran. As usual, rumors ran rampant through the regiments. Some said that they had done their part in the war, that one of the un-bloodied divisions in Africa would take their place, and they would be sent back the States for a well-deserved rest. Others had the men being given thirty days leaves in Oran for a little rest and relaxation (R&R). Of course the GIs liked the one about going home the best.

It was summer and hot when the 1st Division's dog face soldiers unloaded at their temporary base near Oran. The first thing they noticed was that the Service of Supply troops, long stationed in Oran, most of whom had never been close enough to the front lines to even hear cannonading in the distance, were dressed in the cooler cotton khaki uniforms. The combat seasoned soldiers of the Big Red One had only their hot, heavy, woolen ODs to wear, the same clothes they had worn throughout the campaign. There had been a suggestion at Corps Headquarters that the combat troops be issued khakis, but General Bradley rejected it. He thought khakis were impractical to wear in the field, and besides, the changeover would unnecessarily burden supply he said. He also said that the change back to ODs would be a giveaway to the enemy as to when the next offensive action was about to begin. Where Bradley got his information that khakis were less practical than wool ODs for field wear, especially in the hot summer heat of the Mediterranean area, is an un-answered question. Khakis had been commonly worn by civilian working men for years, and the new, all cotton fatigue uniform would soon replaced the wool ODs for field use.

Already hot and irritated, the men of the Big Red One were sorely disappointed when they learned that they were not being sent home or even being given a long rest, but were scheduled to go right back into training and preparing for the next combat operation, the invasion of Sicily. Then, when some of them got passes to go into Oran for a little fun, they found that the service clubs there were reserved for the SOS troops and closed to the men dressed in the hot, woolen ODs. It was more than they could take, and they proceeded to liberate Oran for the second time. There were many fights of near riot proportions between the SOS men in their khakis, and the rugged men of the 1st Division. The soldiers with the Combat Infantryman's Badges on their chests almost always won. After all, they had taken on the best the Africa Corps had to offer. General Bradley wrote that "bands of the 1st Division hunted down khaki clad service troops," and they "left a trail of looted wine shops and outraged mayors." The Provost Marshall and the Inspector General began to look on the Division as a menace to the orderly management of troops overseas.[67]

Terry and Ted initially did little to quell the unruly actions of their belligerent and cocky troops. Ted's history of failing to insist on strict discipline by his combat-seasoned troops while they were in the rear areas went all the way back to France during World War I, and the time some of his men had been given a seven day R&R leave. When their leave was almost over, and the men were aboard a train going back to camp, some of them leaned out of a window at one of the stops and began talking to some Military Policemen standing nearby. They told the MPs that they were newly arrived members of the "Arkansas Balloon Corps," and asked them to tell them what it was like to be in combat. When the MPs began telling them dramatic war stories, as if they had been there, and edged close to the train, Ted's men doused them good with water just as the training was pulling out. A short time after his doughboys returned to camp, Ted was instructed by higher headquarters to investigate the incident and "fix the responsibility." He didn't have to investigate the matter; he already unofficially knew who the guilty men were. In his reply to the order, Ted said that his men were innocent and that the higher ups should look into the activities of some other unit.[68]

General Omar Bradley was already upset with Terry Allen for incurring heavy losses while making a completely unauthorized attack, and he thought seriously about relieving him on the spot for his independent action; however, the Allies were on the threshold of a great victory, and he changed his mind. Bradley also directly blamed both Allen and Roosevelt for the breakdown in 1st Division discipline, writing, "They (Allen and Roosevelt) looked upon discipline as an unwelcome crutch to be used by less able and personable commanders." He said that Allen was a rebel himself, who "had long ago disproved the maxim that discipline makes the soldier," and he commented that Roosevelt told some of the GIs that once they licked the Boche, "we'll go back to Oran and beat up every MP in town." It also got back to him that Ted said, "The United States Army consists of the 1st Division and 11 million replacements." Brad (Bradley) thought Ted and Terry were not good team players. He and the other big brass at corps and army level, were beginning to talk about relieving both of them of their duties with the Big Red One as soon as the Germans were defeated in Sicily. In fact, Omar Bradley had already made up his mind, he would sack them both. George Patton agreed with Brad with respect to Allen, but thought that Ted should be retained and given command of the Division after Terry was gone. [69]

In order to finally get a handle on the disciplinary problem, Ted and Terry initiated a training regimen designed to keep the men as busy as possible, so they wouldn't have time to think about their misfortune. Passes were restricted, new equipment and new woolen ODs were issued. Close order drill, inspections, guard duty, military ceremonies, kitchen police duty, as well as instruction in the familiar first aid, communication, field problems, amphibious training, etc. was initiated. [70]

As soon as Quentin was physically able to travel, he was sent back to the States and was given a recuperative leave. Eleanor immediately left the UK and returned to Oyster Bay to look after Quentin. Ted, thinking of his wife and the wedding anniversary they had coming up soon, sent her a V-Mail letter that many consider to be one of the most meaningful and poignant love letters they have ever read, especially when the writer was not gripped by the passions of youth. It stated:

Dearest Bunny,
Do you know what this is—a wedding anniversary letter. I think it should arrive about on the right date. Do you remember that hot June day thirty-three years ago?—the church jammed—Father with a lovely waistcoat with small blue spots—the Rough Riders—the ushers in cutaways—the crowds in the street—your long white veil and tight little bodice—the reception at Aunt Harriets"s—Uncle Ed - Your mother with one of her extraordinary hats that stood straight up. And do you remember what the world was then—little and cozy—a different order of things, wars considered on the basis of a Dick Davis novel—

a sort of "as it was in the beginning etc" atmosphere over life. We've come a long way down a strange road since. Nothing has happened as we imagined it would except our children. We never thought our occupations and interests would cover such a range. We never thought that our thirty-third anniversary would find us deep in our second war and me again at the front—Well, darling, we've lived up to the most important part of the ceremony, "In sickness and in health, for richer and for poorer, till death do you part."
Much, much love,
Ted.[71]

June 7th was a depressing day for Ted. He got word that his brother Kermit committed suicide while on duty in Alaska, and, if that wasn't enough, he had to write condolence letters to the next of kin of the 1st Division soldiers that had been killed during the North African campaign. This was always a depressing chore. Besides expressing his personal sympathy, Ted always put something in those letters to, hopefully, make the addressee feel that his or her loved one was special. A typical sentence in one of his letters would be, "His name now stands with those of the other young men on our Nation's roll of honor, the young men who, since the beginning of our Nation have paid the greatest sacrifice and, therefore, have done the most." He also wrote Eleanor a pensive letter in which he reminisced about growing up with Kermit and the things they had done together in years past, and he speculated that, with Kermit's death, Belle would drift away from the family.[72]

From the many letters Ted wrote to his wife and other members of the family, it is obvious that the months of May and June, '43 were tough on him emotionally, especially after he learned of the death of his brother. In every letter to Eleanor, he told her how much he missed her and how much he wanted to be at home. He wrote his sister Ethel Derby, that he "wishes he could be at Oyster Bay if only for a minute."[73]

Operation Husky, the invasion of Sicily, had been agreed upon by the Allies in January, 1943, at the Casablanca Conference. The purpose of the Sicilian campaign was threefold. Primarily, it was to draw Axis forces away from the Russian front, but also it was intended to make the Mediterranean area safe for Allied shipping, and to possibly knock Italy out of the war.

The general plan for the invasion of Sicily called for the British Eighth Army (General Montgomery CO) to land forces on the southeastern corner of that triangular shaped island and then race to Messina, a city on the northeastern corner. With Messina in Allied hands, the enemy would no longer be able to escape across the Strait of Messina into Italy, a distance of only four miles. American forces, including the Big Red One, would land along the southern shore, to the west of the British, and give the Eighth Army protection on its left flank as it fought its way north along the coast toward Messina. D-Day for the invasion was set for July 10th.

The 1st Infantry Division's orders called for it to land on the beaches near the town of Gela, to secure that city as quickly as possible, and then to move inland and capture the Ponte-Olivo Airport.[74]

As the date for embarkation approached, Ted was pleased with how the Big Red One looked during its training. The new replacements had been with them for several weeks and had received some valuable instructions, especially involving amphibious landings. The enthusiastic rookies interspersed among the many steady combat veterans made the Division a powerful force indeed.[75]

On June 24th, Terry and Ted led the Division in a large-scale practice landing near Zeralda, Algeria. Generals Eisenhower, Bradley, Patton, and Marshall observed from the beach. The Navy missed putting the men ashore at the proper place by half a mile. While it certainly was not intended as such, the misplacing of the assault waves on that Algerian beach gave Ted a valuable rehearsal for another misplaced D-Day landing that would be made less than a year in the future on the coast of Normandy, France, at a place code named, "Utah Beach." By now, Dwight Eisenhower had changed his opinion about the quality of the leadership provided by the American junior officers; he knew it was outstanding. The brass saw that the Big Red One was in top form. Terry and Ted had the men as ready as they could make them.[76]

General Allen, with the Division CP detachment, boarded the USS Samuel Chase, and Ted, with the alternate CP group, boarded the USS Bayfield in Algiers Harbor. On July 5th, they set sail in rough seas for the Sicilian invasion beaches. After rendezvousing with the entire invasion convoy on the 8th, the ships transporting the 1st Division dropped anchor off the coast of Gela, Sicily on the night of July 9th.[77]

The men making up the initial assault waves climbed down the rope nets dropped from the sides of the troop ships, and jumped into the landing craft. As in North Africa, Ted was in the first wave. After pre-invasion bombing raids by the air corps and shelling by naval warships, the first wave boats began the seven-mile run to shore. The seas were high. The landing craft reached the beach at 0245 hours. Ted described the landing as:

We guided on the burning buildings fired by our air bombardment. We landed and went up over the beach through machinegun bullets, worked through sand dunes, clearing out nests of Italians. They fought only until we got close to them, then surrendered. During the dark hours I worked up and down the beach, puffing through heavy sand, straightening out units. As day broke I worked to where the advance C.P. of the Division was to be established. Prisoners were streaming by, mostly Italians, some few Germans. The Italians behaved like a combination of a little boy and a puppy wagging its tail. The Germans held themselves aloof, but were not as tough-looking as those we had met in Africa.[78]

Ted knew all the details of the Big Red One's part of the invasion, including the order and location the various companies of the Division were to land. His initial duty on the beach was to see that the units came in when and where they were scheduled and to straighten out any problems that came up. Next, he was to get the assault waves off the beach, over the sand dunes, and clear out any pockets of resistance in the area. The landing went smooth; there were no major foul-ups. By dawn, a satisfactory toehold had been established. He then supervised the various units as they went inland to accomplish their next mission, the capture of Gela, its small seaport, and the nearby airport.[79]

The Allies did not have air supremacy at this time in the war and the only air cover over the invasion beaches was supplied by a few British Spitfires. The American Air Corps was occupied with strategic missions further inland. During that first day, there were a number of air raids by squadrons of German JU-88 bombers, aimed primarily at the invasion fleet lying offshore, and at the town of Gela. In the middle of D-Day afternoon, after Gela had been secured, Stevie drove Ted into the town to meet General Patton, who was now the Commander of all American Army forces involved in the invasion, and guide him back toward the beach to where the Division CP was located. As they were headed to the CP, a flight of twelve JU-88s came in and began bombing Gela and the ships anchored offshore. While the bombs were not hitting close to their vehicles, Patton's command car stopped and all in his party ran for cover except Patton. He got out and watched the bombers through his binoculars. Apparently, he wanted to impress the men around him. Seeing the Patton vehicle stop, Ted and Stevie stopped and just stood there and watched in amazement. After the raid was over, all of them got back in their vehicles and continued on to the CP where Patton conferred with General Allen.[80]

As the sun went down at the end of that first day, the troops dug in for the night, but they were still shy of the Ponte-Oliva Airport. Early the next morning, J.J. Cunningham of Pensacola, Florida, who was a member of the 18th Infantry, awoke from what little sleep he had been able to get. He was sure that his squad was the most forward element in his battalion. Not yet having received any orders to move, Cunningham and the men with him began digging their fox holes deeper. All at once, Ted Roosevelt appeared from the German side of the line. He smiled at the men and said, "When you get through digging those shit holes, get in them." The men got a chuckle out of his remark, and the General walked on off.[81]

Ted had an eerie sense that enabled him to know when and where the next enemy attack would take place. He would always be at the hot spot in the line to give any help he could. By 0630 on D plus 1 (D for the day the invasion took place. Plus 1 meaning the day after D-Day) he was with the 26th Infantry Regiment observing an incoming attack by a group of German light tanks. The situation at that particular time was not critical, but it was delaying the capture of the airport. At 0640 Ted got General Allen on the field telephone and said:

> Terry—look. The situation is not very comfortable out here. The 3rd Battalion has been attacked by tanks, and has been penetrated. The 2nd Battalion is in support, but that is not enough. If we could Get a company of medium tanks, it sure would help. If we are to take the Ponte Olivo Airport, we must have those medium tanks.[82]

Both Ted and Stevie were still with the 26th Infantry watching the German light tank attack when, at 1030 hours, they looked to the extreme right and spotted a group of fifty German Mark IV heavy tanks approaching down the valley. Realizing there was nothing to stop them before the enemy force got all the way to the beaches, Ted and his aide jumped in their jeep and hightailed it down the road leading to the Division CP, barely making it past the most advanced German tanks before the road was cut. As they were racing toward the CP, they came upon the Cannon Company of the 16th Infantry Regiment, and warned the Company CO of the approaching Kraut armor. As fast as possible, the company's artillery was put in place on the forward slope of a hill where there was a good view of the fast approaching Mark IVs, and started firing at almost point blank range. Ted managed to get General Allen on the phone again, and warned him of this major German attack then in progress. There was still no air to ground support, but all available artillery and naval gunfire was called in. Before the attack was beaten back, the enemy tanks got within a thousand yards of the beach. Ted remained at the front and personally directed the defense. A large number of the enemy tanks were destroyed, including seventeen by the 16th's Cannon Company.[83]

While the German attack was still in progress, Wesley C. Henson of Hope Valley, RI, and several other men in the 1st Battalion, 7th Field Artillery Regiment, were trying to find their Battalion Headquarters. Hearing of the approaching German tank attack, and being unable to find the headquarters, they turned around and headed back toward the beach. Ted must have seen the men retreating, for he came roaring up in the Rough Rider and asked them where they were going. When they told him, Ted, whose arthritis had worsened and now always walked with a cane, shook his stick at them and bellowed, "Never turn your ass on the enemy." His driver (almost certainly Stevie) then wheeled the jeep around and drove back in the direction of the Krauts. In describing the incident to the author, Henson's words were "We followed—we did not dare not! What a man he was."[84]

Later on, after time for reflection, General Omar Bradley wondered whether any other division in the U.S. Army could have repelled such a determined German attack, especially since it had been led by the elite Hermann Goering Division.[85]

For his actions during the first two days of the Sicilian invasion, Ted was awarded the Silver Star. Since this was his fourth such award in two wars, he would now wear three Oak Leaf Clusters on his Silver Star ribbon.[86]

The Division now resumed the offensive, and on July 13th succeeded in capturing the Ponte Olivo Airport. As soon as the Germans had been pushed back far enough to put the airfield out of artillery range, the airport was put in operation. Air supremacy then shifted to the Allies. Over the next ten days, the Big Red One advanced seventy miles. From this point on until Sicily fell about four weeks later, the Axis forces were fighting a delaying action to allow as many of their troops as possible to be evacuated from Sicily across the narrow Strait of Messina into Italy.

Early in the campaign, the famous journalist Quentin Reynolds gave ten to one odds and bet a member of the Division staff $10 that Ted would be killed within the next two weeks. The officer said he took the bet, not because he thought he would win it, but because he would take any bet with ten-to-one odds. Later, when Ted heard about Reynolds' loosing bet, he laughed and gave his friend a stern lecture against the evils of reckless gambling. Quentin Reynolds had more than friendship for Ted Roosevelt, he had great respect. Speaking of him, Reynolds said, "He is perhaps the only man I've ever met who is impervious to fear."[87]

From the standpoint of the GIs in the Big Red One, the Sicilian Campaign developed into beginning an attack each day or night against a German or Italian force well entrenched on some steep mountaintop, where the enemy had the high ground and the advantages that good observation affords. Mules were often used to haul the supplies and equipment up the narrow mountain trails. Sometimes the terrain was so sheer that the men had to use ropes to make the climb. It was a situation of taking one poor, dirty, mountain town after the other. One of the municipalities the Division captured was Enna, the capital of Sicily. The infantry paid for each mile advanced with heavy casualties.

On July 15th, the 70th Tank Battalion was attached to the 1st Division and immediately prepared to make an attack on the town of Barrafranca. A combat team, self named the "Rough Riders," led by Ted and made up of the 70th Tank

Bn., the 1st Division's Reconnaissance Troop, and the 1st Division's Engineer Bn., jumped off in the attack at dawn on the 17th. Opposition was light and they quickly secured a critical cross roads needed for the final advancement to the objective. Then the Wehrmacht began to put up fierce resistance with tanks, heavy artillery, mortars, and nebelwerfers (the famous screaming meemie). The men of the 70th had never heard anything as terrifying as the screaming meemie before. Lieutenant John Ahearn described the sound as, "a freight train coming out of the sky." Sergeant Walter Waszyn said, "The nebelwerfer fire absolutely froze us. Six shells coming at you at one time." The attack bogged down, and some of the men began pulling back. At that instant, Ted appeared out of nowhere. He was bareheaded and began chasing the retreating troops back to the line with his cane and yelling:[88]

Follow me you sons-of-bitches, we're going after them.[89]

Stevie wrote that it was the second time in less than a week that General Roosevelt had saved the day. Through the joint efforts of the 1st Division and the 70th Tank Battalion, Barrafranca fell that very day.[90]

While the Allies now had air supremacy, they didn't have total control of the skies. Late in the day of July 15th, Ted was in a conference at 70th Tank Battalion Headquarters when a Luftwaffe bombing raid came in. All of the officers there made a run for protection in a nearby cave. Lieutenant Hirsch of the 70th, being young and fast, was the first to reach the cave entrance. Realizing that the General was hobbling along and bringing up the rear, the Lieutenant stopped and stepped back to allow Ted to enter first. With the aerial bombs exploding all around, Ted uttered the words that were, at the time, famous to the GI's,

Go ahead Lieutenant, there is no rank in a situation like this![91]

Sergeant Andrew F. Favara of New Egypt, NJ, a member of the 1st Engineer Battalion, had a similar experience with General Roosevelt when they both took shelter in an old, abandoned building as a low-flying Messerschmit came in with its machineguns blazing away.[92]

Ted had encountered the 70th Tank Battalion back in early 1942, when they all thought they were going to invade Martinique. By now the men of the 70th and the General were old friends, and each had the utmost respect for the other. Ted felt that the 70th fit in well with his style of leadership, and the 70th considered the feisty old General to be one of their own.

The style of leadership of some commanding officers, even some West Point commanding officers, is to drive his men, and drive his men, and drive his men to the point of exhaustion, and then drive them some more. The trick is, they say, to know when the men have actually reached the point from which they can go no more, and the breaking point differs with each individual. After the Big Red One had been in combat everyday for two weeks and all its troops were exhausted from starting a new attack every day, Ted wrote Eleanor a letter critical of the high command. He wrote that the men in the Division were tired, and that each day they faced fresh Axis troops. He couldn't understand why the top brass didn't commit rested American troops rather than continue using the same old worn out bunch. He wrote:

It's due, I guess, to a desire on the part of our command to get as far as they can without committing troops. It's a gamble I would not take if I were in their place, for the stakes are too high. Also, never having commanded troops in action, they do not understand how exhausted soldiers get. Often it is not a question of losses but of extreme exhaustion. The soldier who has hiked, climbed and fought for days on end is completely done up. That's the case with some of units now. There's a fool saying to the effect that there's always one step more in a doughboy. Yes, but how about it when he's taken that step? Well so be it. As Nicias said when the Athenians commenced their retreat on this same island: "Man does what he can, and bears what he must."[93]

The Battle of Sicily ground on. The 1st Division attacked almost every day and would make some hard fought advancements. Then it would get to the next defended mountain. By the last days in July, Nicosia had fallen and the Division received orders to assault and capture Troina, the highest town in Sicily. By now the Axis had pulled its forces into the northeastern corner of the island and was evacuating units across the Messina Strait as fast as possible. Allied intelligence was aware that the Germans would fight hard to hold Troina to gain time to complete the removal of their forces from the island. Elements of several divisions had been placed in and around the town for defensive purposes. These defenders included the infamous Herman Goering Division and the experienced 15th SS Panzer Division.

The assault on Troina began on August 1st. It was a grinding, hot, and dirty onslaught for six days. Omar Bradley thought Terry Allen's tactical planning for the initial assault was poor because he miscalculated the enemy's strength, and he failed to heed to some of the suggestions Bradley offered. Any remaining doubt about relieving Allen and Ted was now a thing of the past.[94]

During the Troina battle, there occurred two somewhat similar incidents that, perhaps, more than anything else, show the difference between the personalities and leadership styles of the aggressive, quasi-psychotic George Patton and the polite, likable Theodore Roosevelt, Jr. Both incidents involved soldiers under medical care for conditions suffered in combat. One was the famous slapping episode when Patton slapped a combat fatigued soldier in a field hospital. The other occurred when Ted was visiting an aid station and spotted Lieutenant John Finke, who he knew by name and by the fact that they both had Dutch ancestry. The Lieutenant was sitting on the aid station floor with a bloody turban bandage around his head. Walking over to him, Ted said, "Hell, Finke, they sure picked the wrong place to shoot a Dutchman, didn't they?" Even though he had a splitting headache, the Lieutenant, and everyone else there, roared with laughter.[95]

Finally on August 6th, after repelling twenty-four counterattacks, and even getting some air support from the U.S. Air Corps, the Big Red One captured the town of Tronia. The Division was immediately pulled out of the line. The twenty-seven consecutive days in front line combat cost the First Infantry Division 1,788 casualties. Ted was never considered one of the injured, nor did he get a Purple Heart, even though he suffered two broken teeth when he was hit in the mouth by shrapnel.[96]

Right after the Division was pulled from the front, Ted and Terry were told to report to II Corps Headquarters. Arriving as ordered, they were met by Generals Bradley and Patton who wasted no time in summarily relieving them of their duties with the 1st Division and telling them that they were both being sent back to the States to train new recruits. Even though taking this drastic action had been discussed by Generals Bradley, Patton, and Eisenhower for three months, it was not irrevocably agreed upon until late in July. While there is some indication that their impending transfers were mentioned in routine paperwork received by 1st Division Headquarters from II Corps Headquarters, there is no record that either Terry or Ted saw it. Apparently the first notification they had was when they were personally informed by Bradley and Patton after the Battle for Tronia had been successfully concluded.[97]

Later, both Bradley and Patton tried to take full credit for relieving their best commanders, from their best division. They both claimed that he was the one that made the decision and that the other didn't have anything to do with it. At the time Patton commanded an Army and Bradley a Corps, so Patton was Bradley's immediate superior officer. Whichever one of them was the primary force behind the decision, it didn't seem to trouble Patton, but General Bradley anguished over it. He wrote that it was an extremely unpleasant event and was one of the hardest things he had to do during the entire war. Brad discussed the matter at length in his books, *A Soldier's Story* and *A General's Life*, writing that the problem with Terry and Ted was caused by "too much brilliance, too much success, too much personality, and too strong an attachment of two men for the 1st Division." From a realistic standpoint, it is easy to see why Ted had to be relieved if they were going to relieve Terry Allen and not make Ted the Division Commander. There were any number of high-ranking regular army officers dying for division command, especially command of the Big Red One. Ted was a reserve officer with a total of only four years active duty experience. No matter what his war record was, how could they give the Division to Ted? The men of the 1st Division revered Ted Roosevelt. If they left Ted as assistant CO, the troops would naturally look to him rather than the new commander, and this would be a problem. While Bradley thought Ted was too close to the troops, the real reason he was fired was because they couldn't make him CO and it would create new problems if they let him stay.

The Terry and Teddy show was over. No matter how it's analyzed, it is hard to justify firing both the coach and the quarterback right after they get the team to the Super Bowl. Perhaps as a consolation prize, Ted was awarded the Legion of Merit. The citation reads, "For his able training of First Division troops, his inspiring leadership of them in combat, and his continual personal example of absolute fearlessness and determination in the performance of his duties in North Africa and Sicily."[98]

While it had nothing whatsoever to do with them being replaced, an amusing incident occurred while Ted and Terry were on their way back to Corps Headquarters that typifies, in many ways, the problems the top brass had with these two strong and unconventional personalities. An MP stopped their jeep and gave them both a ticket for being out of uniform. Neither had his helmet on in violation of regulations. Terry had his in his lap, while Ted had on one of the wool caps that were suppose to be worn under a helmet; he hated helmets and didn't even have his with him. Arriving at Corps, and apparently having no inkling of what was about to happen, Ted walked in, told Bradley about the tickets and said, "we get along a helluva lot better with the Krauts up front than we do with your people back here in the rear."[99]

As dismayed and hurt as he was, Ted immediately left Corps Headquarters. He went back to his quarters, and wrote an open letter to the Officers and Men of the 1st Division, saying:

> More that 26 years ago the 1st Division was formed, and I joined it at that time, I have served with it in two wars and have served with no other unit.
>
> We have been together in combat; we know each other as men do only when they have been battle comrades. I do not have to tell you what I think of you, for you know. You will always be in my heart.
>
> I have been ordered away. It is a great grief to me, and my hope is that sometime I may return, for it is with you that I feel I belong.
>
> Your record is splendid. You are known as assault troops the world over. You will add in the future new honors to our history.

May luck go with your battle worn colors as glory always has.[100]

During the two wars in which Ted had been a member of the First Infantry Division, it added the following battle streamers to its flagstaff: Lorraine, Aisne-Marne, Picardy, Montdidier-Noyone, St. Mihiel, and Meuse-Argonne from World War I; and Algeria-French Morocco, Tunisia, and Sicily from World War II.[101]

Three days after he was relieved, *Time Magazine* put Terry Allen's picture on its cover and ran a long story lauding his abilities. When he got back to the States, Allen was given command of the newly formed 104th Infantry Division. After training his new Division, he took it to Europe where both he and the 104th Division served with distinction for the rest of the war. In final analysis, Terry Allen is probably the finest CO of an infantry division in combat that the Unites States has ever produced.[102]

Major General Clarence R. Huebner, the new Division CO, had none of the color of Terry Allen, and he was a strict disciplinarian. Upon assuming command, he initiated a regimented basic training schedule, including close order drill, personal inspections, quarters inspections, etc., which the men termed as "chickenshit." Huebner said the men loved Allen, but respected him. Whether the men respected him or simply thought he was chickenshit, the Big Red One was transferred to England after the Battle of Sicily was over to train for operation Overlord, the D-Day invasion of France. Huebner remained the Division's Commanding Officer during the hell of Omaha Beach on June 6, 1944, and for six months thereafter.[103]

All politically powerful people have big egos. In fact, some of President Teddy Roosevelt's detractors nicknamed him, "Egotisticus Americanus." Ted had inherited a lot of ego in his genes. Here he was, doing a magnificent job, in the front lines every day, getting practically no press coverage because of some censorship order, and had now been relieved of his duties. Instead of returning home the conquering hero, he would be returning home as an incompetent officer who had been booted out of his job. This he couldn't accept. He knew he didn't deserve to be treated this way, and he was determined to do something about it.

After a goodbye dinner with the 1st Division staff and some of the officers that were his close friends, Ted, with Stevie, caught the first plane available to Algiers and immediately went to Allied Force Headquarters and saw General Walter Bedell Smith, Dwight Eisenhower's Chief of Staff. "Beetle" Smith and Ted had a frank discussion about the situation, and Smith explained to him that it would be unfair to any new commander of the Division to leave him in it. He also said that General Patton considered him technically not qualified for division command. This remark Patton made didn't surprise TRJr too much. He had already heard via the grape vine that George Patton was embarrassed about the time in North Africa when Ted got up out of his foxhole and gave it to Patton while Luftwaffe bombs were falling all around. Patton seemed to think that this had made him the target of the GI's jokes and laughter and he held it against Ted. At the time, neither Ted nor Smith knew that less than three months previously Patton had written in his personal diary that Ted should be made the 1st Division CO after Allen was sacked. General Smith did, however, give a sympathetic ear to Ted's plea that he wanted to stay overseas with troops rather than be sent back home. He got new orders drawn up assigning Ted to Mark Clark's Fifth Army as Chief Liaison Officer to the French Expeditionary Corps.[104]

The Terry and Teddy Show
Source Notes

1. Stanton p 75; McCormick Research Center, First Division Museum, Cantigny.

2. Collier p 399; Roosevelt, Mrs. T Jr., p 419.

3. Roosevelt, Mrs. T Jr., p 419, 423; LOC container-6; Ingersoll p 189; Roosevelt, T. Jr., All In the Family, p 22; Stevie's Notes.

4. Andrus p 8; Finke p 37; McCormick Research Center.

5. Eleanor's letter to Cornelius, 8/14/41, LOC c-6; Eleanor's letter to Alex Woollcott, 6/13/41, Theodore Roosevelt Collection, Harvard University, bms Am 1449 (1417)

6. Roosevelt, Mrs. T Jr., p 419.

7. Eleanor's letter to Cornelius. 9/14/41, LOC c-6; TR Coll. H.U., bMS Am 1449 (1421).

8. Eleanor's letter to Cornelius of. 11/4/41, LOC c-6.

9. Roosevelt, Mrs. T. Jr., p 420.

10. LOC c-6.

11. Eleanor's letter to Gracie, 12/16/41, LOC c-6; Ted's letter to Edith, 12/15/41, LOC c-9.

12. Julius Adler's letter to Eleanor after T's death, LOC c-32; Eleanor's letter to Gracie, 12.16.41, LOC c-6; Official Army Records, St. Louis, Mo.

13. Recollections of Major Raphael Uffner, First Division at Cantigny; Jensen p 17, 18; TRJr. Collection, Sagamore Hill; Author interviews with 1st Div. Vets. Joseph S. Kowalski, John Morello, and Louis Newman.

14. Roosevelt, Mrs. T. Jr. p 421.

15. Eleanor's letter to Cornelius., 3/17/42, LOC c-6.; Roosevelt, Mrs. T. Jr. p 422.

16. Jacksonville Journal of 8/14/43

17. Roosevelt, Mrs. T. Jr., p 386.

18. Hoyt p 63, 64.

19. Jacksonville Journal 8/14/43; Katcher p 4; Official Army Records; Personal interview with Henry Bowles.

20. Hoyt p 63; Katcher p 4.

21. Roosevelt, Mrs. T. Jr., p 423, 424.

22. Hoyt p 63.

23. Hoyt p 63, 64; Katcher p 4.

24. Hoyt p 73.

25. Roosevelt, Mrs. T. Jr., p 328, 329.

26. Hoyt p 79.

27. Roosevelt, Mrs. T. Jr., p 430–432; Author interview with 1st Div. vet. Joe Morell)

28. Katcher p 4.

29. Downs p 2.

30. Butcher p 148.

31. Ted's letter to Eleanor of 7/30/43, LOC c-61; Stevie's Notes. Diary entries of 3/5/1922, 6/20/22, 6/27/22, and 6/29/22, pages 205, 318, 324, and 326 respectively, LOC c-1.

32. Ted's letter to Eleanor of 12/26/42, LOC c-6; Roosevelt, Mrs. T. Jr., p 437.

33. Recommendation for the DSM by Major Critz and favorable endorsement by General Allen, LOC c-39; Terry Allen papers; Stevie's Notes.

34. Stevie's Notes, Citation for Bronze Star, LOC c-39; Statement of John Bowen, LOC c-39; Hamilton p 31; Knickerbocker et al p 10–11; Personal interview with Thomas Bowles.

35. Critz recommendation and Allen endorsement, LOC c-39.

36. Stevoe's Notes; Terry Allen papers; Roosevelt, Mrs. T. Jr., p 428; Butcher p 288.

37. Katcher p 6.

38. Russell Landstrom story in clipping file, TR Collection, Harvard U.; Roosevelt, Mrs. T. Jr., p 238–240.

39. Stevie's Notes.

40. Stevie's Notes; Ernie Pyle's column written at the Tunisian front on 2/19/43.

41. Letter from Mr. Anderson to author.

42. Stevie's Notes; TRJr letter to Ethel Derby, 2/10/43, TR Coll. H.U. 87M-100.

43. Nicholas Roosevelt p 35; Hamilton, "Jr. In Name Only" p 32; AP story written by Wendell Phillippi appearing in the 9/9/62 issue of the Corpus Christi Caller-Times; Bradley, Soldiers Story, p 119.

44. Stevie's Notes.

45. LOC c-56

46. Eleanor's letter to Ted of 12/26/43, LOC c-6; Roosevelt, Mrs. T. Jr., p 438–440

47. Stevie's Notes; Poem by Grantland Rice.

48. Roosevelt, Mrs. T Jr., p 443.

49. TRJr. letter to Ethel Derby, 3/7/43, TR Collection, H.U., 87M-100; DBY p 441.

50. New York Times 7/9/43; LOC c-39.

51. Terry Allen papers; Stevie's Notes.

52. Blumenson p 190.

53. Stevie's Notes.

54. Stevie's Notes; Terry Allen papers.

55. Finke p 104.

56. Stevie's Notes; Terry Allen papers.

57. Stevie's Notes; Terry Allen papers; TRJr. letter to Eleanor., LOC c-61.

58. LOC c-56.

59. Terry Allen papers; Katcher p 7; Patton letter, LOC c-39 (World War II folder)

60. LOC c-39.

61. D'Este p 466; Astor p 312.

62. Stevie's Notes.

63. Terry Allen papers; Stevie's Notes.

64. Stevie's Notes.

65. Terry Allen papers; LOC c-61

66. Andrus p 12.

67. Bradley, Soldiers Story, p 118; Hoyt p 202–203.

68. Roosevelt, T. Jr., Average Americans. p 197–198.

69. Blumenson p 270; Bradley, A Generals Life p 158; Bradley, Soldiers Story p 118–119; Miller, Merle p 501.

70. Stevie's Notes; Finke p 284.

71. LOC c-10; Tamplin p 23.

72. TR Coll. H.U. MC 56; LOC c-10.

73. Ted's Letters to Eleanor., LOC c-10; Ted's letter to Ethel, TR Coll. 87M-100.

74. Terry Allen papers; Finke p 285.

75. TRJr letter to Dick Derby, TR Coll 87M-100.

76. Bradley, SS, p 127; Finke p 285.

77. Finke p 285.

78. Ted's letter to Eleanor of 7/14/43; Stevie's Notes.

79. Stevie's Notes

80. Stevie's Notes; Blumenson, Patton, The Man Behind, p 198.

81. Author interview with J.J. Cunningham.

82. Terry Allen papers.

83. Stevie's Notes; Knickerbocker p 105; Terry Allen papers; Ted's letter to Eleanor of 7/22/43, LOC c-61.

84. Henson's letter to author.

85. Katcher p 11.

86. LOC c-55

87. LOC c-56.

88. Knickerbocker p 115; Jensen, Common Men, Uncommon Valor.

89. Statement of Marvin Jensen, Sagamore Hill archives.

90. Stevie's Notes

91. Ibid

92. Letter to author from Andrew Favara

93. Ted's letter to Eleanor of 7/23/43, LOC c-61.

94. Bradley, General's Life, p 195

95. Finke p 161.

96. Katcher p 14; Phillippi article of 9/9/62

97. Stevie's Notes.

98. Bradley, A Soldiers Story p 160–163; Bradley, A General's Life, p 195.

99. Bradley, A Soldier's Story, p 161–162.

100. Military History Institute correspondence with author.

101. Knickerbocker p 405–406.

102. Time Magazine 8/9/43.

103. Davis, Kenneth S., Experience of War, p 421; Mansoor p 106.

104. Stevie's Notes; LOC C-61.

IN LIMBO

Ted promptly reported to General Mark Clark at his North African Headquarters. Clark told Ted he would place him with American troops as soon as something became available, but that he didn't know long it would be. Until then, he would be working with the French.

On August 18th, Ted began working at his new job. While the Allied invasion of Italy would not take place for several weeks yet, the French Expeditionary Corps was training in North Africa in preparation for going to the anticipated Italian front. Since the French had insufficient supplies and equipment of their own, American uniforms, armor, ammo, rations, etc. would be utilized to maintain the Corps. Ted's job would be to handle any problems that arose from their use of the unfamiliar materials and equipment, to aid in training the unit for combat, and to take care of any diplomatic problems that might arise between Mark Clarks V Army and the French Corps.

The French and the American one star general immediately hit it off on the right foot. They knew of Ted's splendid record from the Great War. Some of the soldiers in the French Expeditionary Corps had fought against the 1st Division in Oran, and others had been involved with Groupment Roosevelt in North Africa. Ted had a high regard for the French and he said he could speak their language. Stevie disagreed with his bosses claimed French linguistic skills, however, saying, "His French was a combination of Spanish, which he spoke very well, some pidgin-Italian, and a few phrases from restaurant menus."

At this point, Ted was glad to still be in a war zone, but he was afraid that he was at a dead end with respect to getting back with American combat troops. He wrote Eleanor, asking her to go to see Army Chief of Staff General George C. Marshall, in Washington, and request that he send Quentin and him out to assist General Joseph Stillwell in the Far East, or put him back with American troops in any war zone. Even though his and Marshall's relationship went all the way back to the Great War, Ted was concerned that Marshall might think of him as incompetent because he had been relieved of his job. He suggested to his wife that she ask General Marshall check with the current 1st Division staff as to whether or not he was qualified for command. He also wanted her to remind the Chief of Staff that he had been in front line combat longer than any other general officer in the Army and that he had never been involved in an unsuccessful military campaign. When Eleanor met with Marshall, he was cordial, but said that Ted was too close to the men and he did not make any commitment to help Ted out of his predicament.[1]

For about a month Ted assisted in training the French Corps. Each day he would go out to some unit to observe the activities and make any comments and recommendations he thought would be helpful. The way the French troops were looking in their training impressed him, and he became close friends with General Alphonse Juin, the Corps Commander.[2]

Months before the Sicilian invasion,, the Allied intelligence services concocted a number of ruses meant to deceive the Germans and Italians into believing that the next offensive move by the Americans and English would be an invasion of Sardinia and/or Corsica rather than Sicily. One of these hoaxes was described in the Hollywood movie entitled *The Man Who Never Was* that was popularized by actor Clifton Webb. The Krauts and Eyeties fell for the trickery and transferred strong military forces to both Sardinia and Corsica. By the middle of September, the Germans had recalled most of their forces from those islands, but the Italians had not. About 20,000 German and 200,000 Italian troops were still stationed there. The American Office of Strategic Services, a.k.a. OSS, (In 1943 the OSS was headed by Ted's old World War I friend, William Donovan. The OSS was the predecessor of the CIA) and the British intelligence service (Officially named the Special Operations Executive, a.k.a. SOE) thought that the Germans would withdraw the rest of their forces from Corsica and Sardinia for use elsewhere, but they were unsure as to what the Italians would do with respect to continuing to resist the Allies, and they also had questions as to whether or not the air fields and harbors on the islands were in condition to be useful for military purposes.. At this point, Allied Force Headquarters and the intelligence services decided they had need of Ted Roosevelt for a special mission. They sent for him.

Ted's special assignment was to take a radio operator and two interpreters, along with a personal letter of introduction from General Eisenhower, and go by PT boat to Sardinia. There he would meet an OSS team that had previously been parachuted in, and confer with Italian General Basso, the commander of all Italian forces on Sardinia and Corsica. Basso would, hopefully, confirm that the Italians were friendly and ready to cease their resistance to the Allies. After that, Ted was to make an inspection of airfields and harbor facilities on the islands and report on their condition for use by the U. S. military.[3]

On September 16th, Ted journeyed to Allied Headquarters in Algiers, where he was briefed by Generals "Beetle" Smith and Harold Alexander. He would depart after dark. At the last minute the boat developed engine trouble, so his departure was delayed for twenty-four hours. With time to kill, Ted visited the ruins of Carthage, went to a museum, and did some shopping in a bookstore. Finally getting underway on the 17th, his boat was met the next day off the coast of Sardinia by a harbor tug and led through the German minefield. As they pulled up to the wharf at Cagliari, Sardinia, where he was to meet the OSS team, Ted was surprised to see that one of the men waiting there was his old acquaintance, Serge Obolensky.[4]

Serge Obolensky was certainly an interesting fellow. An Oxford educated, Russian-born Prince, Serge was only three years younger than Ted, and had fought heroically with the Russian Army against the Germans in the First World War. After Russia withdrew from the war, he fought the Bolsheviks in the Russian Revolution, then he fled Russia and lived and worked in England and Australia for several years. In 1924, he married the extremely wealthy Alice Astor, of the John Jacob Astor, Rhinebeck, New York, Astors, and lived a life of leisure for the next several years, with continuous holidays and parties in France, New York, London, etc (A jet-set lifestyle before Lindberg flew the Atlantic). In the late '20s, he and Alice were divorced, and he went to work in New York City. In 1931, Serge was granted what he said was one of the world's greatest gifts, American citizenship. Later in the '30s, his former brother-in-law, Vincent Astor, gave him a job in the hotel business. A few years later, Serge quit his job and enlisted in the New York State Guard as a private in the infantry. Shortly after Pearl Harbor, he took the officer's exam and was made a 2nd lieutenant. In a short time, he was made a company commander and promoted to captain. Bill Donovan accepted his application into the OSS, where he received commando instruction and special training in guerrilla tactics. He then went to jump school at Ft. Benning and Glider School at Ft. Bragg. He was a Lieutenant Colonel by the time he studied tank tactics at Ft. Knox. He took marine training at Pendleton and additional commando training at Ft. Hood. The night-jump into Sardinia in mid-September to meet Ted was his first mission as an OSS operative.[5]

Serge and Alice and Ted and Eleanor had known each other casually for years, but the Obolenskys were actually closer friends with FDR and his Eleanor, and Ted's brother and sister-in-law, Kermit and Belle.

Colonel Obolensky arrived in Sardinia a couple of days before Ted, and he had already conferred with Colonel Bruno, the Italian Chief of Staff, and with General Basso, the CO. They told him that the Germans were withdrawing, and they assured him that the Italians would abide by the instructions that had been given them by their King and not give the Allies any problems. They did, however, warn him of the presence on Sardinia of the elite and possibly hostile Nembo Division, made up of tough Italian paratroopers. Unlike most of the other Italian military units, the Nembo Division had fought valiantly against the Allies all through the North African campaign, and had displayed a loyalty to the Germans. One battalion had even mutinied and left Sardinia to join up with the Germans. When a senior officer tried to talk them out of it, they shot him in cold blood. The rest of the Division was still on the island, but it was in a state of turmoil.[6]

After disembarking, Ted had Serge brief him on the situation in Sardinia, and then they made a call on General Basso at his headquarters. After going to their quarters that night, Serge got around to telling Ted about the unstable situation involving the Nembo Division. Ted thought for a minute and then told Serge he wanted to review the Division the next morning, and to set it up with Colonel Bruno. Serge tried to dissuade Ted from doing this, but to no avail.

Leaving Ted at their quarters, Serge immediately went to Bruno and instructed him to have the Nembos on the parade ground the next morning at 0830 hours for a review by General Roosevelt. Hearing this, the Colonel was horrified, saying, "Oh my God! You must change his mind." When told Roosevelt was insistent, Bruno said they would kill him, "A Roosevelt murdered reviewing our troops!— and you too!"

When they drove up to the parade ground the next morning and saw the surly Nembo Division assembled, Ted told Serge they would leave their pistols in the car adding, "We'll use only our swagger sticks." Walking up to the formation, Ted immediately went up to the Division Sergeant Major, who was an enormous hulk of muscle with a chest full of ribbons. Complementing the Sergeant on his appearance, Ted asked him how he had earned all his decorations. The big Sergeant smirked and responded that he had earned them fighting against the Americans, and he named the battles. Ted said,

Splendid! If we'd had troops like you on our side, we'd have really done a job. You gave us one hell of a time! I congratulate you on your accomplishments.

The Sergeant Major's smirk turned into a smile, and all the men who could hear the conversation began to grin. Then Ted asked him what else he did and was told he was a boxer. After talking a minute about boxing, Ted had all the men who did some boxing to step forward, and he had a few words with them about that activity. Some of the men began to chuckle over Ted's bad Italian. Serge said he could see the ice melting away. Then Ted went down the ranks, looking at the men and stopping to talk informally with many of them. He asked them things like what battles they had been in and the names of their hometowns, and other harmless chatter. Serge said it was an astonishing thing to hear the men cheer Ted when he had finished and turned to walked away.

After Serge and Ted returned to their quarters, Serge asked him how in the world he did it? Ted replied:

Sergie, it's really very simple. When I was a boy, Father always took my brothers and me on his campaign trips. I learned a few helpful things on those trips. Father always had to have a rope put up ten feet away around his observation-car platform to keep the crowd back. They always pressed up against it, and when Father came to the proper moment in his speech, he would shout, Take away that rope! The people always cheered, and when the rope was removed they all rushed up to shake his hand. Serge, I tell you. You can't do without that rope.

Very early the next morning, the officers of the Nembo Division sent word to Ted and Serge that they would like them to join them for breakfast. Both American officers were delighted to accept the honor. After the meal was finished, many of the former enemy soldiers voluntarily joined with the Allies to fight the Nazis.[7]

By now the Germans had completely evacuated the islands. Ted and Serge spent several days touring Sardinia and Corsica, looking over airfields, naval installations, ports, and other facilities which Ted thought might be of benefit to the Allies. During their travels, the local citizens always gave them an enthusiastic welcome.[8]

After about ten days, the two American officers flew to Algiers, where they were met by a large group of war correspondents who had heard about their coup in Sardinia. Ted lauded Colonel Obolensky and told the reporters he (Obolensky) was the one responsible for the success of their mission. Either because of the censorship order or because of Ted's humility, Serge, and not Ted, was acclaimed by the American media. Serge later received a very nice citation from Wild Bill Donovan, the chief of the OSS.[9]

At the conclusion of the Sardinia affair, Serge was ordered back to London, and was later parachuted into German occupied France, where he worked with the French Resistance. After the war, he returned to the U.S. to complete a very successful career in the hotel business.

As an interesting sequel to the Sardinia mission, in the mid-1950s, Serge had an occasion to meet a Captain Minietto, who had been in the Nembo Division when he and Ted made their inspection. The captain told him that he and five other officers made plans to assassinate Ted when he came to review the Division, but that they were so impressed by Ted's manner and the fact that he was unarmed and had no armed bodyguards, that the plot was called off. All six of those officers ended up joining the Allies in the fight against the Germans.[10]

Back with the French by mid-October, Ted again went to work helping get the Corps ready for combat. He traveled to different regiments and battalions each day, observing training, advising, and assisting in any way he thought would help. At the same time, he began a relentless campaign to get out of the rut he perceived himself to be in, and get sent back to American troops. What he really wanted, though, was to get in on the upcoming cross channel invasion of France. Everyone, including the Germans, knew the invasion would be soon, they just didn't know exactly where or when. Ted contacted General Mathew Ridgeway, who, as Major Ridgeway, had been his military advisor when he was Governor General of the Philippines. Ridgeway promised to help. He also stayed in close touch with "Beetle" Smith and began writing letters to Omar Bradley, who had been transferred to England to work on the invasion. He was begging everybody he had any influence with to help get him back with American troops for the "Big Show." At first, Brad didn't even answer his letters.

The invasion of Italy took place in September, but it was not until December that the French Corps was pronounced ready for combat and put at the front near the Nazi stronghold at Cassino. Ted took right up where he left off with the 1st Division, visiting different units in the line each day, trying to cheer the men and assist them when he could. From experience he knew that the junior officers and men in the lines faced far greater dangers than he did, and they didn't enjoy the comfort of being able to go back to a cot at headquarters each night. He called the young French soldiers "the soul of France." During this early period at the front Ted and General Alphonse Juin, the Corps Commander, worked together closely and recognized that they were alike in many ways. For one thing, they both had the same philosophy of leadership, that it should be from ahead and not from the rear, in contrast to the style of many American senior officers. The famous war correspondent, Drew Middleton, wrote of Ted's manner of leadership, "He never said, 'Go!' He said 'Come!'" After the war, when he was a Field Marshall and Chief of Staff of the French Army, Alphonse Juin said, with tears in his eyes, that Ted had the admiration of the entire French Army, and "no man had more courage, stamina, and cheerfulness than Theodore Roosevelt, Jr."[11]

Kurt Show, Ted's driver, was an uplifting personality to have around, and Ted was always laughing at something he said. One time, General Sir Harold Alexander, the Allied Deputy Commanding Officer, was in the area and invited Ted to have dinner with him. Ted, for the first time in weeks, had to take a bath, change out of his dirty combat clothes, and put on his clean, pressed class A uniform. Show looked him over admiringly, and said he "looked like a general." Another time, Ted, Stevie, and Show had gotten a new pump style gasoline lantern for their quarters. Show was explaining that it was simple to operate. When Ted interrupted to say he could work it, Show retorted, "The General can use it, that proves it's simple."[12]

The French Expeditionary Corps was fighting right next to American units, so Ted had many occasions to see and talk with his fellow countrymen. One of the Americans he ran into was Sergeant Rocco (Rocky) Napoli of Oyster Bay, who Ted had given carnival tickets to when Rocky was a boy. As Ted approached, Sergeant Napoli came to attention, saluted, and told Ted his name and where he was from. Ted ignored the salute. He just started laughing and grabbed Rocky's hand. They had a nice conversation about old times in Oyster Bay. Later, the young Sergeant told his commanding officer that he should have more respect for him now that he knew who his friends were.[13]

Another time Ted ran into some Americans was when he chanced upon the headquarters of a U.S. heavy mortar company set up in a battered old house in a war-torn Italian town. The GIs gave Ted some coffee and fixed him some food when they found out he hadn't eaten anything since the day before. Ted said, "I never tasted anything as good as that coffee, bacon, and toast." As he was eating, they talked about the war, the company CO's family back in Boulder, Colorado, and a myriad of other subjects. After he left and had gotten some distance away, a flight of Luftwaffe planes came over and bombed the already ravished town. Ted later found out one of the bombs scored a direct hit on the mortar company's headquarters and killed all the men he had just been talking with.[14]

In their exchange of almost daily letters, Ted and Eleanor wrote to each other about everything: the family, Old Orchard, friends at Oyster Bay, after the war plans, how Ted huffs and puffs when he has to walk up a hill, how weary he gets from the riggers of combat, how cold it is, etc. In one letter, he said he couldn't wait to see and play with his new grandson, TR IV. In another, he told of a highway sign that particularly impressed him, it read *"Vino, Speedo, Morto."* Ted's letters were especially descriptive of the war in Italy, with such words and phrases as "dirty," "unshaven," "up and down," "mules," "wet," "stretchers," "walking wounded," "frozen feet," "heavy casualties," and "bone tired." In one letter he talked about the terrain on which they were fighting, saying:

> It is a jumble of sheer, rocky hills and mountains so steep that they seem about to tumble on you. The soldiers assault them in the face of hostile fire, often climbing hand over hand. Then there's the rain and snow on the heights. Roads either do not exist or have been destroyed. Every mile or so a bridge is blown out, and the Germans are covering the gap with fire. The infantry has to drive them from the heights before the engineers can start repair work. The time comes when you'd rather get hit than throw yourself down and have to get up.[15]

In another particularly realistic depiction of the war, Ted wrote:

From the right flank I move to the center. There I got a position from where I could look over the front from the crest of a hill. In a battle, nine times out of ten it's impossible to see anything as the country is so large and the men so few. Here this is particularly true as it's mountainous and rugged, and both sides take advantage of every bit of cover.

If one is battle-wise one senses things from small indications difficult to explain. For example I can tell by sounds a great deal of what's going on. German machine guns sound like ripping cloth—ours are slower. Mortar shell bursts are different from artillery. Various caliber bursts are distinguishable. Once I woke in the middle of the night because I'd heard in my sleep a German M.G. where it had no business to be. I went forward and found a heavy German attack was through our lines. If our M.G.s fire short business-like bursts, all is well. If they rattle wildly, it's another story.[16]

After the war was over, it was learned that some of the Jewish slave laborers that the Nazis had forced to work in munitions plants had sabotaged many of the artillery shells so that they would not explode. Not knowing the reason, Ted noticed that an inordinate number of German shells were duds. He was particularly glad that one shell that hit only a few yards from him failed to explode. Another time though, as they were driving along, a shell hit and exploded right in front of Rough Rider. Ted and Stevie were not injured, but they had to stop and fix the leaks in the radiator. They stuffed rifle-cleaning patches in holes in order to get back to their quarters.[17]

Still upset over being relieved of his job with the Big Red One, Ted wrote Eleanor that, while he hated war, if the U.S. was in one, his place was where the fighting was fiercest. After Germany was beaten, he wanted to be sent straight to the Pacific to fight rather than come home. He said that it would be too hard to come home for a short while and then have to turn around and leave. When he finally did get home, his only ambitions were to work for Doubleday, Doran, enjoy life, and never stray far from Old Orchard again.[18]

By the end of January, the French had come to greatly admire Ted for his bravery, ability, and constant appearances at the front. They consulted him on strategy and tactical matters, and considered him to be one of their own generals, rather than simply a liaison officer. One day, they invited him to attend a military awards ceremony to be held just behind the front lines. The French Army Commander, General Henri Giraud, was to decorate some of the French heroes. The men to be decorated had just come off the front lines and were still in their battle dress. Just as the ceremony began, Giraud suddenly turned to Ted and said,

"General, take your place at the right of the line." Ted, surprised, peeled off his grimy trenchcoat, handed it and his walking cane to Stevie, and in his mud-splattered combat jacket took his place as directed. Then General Giraud read the citation for the unexpected award, *Au nom de la France,* etc, tapped Ted on each shoulder with a bayonet, and made him an Officer of the French Legion of Honor. Since Ted had been awarded the Legion of Honor with the rank of Chevalier in World War I, he became the only American soldier to have received this distinction in both major world wars. [19]

Not long after the awards ceremony, Ted caught what he thought was the flu. By the last of February, he was so sick he required hospitalization. The diagnosis was pneumonia. At about the same time he was admitted to the hospital, General Omar Bradley received Ted's most recent letter begging for a job with American troops for the invasion. He said in the letter, "If you ask me I'll swim in with a 105 strapped to my back. Anything at all. Just help me get out of this rats' nest down here." This letter finally got results. Years later, in writing about his decision to bring Ted to the UK to help with the D-Day invasion, Bradley said he knew Ted was "immune to fear," "would stroll casually about under fire while troops about him scrambled for cover," and "would banter with them and urge them forward." He now decided Ted could help and notified him that he could have a job serving with a green division to steady it under fire. Bradley wrote, "You'll probably get killed on the job." As sick as he was, TRJr was electrified, he was back with his countrymen. [20]

Writing Eleanor that he was on his way, but not bothering to write General Bradley of his acceptance, Ted, with a fever of 102.5 degrees, checked himself out of the hospital. Packing his belongings was simple, for beside his clothing and bed roll, all he had were his dozens of pictures of Eleanor and the family, and the books he always carried with him, which include a volume of Shakespeare's works, a Bible and a copy of *Pilgrim's Progress.* That night, his French friends gave him a farewell dinner, during which General Juin embraced him twice and told him, "All French soldiers in the Army know and love you." The next day, he and Stevie caught a plane and flew to Algiers, the first leg of the trip to London, where he would report to Supreme Headquarters, Allied Expeditionary Force (SHAEF). That night in the hotel room, Ted was delirious and unable to eat. [21]

In Limbo Source Notes

1. Ted's letters to Eleanor, LOC c-61; Roosevelt, Mrs. T. Jr., p 450.

2. Stevie's Notes

3. Ibid.

4. LOC c-61; Obolensky p 365; Roosevelt, Mrs. T. Jr., p 445–447.

5. Obolensky p 1–325
6. Obolensky p 362.
7. Obolensky p 367
8. LOC c-61.
9. Obolensky p 372.
10. Obolensky p 367
11. TR Collection TRJ-87–44; Ted's letters to Eleanor, LOC c-61; NY Times 4/8/45.
12. Ted's letters of Eleanor of 1/12/44 & 1/13/44, LOC c-61
13. Anton Community Newspaper of 10/12/89, Sagamore Hill Archives
14. Ted's letters to Eleanor LOC c-61.
15. Ibid
16. Ibid.
17. Stevie's Notes; Ted's letters to Eleanor, LOC c-61.
18. Ted's letters to Eleanor, LOC c-61.
19. Ibid.
20. Bradley, Soldier's Story, p 332.
21. Ted's letters to Eleanor, LOC c-61; Phillippi article of 9/9/62; LOC c-56.

HIS FINEST HOUR

From Algiers, Ted and Stevie caught a military plane to Oran, where Ted spent the two-day layover in bed, then they caught a flight to Casablanca and on to the United Kingdom, arriving on February 27, 1944. When he walked into the Supreme Headquarters of the Allied Expeditionary Force in London to report to General Beetle Smith, Ted was staggering and almost out on his feet from his raging fever. Beetle, who had become Ted's good friend, was General Eisenhower's Chief of Staff, and told him that when his last letter arrived, he (Smith), Ike, and Bradley decided they needed to get him to England to help get ready for the invasion. When Ted came out of the headquarters, he had a grin on his face that went from ear to ear and he told Stevie that he had been attached to the 4th Infantry (Ivy) Division as a spare brigadier, but had been ordered to first check himself into the hospital.[1]

The hospital staff didn't consider the General to be a very good patient. He had all that energy and stamina, and he wasn't used to being confined to a building, much less a hospital room. He didn't like the orderlies and nurses hovering over him, and constantly coming at him with thermometers, needles, and medicine. After his fever broke, they couldn't keep him in bed, nor could they figure out where he was getting the cigarettes they were continually catching him with. Ted wrote of his feelings:

I haven't missed any of the shows here yet, and I don't want to be left out of any of the ones to come. I want to be right there in the first assault boat.

Honestly, I don't see why they want to keep me in a hospital. I suppose it would be alright in peacetime, but not when there is a war going on. I've tried to tell them that if I were in battle I'd be taking far greater chances and nobody would expect otherwise. Well, we're still in the war, aren't we? Why do I have to be so damned careful now?[2]

It wasn't long before he began to have visitors. One of the first to come was

Quentin, who in the fall of 1943 had been classified fit for duty and sent back to the First Infantry Division to train for D-Day. During the time Quentin and Ted served together in the Big Red One in pre-war days, he was able to spend a lot of time with his youngest son, and had perhaps developed a closer bond with Quentin than with his older sons. Quentin surprised his father by telling him that after being posted to England, he had met and fallen in love with Francis Webb, an American Red Cross girl from Kansas City who was stationed in London. They planned to be married on April 12th. Even though Quentin had been pronounced recovered by the Army doctors, when Ted saw him, he knew his son was not back physically to where he was before he was wounded. Concerned, Ted sent for his old friend from training days in Scotland, Kenneth T. Downs, who had been transferred back to the OSS. Colonel Downs immediately went to the hospital. When he first entered the room, the nurse told him that Ted was gravely ill and that he could not stay very long. Downs was somewhat shocked at how much weight his friend had lost since they had last seen each other in Sicily, but when Ted gave him a big Teddy Roosevelt smile and sneaked out a hidden cigarette, the Colonel realized Ted was not as sick as he looked. Taking on a serious look, Ted said:

> Don't pay any attention to her. Stay as long as you like. Now, Ken, apart from the pleasure of seeing you again, I asked you over today to ask a favor. The coming operation will be my last one. I won't come back from this one. No, no, don't interrupt, please, just listen to me. When I am dead, I want you to get Quentin transferred to the OSS. As you probably know, he is back with the 1st Division, but he was pretty badly hit in Tunisia and he is not strong enough, physically, to serve with an infantry division. He thinks he is, but he is not. He should not be denied the invasion, of course, but he is not strong enough for the long continued grind afterward. He is an intelligent, well-educated boy and should be of great value to the OSS.[3]

Knowing of the General's reputation for always being at the front where the fighting was fiercest and of his indifference to enemy fire, Colonel Downs had a eerie feeling that Ted's premonition of death might be right and he solemnly promised that he would take care of Quentin.[4]

Pursuant to his habit of writing Eleanor about everything, Ted wrote of seeing Quentin and of their son's marriage plans. It developed that Francis and Quentin had both written letters to their mothers telling them they had fallen in love and of their upcoming wedding, but Quentin had stuck both letters in his pocket and had forgotten to mail them. The news in Ted's letter was the first knowledge Eleanor had of her son's impending marriage. Assuming Francis' parents knew of the plans, Eleanor phoned them to get acquainted. The Webbs didn't know anything of the wedding and were upset by Eleanor's call. They thought she was telling them that their daughter was going to marry Elliott Roosevelt, FDR's son. Their anguish didn't last long, however, for Eleanor quickly straightened the matter out.[5]

At long last out of the hospital, where a few weeks seemed like a few years, Ted reported to Major General Raymond O. Barton, the CO of the 4th Infantry Division, on March 25th. Ted and Barton had never met before, although the Division Commander had the occasion in past times to meet Ted's brother, Archie. General Barton was well aware that he needed all the help he could get in taking his totally green division into combat, but at first he was apprehensive about having Ted, who he considered to be a celebrity, as a spare brigadier general attached to his unit.[6]

When General Barton found out Ted had not yet found quarters, he suggested that he share a private home he and six other 4th Division officers had rented in the nearby town of Tiverton. Ted took his CO up on the offer and he moved in with what turned out to be the most interesting and congenial group he had been with since those long ago days at Harvard. General Barton's aide, Captain Lewis Fiset, was one of the officers quartered in the home. Fiset remembers well the very busy days during the two months they lived there with Ted. If there were no conferences or night problems, the group would get together at night and sit around drinking Scotch and discussing and arguing over many interesting subjects. One time, they were in an argument over the Jewish Passover and needed a Bible to settle the question. Ted was the only one in the group that had one handy; he got it and the argument was settled.

Fiset remembers Roosevelt as being "a kind and charming man and easy to get acquainted with." One particular thing that stuck in the Captain's mind about Ted was the fact that he was a small man with very small feet. His feet were so small that the Army was not able to fit him with combat boots; he had to get Eleanor to send him a pair from Abercrombie & Fitch. During this period, if he could get away a couple of hours early, Ted liked nothing better than to go trout fishing in one of the nearby streams. One time he caught a sixteen-inch trout.[7]

The general plan for the invasion was code named Overlord, and called for the Allies to invade the Normandy coast of France on June 5th. Five separate beaches would be simultaneously assaulted by ground troops transported to shore by landing craft of various sizes and types. Each of the five beaches on which the initial landings were to be made was given a different code name: Omaha, Juno, Gold, Sword, and Utah. Omaha Beach would be assaulted by the Big Red One and the U.S. 29th Infantry Division. British, Canadian, and French units would land on Gold, Juno and Sword Beaches.

Utah Beach was on the west flank of the five beaches. The plan called for the U.S. 82nd and 101st Airborne Divisions to be dropped a few miles inland from Utah Beach before dawn on June 5th. The actual beach area was to be assaulted from the sea immediately after daybreak by the U.S. 4th Infantry Division. The initial waves of infantry would touch shore at low tide so that the beach obstacles that had been placed by the Germans would be exposed for destruction by the special demolition teams that would accompany the infantry. All the beaches would receive a bombardment from the air and from naval warships before the ground assault units were to land. The overall invasion scheme was the most elaborate and complicated such plan ever devised.

Only a day or two after he was settled in his new quarters, Ted went on one of the several amphibious training exercises the 4th Division participated in at Slapton Sands, on the Devon coast. To make the exercise as realistic as possible, the Division combat loaded onto troop ships, sailed to the Slapton Sands coastal area, then climbed into Higgins Boats, and assaulted the beaches. Opposition was provided by an entrenched aggressor force. The weather was windy and cold. When he held up to the rigors of this three-day maneuver, Ted felt he was over his illness. The Division then went back to the Tiverton area, where the normal training schedule was resumed. General Barton gave Ted a free hand, allowing him to go to a different 4th Division unit each day to observe training and offer what advice and good cheer he could, just like he had done with the Big Red One and the Free French. Very quickly, Ted learned the names of most of the officers and a good many of the enlisted men in the Division. He told Captain Fiset that he developed his almost uncanny ability to remember names during the time his father was in the White House.[8]

Russell "Red" Reeder, with orders to report to General Barton and assume command of the 4th Division's 12th Infantry Regiment, arrived at Division HQ on April 1st, and for the first time met General Roosevelt. Colonel Reeder was immediately impressed with Ted's gregarious and garrulous personality. He said Ted gave him a big smile and grabbed his hand, saying all in one breath, "Well, Red Reeder, where have you been? For a week we've been looking for you. I read *Fighting on Guadalcanal* (Reeder had recently been transferred from Guadalcanal. The book was a publication of the U.S. Army). What a job! Sit down and relax, Tell me about your trip over. What's going on in the States?" When the conversation turned to President Teddy Roosevelt, Ted replied, "Father was quite a man," but Reeder thought he could detect a tone of contention in his voice. Red said that it didn't take him long to realize that Ted loved everybody and everybody loved the little general.[9]

Ted was best man at his son's wedding at the Church of St. Peter and St. Paul in Blandford, England. He wrote Eleanor all about the ceremony and the wedding breakfast, saying, "Thank God I was here at this time, but I miss you something awful." Quentin got a five-day honeymoon leave, which he and his bride spent at a seaside resort. A gossip column in a London newspaper ran an item on the wedding and reported that Ted was attached to the 4th Division and served as his son's best man. This was local news and not subject to the censorship order. The *New York Times* picked up the story and reported that Ted was under a strict censorship order and for that reason, news accounts of his combat exploits were not appearing in the newspapers.[10]

As April drew to a close, the entire U.S. VII Corps (made up of several divisions, including the 4th Inf. Div., and the 101st and 82nd Airborne Divs.) held a final, full-scale, dress rehearsal of the Utah segment of the invasion. This most important practice landing was code named "Exercise Tiger," and was again at Slapton Sands. The brass in charge of training selected that particular beach area for training purposes because of its similarity to the Normandy coastline. The civilian population in the vicinity of Slapton Sands had been forced to evacuate for security and safety reasons. The Troops and equipment were combat loaded and there was an airborne assault, shore bombardment and a storming of the beach, as near the real thing as they could make it. This time, however, a flotilla of German E-Boats slipped between some of the troop transports and the shore one night, and sank two fully loaded LSTs. Losses were high, mostly from drowning, and many men were missing. A final official tally indicated 749 U.S. servicemen (mostly army engineer and quartermaster troops) died and about twice that many were injured. Many of those young Americans died because they had not been given instructions on how to use a new type of life preserver that wrapped around the waist, rather than the old style where the arms are slipped through the holes and the preserver is tied around the chest like a vest. There was an instant panic among the top brass and the Allied intelligence community because a few of the officers that were missing were bigots, which meant they had already been briefed on some of the details of the invasion. There was a fear that the German E-boats might have captured one or more of the unaccounted for officers. Within a few days, though, the worried brass could relax, because the bodies of all the missing bigoted officers were recovered from the sea.

At the time of Exercise Tiger, the Allied chain of command went down from Supreme Commander Eisenhower to British General Montgomery (CO of all Land Forces), to Omar Bradley (Commander of the U.S. First Army, who had charge of both the U.S. V Corps at Omaha Beach and the U.S. VII Corps at Utah Beach). Major General Joseph Lawton Collins, the CO of the VII Corps, served directly under Bradley. Admiral Don Moon was in charge of the naval forces scheduled for Utah Beach. A complete news blackout was imposed on the Slapton Sands training disaster and all the servicemen with any knowledge of the tragedy were sworn to secrecy, under threat of court martial. There was no official investigation ordered or conducted.

It is understandable why the event was initially hidden from the public. It occurred only six weeks prior to D-Day and there was concern that the Nazis might garner valuable intelligence information from any pre-invasion announcement of the sinkings and corresponding loss of life. In the 1980s rumors began to spread that there had been an official "cover up" of the disaster that occurred during Exercise Tiger and that there had been many more than the reported 749 deaths. However, any cover-up has been disputed in several books and articles written in the 1980s and '90s. One writer claims that SHAEF made an official announcement about the catastrophe in July of 1944, but, if that is so, it apparently escaped public notice. One current rumor is that the families of the dead American boys were notified that their loved ones were missing in action, but were never told the truth. Several years after the War, General Omar Bradley wrote that General Collins misled him with respect to the number of casualties at Tiger and that for several years he thought personnel losses were minimal. While an in-depth study of the Slapton Sands incident is beyond the scope of this book, there are a number of known instances where the U.S. military has misled the public in the name of national security. A somewhat similar occurrence took place at the West Lock area at Pearl Harbor in May of 1944, when several LSTs loaded with ammunition blew up and sank, killing over 160 sailors. Like Slapton Sands, there was a complete news blackout, but, unlike Slapton Sands, an official investigation was ordered. No cause for the West Lock event was ever proved. It was apparently either sabotage or a careless accident. In any event, the Navy finally declassified the reports and other documents in the 1960s and the public became aware of what happened. There is no surviving record of what knowledge General Roosevelt had with respect to the Exercise Tiger debacle, but he obviously had nothing to do with the planning or cover-up because that was done on a higher level of command. Assuming General Bradley's innocence, as he proclaimed, it's impossible to believe Army Group Commander Montgomery and/or Supreme Commander Eisenhower had more knowledge of the disaster than Bradley, who was their immediate subordinate. How did the Krauts learn of the operation in time to have their E-Boats there at the right time and place. This leads to the question of why General Collins and Admiral Moon didn't find the tragic loss of 749, or more, of their young men important enough to conduct, or at least recommend, an investigation.[11]

By now Ted was very comfortable with his place in the 4th Division, and used the word "splendid" to describe his opinion of its fighting qualities. General Barton had come to like Ted, and Ted certainly thought a lot of his CO. He wrote Eleanor that everyone called Barton "Tubby," and that he was a hardworking, knowledgeable man and so "square you wouldn't believe it." General Barton and Terry Allen had been close friends and classmates at West Point, and Terry had put in a good word for Ted with his new CO. The other officers and men in the Division also appreciated what the new brigadier general brought to the unit. Regimental Commander Red Reeder said Ted was "the first general I ever liked to see coming, and begged to come back soon."[12]

As the month of May arrived and training continued, Ted was out in the field with the men everyday. He was cheerful and helpful; in fact, one private said, "He exudes cheer." Ted often said that morale was his business and some of the GIs called him the Division Morale Officer. In many ways, the general was more of an enlisted man than an officer anyway. Despite his fifty-six years, he went out with them on their full field pack marches and maneuvers, and he slogged along in the mud and rain, just like they did. He was probably the only general in the European Theater of Operations (ETO) that knew how heavy a soldier's pack could get. Most of the big brass had no combat experience on the level of the dog face soldier, and didn't realize how burdening it was to carry a pack loaded with unnecessary equipment. Ted told Stevie one day that if he had his way the rifleman would carry into combat only his rifle, ammo, water, and rations. Another thing that the ordinary GI admired Ted for was the fact that he certainly didn't look like a general. Some of them thought he looked like Knute Rockne of Notre Dame. Marvin Pike of the 4th Division said Ted was only about 5'6," 140 lbs., and sloppy in his dress. "He didn't dress neat like most generals did, but he was a real fine guy with a lot of humor and he just mixed with the rest of the GIs and everybody liked him." Joel Thomason, the CO of the 29th Field Artillery Battalion, said Ted "was the worst looking soldier I ever saw."[13] In describing his boss, Stevie wrote:

> The old man was the most disreputable looking general I ever saw. He was dressed in ancient combat clothes and always covered with dust or mud, depending on the weather. He went into battle armed with nothing but a .45, his walking stick, his eyeglasses and an old briefcase full of maps. Half the time he forgot his helmet, which he hated anyway, and wore an old woolen cap. Fortunately he made a lot of noise—his normal speaking voice was a bellow which could be heard across a field—and everybody in combat knew him by sight anyway. Otherwise he would frequently have been mistaken, if you were too far away to see the star, for the most beat-up GI in the place.[14]

Perhaps it was because he was the son of a former President, or perhaps it was because of his unique personality, but for whatever reason, it is amazing how many World War II veterans, particularly those of the 1st and 4th Divisions, and the 70th Tank Battalion remember Ted Roosevelt and have anecdotes about him. They knew he was just like they were. Captain Francis (Frank) Glaze, Jr., CO of Headquarters Company, 8th Infantry Regiment, 4th Infantry Division, recalls the time his regiment was put in formation around an outdoor boxing ring; no one knew why. All of a sudden several staff cars wheeled up and stopped, and out stepped Generals Eisenhower, Montgomery, Bradley, Patton, Barton, Ted Roosevelt, Air Marshall Sir Arthur Tedder, and Prime Minister Winston Churchill. That's when the GIs were told that the 4th Division would be one of the assault divisions on D-Day and that Colonel James Van Fleet's 8th Infantry Regiment of the 4th would be the first to land on Utah Beach. It wasn't surprising that the 8th Infantry was picked to spearhead that segment of the invasion, for among its former commanders were Tubby Barton and none other than Army Chief of Staff, General George C. Marshall. Captain Glaze said they first took being picked to make the initial assault on Utah as an honor, but after thinking about it, said "Oh, Shit!" Years later, when he was writing of his war time experiences for the book *WarStories: Utah Beach to Pleiku,* Frank Glaze began his tale, not by writing, "The time I saw Winston Churchill," or "Ike", or "Monty," or "All the big brass," but by writing, "The first time I saw Ted Roosevelt."[15]

On May 13th, Ted and nineteen other British and American officers were called to London as honored guests of General Eisenhower to attend a luncheon to celebrate the anniversary of the fall of Tunis. Ike said he brought them together because he thought they would enjoy getting together before they took off on the next endeavor of the great adventure. Ted had a wonderful time, laughing, and socializing, and being with some old friends he hadn't seen for a while. "Beetle" Smith invited him to spend the night, and he accepted. The next day, he was able to have lunch with Quentin and Francis. On the 15th, Ted attended the famous high-level briefing given by Field Marshall Bernard Montgomery at his headquarters at St. Paul's School. General Eisenhower made some remarks, as did the King of England. Prime Minister Winston Churchill reminded everyone that bravery, ingenuity and persistence are of more importance than the quantity and quality of equipment. It was confirmed that D-Day was scheduled for June 5th.[16]

A couple of weeks before D-Day, General Omar Bradley, who was by now the CO of the American First Army with the responsibility of both Utah and Omaha Beaches, called a conference of nearly a thousand of the American officers who would be involved in the invasion. Bradley wanted to discuss the plan and give them some idea of the overall picture. As the meeting got underway, Bradley rose to the rostrum for some opening remarks. His first comment was that the men sitting out there would have grandstand seats to the greatest show on earth. Before he could continue, the Army Commander was interrupted by Ted's resonating whisper of, "Hell, goddamn! We won't be in the grandstand, we'll be on the playing field." All those around, including Brad, got a good chuckle.[17]

As soon as Ted found out that the Ivy Division would be the initial assault unit on Utah Beach, he made it a point to meet privately with General Barton. He asked the Division CO for permission to land in the first wave of troops. Barton immediately denied his request. After waiting a few days, Ted again talked to the Division CO, but he was turned down a second time. (No doubt General Barton felt the same as Italian Colonel Bruno on Sardinia, he didn't want a Roosevelt killed on his watch.) After what Generals Bradley and Smith had told him when he first reported to General Eisenhower's headquarters in late February, Ted felt sure his request would be granted on a higher level, but he didn't want to go over Tubby Barton's head. So on May 26th, he wrote the following letter:

To; Major General R. O. Barton, CG 4th Inf. Div.
Since your informal refusal of my request to go with the assault companies I have given much thought to the question and decided to request reconsideration because of the following facts:
1. The force and skill with which the first elements hit the beach and proceed may determine the ultimate success of the operation.
2. The rapid advance inland of the assault companies is vital to our effort as the removal of underwater obstacles cannot be accomplished unless the beach is free from small arms fire.
3. With troops engaged for the first time the behavior pattern of all is apt to be set by those first engaged.
4. Considered, accurate information of the existing situation should be available for each succeeding element as it lands.
5. You should have when you get ashore an overall picture in which you can place confidence.
6. I believe I can contribute materially on all of the above by going with the assault companies. Furthermore, I know personally both officers and men of these advance units and believe that it will steady them to know I am with them.
THEODORE ROOSEVELT
Brigadier General, U.S.A.[18]

When Ted handed the letter to General Barton, he said, "I'd rather go on and do this invasion than anything else in the world." Mustering all his diplomacy, he told his CO that he would take the matter all the way up to Ike if necessary. The Division Commander carefully read the letter and realized that every point made was valid. He mulled things over in his mind for a minute and then reluctantly agreed to let him go in with the first wave as requested. This would be Ted's third first wave landing of the war, fourth if Sardinia is counted. Tubby Barton later confessed that he thought Ted would never live through the D-Day landings.[19]

After giving in to Ted's insistence, General Barton told Colonel James Van Fleet, the Commander of the 8th Infantry Regiment (the unit selected to make the initial assault) to place Ted on one of the first wave landing craft. Van Fleet met with Captain Robert C. Crisson, the CO of Company C, 8th Inf. Reg. (one of the first wave companies) and asked him if Ted could go in on one of his boats. Crisson emphatically said no; he didn't have anything against Roosevelt, but he was a new company commander and didn't want to be interfered with. He told Van Fleet that if he didn't have confidence in him, he should give the company to someone else. After being rebuffed by Crisson, the Regimental Commander prevailed upon Captain Howard Lees, the CO of E Company, to allow Ted to go in on one of his boats.[20]

Toward the latter part of May, the Ivy Division was loaded on trucks and began moving from the training camp area to one of the many Tent Cities (Called by some, Sausages) that had been set up close to the English Channel coast. As the truck convoys rolled over the British countryside and through the towns and villages, the people lined the streets and roads. A few waved, a few cried, but most just silently watched. After having lived through the Nazi blitz and abuse for four years, these people, stoic by nature, had an inner feeling that this was it; the long awaited invasion was at hand. They knew that many of those young American boys passing by in the trucks would never return. It was true that the English people complained that the GIs were "overpaid, oversexed, and over here," but they had lived among those brash, energetic Colonists for a long time now and were attached to them. They appreciated what they were there for. It was an emotional time in British history. One Ivy Division soldier described the ride to the Tent City as "like a death march."[21]

Security was tight in all the Tent Cities. A heavy barbed wire fence completely encircled the areas, and MPs were everywhere. There the troops were issued clothing specially treated to prevent penetration by poison gas, in case Hitler decided to use gas as a weapon. French invasion money was distributed. No telephone calls to the outside were permitted. During the several days spent in these restricted compounds, the men cleaned their weapons and were given lectures on their various missions and objectives. Life-like models of Utah Beach and the other invasion beaches were used as teaching aids. Many of the men wrote if-I-don't-make-it letters home to loved ones. Ted wrote "Bunny"

We've had a grand life, and I hope there will be more. Should it change *****
at least we can say that in our years together we've packed enough for ten
ordinary lives. We've known joy and sorrow, triumph and disaster, all that goes
to fill the pattern of human existence.
Much much love,
Ted[22]

Late one night, as May came to a close, Captain George Mabry, the operations officer for one of the assault battalions, was burning the midnight oil in his office, pondering over the invasion plans for his unit, when in walked General Roosevelt who asked, "What the hell are you up to, George?" When Mabry said he was thinking about how he could improve the plans for his battalion, Ted said, "Whatever you plan, the boys are just going right in there and throw in all they've got. So what do you want with all this paper?" Mabry, who would go on to win the Congressional Medal of Honor and years later retire from the Army as a Lieutenant General, instantly felt better. He put his paperwork aside and went to bed.[23]

On June 3rd, when he boarded a tender for shuttle to the troopship, USS Bayfield, anchored in the bay at Torquay, Ted felt that the 4th Infantry Division was as ready as they could make it for D-Day in Normandy, still scheduled for June 5th. He assessed the officers and men to be confident, alert and tough; he knew they would give a good account of themselves. Since the Bayfield was the same ship that had transported Stevie and him for the Sicilian invasion, Ted was very familiar with it. They were even assigned to the same cabin they had nearly a year earlier. Ted jokingly told some of the crew that he wanted them to put a fresh coat of paint in his little shower before the next invasion. He then sat down at the small desk and wrote Eleanor a twenty-four page letter, stating in part:

> We are starting on the great venture of this war and by the time you get this letter, for better or for worse, it will be history.
>
> We are attacking in daylight the most heavily fortified shore in history, a shore held by excellent troops. We are throwing against it excellent troops, well armed and backed by superb air and good naval support.
>
> We are on our transports, buttoned up. Our next stop Europe. The Germans know we are coming for the harbors of southern England have been crowded with our shipping and the roads choked with our convoys.

In part of the letter Ted is philosophical and nostalgic, and he speaks of their wedding and how much has happened to them over the years. It concludes, "Much, Much Love. I pray that we may be together again, Ted"[24]

As soon as he got settled in his cabin, Ted went out on deck to talk with the men and ease some of their tension. It was more of what he termed as "banal talk," but it helped. As one particularly small soldier was lugging a heavy mortar base plate up the gangplank, George Mabry heard Ted boom, "The army hasn't changed in a hundred years, always the little guy gets the biggest load." Hearing this, the little infantryman grinned from ear to ear, straightened his shoulders, and somehow his burden was a little lighter. As Sergeant John Beck of the 87th

Chemical Mortar Battalion was boarding the ship, a man with a star on his shoulder asked him, "How are you, son?" He later found out it was General Roosevelt. Sergeant Beck never forgot that seemingly minor incident.[25]

Having fought alongside of the 70th Tank Battalion in Sicily, Ted was familiar with the fighting qualities of the unit, and knew it was a crack outfit. On one of the training exercises at Slapton Sands, Ted learned that the 70th was in England training for the invasion. He wasted no time in making a recommendation to the top brass that it be attached to the 4th Infantry Division. Ted's advice was followed and the combat experienced 70th Tank Battalion was assigned to the inexperienced Ivy Division to assist in the D-Day landing. On board the Bayfield, Ted recognized the distinctive 70th Tank Battalion shoulder patch on a lieutenant and he sent Stevie to get young officer. When the lieutenant reported, Ted asked him why he was on the Bayfield rather than on the ship that had been assigned to his battalion. The tanker, Franklin Anderson, explained that he had been temporarily assigned to the 4th Division combat engineers, then on the Bayfield. With that, Ted sent for another cot to be set up in his cabin and had Lieutenant Anderson moved in with Stevie and him for the next two nights.

About the same time Lieutenant Anderson was moving into Ted's quarters, General Eisenhower delayed the invasion for twenty-four hours because of stormy weather over the English Channel. The 4th Division had loaded on its assigned troop ships at Dartmouth, Exmouth, and Torquay and by the time Ike delayed D-Day until the 6th, the Division was too far out at sea to return to port. They had to wait out the storm on board. The ships circled out in the English Channel off of the Isle of Wight. Warships surrounded them for protection; they didn't want another Exercise Tiger on their hands. The men were miserable.[26]

At various times on the 3rd, 4th, and 5th, Ted was out on deck talking to the men to reassure them and alleviate some of their fears. Louis Putnoky remembers him being on the fantail of the Bayfield as she plowed her way over the rough channel toward the Normandy Coast. It was nothing like a speech, more like just shooting the bull, Putnoky said. Ted and the men talked about various things, but when the subject of combat came up, he talked to them like a father and told them to do the best they could and everything would be alright.[27] Marvin Pike remembers that at about 7:00 p.m. on the 5th, a stand by order came over the ship's PA system, then Ted came on and said:

Tomorrow morning at 6:30, we land on Utah Beach. I'll be there with you. I'm going in on Captain Lees' boat. I'll be in the first wave. Just wanted to wish you guys good hunting.[28]

After Ted's short remark, the following order of the day from Supreme Commander Eisenhower was read:

Soldiers, Sailors, and Airmen of the Allied Expeditionary Forces: You are about to embark on the Great Crusade, toward which we have striven these many months. The eyes of the world are upon you. The hopes and fears of liberty-loving people everywhere march with you. In company with our brave Allies and brothers-in-arms on other fronts you will bring about the destruction of the German war machine, the elimination of Nazi tyranny over the oppressed peoples of Europe, and security for ourselves in a free world. ******

Then a recorded speech by President Franklin Roosevelt was played, the chaplains held a service, and a meal was served. After this, Ted and Stevie went back to their cabin to rest and, hopefully, get a short nap before being called on deck to get into their assigned landing craft. Ted promised his loyal aide that he would get him promoted to captain "if we make it." When Stevie reminded him that the Army Table of Organization called for him to hold the rank of only a lieutenant, his boss replied, "Oh, the hell with the TO. I'll fix it. Is that a bargain?" Naturally Stevie said yes. Shortly after D-Day Lieutenant Stevenson became Captain Stevenson.[29]

Not long after midnight, the Bayfield and the 874 other naval vessels assigned to the Utah segment of the Normandy invasion reached the proper location and dropped anchor. They were some fourteen miles off the Normandy shore. Soon the call went out for the first wave troops to prepare to come up on deck and man their assigned Higgins boats, technically called LCVPs. Getting his personal equipment together was easy for Ted. All he carried with him was his .45 automatic with only one clip of ammo, shoulder holster, a first aid pouch, a bar of chocolate, the two small books he took on every invasion, his walking cane, and a supply of cigarettes which he put into a waterproof receptacle normally used for an entirely different purpose. For the most important invasion in the history of the world, he wore the same beat-up coveralls he fought the Sicilian campaign in, a pair of canvas leggings, an old combat jacket, and his woolen cap rather than his hated steel helmet. George Mabry happened to walk by and thought the General sounded a little nervous when he heard him ask his aide, "Where in hell is my life belt?" Stevie replied that he had given him three already. "Well give me another, I've lost the whole damned lot." Stevie left and in a couple of minutes was back with another one. Now, as Ted put it, he was ready to march to the sound of the guns.[30]

At 0200, the first wave troops were called up on deck to load into their landing craft. Looking toward shore, they could see flares and tracer fire in the sky, and hear the drone of planes and the bursting of shells fired by antiaircraft artillery in the distance. They all knew the gunfire was directed at the paratroopers of the 82nd and 101st Airborne Divisions, at that minute being dropped into Normandy. D-Day, the most important day in the twentieth century, had begun. The events of that day would be forever etched into the minds of all the men and women who were there, be they American, English, Canadian, French, Polish, Russian, Asian or German.

Most of the Higgins boats were already in the water alongside the Bayfield, and the men would climb down the heavy rope nets thrown over the side of the ship and jump down into their specified craft. Ted's particular assigned craft was on the deck of the Bayfield and was to be rail loaded. This required the men to climb a ladder up the side of the Higgins boat and then jump the approximately five feet down to the landing craft's deck. When Ted reached the top of the side and was preparing to jump in, a kind hearted GI already in the boat stuck his hand up to assist the General. Insulted at the offer of help, Ted snapped, "Get the hell out of my way. I can jump in there by myself. You know I can take it as well as any of you." None of the thirty scared, young infantrymen in the boat could suppress a smile. [31]

When all the first wave boats were loaded and in the water, they started circling while the boats of the two following waves were loaded. At exactly 0330, the circle of first wave boats straightened out into a horizontal line and headed toward shore. No one knew that only one of the four guide boats assigned to make sure the first wave landed at the right place was actually on station. One had hit a mine and sunk, one had fouled its prop, and one had been diverted to another mission. As the LCVPs plowed toward shore, Ernest Hemingway, one of the reporters with the Utah Beach convoy, described the crowded, uncomfortable, little landing craft as being shaped like coffins. [32]

The plan called for intensive bombing of the beach area by flights of medium bombers, followed by a shore bombardment by naval warships, including the USS Nevada, that had been re-floated and refitted after having been grounded during the Pearl Harbor attack. Lastly, there would be a rocket concentration fired at the beach by special rocket boats. Then, after all this beach preparation, the first wave of troops would land. From the shoreline, sandy Utah Beach gently sloped upward for about three hundred yards to a four-foot to six-foot high seawall. Inland from the seawall were some low sand dunes for about one hundred yards and then there was a low bottomland farming area extending inland for about two miles. A series of drainage ditches ran through these lowlands. The Germans had flooded much of the bottoms so that it was, in effect, an area of murky, shallow, man-made swamps of about four feet in depth, except there was a sudden drop-off to about eight feet where the drainage ditches were located. History has christened these flooded lands as the "inundated area." Every mile or so along Utah Beach, higher causeways (called exits) extended inland from the beach, through the inundated area, to the higher ground about two or three miles from the coast. These causeways were of sufficient width and compaction for use by armor and other military vehicles. The Germans defended the Utah Beach area with randomly placed pillboxes and trenches. Tank turrets mounted on concrete structures were placed among the sand dunes near the shoreline. These formidable emplacements were manned by infantry with rifles and machineguns. The Germans had laid mines, driven large steel stakes into the sand, and placed hedgehogs and Belgian Gates at various locations along the beach. The Kraut medium and heavy artillery batteries were located some two to five miles inland from the coast.

Ted wrote of the run in to the beach:

At the signal we climbed into our craft which was still on the davits. The ropes whined through the pulleys, we landed on the water and cast off. It was rough and spray burst over us, soaking us to the skin and leaving us shivering with cold. In the darkness the boats circled in their rendezvous stations, cock swain calling to cock swain to gather the different waves and sort them out. Then began our long run to the beach—the transport area was some fourteen miles off the coast.

For some three hours we jockeyed and pushed toward shore and then the naval bombardment began. In the dusk flashes came from the big ships as the great guns were fired. Gradually it became brighter and I could make out on all sides the craft of the flotilla—most were our small landing launches with the assault troops. There were also destroyers on our flanks, rocket ships with racks for their rockets and many smaller craft—L.C.S.s—land craft support ships with m.g.s to run close to the shore and fire.

Now we began to make out the low line of the shore—revealed by the flash of the explosions as the naval shells landed—and now German shells began landing among us, sending up towers of spray.

Suddenly we heard the drone of planes, and silhouetted against the colored clouds of dawn, formations of planes swept by and passed toward shore. Flight after flight dropped its bombs on the German emplacements. There'd be a ripple of thunder, blazes of light, clouds of dust, and the planes would pass us again on their way home. One fell by me, flaming like a meteor. We passed a capsized craft, some men clinging to it, others bobbing in the waves.

The little boats were now going full speed, slapping the waves with their blunt prows. As we peered over the gunwale the shore seemed nearer, but veiled as it was in the smoke and dust of the bombardment, it was hard to make it out.[33]

Rough seas caused the landing boats to violently pitch and roll. A frigidly cold ocean spray drenched the crowded young soldiers as the open little craft struggled toward shore. Many of the men got seasick. The smell of the diesel oil from the motors, combined with the putrid odors of the vomit, added to the misery and terror of the green assault troops. General Eisenhower later said that the Higgins Boat greatly contributed to the U.S. winning the war, but on that cold, rough sea, packed with thirty men and their equipment, a Higgins Boat was a terrible place to be, especially if you're young, green, and scared. One miserable, seasick 4th Division soldier said, "That son-of-a-bitch Higgins hasn't got nothing to be proud about inventing this boat."[34]

Ted was aboard one of the twenty Higgins Boats making up the first wave. In actuality, his boat was the first to grind to a halt on a sand bar and lower its ramp. Ted was the first to jump off into the cold, four-foot deep water and, wearing his beloved old wool cap rather than his helmet, he began to wade the one hundred or so yards to shore. With this, Ted became the only general to land in the first wave and, at fifty-six, he was the oldest soldier to land on D-Day. Since Quentin landed with the First Infantry Division on Omaha Beach at H Hour plus sixty minutes, Ted and Quentin became the only father/son team in American Army uniforms to set foot on the soil of France on D-Day.

As soon as he made it to shore and looked around, Ted realized something was wrong. He didn't see any of the landmarks he was supposed to see. The loss of three out of the four control boats, along with the smoke from the naval and air bombardments, and a strong current had caused the first wave to land in the wrong place. Ted described his landing:

Suddenly the beach appeared before us—a long stretch of sand studded with wire and obstacles. Then with a crunch we grounded, the ramp lowered and we jumped into water waist-deep and started for the shore. We splashed and floundered through some hundred yards of water while German salvos fell. Men dropped, some silent, some screaming. Up the four hundred yards of beach we ran—Grandfather puffed a bit—then we reached the seawall. ******.

The moment I arrived at the beach I knew something was wrong, for there was a house by the seawall where none should have been were we in the right place. It was imperative that I should find out where we were in order to set the maneuver. I scrambled up on the dunes and was lucky in finding a windmill which I recognized. We'd been put ashore a mile too far to the south. That meant I had to hotfoot it from left to right and back again setting the various COs straight and changing task.[35]

The initial mission of the two first wave battalions was to subdue the beach defenses and then proceed across the inundated area on a particular two of the causeways that ran inland from Utah Beach. When the inundated area was cleared, they were then to attack some specific targets. All the while they would be joining up with the 82nd and 101st paratroopers that had been dropped in several hours before. Where the first wave actually landed there was only one causeway, and it was not either of the causeways they were supposed to land near. The first wave should have landed a mile to the north, and the following waves would soon be coming in. Ted was by far the highest-ranking officer on the beach, everybody there would look to him. His problem was what to do. While there was some German artillery and small arms fire, the opposition was not as heavy as had been expected, certainly nothing like the murderous fire that was being experienced twenty miles away at the other American beach, Bloody Omaha. Should Ted order the six hundred men making up the first wave to fight their way up the beach a mile to where they should have landed, or should he have them eliminate the beach defenses where they were and then assign them new tasks going inland? If he elected to have the men go inland from where they were, the Division would initially have access to only one causeway, and this might create a terrible bottleneck for the thousands of troops and vehicles soon to land in the following waves. Or should the first wave be written off and the following waves directed a mile north to the planned location? Jack Tallant, who was an aid man with Company E, 2nd Battalion, 8th Inf. Regiment, came in on Ted's boat and was right with him when they got to shore, said,

> I went in on the same boat that Roosevelt did. Our boat was the first one to land on Utah Beach. When the ramp went down we waded to shore and then went on inland several hundred feet and took cover behind a wall that ran along the beach. We were under small arms fire and also some artillery shelling at the time. General Roosevelt was right up there looking at his map. Within 1 or 2 minutes after we reached the wall, I heard Roosevelt say, "We're not where we are supposed to be, we should be over there (pointing down the beach). Well it's too late to do anything about it now, over the wall, over the wall." The troops then started climbing over the seawall and moving inland. About that time I got busy treating a soldier who had been shot, so I remained there behind the wall for about 15 minutes before I moved on inland also. The wounded man died. He was a friend of mine.[36]

Ted's extensive combat experience, as well as the experience of having landed at the wrong location during a practice landing in North Africa a year earlier, paid off. He realized that it was vital to seize other causeways and link up with the 82nd and 101st paratroopers. He made his decision, he would have the first wave troops eliminate the beach defenses in the immediate area, and then order them to go inland before proceeding to the north to secure additional causeways. This is when he uttered the famous phrase, "We'll start the war from here." Millions of people heard it repeated by Henry Fonda in the movie *The Longest Day*. These words instantly told the troops what to do. Over the course of the next three hours Ted repeated the phrase to a number of men on the beach, including Pfc Joseph Blaylock, Sgt. Marvin Pike, and Captain Francis Glaze. Probably every one of the men in the first wave were aware of the presence of the general, even if they did not personally talk to him. Ted ordered colorful beach markers put out as signals for the following boats to come in. When Colonel Eugene Caffey of the engineers landed in the third wave, Ted told him they would "start the war from here," and then had him radio the Navy to keep sending the landing craft to where the first wave had come ashore.[37]

Having made sure the rest of the 4th Division would follow behind the first wave, Ted, still under fire, remained exposed on the beach for the next three to four hours, directing the follow-up troops inland. Harper Coleman, who came in a little before 0700, said, "General Theodore Roosevelt was standing there waving his cane and giving out instructions as only he could do. If we were afraid of the enemy, we were more afraid of him and could not have stopped on the beach had we wanted to." Captain John Ahern, CO of Company C, 70th Tank Bn. drove his tank ashore shortly after H hour and reported to Ted on the beach. The general ordered Ahern to take his company of fourteen tanks and secure the lateral parts of the beach. After sending half his tanks north along the beach, Ahern took the seven remaining tanks and proceeded to the south.[38]

Just as he reached the shoreline, Sergeant Harry Brown saw a mortar shell explode near Ted throwing sand on him. Acting annoyed, Ted simply brushed himself off. Another 4th Division rifleman, entering combat for the first time, laughed when he saw Ted do a little dance step there on the Utah shore. That laugh gave the rookie infantryman the energy and courage to keep moving forward. About 1030 hours, when Robert Kaufman and Goldie Goldstein landed amidst intense German artillery fire, there was Ted walking on the beach, waving his walking stick and urging the troops to get across the beach and move inland. Some of the hundreds of others on Utah Beach that morning who the General hurried to get inland included Joseph Owens, Donald Ellis, Morris Austein, Tom Primm, Dennis Gray, George Mayberry, Bill Davis, and Charles Mastro.[39]

By late morning when General Barton got to the shore, the beach defenses had been silenced, but the area was still under German artillery fire. A second causeway through the inundated area had been opened. Both Tubby and Ted knew the importance of building up the forces and getting the troops and armor inland.

When the traffic began to back up, the two Generals acted like traffic cops and sent the vehicles and armor north to a newly opened causeway. Red Reeder, the Commander of the 12th Infantry Regiment, came ashore about mid-day. He met Ted on top of the sand dunes and was told, "Red, the causeways leading inland are all clogged up. Look at it! A procession of jeeps and not a wheel turning. Something's wrong." Colonel Reeder said, "Roosevelt looked tired and the cane he leaned on heightened the impression." After Ted's remark, Reeder signaled his men to ignore the causeways and make their way inland by wading across the flooded area.[40]

Shortly after running into Col. Reeder, Ted and Stevie went inland on the jammed up causeway to find out what the trouble was. Before going far, they discovered the tank leading the column had come to a deep bomb crater and could go no further. The combat-inexperienced troops were just standing around not knowing what to do. Taking one look at the situation, Ted ordered the men to get axes off the tank and other vehicles, and then cut down some nearby trees and throw them in the hole. When this makeshift bridge was completed, the column began to move forward again. Ted had Stevie get the name of the officer in charge, telling him, "We've got to get rid of him. That damn fool might have let every one of these men get killed."[41]

Describing what he did to his wife, Ted wrote:

As the succeeding waves landed I pushed them inland if they halted, and redirected them when they started wrong. Shells continually burst around us but all I got was a slight scratch on one hand. The day gradually wore on. More and more landed. Our ships shifted their bombardments to the flanks.

Then General Barton arrived and we set up our C.P. in earnest. By this time the immediate beach was cleared of Germans and the soldiers began to push their way inland over a flooded area about two miles broad. This had been inundated by the Germans by damming the streams ***

I must have walked twenty miles up and down that beach and over the causeways. Towards afternoon I went inland myself, Everything was in wild confusion still. It always is on a landing. Soldiers were everywhere. Occasionally groups of prisoners would pass, disheveled, dirty, unshaven. There was the continuous rattle of rifle and m.g. I managed to see the three regimental COs. All were well set and confident. My sole food was a cake of D Ration chocolate but I did not feel hungry.

By this time the Rough Rider was ashore and Stevie and I were set. When night fell and we got back to the Division CP. I was delighted to find Show with the $\frac{1}{4}$ ton trailer. That meant our bedding-rolls. I was still soaking wet and shivering with cold. I did my old trick—took off shoes and socks and went to bed in my wet clothes. At the end of the three hours sleep the situation allowed I was dry.[42]

General Barton and everyone else on Utah Beach that morning, credited Ted with saving the day with his on-the-spot change of the invasion plan and with his heroism in calmly staying on the beach for several hours while under fire to keep the green, terrified troops moving inland. It was as if his total life experiences were meant to prepare him for what he did that morning. His actions were superb, there is no other word for it. Speaking of Ted and the D-Day landing as he saw it, Lieutenant R. W. Chambers wrote:

He's the most remarkable guy you have ever known. With hell all around us, he walked up and down, carrying only a little swagger-stick which he would poke into the back of some man who was panicky, with a cheerful 'What's the matter boy? Get into it.' At one point when panic swept over one particular section of beach, it was thanks to General Theodore Roosevelt, Jr. that our men held it. He restored morale by his calm and complete fearlessness, going forward with nothing but his swagger stick in the way of a weapon as if he were walking along the Champs Elysses in spring. All of the men worshipped him. Tales of his bravery are endless.

Captain W. Amos Buck of the 1106th Engineer Combat Group wrote a Colonel friend of his:

We were read messages from all the generals and from the President with the last, and the one to be remembered, coming from General Teddy Roosevelt. It was an impromptu affair from the man's warm heart and was short and to the point. He has been through several landings and knows whereof he speaks. Further than that the men all know he is a front line general and respect and love him. I had the pleasure of meeting him several times. The man has a remarkable memory too. ****** you have no idea how much good a man of that type does with a bunch of scared and inexperienced GIs. I later saw him on the beach—as forward as the doughboys he leads. Do you think they will ever forget seeing him in such a spot? I do not think so. A grand old guy—he takes everything the younger men do. Sure it hurts, but he keeps going.[43]

From D-Day on for the next three weeks the 4th Division was in constant combat and the Division Commander had scant time to think, much less to do paperwork that was not absolutely required. On June 27th, at his first opportunity,

General Barton filled out the necessary papers to put Ted in for the Congressional Medal of Honor, giving as his reasons, in part:

> General Roosevelt, with utter disregard for his own personal safety, in the face of grazing small arms and machine gun fire, led groups of the assault troops over the seawall, establishing them inland, returning only to lead others in the same fashion. He left the beach only after all assault troops had been cleared, proceeding inland to the most forward elements of the combat battalions in contact with the enemy ******* far above and beyond the call of duty.

Barton's Medal of Honor recommendation was supported by affidavits from Lt. Col. Carlton O. MacNeely, the C.O. of one of the first wave battalions, and from Colonel James A. Van Fleet, the C.O. of the initial assault regiment. Van Fleet said that Ted, "Repeatedly moved from one unit to another with complete disregard for his own safety, above and beyond the call of duty, that his acts conspicuously distinguished him for gallantry and intrepidity above all the officers and men on the beach," and that his actions made possible "a brilliant and successful landing." MacNeely stated, in part:

> With complete disregard for his own life and with utter contempt for heavy hostile artillery, machine gun and small arms fire, he immediately went on a personal reconnaissance of the beach to determine the position of the troops in relation to previous designated points of exodus from the beach inland. At the time of General Roosevelt's reconnaissance, strong enemy positions were firing at point blank range upon the assault troops and upon him from a distance of a little over 100 yards. Returning to the point of landing, he contacted the commanders of the 1st and 2nd Battalions, and coordinated and personally led the organizations in the assault of heavy fortified enemy positions. General Roosevelt's heroism, leadership and presence in the very front of the attack, and his complete unconcern at being under heavy direct fire, inspired the troops to the heights of enthusiasm and self-confidence. Although the enemy had beach "Uncle Red" under constant direct fire, General Roosevelt moved from one locality to another, and rallying men around him, directed and personally led them against the enemy. Under his seasoned, precise, calm, unfaltering leadership assault troops reduced beach strong points and rapidly moved inland with minimum casualties. General Roosevelt's actions conspicuously distinguished him by gallantry and intrepidity at the risk of his own life, above and beyond the call of duty in a manner which sets him above and apart from his fellow officers and enlisted men of his command. His extraordinary courage and deep sense of responsibility to his men, to his higher commanders and to

the American people during this decisive and vastly significant engagement, reflects great credit upon himself, the service and the entire American nation.[44]

Beginning early on the morning of June 7th, Ted and Stevie did their usual visiting of different units of the Division, trying to be at the hot spots at the hot time, just like they had done in North Africa, Sicily, and Italy.[45]

After the Utah Beachhead was firmly established and other American divisions had landed, the 4th Division began to concentrate on its next objective, the liberation of the port city of Cherbourg. The Ivy Division first had to fight its way inland into the agricultural areas of the Cotentin Peninsula of Normandy. There, the troops encountered the Norman hedgerows for the first time. For hundreds or even thousands of years these tall, thick, elongated mounds with trees and bushes on top, held together by masses of roots growing into the compacted soil underneath had acted as fences around the irregularly shaped fields. Some of the hedgerows were as high as fifteen feet and as thick as twenty feet. For some unknown reason, Allied intelligence had failed to appreciate the significance of these terrain features and the value they would have to the German defenders. The enemy troops would lay behind the hedgerows, protected from anything but a direct mortar or artillery hit, and have good fields of fire on the Americans as they tried to advance from one field to another. As one dog face GI said, "Every god dam field in this hedgerow country is a battlefield."[46]

General Barton assigned Ted the job of trying to come up with some system to advance over the hedgerow-bordered fields without suffering horrendous losses. One idea he came up with was to use tank-dozers against those formable obstacles. This worked fairly well against some of the smaller hedgerows. Then Ted talked with Captain Harold Blackwell, the CO of an anti-aircraft battery assigned to the 4th Div., and had Blackie's unit spray the hedgerow that the infantry was assaulting with half-track mounted 40 mm and quad-50 caliber fire. This kept the Germans pinned down until the foot soldiers got close enough to use their flame-throwers and grenades on the defenders. The infantry would then shoot up a flare or throw a smoke grenade as a signal to lift the anti-aircraft fire and then they would climb over the hedgerow and assault the defenders. This tactic worked fairly well also, but it wasn't long before American ingenuity came up with a special steel prong to weld onto the front of tanks that would allow the tank to bust right through most of the hedgerows. However, before the battle for Normandy was over, the hedgerows cost many a World War II doughboy his life.[47]

As yet, the American forces had captured no port through which to supply the troops, and considered it vital to capture the channel coast city of Cherbourg for that purpose. Toward the end of June, the 4th Infantry Division, in partnership with several other American divisions, was closing in on this objective. Ted was on the front lines most of the time. On one occasion he put chewing gum over the star on his helmet so the Huns would not be able to see that he was an officer and led a reconnaissance patrol through the German-infested eastern outskirts of Cherbourg all the way to the sea. They had to turn back, however, because they could not be reinforced. Some of the Ivy Division soldiers realized the difficulty of this feat, and considered it to be one of the bravest acts of the war.[48]

Before Cherbourg finally fell to the American divisions on June 26th, the surrounded Germans established themselves in defensive perimeters in depth, with the final defensive positions being in an old fort in the Cherbourg inner city. During the final battle, American artillery bombarded the Germans relentlessly and the town was ablaze. Late into the night of the 25th and into the early hours of the 26th, Ted and some of the other 4th Division personnel, including Captain Lewis Fiset, along with Gault MacGowan, a correspondent with the New York Sun, stood on a hill overlooking the old city and watched the shelling against the background of flames. All the men watching were impressed with the dramatic scene, and remembered the poem Ted was reciting at the time, Alan Seeger's, I Have a Rendezvous With Death, in part:[49]

But I've a rendezvous with Death
At midnight in some flaming town.

After Cherbourg fell, Division headquarters was moved into the Grand Hotel Atlantique, and the Corps Commander left the 4th ID alone for a few days of well-deserved rest. Ted was made the Military Governor of the city for a period of two days, during which the Luftwaffe bombed the city twice. All of the city's utilities had been knocked out, so Ted put all the local electricians and plumbers he could find to work on the repair of the electric and water services. June 28th was declared Liberation Day, and the French Maire was installed in a ceremony in which General Collins made a speech. Kenneth Downs, Ted's friend from the OSS, was there, and Ted reminded him of his promise to get Quentin out of harm's way. Downs, who happened to have his boss with him, confirmed Quentin's impending transfer.[50]

One of the first things General Barton did during this short lull after Cherbourg fell, was to formally file his recommendation for Ted to be awarded the nation's highest military decoration, the Congressional Medal of Honor. Aware of the recommendation, Ted wrote Eleanor that the Division CO and many others gave him far more credit than he deserved. He said that while he would cherish such a prestigious honor, he probably wouldn't receive it because General Collins, the Corps Commander, didn't like him and would probably disapprove it when the recommendation was passed on up the chain of command. The final decision, however, rested with the War Department and the President. As Ted predicted, when the recommendation reached VII Corps Headquarters, J. Lawton Collins, the West Pointer who had no combat experience during World War I and whose combat experience in World War II was as a division commander and corps commander; who had never been shot at and who fit to a tee Ted's complaint about top brass who didn't know how heavy a foot soldier's pack gets; who must have been at least partially responsible for the Slapton Sands disaster and/or cover-up; who respected World War II author and historian John Keegan said, "had a disregard for casualties more typical of an American Civil War general than a Second World War general;" who once chewed General Roosevelt out in the presence of some of the enlisted men for not wearing his helmet; who, on another occasion, carefully explained to Ted that while everyone considered him to be the Assistant 4th Division Commander, he was only attached to the division rather than assigned to it and was really not even in the chain of command; who liked to refer to himself as "Lightning Joe;" and who fit the typical West Point mould described by columnist Drew Middleton, as being "suspicious of anything not included in the Academy's curriculum;" recommended the award be reduced to the Distinguished Service Cross.

Other than personal animosity, intolerance of someone he considered to be un-deserving, or jealously, there is no reasonable way to explain Collins' action, especially in view of the strong recommendation and affidavits from the senior officers who were on the beach and personally observed Ted's heroics. Collins' failure to favorably endorse the MOH recommendation was also a personal slap at Tubby Barton, and Colonels MacNeely and Van Fleet. When the matter reached General Bradley at First Army Headquarters, Brad was in the middle of the situation and had a war to run. He did what he thought was the proper thing and went along with the recommendation of his immediate subordinate (Collins), and approved the awarding of the DSC. The funny thing though was that Ted was never informed of either Collins' or Bradley's action, nor was he awarded the DSC decoration, nor was the matter referred on up to General Eisenhower's headquarters, as regulations required.[51]

In early July, Secretary of War Henry Stimson paid a personal visit to the Normandy area. On his trip, someone, probably either Ted or General Barton, gave him a copy of the Medal of Honor recommendation and the supporting affidavits.[52]

Before the end of the first week in July, the headquarters of the 4th Division had been relocated near Groult, still in the Normandy orchard and hedgerow country, and the Division was back in the line. Again, Ted was constantly at the front, shooting the bull, joking, advising, and trying to be helpful. One time, when he was visiting one of the unit headquarters, he climbed up on top of a hedgerow and had just begun to relieve himself when enemy shells started falling in the immediate area. Everyone around instantly hit the dirt. When the brief barrage lifted, Arnold Devincenzo happened to look up and there General Roosevelt was, still standing up there on the hedgerow, urinating. Not long afterwards, Ted, Colonel Van Fleet and Captain Francis Glaze were conversing in the middle of a road near the CP of one of the 8th Inf. Battalions, when a German artillery barrage came in. Glaze dove into a ditch, but Roosevelt and Van Fleet just stood there and continued to talk. After finishing their conversation, Ted looked down at Captain Glaze, who was still lying in the ditch, and said, "You are probably smarter than we are. Why don't you lead us back out of here? We've been brave and stupid long enough."[53]

Not long after meeting with Van Fleet and Glaze, Ted and Stevie went to the headquarters of one of the D-Day assault battalions and found its CO, Colonel MacNeely in critical condition from a head wound he received from an enemy shell-burst. Nearby lay "Smokie," MacNeely's aide, also badly injured. Ted spoke to the Colonel and he responded. Later, Eleanor received Ted's letter describing the event. He wrote that he prayed for MacNeely's recovery. Ted's prayers were answered; Colonel Carlton MacNeely survived his wound and eventually made a good recovery.[54]

General Bradley had been disappointed with the performance of the green 90th Infantry Division since shortly after D-Day, when it first entered combat. The Division Commander was relieved in mid-June and the Deputy VII Corps Commander was made Division CO, at the insistence of General Collins. When this move didn't improve the Division's combat performance, some of the 1st Army staff recommended that the 90th be scrapped and that its officers and men be sent out as replacements in other divisions. But Bradley wanted to give the unit one more chance, and he began to think. What could he do to solve the problem? Then the solution suddenly came to him. While he and Ike had agreed back in Sicily that Ted Roosevelt was "too softhearted, and too much like one of the boys" to command a division, things had now changed. He reasoned that what the 90th Infantry Division needed as its commander was, in Brad's words:

*** A man with vitality and courage, a man who could pick up the Division single-handedly and give it confidence in itself.

Bradley knew that of all the general officers that were available, Ted had earned and deserved a division command. He was sure that if he gave the division to Ted and made some strict disciplinarian the assistant division CO, the 90th would be giving Jerry hell within a week or two.[55]

On the 11th of July, Bradley's headquarters informally notified Ted that the

CO of the 90th Infantry Division was going to be relieved and that he would likely be given the command. TRJr was elated. In a sense this would fulfill a lifetime ambition because it would give him a place in American history that he had earned on his own. No one could say he had been made a division commander because his father was Teddy Roosevelt. They had both been regimental commanders, and while Ted had been an assistant division commander, that was just not the same as being the CO of a large size unit, especially a division. Division command would mean an automatic promotion to Major General. Also, both he and his father had been recommended for the Congressional Medal of Honor, but nether had received the prestigious award. Ted, because of General Collins, didn't have much hope of ever getting it.

Even though he was thrilled at the news, Ted actually felt awful and the fact that it rained all day and he was soaked didn't help any. He and Stevie made their usual rounds to various 4th Division units, but Stevie could tell that his boss was not his normal jovial, enthusiastic self. When they stopped by Harold Blackwell's anti-aircraft battery, Ted pulled Blackie off to the side and told him it looked like he would be leaving the 4th Division to assume command of the 90th Infantry Division. That night, back at division headquarters, when Ted was reporting his daily activities and observations to the division CO, Tubby realized that Ted was sick and ordered him to see the doctor. He also instructed him not to go out the next day unless he (Barton) personally gave the OK.[56]

Orderly-driver Sergeant Kurt Show was a master at scrounging, and had recently liberated a captured German trailer and diverted it to his boss's use. In it he had put a real bed, a writing desk, a radio, an electric light, and a few other comforts of home. Ted was tickled with his new quarters. That night, before he retired, the division surgeon came in and gave Ted a cursory examination. Finding nothing wrong, the doctor said the trouble was that Ted was trying to do things twenty -year-olds did, with a fifty-six year old body, and gave him a sleeping pill. The next morning Ted felt fine, back to his old self. Dutifully he went to General Barton and said that whatever was wrong with him the day before was gone, and he was now feeling fine. The CO agreed for Ted to go out among the units, but told him he could not get any nearer to the front lines than the headquarters of the various 4th Division regiments. This would generally keep him more than a mile behind the front lines.[57]

Making his rounds on July 12th, Ted obeyed General Barton and did not get any closer to the front than the headquarters of the regiments. But his boss did not tell him he couldn't climb trees and church steeples to get a better look at the front and the surrounding terrain, so Ted didn't consider himself disobeying orders when he did this several times during the day. By now, General Bradley's headquarters had confirmed to Ted that the CO of the 90th Infantry Division was being relieved and that, subject only to Ike's expected approval, Ted would definitely be appointed its new commander. On his way back to his little trailer-home that night, Ted again stopped by Blackie's AA battery to tell his friend goodbye. He told Blackie how much he had wanted a division command and that the next day he was going over to the 90th to look things over and meet the division staff.[58]

The 4th Infantry Division Headquarters and Ted's little trailer had been moved to the town of Meautis, and he arrived there about 1800 hours. After making his nightly report to General Barton, he chatted a bit with the staff. About 1930 hours, who should drive up unexpectedly but his son Quentin, and a few minutes later his old friend Colonel Clancy Beck. Clancy was the officer Ted borrowed a dirty white undershirt from to tie onto his half-track almost two years before when he and Bill Gordon drove down into Vichy French occupied Oran and negotiated the surrender of the French forces. Both Quentin and Clancy were still with the Big Red One. Ted was surprised and delighted to see them both. Show had gone out that day and procured chickens, fresh peas, fresh onions, and a couple of bottles of good French red wine. They all, including Stevie, had their best meal since leaving England a month and a half before. After a couple of hours of eating and talking, Clancy left, but Quentin stayed for a while longer. He and his dad talked about more personal things, like Old Orchard, family, and after the war plans. Ted told his son he had been having some chest pains and what he thought were small heart attacks, but to Quentin his father seemed perfectly happy and normal. Quentin left a little after 2200 and drove back to the Big Red One.[59]

As soon as Quentin left, Ted, planning a busy day tomorrow, went to bed. Stevie's cot was out under a tree only about twenty feet from his boss's, and he retired right after Ted. Just as Stevie was dozing off, the air raid alarm sounded and some Luftwaffe planes came in on a strafing and bombing raid on a nearby area. Stevie ran to Ted's trailer to warn him of the danger. When he burst in and found his boss half sitting and half lying in bed with his face contorted in pain, he knew Ted was in distress. Ted's last words were, "Stevie, get the doctor." Stevie ran and got the division surgeon, whose tent was nearby. Ted was unconscious by the time the doctor got there. He died at 11:50 p.m. on July 12, 1944.[60]

Quentin was notified, and he immediately returned to Meautis to make funeral arrangements. He wrote his mother a touching letter. It began, "The Lion is dead."[61]

Omar Bradley, who was miles away at First Army Headquarters, had no idea Ted was having physical problems. At about the same time Ted died, Bradley phoned Supreme Headquarters, Allied Expeditionary Force (SHAEF) to get General Eisenhower's approval of Roosevelt being given command of the 90th Infantry Division and to suggest that the paper work for Ted's promotion to Major

General be sent on to the War Department. The Supreme Commander wasn't available, so he passed the information on to the Chief of Staff, Beetle Smith. Smith said he would talk with Ike about Ted's new job and promotion the first thing in the morning and get back in touch when he had an answer. Very early on the 13th, Beetle telephoned Brad and said, "I've got the answer for you on Roosevelt, Ike said OK. It's the right thing to do." In the meantime, Bradley had received word of Ted's death from 4th Division Headquarters and he gave General Smith the tragic news.[62]

Immediately the censorship order that had prevented Ted's name being mentioned in hundreds of news reports was revoked, and the front pages of newspapers and radio broadcasts all over the U.S. were full of stories about him and his bravery. While the American war correspondents in Europe had not been allowed to use Ted's name in their press reports, they were personally aware of many of his heroic actions. Quentin Reynolds wrote that Ted was the bravest man he ever saw; that he "Couldn't tell whether Ted Roosevelt had learned how to conquer fear or whether he simply didn't understand what fear was." In his radio program on July 13th, Gabriel Heater spoke of Ted's tolerance toward others and of his belief in the young people of America. General Tubby Barton said, "He was the most gallant soldier and officer and gentleman that I have ever known, and I make no exceptions."[63]

A column by Westbrook Pegler pointed out that Ted was so small physically, and so congenial and polite that it was easy for people to pass him by without realizing that he was a man of great personal honor and that he was "One of the finest American soldiers and one of the great patriots in American history."[64]

The Board of Directors of the American Express Company adopted a resolution recognizing its former Board Chairman's gallantry. It stated, in part:

In business life, his association was valued not only for his distinguished military and civil services, but for his high ideals in public and private life. His enthusiasm and ready grasp of business problems was at all times a valued asset. His high respect for character and justice was an inspiration.[65]

In a press dispatch, correspondent Clark Lee wrote that Ted had probably been under enemy fire more than any other American and he referred to Ted's ability to instill confidence and alleviate fear in the troops with his calmness and friendliness in stressful situations. Mr. Lee also wrote about the censorship order preventing news stories being written about Ted. He reported that when the correspondents protested the matter directly to Ted, Ted laughed and responded that he didn't want publicity, and that anyway, "I belong to the wrong Roosevelts, the Oyster Bay Roosevelts. We are out of season."

The British Ministry of Information had issued the classified censorship order for the "Official Use of Censors Only." It was a guide as to what the men and women actually doing the censoring could approve for publication. The copy of the order given to Eleanor was dated 11/26/42, and states that it cancels and supersedes a previous order. The complete order is several typed pages in length and covers a wide variety of matters a reporter might desire to put in a news report. It names some sixty high ranking military officers in the European Theater of Operations that the correspondents were free to write about without fear of all or part of the report being deleted by a censor. This privileged list included Eisenhower, Patton, Bradley, Mark Clark, etc. Stories about certain people and things were to be submitted to the U.S. Advisers for approval. Ted's name was to automatically be removed from any news story, no matter what else might be in the copy. Ted, Quentin, and Henry Wallace, Jr., the son of the U.S. Vice-President, are the only names listed in the entire order that could not be mentioned in a news article under any conditions. With respect to these three men, the order states:

> There is a specific stop on the following: Brig. General Theodore Roosevelt and his nephew Quentin Roosevelt; Mr. Henry Wallace Jr., the son of the U.S. Vice-President.[66]

The officer that provided Eleanor with a copy of the order said that he had no doubts that it originated in the White House to put the wraps on war news about the Republican Roosevelts. The previous order, of which no copy has been found, obviously also banned articles naming Ted because his name was not mentioned in the reports describing the 11/8/42 invasion of North Africa.[67]

Some years after the war, Mrs. TRJr made an attempt to find out who the originator of the prejudicial censorship order was. The British reported that the part of the order concerning Ted, Quentin and Henry Wallace, Jr. was placed at the request of "U.S. Advisers," but they didn't know specifically who those advisers were. In her efforts, she wrote former Vice President Henry Agaard (a.k.a. Agard) Wallace and asked if he knew anything about the matter. Mr. Wallace promptly replied that he, "Had never heard of the Censorship stop to which you refer."[68]

Logically, there are only two sources from which the order could have originated. One would be from some clerk or some low-level political hack in uniform as a U.S. Adviser, who didn't have enough to do that day and acted without authority. The other would, of course, be the White House. And there is a strong circumstantial case that the White House was the guilty party.

From the early 1920s on through the general election in the fall of 1940, Ted actively campaigned hard in behalf of the Republican Party and he publicly lambasted at every opportunity the Democrats in general, and the New Deal policies of his cousin, FDR, in particular. Franklin Roosevelt, being the political genius that he was, with few exceptions, simply ignored Ted's criticisms, or so it seemed. Shortly after Pearl Harbor and his promotion to Brigadier General, Ted made a courtesy call on the President. The *New York Times* reported that when he emerged from the White House, Ted said, "It is our country, our war and our President," and he expressed hope that the First Infantry Division would be sent abroad soon. At that time, Ted was only fifty-four years old. To Ted, his public comment may have been a peace offering, but to FDR, it might have sounded like a patriotic statement from a politician with after-the-war political ambitions.[69]

In May of '42, shortly before the 1st Division was sent to England, Ted wrote FDR a one-page, handwritten note on Headquarters First Division stationary, essentially saying, you are doing a good job, Good luck, Ted. FDR and his personal advisors were aware that Ted's exemplary war record from World War I had received extensive press coverage, and that Ted had used this as a tool in his political campaigns for the state legislature and governor. Instead of the peace offerings that Ted intended, the White House visit and personal note were like mistaking gasoline for water when fighting a fire, with respect to President Franklin Roosevelt's reaction.[70]

Any thought that the censorship stop order was for the purpose of protecting General Roosevelt, Quentin, and Henry Wallace Jr. by hoping the enemy would not realize who their prisoner was in the event one of them was captured, evaporates when you consider the thousands of famous Americans, and sons of famous Americans who were in the ETO and were not included in the order. In fact, FDR's own sons had admirable combat records and at the same time received good press coverage of their exploits. The argument that the order covers both the Republican Roosevelts and the Democrat Wallace, and is, therefore, politically neutral, fails when it is discovered that there is actually no such person as "Henry Wallace Jr., the son of the U.S. Vice President." Vice President Henry Agaard Wallace had two sons, one of them was named Henry Brown Wallace, and the other was named Robert Brown Wallace. Henry Brown Wallace was, obviously, was not a Jr. and never represented himself as being a Jr., or as being the namesake of his father. During World War II, Henry Brown Wallace was never in the European Theater of Operations. Quentin was Ted's son, rather than nephew, but no censor would realize that and would not approve the publication of a news report about Quentin on that technicality anyway.[71]

It is impossible to believe that the part of the order relating to Ted, Quentin, and the non-existent Henry Wallace, Jr. originated with some low-level person in the U.S. Advisers. It was craftily and deceptively worded to make it appear as having been drafted by someone not well-versed with respect to the individuals involved, but was stated in such a way that it accomplished the purpose intended.

322 / Robert W. Walker

It prevented the public from knowing of the actions and bravery of one of America's greatest war heroes until he was no longer a political threat. At the same time, it damaged Quentin in case he had political ambitions. The entire episode was nothing more than some political shenanigans, in some ways similar to the time during Ted's run for Governor when Mrs. FDR followed Ted around in an automobile disguised as a teapot. The teapot trick was the brainchild of Louis Howe, a journalist and political advisor to Franklin, but he died in the '30s, so Howe could not have been the mastermind behind the scheme. It would have been a simple matter for FDR, himself, to have mentioned the matter to his friend Winston Churchill, or any number of others with duties involving censorship, and had the problem quietly handled. Almost certainly, though, the President would have delegated the dirty work to someone in his small inner circle. Harry L. Hopkins, the President's shrewd political advisor and right hand man, was FDR's personal envoy to Great Britain and was in the European Theater of Operations (including North Africa) a number of times. It would have been easy for him to have clandestinely arranged for the stop order to be issued. It could have possibly been the work of the Chief Executive's Press Secretary, Steve Early, or political advisor and oil tycoon, Ed Pauley, or even Mrs. FDR, but it certainly wasn't the President's trusted friend and advisor George Allen's doings. Allen hailed from Booneville, Mississippi, which is just across the line from the author's Alabama home. No one from Booneville could possibly be capable of such a devious act. Most likely the mystery will never be solved, but, to the author at least, it just smells like Harry Hopkins pinch-hitting for his boss. Whether FDR knew about the order is a wee bit questionable, but he almost certainly did, and, knowing everything is fair in love, war, and politics, had a good laugh.

When Secretary of War Henry L. Stimson got back to Washington in mid July and discovered that the Medal of Honor recommendation for General Roosevelt had not been received by the War Department, he asked General Marshall to check on it. After Marshall made several inquiries to Eisenhower's headquarters, it was admitted that General Bradley had authorized the DSC be awarded in lieu of the MOH based on Collins' recommendation. Bradley had filed away General Barton's MOH recommendation without any intention of passing it on up the line with his favorable or unfavorable endorsement. When Eisenhower finally sent the matter on to the War Department, he went along with the endorsements of Collins and Bradley, his immediate subordinates, who said that the Distinguished Service Cross was the proper award.[72]

By criteria, the Medal of Honor may be awarded to a member of the armed service who distinguishes himself or herself conspicuously by gallantry and intrepidity at the risk of his or her life, above and beyond the call of duty, while engaged in military action against an opposing foreign enemy of the United States.

The deed performed must have been one of personal bravery or self sacrifice so conspicuous as to clearly distinguish the individual above his or her comrades and must have involved risk of life. Incontestable proof of performance is required and each recommendation for the MOH will be considered on the standard of extraordinary merit.

When the formal paperwork was finally received by the War Department in late August, Army Chief of Staff Marshall and Secretary of War Stimson realized that Ted's actions were well within the criteria for the nation's highest military honor to be awarded. They overrode the endorsements of Collins, Bradley, and Eisenhower authorizing the DSC, and recommended to President Franklin Roosevelt that Ted be posthumously awarded the top medal. FDR gave his approval (Maybe he felt a little guilty). General Bradley apparently never completed the paperwork to award the DSC, for there is no mention of it in Ted's Official Army Records.

Neither Eisenhower nor Collins ever made any public comment about whether General Marshall and Secretary Stimson were justified in recommending the MOH posthumously to Ted. However, General Bradley did. In one of his books, Brad describes how on D-Day Ted landed in the first wave of troops on Utah Beach and, while under intense fire, with the aid of his cane calmly walked up and down the beach, encouraging the troops, and instructing them inland, rather than letting them stop and dig in. Bradley knew Ted had set a magnificent example for the green American soldiers, and that by exposing himself to the murderous German fire, Ted had given the scared young GIs the will and confidence to go on in and get the job done. Bradley wrote, "No soldier I know showed more deliberate courage than General Theodore Roosevelt in the Normandy invasion," and, "I have never known a braver man nor a more devoted soldier."[73]

On another occasion, when General Bradley was asked what the bravest act he had ever known of was, he answered by describing Ted's performance on Utah Beach. George Patton said Ted "was one of the bravest men I ever knew."[74]

On September 21, 1944, Eleanor, Cornelius, Quentin, Gracie with her two children, Ted's long time secretary Ms. Margaret Hensey, Generals Marshall and Hap Arnold, and a few other dignitaries, gathered in the Washington D. C. office of Secretary of War Henry Stimson, in the newly constructed Pentagon. There, Eleanor accepted the Congressional Medal of Honor in behalf of her deceased husband. Fifty-seven years later another posthumous MOH ceremony took place. This one was at the White House, where President Bill Clinton presented the award to the descendants of Theodore Roosevelt for the former President's valor on San Juan and Kettle Hills over one hundred years before. The only other father and son to receive the medal is Arthur MacArthur and his son, Douglas.[75]

For his many exploits in two world wars, Ted received at least one of every medal for valor the United States has to offer its front line warriors. He is the most decorated citizen-soldier (meaning nonprofessional or non regular army) in American history. With respect to all the foot soldiers who ever served, only Douglas MacArthur has more.

At the time of the Japanese surprise attack on Pearl Harbor, Douglas MacArthur was in command of all the American and Filipino forces in the Philippine Islands. Even though he was promptly notified of the Pearl Harbor attack, nine hours later when the Japanese struck the Philippines, they caught all of MacArthur's planes lined up on the ground like sitting ducks. The results were devastating. MacArthur had done nothing to prepare his forces for an air attack that was sure to come. The only explanation he ever gave for his failure to prepare was that he "was under the impression" the attack on Pearl Harbor resulted in a victory for the Unites States.[76]

Within days of the December, 1941 Japanese invasion of the Philippine Islands, MacArthur realized his army would not be able to stem the onslaught, and ordered the transfer of all his troops and supplies on Luzon Island to the Bataan Peninsula. In theory, his forces would then be able to hold out long enough for help to arrive from the States. While a plan for the wholesale removal of men and material to Bataan had been in existence for years, there had been no practice or rehearsal of the plan. So when the actual evacuation was attempted, most of the soldiers reached Bataan, but large quantities of food and supplies were left sitting in warehouses in Manila. It's hard to believe, but at the time MacArthur's forces outnumbered those of the enemy. There is no question that had all the food and supplies in the warehouses been removed to Bataan, the Japanese would have been held off much longer. Some historians believe MacArthur's men could have held out long enough for help to arrive from the mainland.

During World War I, Douglas MacArthur had been a fearless front-line leader, and for his many heroic WW I acts was awarded the DSC and one Oak Leaf Cluster, and the Silver Star and six Oak Leaf Clusters. Contrary to his previous conduct, in World War II the General stayed holed up in his bombproof headquarters on Corregidor Island during most of the Japanese siege of Bataan. Only once did he make the short trip over to Bataan, but his visit was brief and he did not go to the front. He was so reclusive on Corregidor that his troops began to refer to him as "Dugout Doug."[77]

In all of American military history there has never been another military man as controversial and as unique as Douglas MacArthur. He was a paragon to some, and a paradox to others. He was either idolized or hated. There was no middle ground. The self centered General was probably unaware of both.

The spring of 1942 was a rough time for the United States. It seemed that everything was going wrong. Japan had defeated the American forces at every opportunity, and German U-boats were playing havoc with U.S. shipping. When it became obvious to FDR that the American forces in the Philippines couldn't hold out much longer, he ordered MacArthur to escape from Corregidor and make his way to Australia to command the Allied Army being built up there. When the General obeyed the President's order and left, some people criticized him for abandoning his men and claimed he was a coward.

It was the perception of President FDR and Chief of Staff George Marshall that the morale of the American public was at a low point. Too, they didn't like anyone calling their commanding general a coward. They decided that if they made MacArthur into a legitimate hero, it would dispel any claim that he was a coward, and it would also give the public a hero figure to look up to which would have an uplifting effect on morale. For these reasons, in March, 1942, the egotistical general was awarded the Congressional Medal of Honor, even though he in no way met the criteria to qualify for the decoration. Had the undeserved award not been made to MacArthur, Ted Roosevelt would be the United States' most decorated soldier.[78]

In 1955, after the Philippine Islands had been a free and independent nation for nearly a decade, Eleanor was invited to be the guest of honor of the Philippine Government and of the exclusive Order of the Knights of Rizal at a ceremony and reception in Manila. The event was a way for the Filipinos to express their admiration and affection for Ted and her. They wanted to honor her deceased spouse for the good work he had done more than twenty years before, while he was Governor General of the Islands. Eleanor was happy to attend; she loved the Philippines and the Filipinos. After arriving from the States, she settled into the quarters she had been provided in the American Embassy. The proceedings would be formal.

On the appointed day and time, a City of Manila police motorcycle detail met her at the Embassy to escort her to the hall where the ceremony was to take place. The colorful displays of the American and Philippine flags added to the pageantry. When they arrived at the hall and Eleanor stepped from the limousine, the Honor Guard was called to attention and the Philippine Naval Band struck up, "Hail to the Chief," in honor of Ted. The last time she had heard that tune when it was being played in honor of her husband was in 1933, when they departed those same islands. Ted was with her, then. This must have been an emotional moment for Eleanor, perhaps as emotional as the time she found her Colonel Roosevelt in the Argonne right after the last shots of the Great War had been fired. As she stood there, listening to that song, the thoughts of what might have been, and the memories of the full and exciting life she and Ted had shared together must have pervaded her mind.[79]

For many years, Ted saw his life as a stage upon which he, as the oldest son and namesake, had a duty to play the part created by his famous father. He looked on his father as perfect in every way. Probably the first difference in overall philosophy between them came about during the Great War, when Ted experienced first-hand the unbelievable horrors of modern warfare. To him, there was nothing romantic about war. He wrote and said many times that everybody loses in war. Teddy, on the other hand, was in actual combat with an enemy for only a few hours during the Spanish-American War. He had always viewed war as a game. He once said that:

Aggressive fighting for the right is the noblest sport the world affords.[80]

In the 1930s, Ted began to take exception to some of TR's progressive, if not liberal, politics, and he emphatically rejected his father's colonialist policies. While they were both social liberals, Ted was more of an economic conservative than was his father.

Both TR and TRJr were liked and admired by the common, ordinary people, but the common man never considered TR to be one of them. He was something special. On the other hand, the doughboys of the Great War, the GIs of World War II, the Puerto Ricans, and the Filipinos felt comfortable when Ted was around and looked on him as a friend. To the soldiers, he was like an enlisted man with a commission. He was one of their own.

For the last six or seven years of his life, Ted was at peace with himself. He no longer felt he had to continue his father's roll. He was free to be his own person. He had done his best to fill his father's shoes and had come up short. But by the time he was fifty, it no longer bothered him. Perhaps by then Ted realized that his own accomplishments were not small and that a person with the abilities, and energy, and charisma of a Theodore Roosevelt comes along only once in a century. He accepted the fact that he, with his own abilities, could not compete with his father, and it no longer mattered. Who is to say how Ted's life would have unfolded had Teddy not talked him out of going to the Unites States Military Academy as he wanted to do when he was sixteen years old. After all, he would have been in that same magical age group as Eisenhower, Bradley, MacArthur, Clark, and Patton, themselves West Pointers.

It has been said that a person can be great and still not be famous. Achievements and thoughts lead to greatness, but only history can grant fame. Theodore Roosevelt, Jr. was a great American, but his father accomplished so much and was so respected that he completely eclipsed whatever fame his namesake might otherwise have had. In a sense, Teddy had unintentionally caused Ted to be denied the place in American history that he had rightfully earned.

As a youth Ted said,

I will always be honest and upright, and I hope someday to be a great soldier, but I will always be spoken of as Theodore Roosevelt's son.[81]

His Finest Hour Source Notes

1. Stevie's Notes; LOC c-39.

2. AP article of 7/14/44 in Stevie's Notes.

3. Downs, Sagamore Hill Archives.

4. Ibid.

5. Roosevelt, Mrs. T. Jr., p 452.

6. R.O. Barton affidavit of 10/20/49, LOC c-56.

7. Personal interview with Major Fiset; Ted's letters to Eleanor LOC c-61.

8. Fiset interview; Roosevelt, Mrs. T. Jr., p 451.

9. Reeder, Born At Reveille, p 227.

10. Roosevelt, Mrs. T. Jr., p 542–543; NY Times 4/14/44.

11. Fiset interview; Bradley, Soldier's Story, p 251–252; Collins p 188; Hoyt, The Invasion Before Normandy, p 11–13.

12. Fiset interview; Ted's letters to Eleanor, LOC c-61; Ted's letter to Dick Derby of 4/19/44, TR Collection 87M-100.

13. Article by Kathleen Young Sheedy, TRJr Archives, Sagamore Hill; Statements by Marvin Pike and John A. Beck, Sr., Eisenhower Center, New Orleans; Joel Thomason's description of his war experiences, Babcock, p 145.

14. Stevie's Notes; LOC c-56.

15. Babcock p 141; Personal interview with Frank Glaze

16. Ted's letters to Eleanor, LOC c-61; Butcher p 539.

17. Ambrose, D-Day June 6, 1944, p 168; Phillippi article of 9/9/62.

18. Neylan

19. General Barton letter of 11/20/49, LOC c-56.

20. Personal interview with Robert Crisson.

21. John A. Beck, Sr. statement, Eisenhower Center

22. Phillippi article

23. David Howarth article in Saturday Evening Post, 4/4/69.

24. Stevie's Notes; Ted's letters to Eleanor, LOC c-61.

25. Howarth, D-Day, paperback p 112; Astor, June 6, 1944, The Voices of D-Day, p 225.

26. Jensen, Common Men, Uncommon Valor, TRJr Archives, Sagamore Hill

27. Personal interview with Mr. Louis Putnoky.

28. Marvin Pike affidavit, Eisenhower Center

29. Stevie's Notes; LOC c-56

30. Stevie's Notes; Howarth, D-Day p 112; TRJr Archives, Sagamore Hill; Jensen p 136.

31. Babcock p 108.

32. Hemingway, Voyage To Victory, Colliers Magazine 7/22/44.

33. Ted's letter to Eleanor of 6/11/44, LOC c-61

34. TRJr Archives, Sagamore Hill; Jensen p 136.

35. Ted's letter to Eleanor of 6/11/44, LOC c-61

36. Personal interview with Mr. Tallant.

37. Dreg p 182; Miller, Russell p 409; Ryan p 178 and 233; Personal interviews with Marvin Pike and Francis Glaze.

38. Statement of Harper Coleman, TRJr Archives, Sagamore Hill; Statement of John Ahern, Eisenhower Center; Dreg p 180.

39. Sheedy, TRJr Archives at Sagamore Hill; Statements of Dr. Robert Kaufman and Dennis Gray, Eisenhower Center; Personal interviews with Goldie Goldstein and Bill Davis; Babcock p 52, 54, 68 and 83; Astor, Voices p 229; Miller, Russell p 412.

40. Ryan p 286; Reeder, Born at Reveille p 248.

41. Stevie's Notes

42. Ted's letter to Eleanor of 6/11/44, LOC c-61.

43. LOC c- 56; Letter written by Capt. W. Amos Buck to Col. Collins, LOC c-39 (WW II folder)

44. Neylan

45. Stevie's Notes.

46. The Story of World War II as Written by the Soldiers, Yank, editor p 46.

47. Babcock p 160–161.

48. AP report of 7/14/44 in Stevie's Notes; LOC c-32.

49. Personal interview with Major Fiset; LOC c-56; Time Magazine, 7/24/44.

50. Unpublished diary of Norborne P. Gatling, Jr. furnished by Mr. Werner Kleeman form his personal library; Downs

51. Keegan p 159; Babcock p 145; National Archives and Record Adm. Record Group 331, Stack area 290, Row 08, Compartment 12, Shelf 03; Interview with Major Fiset.

52. Ibid.

53. Statement of A. Devincenzo, TRJr Archives, Sagamore Hill; Babcock p 141–142.

54. Ted's letters to Eleanor, LOC c-61.

55. Bradley, A Soldier's Story, p 331.

56. Bradley, A Soldier's Story, p 297–298, 331; TRJr Archives, Sagamore Hill; Babcock p 160–161. Hastings, Overlord p 246

57. Stevie's Notes; Statement by General Barton, TRJr Archives, Sagamore Hill.

58. Harold Blackwell's letter, TRJr Archives, Sagamore Hill; Babcock p 160–161.

59. Stevie's Notes; Clarence Beck letter to Eleanor of 5/22/45, LOC c-32; Roosevelt, Mrs. T. Jr., p 457–458.

60. Stevie's Notes; Barton letter to Eleanor of 7/13/44, LOC c-32.

61. Roosevelt, Mrs. T. Jr., p 457.

62. Bradley, Soldier's Story, p 332.

63. LOC c-36 & c-56.

64. Neylan

65. American Express Board of Directors minutes of 8/1/44.

66. LOC c-36

67. Hamilton, The Roosevelt No One Knew.

68. LOC c-36.

69. NY Times of 12/23/41

70. TRJr letter to FDR of 5/7/43, FDR Library

71. LOC c-36; Lord p 48; Schapsneier p 122.

72. National Archives and Records Administration, Record Group 331, Stack Area 290, Row 08, Compartment 12, Shelf 03.

73. TRJr archives, Sagamore Hill; Bradley, A Soldier's Story(paperback) p. 332.

74. Roosevelt, Mrs. T. Jr., p 455; Blumenson, Patton Papers p 480–481

75. NY Herald Tribune of 9/22/44; NY Times of 9/22/44.

76. Manchester p 237.

77. Manchester p 205; MacArthur p 117.

78. Manchester p 275–276; MacArthur p 147, 179.

79. LOC c-56.

80. On the wall at American Museum of Natural History in New York.

81. Miller, N. p 295.

EPILOGUE

After his World War II battle injuries reached maximum improvement and he returned to civilian life, Ted's brother Archie continued to make his home near Oyster Bay and became successful in the bond and brokerage business. Even though he did not drink, out of deference to his brother Kermit and his uncle Elliott, Archie joined Alcoholics Anonymous and maintained an active membership in that organization for many years. Later, after his wife Grace died in a tragic auto accident, Archie moved to Florida, where he resided until he died at age seventy-nine.

Dick and Ethel Roosevelt Derby lived near Oyster Bay until their deaths in the 1970's. Ethel was a guiding force in the Theodore Roosevelt Association and Dick had a successful medical practice.

For the rest of her days, Alice Roosevelt Longworth maintained her residence in the home she and her deceased husband, Nick, bought in Washington D C. A character all her life, Alice was an active player in the Washington social scene until her death, in 1981, at the age of ninety-six. She was Teddy Roosevelt's first born and the last of his offspring to pass on.

Even though she was in failing health as she grew older, Ted's mother, Edith, made her home in Sagamore Hill until her death in 1948. The old home-place was then conveyed by the Roosevelt family to the National Park Service and thereafter opened to the public as the Sagamore Hill National Historic Site.

Ted's daughter and son-in-law, Grace (Gracie) and Bill McMillan, lived in Maryland, where they raised their two children. Gracie, who was active in many community projects, kept in close touch with her mother and visited her often.

Son Cornelius never married, but substituted for his father in many of the family functions. After the war, he made his career with the CIA.

After distinguished service as a naval aviator throughout WW II, Theodore III and Anne made their home in Pennsylvania, where they raised their only child, Theodore Roosevelt IV.

As had been promised to Ted, Quentin was transferred out of the Big Red One and into the OSS, where he finished out the war. Afterwards, Quentin and Frances made their home in China, where both were employed with the CIA, and Quentin held a second job with Pan-American Airlines. In 1949, Quentin was aboard a commercial airliner that mysteriously crashed into a Chinese mountain. There were no survivors. Frances and their three little daughters returned to the U.S. and resided with Eleanor in Old Orchard.

All of Ted's and Eleanor's children, as well the spouses of their children are now deceased, however all six of their grandchildren are alive and well.

Shortly after D-Day, novelist Ernest Hemingway, who was then working as a war correspondent, landed in Normandy and was accompanying the 4th Infantry Division as it advanced across France. After Ted died, Captain Marcus O. Stevenson was assigned as an aide to Hemingway and they became good friends. The famous writer helped the young Captain compose love letters to send to his sweetheart back in the States. When the war was over, Stevie came home and went to work for International Harvester Company, where he remained until his retirement. Ted's loyal and trusted aide died in the late 1980s.

With Ted no longer available, General Bradley appointed Brigadier General Raymond S. McLain commander of the 90th Infantry Division. Whatever ills the division had were straightened out under McLain, and it created a distinctive battle record by the war's end.

The 4th Infantry Division under General Raymond Barton and later under General Harold Blakeley, and the Big Red One under General Clarence Huebner and then General Clift Andrus, remained in almost continuous frontline combat against the Germans until May 1945, when the war in Europe ended. Even though at any one time the normal manpower component of a World War II infantry division was a little less than fifteen thousand officers and men, each of these gallant units suffered over twenty thousand battle casualties (killed, wounded or missing) during the course of World War II.

Although only in her mid-fifties when Ted died, Eleanor, true to the mores of many in her generation, never remarried, but she continued to reside in Old Orchard and live an active life in and around Oyster Bay. In 1958, her best selling autobiography, *Day Before Yesterday,* was published. The last name in the Old Orchard Guest Book was signed on May 27th 1960. Eleanor died two days later. Today, Old Orchard is owned by the National Park Service and is a part of the Sagamore Hill National Historic Site complex.

After World War II ended, the families of the identifiable Americans killed in Europe were given the option of bringing the remains of their loved ones home, or leaving them in a European cemetery. The Roosevelt family felt that by allowing the body of Teddy's son, Quentin, to remain in France after World War I, a precedent of leaving a fallen Roosevelt where he fell had been established and opted to leave Ted's remains where he was buried. Later, all the American dead still buried in Normandy, including Ted, were disinterred and re-buried in the beautiful and poignant American Military Cemetery overlooking Omaha Beach. Still later, the body of Ted's brother, Quentin, was removed from its World War I grave and re-interred beside Ted.

BIBLIOGRAPHY

A significant amount of the material in this book was obtained from sources other than books and articles.

Material from the Theodore Roosevelt Collection in the Harvard University Library, Cambridge, MA is referred to as "TR Collection." or "TR Coll."

Information from the Theodore Roosevelt, Jr. Collection in the Library of Congress is listed as "LOC." The c and number after LOC indicates the container number within the collection.

Invaluable material was obtained from the Theodore Roosevelt, Jr. Archives housed at the Sagamore Hill National Historic Site near Oyster Bay, New York, and is cited as "TRJr. Archives, Sagamore Hill."

Through sheer luck the author stumbled upon Marcus Stephenson, Jr., the son of TRJr's World War II aide, who was extremely kind in allowing access to his father's extensive notes and articles regarding Ted's exploits. Facts from this source are footnoted as "Stevie's Notes." Within Stevie's Notes was some material prepared by General Terry Allen, and this is footnoted as "Terry Allen Material" or "Terry Allen Papers."

Books and Articles

Adams, Jane, Roosevelt, TRJr., et al What I owe My Father

Allen, Terry de L Mesa, A Factual Situation and Operations Report on the Combat Operations of the 1st Infantry Division During Its Campaign in N. Africa and Sicily During the Period 8 Nov. 42 to 7 Aug. 43.

Ambrose, Stephen E. Citizen Soldiers

Ambrose, Stephen E. D-Day, June 6, 1944

American Express Co.—Publisher Promises to Pay

Andrus, Clift The First

Astor, Gerald The Greatest War

Astor, Gerald The Voices of D-Day

Astor, Gerald Terrible Terry Allen

Babcock, Robert O War Stories, Utah Beach to Pleiku

Bagby, Wesley M. The Road to Normalcy

Baker, Carlos Earnest Hemingway, A Life Story

Baker, Roscoe The American Legion and American Foreign Policy

Baldwin, Hanson Battles Lost and Won

Baldwin, Hanson World War I

Bernstein, Davis The Philippine Story

Bishop, Joseph B., editor Theodore Roosevelt's Letters to His Children

Blumenson, Martin, Breakout and Pursuit

Blumenson, Martin Patton, The Man Behind the Legend

Blumenson, Martin Sicily: Whose Victory

Blumenson, Martin The Patton Papers 1940–1945

Bosco, John B. America at War, World War I

Boulle, Pierre The Bridge on the River Kwai

Bradley, Omar N. A General's Life

Bradley, Omar N. A Soldiers Story (paperback)

Brands, H. W. T. R., The Last Romantic

Breuer, William B. Geronimo

Buck, Beaumont B. Memories of Peace and War

Burns, James M. Roosevelt: The Lion and the Fox

Butcher, Harry C. My Three Years With Eisenhower

Caroli, Betty Boyd The Roosevelt Women

Carrion, Arturo Morales Puerto Rico

Cheney, Albert Loren Personal Memoirs of the Home Life of the Late Theodore Roosevelt—Cheney Pub. Co Washington, D.C., 1919.

Clark, Victor S., Staff Director Porto Rico and Its Problems

Cole, Wayne S. America First

Collier, Phillip & Harowitz, David The Roosevelts, An American Saga

Collins, J. Lawton Lightning Joe

Congdon, Don—editor Combat European Theater

Cook, Blanch Wiesen Eleanor Roosevelt, Vol. 1

Davis, Kenneth S. Experience of War

Davis, Kenneth S. FDR: The Beckoning of Destiny

Dalton, Kathleen A Strenuous Life

de Vallavieille, Michel D Day at Utah Beach

D'Este, Carlo Bitter Victory

D'Este, Carlo Patton, A Genius for War

Diffie, Bailey W. and Justine W. Porto Rico: A Broken Pledge

D'Olier, Franklin When We Were Very Young, Article in The American Legion Monthly

Downs, Kenneth T. An Untold Story About General Ted, Printed by Long Island Trust Co.

Drez, Ronald T.—editor Voices of D-Day

Eisenhower, Dwight D. Crusade in Europe

Eldot, Paula Governor Alfred E. Smith

Falls, Cryil The Great War

Felsenthal, Carol Alice Roosevelt Longworth

Finke, Blythe Fote No Mission To Difficult

Freidel, Frank Franklin D. Roosevelt, Vol. 1

Freidel, Frank Franklin D. Roosevelt, Vol. 2

Friend, Theodore Between Two Empires

Garland, Albert N. & Smyth, Howard Sicily and the Surrender of Italy

Gilbert, Martin The First World War

Glad, Betty Charles Evans Hughes

Grunder, Garel & Livezey, William The Philippines and the United States

Hagedorn, Herman The Roosevelt Family of Sagamore Hill

Hamby, Alonzo Man of the People

Hamilton, Maxwell The Roosevelt That No One Knew, article in 5/27/59 issue of Human Events

Hamilton, Maxwell Article in New York World Herald Sunday Magazine, 6/21/59

Hamilton, Maxwell Junior in Name Only, article in June 1981 issue of The Retired Officer

Handlin, Oscar Al Smith and His America

Hanson, Earl Parker Puerto Rico

Hapgood, Norman & Moskowitz, Henry Up From the City Streets

Harbough, William Henry Power and Responsibility

Harrison, Gordon Cross Channel Attack

Hastings, Max Overlord

Hatch, Alden American Express

Hatch, Gardner N. 4th Infantry (Ivy) Division

Hayden, Joseph R. The Philippines

Hemingway, Ernest Voyage to Victory, article in Colliers Magazine, 6/22/44

Hine, Al—editor of American Heritage D-Day The Invasion of Europe

Hoag, C. Leonard Preface to Preparedness

Howarth, David D-Day (paperback)

Howarth, David Utah Beach, article in Saturday Evening Post, 4/4/69

Howe, George F. Northwest Africa

Hoyt, Edwin P. The Invasion Before Normandy

Hoyt, Edwin P. The G I's War

Ingersoll, Joshena M. Golden Years in the Philippines

Jeffers, H. Paul The Life of a War Hero

Jensen, Marvin G. Common Men, Uncommon Valor

Jensen, Marvin G. Strike Swiftly

Johnson, Roberta Ann Puerto Rico

Josephson, Matthew & Hannah Al Smith: Hero of the Cities

Katcher, Philip U. S. 1st Infantry Division

Keegan, John The First World War

Keegan, John Six Armies in Normandy

Keesing, Felix M. & Marie Taming Philippine Headhunters

Kerr, Joan Paterson A Bully Father

Knickerbocker, H. R., et al Danger Forward

Lewis, Gordon K. Puerto Rico

Liebling, A. J.—Reporter at Large New Yorker 7/8/44 & 7/15/44

Longworth, Alice Roosevelt Crowded Hours

Longworth, Alice & Roosevelt, Theodore Jr. Desk Drawer Anthology

Lord, Russell The Wallaces of Iowa

Lynskey, Elizabeth M., et al Puerto Rico and the United States

MacArthur, Douglas Reminiscences

Madaras, Lawrence, PHD Dissertation The Public Career of Theodore Roosevelt, Jr.

Madaras, Lawrence TR Jr vs Al Smith, Article in the October 1966 issue of the Journal of the New York Historical Association

Manchester, William American Ceasar

Mansoor, Peter R. The G I Offensive in Europe

Marshall, George C. Memories of My Service in the World War

Massingill, Reed Becoming American Express

Mathews, Thomas Puerto Rican Politics and the New Deal

McCullough, David Mornings On Horseback

Miller, Henry Russell The First Division

Miller, Merle Ike the Soldier

Miller, Nathan The Roosevelt Chronicles

Miller, Nathan Theodore Roosevelt: A Life

Miller, Russell Nothing Less Than Victory

Mitcham, Samuel Jr. & Stauffenberg, Friedrich Von The Battle of Sicily

Moley, Raymond Jr. The American Legion Story

Morgan, Ted FDR

Morison, Samuel Eliot The Two Ocean War

Morris, Edmund Theodore Rex

Morris, Sylvia Jukes Edith Kermit Roosevelt

Morrison, Elting E., Editor The Letters of Theodore Roosevelt, 8 Vols.

Murphy, Edward F. Heroes of W W II

Nations, Gilbert O. The Political Career of Alfred E. Smith

Neylan, John Francis Beyond the Call of Duty

Nichols, David, Editor Ernie's War

Noggle, Burl Teapot Dome

Office of the Commonwealth of Puerto Rico Puerto Rico, U.S.A.

Patch, Joseph D. A Soldiers War

Patton, George S., Jr. War as I Knew It

Pearlman, Michael Patricians and Preparedness in the Progressive Era

Perry, Ralph Barton, The Plattsburg Movement

Pershing, John J. My Experiences in the World War (2 Vols)

Persico, Joseph E. Roosevelt's Secret War

Phillippi, Wendell Corpus Christi Caller-Times article of 9/9/62

Pringle, Henry F. Big Frogs

Pusey, Merlo J. Charles Evans Hughes Volume 1

Pusey, Merlo J. Charles Evans Hughes Volume 2

Quezon, Manuel The Good Light

Reeder, Russell "Red" Born at Reveille

Reeder, Russell "Red" The Story of the First World War

Renehan, Edward J., Jr. The Lion's Pride

Reynolds, Quentin Sicily Wasn't Easy

Rice, Grantland & Roosevelt, Theodore Jr. Taps

Rizal, Knights of Program Honoring Mrs. Roosevelt

Roderck, David Paul Personal Diary (unpublished)

Rohmer, Richard Patton's Gap

Roosevelt, Eleanor This I Remember

Roosevelt, Elliott, editor F.D.R. His Personal Letters

Roosevelt, Nicholas A Front Row Seat

Roosevelt, Mrs. Theodore Jr. Day Before Yesterday

Roosevelt, Theodore Jr. & Coolidge, Harold Three Kingdoms of Indo-China

Roosevelt, Theodore Jr. & Roosevelt, Kermit East of the Sun and West of the Moon

Roosevelt, Theodore Jr. & Roosevelt, Kermit Trailing the Giant Panda

Roosevelt, Theodore Jr. All In the Family

Roosevelt, Theodore Jr. Average Americans

Roosevelt, Theodore Jr. Colonial Policies of the United States

Roosevelt, Theodore Jr. Rank and File

Roosevelt, Theodore Jr. April 1934 issue of The Geographical Review, p 182–204. Article entitled Land Problems in Puerto Rico and the Philippine Islands.

Rumer, Thomas A. The American Legion

Ruppenthal, Roland Utah Beach to Cherbourg

Ryan, Cornelius The Longest Day

Schapsneier, Edward L. & Fredrick Henry A. Wallace of Iowa

Schriftgiesser, Karl The Amazing Roosevelt Family

Schroeder, Theodore A Different View, article in the 9/30/1931 issue of The Nation

Sellman, R. R. The First World War

Selsenthal, Carol Alice Roosevelt Longworth

Sheedy, Kathleen Young, Theodore Roosevelt, Jr., article in the Sagamore Hill Archives

Snyder, Charles W. Theodore Roosevelt, Jr., article in the Spring 1991 issue of the Theodore Roosevelt Association Journal

Sommers, Martin The Longest Hour in History, article in the 7/8/44 issue of the Saturday Evening Post

Sprout, Harold and Margaret Toward a New Order of Sea Power

Stallings, Laurence The Doughboys

Stanton, Shelby L. Order of Battle, U.S. Army World War II

Stillwell, Paul, Editor Assault on Normandy

Stratton, David H. Tempest Over Teapot Dome

Sullivan, Mark The Great Adventure at Washington

Sullivan, Mark and Rather, Dan Our Times

Tamplin, Ronald—Editor Famous Love Letters

Taylor, George The Philippines and the United States

Thomas, Lowell This Side of Hell

Thomas, Shipley The History of the A.E.F.

Thompson, R. W. D-Day, Spearhead of Invasion

Time Magazine 9/9/43

Toland, John No Man's Land

Truscott, L. K., Jr. Command Missions

Tuchman, Barbara W. The Guns of August

Turner, John Frayn Invasion '44

Tute, Warren The North African War

United States Infantry Association The Infantry Journal, March/April 1934

Wagenknecht, Edward The Seven Worlds of Theodore Roosevelt

Waldman, Louis Albany: The Crisis in Government

Waldman, Louis Labor Lawyer

Ward, Geoffrey C. A First Class Temperament

Ward Geoffrey C. Before the Trumpet

Warner, Philip The D Day Landings

Welsh, Douglas The USA in World War I

Werner, M. R. and Starr, John Teapot Dome

Wheat, George S. The Story of the American Legion

Wheeler, Gerald E. Prelude to Pearl Harbor

Whitehouse, Arch Heroes and Legends of World War I

Wilson, George If You Survive

Other Sources

Eisenhower Center, University of New Orleans, New Orleans, LA.

New York City Public Library.

F.D.R. Library, Hyde Park, N.Y.

Personal Interviews with dozens of WW II vets from the 1st and 4th Infantry Divisions.

American Express Co. provided copies of requested minutes of Board of Directors meetings.

The United States Army provided a copy of desirable portions of Ted's Official Military Records.

The Center for Military History provided a copy of the letter General Roosevelt wrote to the men of the 1st Infantry Division at the time he was relieved as Assistant Division Commander.

The American Legion National Headquarters provided a copy of the minutes of its 1949 National Convention.

The National Archives and Records Center at Silver Springs MD.

INDEX

For sales, editorial information, subsidiary rights information
or a catalog, please write or phone or e-mail

Brick Tower Press
1230 Park Avenue
New York, NY 10128, US
Sales: 1-800-68-BRICK
Tel: 212-427-7139
www.BrickTowerPress.com
email: bricktower@aol.com.

www.Ingram.com

For sales in the UK and Europe please contact our distributor,
Gazelle Book Services
Falcon House, Queens Square
Lancaster, LA1 1RN, UK
Tel: (01524) 68765 Fax: (01524) 63232
email: jacky@gazellebooks.co.uk

Printed in the USA
CPSIA information can be obtained
at www.ICGtesting.com
LVHW020900131023
760941LV00004B/35